AF801169

MARK PEARSON (BA, DipEd, MLitt, LLM, PhD) is Professor of Journalism and Social Media at Griffith University in Queensland, where he is a member of the Griffith Centre for Social and Cultural Research. He is author of *Blogging and Tweeting Without Getting Sued* (Allen & Unwin, 2012) and co-editor of *Mindful Journalism and News Ethics in the Digital Era: A Buddhist Approach* (with Shelton A. Gunaratne and Sugath Senarath, Routledge, 2015), and *Courts and the Media: Challenges in the Era of Digital and Social Media* (with Patrick Keyzer and Jane Johnston, Halstead Press, 2012). He has worked as a journalist with several media organisations, including *The Australian*. He blogs from journlaw.com and tweets from @journlaw.

MARK POLDEN is a Sydney barrister. After ten years in the media law practice group of a national law firm, and then as in-house counsel for Fairfax Media for the best part of two decades, he now advises and acts for Australian and international print, broadcast and online media, film and television production houses and for private clients.

6th EDITION

Mark Pearson & Mark Polden

THE JOURNALIST'S GUIDE TO MEDIA LAW

A handbook for communicators in a digital world

Routledge
Taylor & Francis Group
LONDON AND NEW YORK

First published 2019 by Allen & Unwin

Published 2020 by Routledge
2 Park Square, Milton Park, Abingdon, Oxon OX14 4RN
605 Third Avenue, New York, NY 10017

First issued in hardback 2021

Routledge is an imprint of the Taylor & Francis Group, an informa business

Copyright © Mark Pearson and Mark Polden 2019

All rights reserved. No part of this book may be reprinted or reproduced or utilised in any form or by any electronic, mechanical, or other means, now known or hereafter invented, including photocopying and recording, or in any information storage or retrieval system, without permission in writing from the publishers.

Notice:
Product or corporate names may be trademarks or registered trademarks, and are used only for identification and explanation without intent to infringe.

Publisher's Note
The publisher has gone to great lengths to ensure the quality of this reprint but points out that some imperfections in the original copies may be apparent.

NATIONAL LIBRARY OF AUSTRALIA

A catalogue record for this book is available from the National Library of Australia

Internal design by Squirt Creative
Index by Puddingburn
Set in 11/15 pt Legacy Serif ITC Std by Midland Typesetters, Australia

ISBN 13: 978-0-367-71978-4 (hbk)
ISBN 13: 978-1-76029-784-8 (pbk)

To my grandchildren—Oliver, Josie, Beatrice,
Charlie, Annabelle, Maddox, Harriet and Poppy.
May you be safe. May you be well.
May you be content.
Mark Pearson

To my family.
Mark Polden

CONTENTS

PREFACE TO THE SIXTH EDITION

One of the most exciting aspects of media law is its dynamic and ever-evolving nature. It is shaped by the changing nature of communication careers, rapid developments in technologies and the social dynamics of politics, economics and culture.

In no period of human history have such changes come about as quickly as in these first two decades of the twenty-first century. We have updated this book to reflect the many changes that have occurred in media law and its interpretation since our last edition in 2015.

Our target audience has broadened with each edition as technologies such as the internet and social media have combined to transform journalism and its allied professional communication careers, including public relations, strategic communication, social media management, professional blogging and their many hybrids.

While the book is Australian in its orientation, media law is now international in its application as the internet and its resultant communication platforms leave Australian communicators and their employers vulnerable to publishing laws across hundreds of jurisdictions internationally. The book tries to offer a taste of such risks faced by those working internationally, while still detailing the most important restrictions and defences in Australia's nine jurisdictions at the national, state and territory levels.

Professional communicators are now working in the so-called 'gig economy'. Their contract work might see them working as a freelance journalist on one assignment, as a media adviser in the next stage of their career, or perhaps as a new media entrepreneur hosting public comments on some innovative news platform. At a secondary level, they are also in a 'gig economy' because their outputs can involve many gigabytes of communication in an instant—presenting dangers for those ignorant of the laws and regulations that might apply.

This edition retains the basic chapter structure of its predecessor, but the content within those chapters has been revised to include fresh and ground-breaking new cases, legislative amendments and important new laws and interpretations of some issues. Recent research has shown that media law is no longer a contest between large media organisations and the rich and famous of society. There is a much larger proportion of litigation between ordinary citizens over what they have said about each other on social media or on private websites. This is also reflected in the kinds of cases we profile in this edition.

Some highlights of important new content covered in this edition include:

- consideration of several recent High Court decisions impacting on free expression, publication and media law defences
- legal implications of 'fake' or false news
- a new table summarising the mindful approach to media law practice, mapping situations against approaches
- major criminal cases challenging the boundaries of open justice, including that involving Cardinal George Pell
- new case studies in navigating crime reporting with a focus on the Yahoo!7 story that prompted the discharge of a jury in a murder trial
- significant developments in defamation law, including record damages awards to actor Rebel Wilson (reduced after appeal) and barrister Lloyd Rayney, and litigation involving actor Geoffrey Rush
- important new research showing that many more defamation actions are being brought by private individuals over internet and social media publications, as distinct from celebrities suing the media
- examination of publisher liability for the comments of third parties in the wake of several new cases, with some holding publishers responsible

- an update on confidentiality of sources, including some new breach of confidence actions and some cases testing the limits of new shield laws for journalists
- a review of the suite of new anti-terrorism laws impacting the media's reporting of crime and national security and jeopardising the confidentiality of their sources
- key new intellectual property cases that have shed light on the media's use of material sourced from the internet and social media
- significant cases showing the rapidly developing body of privacy law in the digital era
- new material in the law of freelancing, public relations and new media entrepreneurship showing the growing legal risks and responsibilities at the business end of communication practice.

There is also an increased emphasis on the higher pressure and pace of the 24/7 news cycle across a range of media, exacerbating the risks to communicators and publishers through their own work and the contributions of third-party commenters on their social media feeds and sites.

Like earlier editions, the book aims to give professional communicators and students a basic working understanding of the key areas of media law and ethical regulation likely to affect them in their research, writing and publishing across media platforms. It tries to do this by introducing the basic legal concepts while exploring the ways in which a professional communicator's work practices can be adapted to withstand legal challenges.

We do not aim to prepare all readers to make complex legal decisions. Our modest hope is that the book will help to provide a basic grounding in media law that allows you to make a cursory risk assessment and sound the alarm bells when legal advice might be needed.

We must stress that we do not offer actual legal advice in the pages of this book. That is the role of lawyers. If in any doubt, seek their advice. Many of the cases and examples we have used would never have emerged if legal advice had been sought prior to publication.

ACKNOWLEDGEMENTS

First, we must acknowledge some previous authorship upon which we have drawn to make this edition as fresh and engaging as possible. Some of the sections exploring the application of media law to digital and social media have been adapted from co-author Mark Pearson's *Blogging and Tweeting Without Getting Sued* (Allen & Unwin, 2012). Much of the foundational material stems from the first three editions written by Pearson in 1998, 2004 and 2008. Some other content has been adapted from Pearson's blogs and from some academic articles and commissioned media and online commentaries by both authors.

Many friends and colleagues deserve our thanks.

Our greatest and heartfelt gratitude goes to our respective families for their support throughout the process.

Scores of others deserve thanks too, including teaching colleagues at Griffith University (particularly in the Griffith Centre for Social and Cultural Research); journalists from Fairfax Media, News Corporation, and the ABC, whose real-life examples volunteered in training sessions have enriched the work; journalism and communication education colleagues, who have made insightful suggestions for improvements upon the earlier editions; the journal editors and reviewers for their comments on academic articles that have fed into this edition; international colleagues Kyu Ho Youm, David Goldberg, Judith Townend, Dirk Voorhoof and Doreen Weisenhaus for their global media law perspectives; and students and journalists whose questions in courses helped shape the revisions and the postgraduate students whose special projects and theses have explored useful topics.

As always, the production of the book within a tight deadline has been made possible through the professionalism of the Allen & Unwin team led by publisher Elizabeth Weiss, her assistant Jennifer McGrath, editor Samantha Kent and copyeditor Susan Jarvis, whose patience with our ongoing updates and corrections is appreciated.

And, of course, thank you to the students and journalists who have found the earlier editions useful enough to justify this sixth edition.

Mark Pearson and Mark Polden

ABBREVIATIONS

AANA Australian Association of National Advertisers
AAP Australian Associated Press
AAT Administrative Appeals Tribunal
ABA Australian Broadcasting Authority (now Australian Communications and Media Authority (ACMA))
ABC Australian Broadcasting Corporation
ACCC Australian Competition and Consumer Commission
ACMA Australian Communications and Media Authority
ACT Australian Capital Territory
ACTV Australian Capital Television
AFL Australian Football League
AFP Australian Federal Police
ALRC Australian Law Reform Commission
AMA Australian Medical Association
APC Australian Press Council
ASB Advertising Standards Bureau
ASIC Australian Securities and Investments Commission
ASIO Australian Security Intelligence Organisation
ASIS Australian Secret Intelligence Service
ASQA Australian Skills Quality Authority
auDA .au Domain Administration Ltd
AVO apprehended violence order
BBC British Broadcasting Corporation
BLF Builders' Labourers Federation
CCC Crime and Corruption Commission (Qld)
CMC Crime and Misconduct Commission
COAG Council of Australian Governments
CPJ Committee to Protect Journalists
CPSC Consumer Product Safety Commission (US)
DIGO Defence Imagery and Geospatial Organisation
DIO Defence Intelligence Organisation
DM direct message
DSD Defence Signals Directorate
EPA Environment Protection Authority
FOI freedom of information

HREOC Human Rights and Equal Opportunity Commission
ICAC Independent Commission Against Corruption
ICANN Internet Corporation for Assigned Names and Numbers
IGIS Inspector-General of Intelligence and Security
INSLM Independent National Security Legislation Monitor
INTA International Trademark Association
IoT Internet of Things
IP intellectual property
IP Internet Protocol
IPO initial public offering
ISP Internet service provider
MEAA Media, Entertainment and Arts Alliance
MFI marked for identification
NBN National Broadband Network
NDB Notifiable Data Breaches
NPP National Privacy Principles
NRL National Rugby League
OHCHR Office of the High Commissioner for Human Rights
ONA Office of National Assessments
PIO public information officer
PJCIS Parliamentary Joint Committee on Intelligence and Security
PMW Pacific Media Watch
PPR Professional Public Relations
PRIA Public Relations Institute of Australia
RTI right to information
SBS Special Broadcasting Service
TGA Therapeutic Goods Administration
TPP Trans-Pacific Partnership
TPP-11 Comprehensive and Progressive Agreement for Trans-Pacific Partnership
URL Uniform Resource Locator
VCAT Victorian Civil and Administrative Tribunal
VNR video news release
WARU West Australian Rugby Union
WIPO World Intellectual Property Organization

PART 1

JOURNALISTS, COMMUNICATORS AND THE LEGAL SYSTEM

CHAPTER 1

Media law in the Web 2.0 era

KEY CONCEPTS

Media law
An array of laws affecting journalists and other professional communicators in their research, publishing and social media use. Key areas are defamation, intellectual property, contempt and court publishing restrictions, confidentiality, privacy, national security, discrimination and freedom of information.

Publication
The act of 'publication' is foundational to many media laws because legal responsibility typically applies from the moment material is sent from one person to another. It could be as simple as pressing a Facebook 'like' symbol.

Jurisdiction
This legal term applies to the 'reach' of a particular state or country's legal powers, and can also apply to the power of a particular type of court to hear a civil or criminal case or other dispute.

Self-regulation
A particular profession's system of rules and procedures, including for ethical and other complaints that it can handle internally without involving the criminal or civil powers of a court or government-appointed tribunal. A hybrid system called 'co-regulation' involves a government authority, like the Australian Communications and Media Authority (ACMA), with power to intervene when self-regulation in the broadcast media has failed or a decision has been appealed.

Media law reform
The process of revising existing laws and regulations affecting the media, and of developing proposals for new ones, typically undertaken by law reform

commissions, parliamentary committees or government-appointed inquiry bodies, although sometimes proposed as legislation as a draft Bill in the parliament.

Fake news
Disinformation published on websites and social media for political purposes or to drive web traffic which would not qualify for media law defences requiring truth or factuality as an element.

Advances in communication technology in this new millennium have redefined the ways most of us share news and information. Industry upheaval and technological disruption have prompted many journalists to retool as bloggers, public relations consultants, multimedia producers and social media editors. These roles add exciting new dimensions to journalism and strategic communications—including conversations and engagement with audiences and instant global publishing at the press of a button. But they also present new legal risks that most professional communicators did not envisage in the twentieth century.

The changes have been so profound that they have impacted the ways we live and organise our lives and work practices. It is only when we review some of the milestones of the internet and Web 2.0, together with the legal and regulatory changes they have prompted, that we start to appreciate the need for all professional communicators to be knowledgeable about media law.

BACKGROUND AND INTERNATIONAL CONTEXT

While the worldwide connection of computers, giving rise to the phenomenon we know as the internet, dates back to the early 1980s, it did not start to impact the lives of ordinary citizens until the mid-1990s. Melbourne's *Age* newspaper became one of the first in the world to offer an online edition in 1995 (van Niekerk, 2005). Over the ensuing years, entrepreneurs started to embrace the commercial potential of the World Wide Web, just as consumers began to use it to source products and services, and students began to engage with it as an educational tool—predominantly from their desktop computers. By the end of 2016, there were approximately 13.5 million internet subscribers in Australia (ABS, 2017).

It was not until August 2003 that the first major social networking platform, MySpace, was launched in California. It was the leading social networking site in the world from 2005 until 2008, when it was surpassed in popularity by Facebook, which by 2017 had almost two billion monthly users, including 15 million in Australia (*Media Watch*, 2017). In the six months to June 2016, 93 per cent of internet users aged 18 to 24 used social networking sites (ACMA, 2016: 58). Streaming of entertainment and news has also become part of daily life. In June 2016, 39 per cent of Australian adults had watched Netflix in the previous seven days, while 27 per cent had watched professional content on YouTube and 16 per cent had viewed the pay television service Foxtel (ACMA, 2016: 82). In the United States by 2017, six out of ten young adults were primarily using online streaming to watch television (Rainie, 2017). Associated with this was the remarkable uptake of the mobile telephone and other devices. The iPhone was only launched in 2007, but by 2016 more than three-quarters of Australians owned a smartphone (ACMA, 2016: 18). The iPad was born in mid-2010 into a market segment that many experts thought did not exist, but by 2016 more than half of Australians used or owned a tablet device (ACMA, 2016: 55). Even more technologies are unfolding rapidly, with implications for both the media and the law, with the increasing use of drone devices for news-gathering purposes and the awe-inspiring Internet of Things (IoT), where everyday devices are all interconnected, offering novel news-gathering and delivery systems for the media but also complex legal ramifications—particularly in the realm of privacy and security law.

Governments, courts and other regulators have been forced to decide on the various rights and interests affected by these new media forms, and some of their decisions have taken private enterprise by surprise. It is a far more difficult task, however, to educate the broader community about social media legal risks. The core message is that we are all publishers in the eyes of the law when we publish a blog or post to a social media platform, and in that role all citizens are subject to the same laws that have affected journalists and publishers for centuries. Further, the instantaneous and global nature of the media means that we may also be the subject of foreign laws of countries other than Australia—particularly if we work for a multinational corporation, or choose to travel to, or have had material we wrote downloaded in, a place where our posts might have broken the law or infringed upon someone's rights. These laws include defamation, contempt of court, intellectual property, confidentiality, privacy, discrimination and national security.

DIGITAL DIMENSIONS

As co-author Mark Pearson explained in his book *Blogging and Tweeting Without Getting Sued* (Pearson, 2012), now that ordinary citizens are publishers on social media, they have been caught up in the tangle of media laws. There was the juror Joanne Fraill, who was sentenced to eight months' imprisonment for contempt of court for friending the accused on Facebook (Pearson, 2012: 45). Then there was Andrew Farley, who had only recently finished high school in Orange, NSW, when he launched into a vicious character attack on social media against a former music teacher, making her so upset she had to take extended sick leave. The case became Australia's first Twitter defamation case to proceed through the courts when the District Court judge awarded the teacher $105,000 in damages (*Farley's case*, 2013). Sixteen-year-old Texan teenager Alison Chang flashed a 'V' sign in a travel snap taken by her church youth counsellor. Her image was lifted from Flickr and posted on a bus stop on the other side of the world as part of a Virgin Mobile advertising campaign, triggering an international legal action by her parents over privacy, libel, contract, negligence and copyright. Virgin had put the caption 'Free text virgin to virgin' right under the teenager's image (Pearson, 2012: 1).

Social media platforms might be configured so that people think they are just corresponding with a cosy group of social media friends—all with a shared sense of humour—but the reality is that remarks can go viral very quickly. Thirty-year-old corporate communications senior executive Justine Sacco lost her job at leading internet and media company IAC after she tweeted tasteless remarks to her 170 followers about AIDS in Africa as she was boarding a flight to Cape Town. Her comments went viral over the duration of her eleven-hour flight and she was trolled ruthlessly for months afterwards, at enormous cost to her wellbeing and her career (Ronson, 2015). In another example, up-and-coming fashion designer Dawn Simorangkir was delighted when she was asked to create some clothing for Courtney Love, but ended up getting $430,000 in defamation damages from the rock celebrity after she angered Love by sending her an invoice. The troubled star had fired off scores of blog and Twitter rants, accusing the designer of being a thief, burglar, felon, drug addict, prostitute, embezzler, cocaine dealer and unfit mother. Love issued an unconditional apology as part of a mediated court settlement, only to be sued by her former lawyers over another series of tweets in which she claimed that they had taken a bribe (*Courtney Love case*, 2009; Pearson, 2012: 19).

There is a clear danger here for professional communicators, such as journalists and public relations practitioners, when using social media. You either need a distinct 'firewall' between your work and your private communications and social media accounts, or you need to treat all your communications as though they are professional posts subject to the media laws we discuss in this book, and compliant with the social media policy of your employer. As we explain very carefully in Chapter 2 and throughout this book, you need to develop strategies to be 'mindful' of your media practices and their legal risks in both your personal and professional communications. Social media policies, codes of conduct and social media companies' 'terms of use' arise on many occasions throughout this book, including in the cases we discuss. It is just as important for you to become familiar with these documents as it is to learn about the laws governing what you can and cannot publish.

With global communication becoming so easy, we need to think about the different legal jurisdictions in which we might be subject to a criminal charge or a lawsuit. Each time you post something to your niche news blog or your social media account, you may be subject to the laws of more than 600 nations, provinces, states and territories. Of course, you might not have 600 hits, views or re-tweets, so you might only be reaching some of them. And, of course, authorities and litigants are generally unlikely to pursue you in your home country. But you can never quite be sure where your words, sounds and images might end up and what the legal consequences might be. As professional communicators, we need to at least be aware of those risks and work to minimise them.

Sometimes the same posting can trigger separate legal actions in different places. Courts and prosecutors might be at odds over whether the laws of one state or another—or even more than one—apply to your online publication or social media posting. When lawyers talk about the 'where' element of an action, the legal term they use is 'jurisdiction'. The word can have a range of legal meanings, but for our purposes it applies to where your publication has reached people, and relates to whether a particular state or nation's laws or courts have any authority over it—and you. For most of the last century, that was all fairly straightforward. Most media organisations were focused on audiences living within fairly well defined geographical areas. Even when a television network broadcast or a newspaper circulated across a state border, the media companies and their lawyers were usually only dealing with one or two sets of laws and court systems, or were able to deal with the problem by varying content between local and interstate editions. That became more complex with the advent of truly interstate and international media organisations in the internet era—first national daily newspapers like *USA Today* and *The Australian*; then international broadcasters like CNN and BBC World; and ultimately global media titles like the *Huffington Post* and *BuzzFeed* and social media platforms like Snapchat, Facebook, Instagram and Twitter. Now media professionals have to consider the legal implications of publishing everywhere, every time you upload your words, images and audio. Despite their best efforts, legislators and judges throughout the world—with their nineteenth- and twentieth-century rituals and precedents—are behind the pace of technological change, and are often finding it hard adapting to the cross-border issues triggered by Web 2.0.

The High Court of Australia became the world's first final court of appeal to rule on the time and place of web publication in a trans-Pacific dispute in 2002. In *Dow Jones v Gutnick* (*Gutnick's case*), the court had to decide whether Australian businessman Joseph Gutnick could sue US-based publisher Dow Jones in his home city of Melbourne over the internet version of its weekly financial magazine *Barron's,* which had 550,000 subscribers internationally, of whom only 1700 had Australia-based credit cards. The publisher argued that the article had been 'published from' New Jersey when it was uploaded, but the court ruled that it was actually published every time it was downloaded, read and understood anywhere throughout the world. The decision gave Gutnick the right to sue for defamation in Victoria, his place of primary residence and the location where he was best known, even though only a small proportion of the publication's readers lived there. *Gutnick's case* demonstrates just how long the arm of cyberlaw can be.

Even within Australia, separate state, territory and federal jurisdictions create complexities, because they often have different publishing laws on important matters like identification restrictions in criminal cases involving sexual crimes, juveniles and national security. For example, it is a serious offence to identify the accused in a serious sexual crime before they have been committed for trial in Queensland, the Northern Territory, or South Australia, but this is normally allowed in other jurisdictions. (Identification of the victim in such cases is banned throughout Australia.) This means journalists need a working knowledge of such laws in all jurisdictions because their online stories transcend these borders and they could face a hefty fine or perhaps a prison term by breaching such prohibitions—even if they are not aware of them.

While foreign countries cannot normally enforce their laws beyond their own borders, you might be called to account for your blogs and postings under their laws if you happen to travel there. And citizens in other countries can go to court to get an order against you in your absence, perhaps demanding that you pay a certain sum in damages for something you have published, or a declaration that what you published was false. That happened to US citizen Bill White in 2003 after he had trolled former colleague Dr Trevor Cullen and others with highly defamatory false allegations (*Cullen's case*). Cullen took his action to the Supreme Court of Western Australia in his home state and won a declaratory judgment of $95,000. White did not defend the case and the damages had not been paid at the time of his death in 2004, but Cullen had at least achieved vindication of his good reputation through the courts.

Under international treaties, nations with equivalent laws to those in your own country can seek to extradite you from your homeland to face trial and punishment for serious publishing offences, like trafficking in child pornography or even breach of copyright, as happened to the New Zealand founder of Megaupload, Kim Dotcom, where the US government won an extradition order in the High Court of New Zealand over alleged copyright breaches it deemed 'fraudulent', along with money laundering, racketeering and wire fraud charges (*Dotcom case*, 2017, appeal pending). Foreign governments and lawyers might also seek information about you from internet service providers (ISPs) or social media networks based in another country—even for non-criminal actions like defamation or privacy infringement.

PROFESSIONAL COMMUNICATORS' LEGAL RESPONSIBILITY AS 'PUBLISHERS'

Whether you have thousands of friends on Facebook, a Twitter following of almost 40 million like US President Donald Trump (@realDonaldTrump), or just a single-figure viewing audience for your Instagram photos of a client's media conference, in the eyes of the law you are now a 'publisher'. Nineteenth- and twentieth-century media barons like William Randolph Hearst and Rupert Murdoch had teams of lawyers at their disposal to advise them on the risks they faced as their giant presses rolled. And they had war chests full of cash to stave off an action or appeal it to the highest courts. Today, even the largest media groups have cut back on staff as they struggle for advertising revenue and audiences. Regardless of whether you work for an internet or social media start-up, a boutique publishing house, a public relations consultancy or as a lone freelancer, you are unlikely to have that scale of support when you find yourself in the midst of a legal dispute you could never have anticipated. You might be working as an independent contractor in the so-called 'gig economy' or your employer may not have the wealth to defend a lawsuit or even to raise bail if you are charged with a criminal offence over material you have published or posted.

Large media organisations traditionally paid the legal costs and damages awards for their journalists if they were sued, and gave them the services of their in-house counsel and external lawyers to guide them through any civil or criminal actions. Most of the so-called 'legacy media' (mainstream media) still do that today, but if you are a reporter or columnist thinking of going solo with your blog, you might weigh this up first. Another advantage of writing for a large media group is that your work is more likely to be checked by editors with some legal knowledge, and perhaps even vetted by the company's lawyers before being published. Either way–and certainly if you are a freelancer or public relations consultant–you should investigate insuring yourself against civil damages.

All over the world, a range of online material has been the subject of legal action, or even prior restraint in the form of court orders or restrictive legislation. This has included words, symbols, still and moving images, sounds, illustrations, headlines, captions and links. Sometimes it is the very words alone that are banned (such as the identity of a victim of a sex crime), while on other occasions it is the overall coverage that creates a meaning that damages a reputation or interferes with a criminal trial–such as a photograph of an accused person, or a story that mentions their prior convictions. Specific kinds of material may be associated with particular laws, with trade mark law protecting against the unauthorised use of others' symbols in connection which the supply of a particular product, copyright covering other uses of other creators' words or images, and defamation laws or more ancient offences such as blasphemy, *lèse majesté* or sedition applying to the use of your own words. In some countries, the simple act of publishing without an official permit is banned, as discussed in the next chapter. There are also many work situations where you might find yourself at greater legal risk. We detail these in Chapter 2 and throughout this edition.

TRUTH, 'FAKE NEWS' AND THE LAW

Notions of truth-telling run deep in both the media and the law. As we learn in Chapter 2, the freedom of individuals and the media to speak and publish truths underscores the foundational philosophical principle of freedom of expression in a democracy. Truth and accuracy also underpin many of the key defences to the media laws covered in this book. However, the term 'fake news'–disinformation published on websites and social media for political purposes or to drive web traffic–and 'post truth'–where objective facts are less influential in shaping public opinion than appeals to emotion and personal belief–were named the 'Words of the Year' in 2016 by the *Oxford* and *Macquarie* dictionaries (Flood, 2016; Hunt, 2017). This was because the expressions had become so popularised through their association with the 2016 US presidential campaign, where successful candidate Donald Trump had gained traction by attacking the mainstream media in his speeches and Twitter feed for its 'fake news' portrayal of him and his policies. Co-author of this book, Mark Pearson (2017), explored the legal implications for those who publish falsified news, and identified defamation–where fake news can damage the reputation of real people–and commercial laws like consumer law, injurious falsehood and intellectual property laws as major hazards for those who choose to peddle false information as news. In essence, while 'fake news' might represent a business model for unethical offshore entrepreneurs preying on gullible audiences using social media, there are numerous media laws that would stand in the way of those attempting it in Australia–and the falsity of the material would destroy possible defences.

DEFINING 'THE PUBLIC INTEREST'

Lawyers, prosecutors and judges will also look to the social purpose served by publishing the material you have written. In some places, that may actually form a defence, while on other occasions your motive or purpose in publishing can be your undoing. Many statutes and court rulings use the expression 'public interest' as an element of a defence to a range of publishing crimes and civil wrongs. In such a case, you have to convince the court that some greater public good is being served by publication, and that society benefits in some way as a result. For example, your defence to a claim that your publication should be taken down because it disclosed confidential information might be that it was in the public interest for your audience to learn of an 'iniquity', such as the cover-up of a possible threat to public health.

Sometimes, even though the term 'public interest' is not used, a defence may have come from a balancing of one set of public interests against the rights of others. For example, copyright law in most countries has a range of 'fair dealing' or 'fair use' defences, which allow parts of copyright material to be re-published without permission for the purposes of education, news or critique. Such defences exist because, through its elected representatives, the community has decided that there is a greater 'public interest' in being educated and informed about such important matters than in protecting the intellectual property owned by the creator of the work. As many judges have pointed out, however, what is in the 'public interest' does not always equate with what is simply 'interesting to the public', and you should not be allowed *carte blanche* simply because your gossip is particularly saucy.

SOCIAL MEDIA AND COMMUNICATION LAW IN AUSTRALIA

Individuals and media organisations have been slower to learn the risks of social media. Several prominent Australians have found themselves in legal strife over their posts. For example, former Test cricketer David Warner was fined by Cricket Australia over a Twitter rant against two journalists (Otto, 2013). Experienced journalist 'Human headline' Derryn Hinch (later a Senator) was jailed for refusing to pay a $100,000 fine over charges stemming from blog and Twitter comments he made about the Melbourne murder of Irish woman Jill Meagher, in breach of a suppression order (ABC, 2013). And the former federal treasurer Joe Hockey sued Fairfax Media over tweets containing the words 'Treasurer for Sale' linked to articles about his connections to a Liberal Party fundraising body (*Hockey case*, 2015). There are many other examples, some of which we showcase in this book.

In both mainstream and social media, you also carry a level of responsibility for the comments of other people on your site. The pioneering decision on corporate responsibility for the comments of third parties in social media was an Australian Federal Court case in 2011 involving an alternative health provider called Allergy Pathway and the consumer regulator (see Key Case 1.1). Justice Finkelstein ruled that the company was responsible for statements made by others on sites and social media pages it was hosting. The Federal Court followed that up in 2012 when it found that the Perthnow news website was responsible for the racially discriminatory comments it allowed to be posted to its site by readers about four Aboriginal youths who died in an accident in a car they had stolen, and ordered it to pay $12,000 to their mother (*Perthnow case*, 2012). The Advertising Standards Bureau also ruled that the Facebook pages of VB and Smirnoff Vodka were effectively advertisements, and that those companies were responsible for the discriminatory and obscene comments made there by customers (Smith, 2012: 4–5). As we explain in Chapter 13, this principle of publisher responsibility for the comments of third parties is still alive, with several cases in recent years extending a body of case law dating back to early in the twentieth century with a defamatory statement pinned to a golf club notice board (*Golf Club case*, 1937). Decisions in Canada and Europe have followed a similar approach, determining that the owners of social media sites and websites were responsible for the hateful and defamatory comments made by third parties on those sites once the material came to their knowledge if they did not act to remove them within a reasonable time (Bodrogi, 2016; Saikaley, 2016).

Journalism and communication students are now finding work in emerging careers while at the same time opportunities in the traditional media are declining. We now have positions like 'online producer', 'social media editor', 'social media manager', 'digital media administrator' and 'social media strategist' arising in new media start-ups, government media relations and corporate public relations, all of which call upon the application of old journalism skills like verification and attribution, and new ones like audience comment moderation and social media policy development. Whatever their backgrounds and qualifications, these people are tasked with managing the engagement of their employers—politicians, corporations, government entities and non-government organisations—with their various stakeholders, the bulk of whom are ordinary citizens with a new-found voice and a willingness to use it.

All this requires a new literacy for citizens about the legal risks involved in their social media use—covering the rights and responsibilities of individuals, legal consequences of actions (or, in some cases, inaction) and the systems in which these risks arise. Such a legal literacy is even more relevant to professional communicators. Journalists, public relations practitioners, professional bloggers and corporate relations personnel all have to be completely across media laws—and a large number of business laws—in their new social networking and blogging context. We try to give you that grounding in this book.

THE IMPORTANCE OF MEDIA LAW AND ETHICS

Every day of your working life as a professional communicator—journalist, editor, public relations consultant, media relations officer, social media editor or blogger—you will make decisions that could have legal implications. Whether you are conducting an interview in someone's home, processing a photograph for online publication, writing up a media release, editing news footage for a news bulletin or pressing the 'kill' button during a talkback radio program, you will be exercising a discretion that may need to be defended in court. This happens because your work often involves bringing important news and information to audiences or clients within the constraints of tight deadlines. Some individuals might find journalists' or bloggers' outputs or methods disturbing, threatening, demeaning or offensive. Sometimes the courts or ethical regulators will agree, and journalists and public relations personnel will find themselves admonished, fined, stymied or even jailed. This is the realm of media law: the rules and regulations that affect professional communicators as they go about their work.

Lawyers talk in terms of 'rights' and 'duties'. Every time you sit at the keyboard to draft a blog or dictate your tweet to Siri on your iPhone, you exercise your right to free expression, but at the same time you have a legal duty not to trample on other people's rights in the process. Even in North America and Scandinavia, where free speech has strong constitutional protection, the courts still weigh your 'right to write' against the rights of other citizens—such as their rights to a fair trial, privacy, safety and a good reputation. Nothing will replace the need for sound legal advice if you are thinking of pushing the boundaries of media law—whether in the online environment or elsewhere—but by the end of this book you should at least have a reasonable grasp of the basic legal challenges facing you as a professional communicator in this complex world of cyber-publishing.

Journalists and public relations practitioners often claim to be providing information and commentary for the public good and in the public interest. In that sense, journalism and related fields are among the most public of vocations and it means that any legal or ethical transgression is likely to attract public attention. Many an editor and news director has cited the following anonymous saying to recruits: 'Doctors bury their mistakes. Lawyers jail theirs. But journalists publish theirs for all the world to see.' This makes the study of law vitally important for digital communicators on at least three counts:

- *Public responsibility.* Communication in Australia is freer than that in many other societies. Abuse of that freedom can erode it for others, who may want to use it for the greater public good. Sound legal and ethical practice enhances the standing of journalism in the broader community at a time when many citizens are calling into question the integrity of media professionals and are demanding greater accountability on the part of journalists.
- *Self-protection.* Legal and ethical transgressions can prove costly and painful for professional communicators and their families, friends, colleagues and employers. Defamation actions have the potential to ruin journalists and bloggers financially, and can send

boutique PR companies into receivership. Contempt charges can land journalists in jail for indefinite periods. Ethical breaches can lead to journalists and public relations consultants being stripped of their professional standing, along with any shred of credibility in the eyes of both the public and their peers.

- *Professionalism.* We live in a digital age in which the boundaries of journalism as an occupation are being challenged. Anyone with access to the internet and some basic software can post to social media, set up as a 'content provider' or become a 'citizen journalist'. Journalists and professional communicators can prosper in this environment if they demonstrate a professional knowledge of media law, which sets them apart from the hobbyists and 'fake news' operators.

A sound working knowledge of law should strengthen, rather than shackle, the practices of the professional communicator. Too little knowledge can lead to a journalist or blogger being overly cautious, for fear of committing some vaguely formulated legal or ethical breach. In this sense, ignorance or uncertainty about the law is certainly no excuse: it can have a remarkable 'chilling' effect on reporting and publishing. A solid understanding of media law can be empowering, generating the trust of your employer and allowing you to work to the edge of the law and to the limits of a defence.

KEY CASE 1.1: *ALLERGY PATHWAY CASE*

Australian Competition and Consumer Commission (ACCC) v Allergy Pathway Pty Ltd and Anor (No. 2) [2011] FCA 74

FACTS

In 2009, the Australian Competition and Consumer Commission (ACCC) brought an action against alternative health company Allergy Pathway Pty Ltd, alleging it had engaged in misleading and deceptive conduct, falsely represented goods or services as being of a particular standard or quality and represented that its treatments had unproven benefits, including that they could 'diagnose and treat allergies'. The company did not contest these allegations, and offered undertakings to the court that it would refrain from 'making or publishing or causing to be made or published in any internet website, radio, television or newspaper advertisements or brochures or other written material' any such false and misleading statements.

Despite that, the company continued to allow people to post such claims in testimonials on its website, Facebook page and Twitter feeds. Its breach of the undertaking came before the Federal Court, where an important question was whether Allergy Pathway was responsible for the comments of others on these social media platforms.

LAW

This has become the leading Australian precedent on publishers' responsibility for the comments of others on their websites, Facebook pages and Twitter feeds, and has been followed by other bodies such as the Advertising Standards Bureau. Justice Finkelstein held that the company and its director were in contempt of court. He found that Allergy Pathway's actions in not removing misleading and deceptive claims about its allergy treatments by 'fans' on its social media sites were in breach of the earlier court orders to desist from making them. He fined both the company and director Paul Keir $7500 each for disobedience contempt. Justice Finkelstein's decision established that the host of such a site would need to take reasonable steps to remove any such comments the instant they had been brought to the host's attention. The *Allergy Pathway* decision went to some lengths to define a Facebook 'profile' and 'fan page' and a Twitter feed.

Justice Finkelstein ruled:

> *It has been shown, indeed it was not disputed, that Allergy Pathway knew that persons had published testimonials on its Twitter and Facebook pages and that it took no steps to have them removed . . . While it cannot be said that Allergy Pathway was responsible for the initial publication of the testimonials (the original publisher was the third party who posted the testimonials on Allergy Pathway's Twitter and Facebook pages) it is appropriate to conclude that Allergy Pathway accepted responsibility for the publications when it knew of the publications and decided not to remove them. Hence it became the publisher of the testimonials. In any event it is clear that it caused them to continue to be published from the time it became aware of their existence . . . (paras 32–3)*

LESSONS FOR JOURNALISTS AND PROFESSIONAL COMMUNICATORS

The judge in the *Allergy Pathway case* suggested that the claims should have been removed within a 'reasonable time' during a routine review. But what is a 'reasonable time'? And does that period differ in serious defamation, contempt or race hate examples? The extent to which someone might be immediately liable as a publisher for a seriously offending comment made by a third party on a social media platform, or whether they would be protected by taking it down within a reasonable time, had not been determined as this book went to press. It seems likely, however, that there would be no liability without knowledge or approval of the offending material. This is in line with general principles of responsibility for publication, and is reflected in the Commonwealth *Broadcasting Services Act 1992* (Sch. 5, cl. 91), which provides internet content hosts with protection from liability if they are not aware that they are hosting content of a particular kind—for example, defamatory material. We revisit this line of cases regarding publisher responsibility for the comments of third parties in Chapter 13.

PROFESSIONAL COMMUNICATORS AND LAWS

Courses and texts define 'media law' in a number of ways. At one extreme, you could treat all law as if it applied to journalists and other communicators, as you may well come into contact with any area of law as part of your reporting or publishing work. At the other extreme, it would be possible to narrow down the concept of 'media law' to exclude all laws that do not specifically refer to the media or professional communication. Most laws encountered by communication professionals are the same laws that any citizen would encounter if they went about the same tasks. Professional communicators and journalists have no special legal rights, and have been granted very few special privileges or immunities by law-makers. For example, the laws of defamation, contempt and copyright apply equally to all citizens. That said, sometimes laws do make an exception for journalists or news organisations. Examples include shield laws introduced at federal level and in some states, excusing journalists and news bloggers from having to reveal their confidential sources in court in some circumstances, and protections offered under both consumer and privacy law to the news activities of media companies.

This book sets out to approach media law from the perspective of the journalist and professional communicator, starting with an explanation of the legal system and free expression to establish your digital legal literacy and 'mindful' practice (Part 1), and moving on to examine laws associated with crime and justice (Part 2), the media and reputations (Part 3), terrorism and discrimination (Part 4) and key issues for the digital era (Part 5). These areas of media law are essential knowledge for all professional communicators, although some have more relevance to one occupation or work task than another. For example, the crime and justice material in Part 2 is of most relevance to court reporters, news editors, public information officers and social media editors of public websites where citizens might be tempted to discuss crime. The Part 5 content—particularly that covering basic business law—will be relevant mostly to freelancers, public relations consultants and entrepreneurs starting their own new media businesses.

There are sound reasons why digital communicators should gain some basic understanding of the legal system, and its procedures and terminology, before moving on to a specific study of media law. Clearly, an introductory account of the workings of these fundamentals allows for an informed discussion of those particular areas of the law that affect their work. Together with other professional communication roles, journalism demands an understanding of how laws are made and how to read legislation. This book can deal with the legislative process only in an introductory manner, which it does in Chapter 3. The democratic process benefits from effective reporting, right from the point at which there is an initiative for a new law or a change to existing legislation; through the phase of lobbying and public debate on the proposal; to the drafting of the actual legislation, and readings and debates on it as Bills in parliament; culminating in assent, enactment and actual operation. Democracy requires the robust reporting of this whole process, with a view to highlighting potential impacts on citizens and audiences, and discouraging or exposing the disproportionate influence of vested interests. This is the essence of the news media's role as the 'Fourth Estate' in the democratic system.

SELF-REGULATION AND REFORM

Inquiries into media regulation in the United Kingdom (Leveson, 2012), Australia (Convergence Review, 2012; Finkelstein, 2012) and New Zealand (Law Commission, 2013) recommended major changes to the regulation of media corporations and the ethical practices of journalists. They stemmed, at least ostensibly, from public angst—and subsequent political pressure—over a litany of unethical breaches of citizens' privacy over several years in the United Kingdom, culminating in the *News of the World* scandal and the subsequent revelations at the Leveson Inquiry (2012), all of which had a ripple effect in Australia and New Zealand. Many contextual factors informed the move for reform here, including an element of dissatisfaction over redress for ethical breaches by the media, evidence of mainstream media owners using their influence for political and commercial gain, and the existence of novel public policy challenges facing regulators in an era of multi-platform convergence and citizen-generated content.

The inquiries into the Australian news media prompted a necessary debate over the extent to which rapidly converging and globalised news businesses and platforms might require statutory regulation at a national level. Several regulatory models were proposed, including a News Media Council backed by recourse to the contempt powers of courts; a super self-regulatory body with legislative incentives to join; a strengthened Australian Press Council (APC) policing both print and online media; and a government-appointed Public Interest Media Advocate.

By 2017, only one major legislative reform of the media had been implemented—an abolition of the cross-media ownership laws that had been in place for three decades, as part of a package including a boost to local programming on regional television, limitations on gambling ads and the anti-siphoning list for live sports telecasts, axing of broadcast licence fees and datacasting charges, greater scrutiny of the ABC and the Special Broadcasting Service (SBS), a $60.4 million regional and small publishing subsidy, and an inquiry into the impact of Google and Facebook on Australia's media (AAP, 2017).

The Australian inquiries in 2011 and 2012 acknowledged—and rejected—the notion that a revamped APC would be sufficient reform. (The Press Council was established in 1976 as a newspaper industry 'self-regulatory' body—a purely voluntary entity with no powers under law.) Nevertheless, both during and after these two reports, and with new support from most of its members, the APC moved quickly to ramp up its purview and powers to address many of its documented shortcomings, such as the refusal of some member newspapers to publish its findings and the threat of withdrawal of funding from others (Simpson, 2012). It locked its members into four-year commitments, recruited new members from the online media sector, amended its Statement of Principles and reviewed its content standards.

Over this same period of review of media regulation, several reformulations of existing media laws were being considered by state, territory and federal governments and their respective law-reform bodies. They covered such topics as privacy law, media classification, intellectual property, cyber-bullying, shield laws and national security laws. Of these, new shield laws have subsequently been introduced in six of the nine Australian jurisdictions (Fernandez and Pearson, 2015). (These give partial protection to journalists seeking to protect the identities of their confidential sources in court when they would otherwise be ordered to reveal them.)

In 2017, a Senate Select Committee on the Future of Public Interest Journalism (2018) looked at a range of different legal issues confronting the media—essentially what measures could be taken to help the flagging mainstream media compete with social media and other digital platforms in the era of 'fake news' and the drift of swathes of advertising dollars to offshore operations like Google and Facebook. Three key recommendations were that national security and border protection laws, defamation and whistleblower and shield laws all be reviewed and reformed to help support public interest journalism (Senate Select Committee, 2018: recommendations 6, 7 and 8).

Media law and regulation constitute a field subject to continual scrutiny and change, which makes it even more important for students and professional communicators to keep up to date with developments.

TIPS FOR MINDFUL PRACTICE

- Your work is subject to laws wherever it is downloaded. That means you could be dealing with more than 600 different legal systems, so you need to think globally when you are producing material in social media or online.
- The knowledge of media law you gain from this book does not make you a lawyer. If in doubt about a media law issue, seek professional legal advice.
- Criminal and civil laws apply as much to bloggers and social media users as they do to large media corporations, so ensure the same precautionary editing protocols are followed with your social media and online presence as they are with traditional outputs like magazines, newspapers and broadcast news bulletins.
- Do not post anything unless you are comfortable with it going public—well beyond your immediate friends and contacts. That also means professional communicators need a strict firewall between their private and professional use of social media.
- Watch the reform process carefully. Media laws and regulatory systems are subject to frequent changes. See co-author Mark Pearson's journlaw.com blog for recent developments.

IN A NUTSHELL

- Major changes in technology over recent decades mean most citizens are now 'publishers' and subject to media laws.
- Many more professional communicators now need to know about media law, just as journalists' changing roles require them to have some knowledge of other laws such as contract and negligence.

- You can be held legally responsible for the material posted by others to your blog or social media page.
- Media laws might affect a range of material you publish, including words, symbols, still and moving images, sounds, illustrations, headlines, captions and links.
- The legal understanding of the term 'public interest' is much narrower than that often used by journalists and politicians. Just because something is 'interesting to the public' does not mean it is necessarily 'in the public interest'. It needs to be a matter of legitimate public concern.
- There have been moves to tighten media regulation, and amendments to various laws affecting the media, in recent years. Government reviews have recommended the formation of new media regulatory bodies, and the laws of intellectual property, privacy, national security and confidential sources have all been subject to recent changes.

DISCUSSION QUESTIONS

1.1 Everyone is a 'publisher' now with the advent of social media. Think of some key legal risks that would be faced by a social media editor for a small public relations consultancy and explain how they might differ from those facing an investigative journalist for a major news organisation.

1.2 Why might journalists, public relations practitioners and lawyers take different approaches to a media law issue like confidentiality?

1.3 Which of the following areas of media law is in most need of reform: privacy, copyright, defamation, court publishing restrictions, or shield laws for journalists? Explain your reasoning.

1.4 You are the entertainment editor for a celebrity blog based in Australia. A friend sends you some screen shots of a popular actor's Facebook page with pictures of them using illicit drugs and in a compromising embrace with another actor. Decide whether this material is in the 'public interest' and suggest the legal issues that might arise.

1.5 You are responsible for monitoring the Facebook page of a local government body. You arrive at work at 9.00 am on a Monday to find that on Saturday morning an anonymous person posted a totally false allegation that a leading local businessman is a child molester. You remove it immediately. Is that enough? What legal issues might arise and what work practices might minimise such a legal risk in future?

1.6 Go online and find a recent example of a blogger or social media user getting into trouble with media law. Compare and contrast it with one of the cases in this chapter.

REFERENCES

Australian Associated Press (AAP) 2017, 'Changes to media ownership laws', *SBS News*, 14 September, <www.sbs.com.au/news/article/2017/09/14/changes-media-ownership-laws>.

Australian Broadcasting Corporation (ABC) 2013, 'Melbourne broadcaster Derryn Hinch cops $100,000 contempt of court fine', *ABC News*, 20 October, <www.abc.net.au/news/2013-10-18/melbourne-broadcaster-derryn-hinch-cops-100/5032986>.

Australian Bureau of Statistics (ABS) 2017, Internet Activity, Australia, December 2016, cat. no. 8153, ABS, Canberra, <www.abs.gov.au/ausstats/abs@.nsf/mf/8153.0>.

Australian Communications and Media Authority (ACMA) 2016, *Communications Report 2015–2016*, ACMA, Sydney, <www.acma.gov.au/theACMA/Library/researchacma/Research-reports/communications-report-2015-16>.

Bodrogi, B. 2016, 'The European Court of Human Rights rules again on liability for third party comments', *Media Policy Project Blog*, London School of Economics, 19 February, <http://blogs.lse.ac.uk/mediapolicyproject/2016/02/19/the-european-court-of-human-rights-rules-again-on-liability-for-third-party-comments>.

Convergence Review 2012, *Convergence Review: Final Report*, Department of Broadband, Communications and the Digital Economy, Canberra, <www.dbcde.gov.au/__data/assets/pdf_file/0007/147733/Convergence_Review_Final_Report.pdf>.

Fernandez, J. and Pearson, M. 2015, 'Shield laws in Australia: Legal and ethical implications for journalists and their confidential sources', *Pacific Journalism Review*, 21(1), 61–78.

Finkelstein, R. 2012, *Report of the Independent Inquiry Into the Media and Media Regulation*, Department of Broadband, Communications and the Digital Economy, Canberra, <www.dbcde.gov.au/__data/assets/pdf_file/0006/146994/Report-of-the-Independent-Inquiry-into-the-Media-and-Media-Regulation-web.pdf>.

Flood, A. 2016, '"Post-truth" named word of the year by *Oxford Dictionaries*', *The Guardian*, 16 November, <www.theguardian.com/books/2016/nov/15/post-truth-named-word-of-the-year-by-oxford-dictionaries>.

Hunt, E. 2017, '"Fake news" named word of the year by *Macquarie Dictionary*', *The Guardian* (Australian edition), 25 January, <www.theguardian.com/australia-news/2017/jan/25/fake-news-named-word-of-the-year-by-macquarie-dictionary>.

Law Commission (NZ) 2013, *The News Media Meets 'New Media': Rights, Responsibilities and Regulation in the Digital Age*, Law Commission, Wellington.

Leveson, B. 2012, *Report of an Inquiry into the Culture, Practice and Ethics of the Press*, The Stationery Office, London [Leveson Report].

Media Watch 2017, 'State of play: news media versus the digital giants', ABC TV, 10 July, <www.abc.net.au/mediawatch/transcripts/s4699615.htm>.

Otto, T. 2013, 'Cricket Australia fines David Warner $5750 over Twitter rant', *Daily Telegraph*, 23 May, <www.dailytelegraph.com.au/sport/cricket/cricket-australia-fines-david-warner-5750-over-twitter-rant/story-fni2fnmo-1226648382977>.

Pearson, M. 2012, *Blogging and Tweeting Without Getting Sued: A Global Guide to the Law for Anyone Writing Online*, Allen & Unwin, Sydney.

—— 2017, 'Teaching media law in a post-truth context: Strategies for enhancing learning about the legal risks of fake news and alternative facts', *Asia Pacific Media Educator*, 27(1), 17–26.

Rainie, L. 2017, 'About 6 in 10 young adults in US primarily use online streaming to watch TV', *FactTank—News in the Numbers*, Pew Research Center, Washington, DC, <www.pewresearch.org/fact-tank/2017/09/13/about-6-in-10-young-adults-in-u-s-primarily-use-online-streaming-to-watch-tv>.

Ronson, J. 2015, 'How one stupid tweet blew up Justine Sacco's life', *New York Times Magazine*, 12 February, <www.nytimes.com/2015/02/15/magazine/how-one-stupid-tweet-ruined-justine-saccos-life.html?mcubz=0>.

Saikaley, J. 2016, 'Can you be held liable for comments of others to your posting on your Facebook page?', *CazaSaikaley blog*, 27 April, <www.plaideurs.ca/en/liability-for-comments-posted-online-by-third-parties>.

Senate Select Committee on the Future of Public Interest Journalism 2018, *Report*, Commonwealth of Australia, Canberra, <www.aph.gov.au/Parliamentary_Business/Committees/Senate/Future_of_Public_Interest_Journalism/PublicInterestJournalism/Report>.

Simpson, K. 2012, 'Journalism standards set for an updating', *Sydney Morning Herald*, 20 July, <www.smh.com.au/business/journalism-standards-set-for-an-updating-20120719-22czm.html>.

Smith, D. 2012, 'September, social media marketing', *E-Commerce Law Reports*, 12(4), 4–5.

van Niekerk, M. 2005, 'Online to the future', *The Age*, 28 January, <www.theage.com.au/news/National/Online-to-the-future/2005/01/27/1106415726255.html>.

CASES CITED

Allergy Pathway case: Australian Competition and Consumer Commission (ACCC) v Allergy Pathway Pty Ltd and Anor (No. 2) [2011] FCA 74, <www.austlii.edu.au/au/cases/cth/FCA/2011/74.html>.

Courtney Love case: Dawn Simorangkir, aka Dawn Younger-Smith, aka Boudoir Queen, an individual v Courtney Michelle Love (5 May 2009) BC410593.

Cullen's case: Cullen v White (2003) WA Supreme Court 153.

Dotcom case: Ortmann v United States of America [2017] NZHC 189 (20 February 2017), <www.nzlii.org/nz/cases/NZHC/2017/189.html>.

Farley's case: Mickle v Farley [2013] NSWDC 295, <www.caselaw.nsw.gov.au/decision/54a63cd93004de94513db98f>.

Golf Club case: Byrne v Deane [1937] 2 All ER 204; [1937] 1 KB 818.

Gutnick's case: Dow Jones and Company Inc. v Gutnick (2002) HC 56; 210 GLR 575; 194 ALR 433; 77ALSR 255.

Hockey case: Hockey v Fairfax Media Publications Pty Limited [2015] FCA 652, <www.judgments.fedcourt.gov.au/judgments/Judgments/fca/single/2015/2015fca0652>.

Perthnow case: Clarke v Nationwide News Pty Ltd trading as The Sunday Times [2012] FCA 307, <www.judgments.fedcourt.gov.au/judgments/Judgments/fca/single/2012/2012fca0307>.

CHAPTER 2

Free expression and mindful practice

KEY CONCEPTS

Freedom of expression
The ideal that all human communication in a democratic society should be unshackled by laws or censorship—subject to the impact on other human rights.

Freedom of the press
The term applied to freedom of the media for more than five centuries. (For most of that time, print was the only mass communication medium in existence.) Today, the expression is used interchangeably with 'media freedom'.

Prior restraint
Any legislative or judicial intervention—by law or ruling—that prohibits a communication before it has been published, broadcast or uploaded.

First Amendment
The words included in the US Bill of Rights that prohibit Congress enacting laws abridging free speech or a free press. Sometimes used as a synonym for 'free expression'.

Implied freedom
A freedom that is not expressed in writing in the Constitution, but implied because of the context and conventions of a democratic system of responsible and representative government. The implied freedom to communicate on matters of politics and government is our key example.

Mindful practice
The ability of a practitioner to pause and reflect professionally on an ethical or legal issue as it arises in the workplace, envisage potential pitfalls and devise an approach that serves the greater public interest, cognisant of the implications for all key stakeholders.

BACKGROUND AND INTERNATIONAL CONTEXT

Professional communicators can only work effectively if they have a deep understanding of the level of free expression tolerated in the societies in which they work. Now that so much communication is global, it is vital that we understand different approaches taken to media and communication throughout the world. We are sometimes called upon to defend free expression against those who are critical of the media and its operations. To remain silent when a politician or a judge is proposing censorship or control of those freedoms is to contribute to their erosion. It is important that all professional communicators have a grasp of the principles of free expression, media freedom and their historical context. Public relations practitioners will often have to explain to managers and clients why journalists are able to pursue stories so vigorously and why it is important to be transparent and truthful in the midst of a crisis. Lawyers will need to understand this principle to defend a media client and to oppose a suppression order in court.

The free expression of certain facts and views has always been a dangerous practice, with countless people put to death throughout history for expressing religious or political views. Many more have been imprisoned, tortured or punished for such expression. In 399 BCE, Socrates elected to drink a poison–hemlock–rather than recant his philosophical questioning of the edicts of his city-state, Athens (Brasch and Ulloth, 1986: 9). The history of freedom of expression is also a history of censorship, because when free expression has been threatened, intellectuals have been called upon to defend it. It was Johann Gutenberg's invention of movable type in about 1450, and the massive growth in the publishing industry over the sixteenth and seventeenth centuries in the form of newsbooks and the activities of 'pamphleteers', that first triggered repressive laws, and then the movement for press freedom (Feather, 1988: 46). (It is interesting that these small radical publishers were similar to the citizen journalists and bloggers we know today–often highly opinionated and quick to publish speculation and rumour.)

The pamphleteers took umbrage at government attempts to impose a licensing system for printers from the mid-sixteenth century

(Overbeck, 2001: 34). Political philosopher and poet John Milton targeted this in 1644 with *Areopagitica*, a speech to the parliament appealing for freedom of the presses. He went on to utter the famous free speech principle, 'Give me the liberty to know, to utter, and to argue freely according to conscience, above all liberties' (Patrides, 1985: 241). Milton inscribed his name on the title page of his unlicensed work in bold defiance of the law he was criticising. The notion of free expression had spawned its offspring: press freedom.

Part of Milton's argument centred on the 'marketplace of ideas'—the belief that truth will win over falsehood when the two compete. This proposition of a contest between truth and falsehood was often used during the seventeenth and eighteenth centuries to justify freedom of expression (Smith, 1988: 31). It continues in public discourse today.

Philosopher and political theorist John Locke took up the fight after Milton's death. Under his social contract theory, governments are there to serve the people, and central to this is freedom of expression (Overbeck, 2001: 36). Of the temptation to suppress truth and new ideas, Locke (1690) wrote in his preamble to an 'Essay Concerning Human Understanding':

> *Truth scarce ever yet carried it by vote anywhere at its first appearance: new opinions are always suspected, and usually opposed, without any other reason but because they are not already common. But truth, like gold, is not the less so for being newly brought out of the mine. It is trial and examination must give it price . . .*

Like Milton, Locke campaigned to abolish the English printing licence system, which expired in 1694 (Overbeck, 2001: 36). Those to speak out against restrictions on press freedom at the turn of the eighteenth century included novelist and journalist Daniel Defoe, who wrote 'An Essay Upon the Regulation of the Press' around 1704 (Brasch and Ulloth, 1986: 62), and John Trenchard and Thomas Gordon who, under the pen name 'Cato', wrote a series of letters about freedom in the 1720s (Brasch and Ulloth, 1986: 64–8).

England's foremost philosopher of the late nineteenth century, John Stuart Mill (1991), articulated the need for free speech in a liberal democratic society in *On Liberty*, first published in 1859. He wrote (1991: 20):

> *The time, it is to be hoped, is gone by, when any defence would be necessary of the 'liberty of the press' as one of the securities against corrupt or tyrannical government. No argument . . . can now be needed, against permitting a legislature or an executive, not identified in interest with the people, to prescribe opinions to them, and determine what doctrines or what arguments they shall be allowed to hear.*

Mill's *On Liberty* built on Milton's 'marketplace of ideas' to define the boundaries of freedom of expression in the modern nation-state.

One of the great legal minds of the eighteenth century, Sir William Blackstone (1765–69: 151–2), had a great impact on the evolution of press freedom in his *Commentaries on the Laws of England* by defining it as the absence of 'previous restraints upon publications':

> *The liberty of the press is indeed essential to the nature of a free state; but this consists in laying no previous restraints upon publications, and not in freedom from censure for criminal matter when published. Every freeman has an undoubted right to lay what sentiments he pleases before the public; to forbid this, is to destroy the freedom of the press: but if he publishes what is improper, mischievous, or illegal, he must take the consequences of his own temerity.*

Blackstone's notion of 'prior restraint' has underscored the development of media law in the United States. The idea was that freedom of the press could tolerate no restrictions before publication, such as licensing and taxes that had been imposed in Britain, but that the law should take its course after publication to punish those who abused this freedom. Publications should be tax and licence free, but subject to laws like defamation and contempt once published. In both Britain and its colonies, a common weapon for silencing the press had been the crime of 'seditious libel'—any serious criticism of government or the Crown, whether or not the criticism was truthful. William Murray, Lord Chief Justice and Earl of Mansfield (1704–93), coined the expression 'the greater the truth, the greater the libel' (Whitton, 1998), ensuring that truth would not stand up as a defence to seditious libel.

Despite these restrictions, basic press freedom had taken hold in Britain. Indeed, some thought the press had gone too far. In this context, the expression 'the Fourth Estate' was coined. At that time, there were said to be three 'estates of the realm'—the Lords Spiritual, the Lords Temporal and the Lords Common. In 1790, English statesman Edmund Burke is said to have pointed to the press gallery in parliament and said, 'There are three estates in Parliament but in the reporters' gallery yonder sits a fourth estate more important far than they all' (Inglebart, 1987: 143).

The libertarian ideals on which press freedom is based were not confined to Britain. The movement for civil rights and individual liberties spread throughout Western Europe during the seventeenth to nineteenth centuries, epitomised by the French Revolution in 1789, leaving a legacy of press freedom throughout that region and in its colonial outposts. The key document of the French Revolution was the Declaration of Rights of Man, approved by the National Assembly of France on 26 August 1789. Its Article 11 stated (Avalon Project, 2002):

> *The free communication of ideas and opinions is one of the most precious of the rights of man. Every citizen may, accordingly, speak, write, and print with freedom, but shall be responsible for such abuses of this freedom as shall be defined by law.*

Note the important qualification: people should be responsible for abuses of this freedom 'as defined by law', a common theme to such provisions and a central thread of our study of media law.

PRESS FREEDOM INTERNATIONALLY

In Western democratic societies, we often take our liberties for granted. But there has never been utterly unshackled free speech or a completely free media: we operate on an international and historical continuum of free expression through to censorship. It is only over the past half-century that the notion of free expression and a free media has gained traction on a broader international scale.

There is no enforceable worldwide agreement on free expression as a fundamental human right, although some nations and regions have entrenched free expression in their constitutions. The key international document is the United Nations Universal Declaration of Human Rights, which in 1948 enshrined free expression at Article 19:

> *Everyone has the right to freedom of opinion and expression; this right includes freedom to hold opinions without interference and to seek, receive and impart information and ideas through any media regardless of frontiers.*

At face value, this statement seems to give all the world's citizens a right to free expression. While a declaration of a lofty goal, it has many limitations, as we will see.

Stronger protections came internationally in 1966 when the United Nations adopted the International Covenant on Civil and Political Rights (Office of the High Commissioner for Human Rights, 1976), prompting a series of binding treaties. The covenant introduced a right to free expression for all the world's citizens, again at Article 19. However, the right is limited because the covenant also recognises duties, responsibilities and restrictions covering respect for the rights and reputations of others, and the protection of national security, public order, public health and morals. Add to this the fact that many countries either have not ratified the covenant, or have not incorporated its provisions to make them part of their domestic law—as in the case of Australia.

At least four major democratic English-speaking nations have Bills of Rights enshrining free speech. The First Amendment to the US Constitution in 1791 guaranteed free speech and a free press. The Canadian Charter of Rights and Freedoms (1982), at section 2(b), confers upon every citizen 'freedom of thought, belief, opinion and expression, including freedom of the press and other media of communication'. The legislation in the United Kingdom and New Zealand does not mention media freedom, opting instead for the broader term 'freedom of expression'.

The European Convention on Human Rights has had a strong impact on the laws of countries on that continent, as well as in the United Kingdom via the *Human Rights Act 1988*. Free expression is protected in Article 10, and it carries with it similar responsibilities to those in the Universal Declaration of Human Rights (United Nations, 1948). European countries vary greatly in their levels of free expression. In 2017, they occupied fifteen of the top 20 places in the Reporters Without Borders World Press Freedom Index (Reporters Without Borders, 2017). The highest levels of free expression were in north-western Europe, with Norway, Sweden, Finland, Denmark and the Netherlands in the top five positions.

New Zealand enshrined free expression at section 14 of its *Bill of Rights Act 1990* (BoRA) In 2011, the New Zealand Supreme Court found that the right protected Valerie Morse, an anti-war protester who burned her country's flag during a dawn memorial service in Wellington. Her conviction for offensive behaviour was set aside (*Flag Burning case*, 2011).

Some countries have laws making it an offence to insult their royal family, with Thailand—a nation with an otherwise free and vibrant media—the most active in the use of such laws. These laws are known as *lèse majesté*, and in Thailand a breach can carry a maximum jail term of fifteen years. Authorities have charged as many as 100 people a year with the offence in recent years, with several unsuspecting foreigners languishing in prison. In 2017, Thai law student and activist Jatupat Boonpattararaksa ('Pai Dao Din') received a prestigious human rights award despite facing *lèse majesté* charges for sharing on Facebook a British Broadcasting Corporation (BBC) profile of the new king of Thailand. More than 2000 people had reportedly shared the BBC item, but only Boonpattararaksa was charged; he received a two-and-a-half year sentence (Cochrane, 2017; Amnesty International, 2017). In 2008, Australian Harry Nicolaides spent six months in prison over a passage regarded as offensive to the Crown Prince had appeared in his self-published novel: it sold only a few copies, but extracts had been published on a US-based website (Akha Heritage Foundation, 2009). Other nations, including Kuwait, also have *lèse majesté* laws or similar.

For many truth-seekers and truth-tellers, the commitment to free expression has taken the form of physical injury or danger—even death. The Committee to Protect Journalists (CPJ) lists more than 1250 journalists confirmed as killed in the course of their work since 1992, including 79 in 2016 (CPJ, 2017). Throughout the Asia-Pacific region, many others suffer violence or are imprisoned for what they report. Some have suffered in other ways, as the victims of lawsuits by those who set out to gag them.

THE US EXPERIENCE

British and European liberal ideals found their way into the wording of the American Declaration of Independence in 1776, the US Constitution in 1789 and the US Bill of Rights in 1791. Central to the Bill of Rights was the First Amendment to the US Constitution:

> *Congress shall make no law respecting an establishment of religion, or prohibiting the free exercise thereof; or abridging the freedom of speech, or of the press; or the right of the people peaceably to assemble, and to petition the Government for a redress of grievances.*

In the context of lively public debate over the wording of the First Amendment and during debates over its ratification, Thomas Jefferson—a future US president and perhaps the greatest advocate of press freedom—coined some famous lines:

> *The basis of our government being the opinion of the people, the very first object should be to keep that right; and were it left to me to decide whether we should have a government without newspapers or newspapers without a government, I should not hesitate a moment to prefer the latter. (To Edward Carrington in 1787, cited in Inglebart, 1987: 124)*

The First Amendment has allowed members of the US media to act with fewer restraints than their colleagues in almost any other country. Nevertheless, their behaviour is not unrestricted, and in the two centuries since the US Bill of Rights was enacted, there have been court and parliamentary battles against attempts to read it narrowly. Many battles have been lost, with courts and legislatures maintaining that other rights—like national security—take precedence.

The twentieth-century platform for the US press freedom battle was the issue of seditious libel and the right to criticise the US government. Pember (2001: 60–1) explains that the first sedition laws in the United States, the Alien and Sedition Acts, were passed in 1798, just after the First Amendment. The laws made it a crime to criticise the president and the government, and many editors and politicians were prosecuted. Sedition prosecutions in the early twentieth century prompted the US Supreme Court to interpret the meaning of the First Amendment in relation to public protests and criticisms of government. In 1925, the court ruled that the First Amendment offered protection from censorship by all levels of government (2001: 61). Another sedition law was adopted in 1940—the Smith Act, which prohibited advocating the violent overthrow of government. The Supreme Court read the law down in the light of the First Amendment: in 1957 in *Yates' case* to say that the accused must have advocated 'specific violent or forcible action toward the overthrow of the government'; and again in 1969 when it ruled in *Brandenburg's case* that the Constitution protected advocacy of unlawful conduct unless it was inciting imminent lawless action (2001: 61).

US government attempts to restrain publication in the national interest have usually failed on First Amendment grounds. The principle was established firmly in the *Minnesota case* (1931), when the state of Minnesota suspended publication of a small weekly newspaper, *The Saturday Press*, because of its defamatory articles exposing corruption. The Supreme Court overturned the suspension, ruling that prior censorship is allowable only in extreme circumstances (Pember, 2001: 67). At least three major cases later in the twentieth century tested this principle. One was the *Pentagon Papers case* (1971) in which *The New York Times* and *The Washington Post* were blocked for two weeks from publishing sensitive documents exposing the facts behind the US government's secret involvement in Vietnam. (It was a prescient case, in view of the more recent WikiLeaks, Edward Snowden-NSA, Panama Papers and Paradise Papers exposés.)

The most significant First Amendment case was *Sullivan's case* (1964), in which an elected Alabama official claimed that *The New York Times* defamed him in an advertisement that alleged police under his supervision were violent and intimidating towards African-American civil rights protesters. The US Supreme Court invoked the First Amendment to rule that public officials had to pass tough new tests before they could succeed in a defamation action, even if the allegations were false.

The 9/11 terrorist attacks on the United States in 2001 brought new threats to media freedom as governments engaged in the so-called 'war against terror' enacted legislation to help police and intelligence agencies to identify and pursue suspects. While media outlets acknowledged the need for more effective security measures, most objected to the resulting curtailment of press freedom. The first major legislation was the USA Patriot Act 2001, with the full title 'Uniting and Strengthening America by Providing Appropriate Tools Required to Intercept and Obstruct Terrorism (USA Patriot Act) Act of 2001'. First Amendment expert Paul K. McMaster (2005) described it as 'a law drenched in secrecy' because of its provisions for secret searches, enforcement provisions and restrictions upon what courts could make public about Patriot Act cases.

More recently, there has been a high level of concern expressed by the Australian media over the extent to which anti-terror and espionage legislation was passed in years following the 9/11 terrorism attacks on the United States and how by 2017 such laws had usurped freedom of expression and exposed journalists to criminal prosecution (MEAA, 2017). We look at these limitations more closely in Chapter 10.

DIGITAL DIMENSIONS

Web 2.0 communication has further empowered ordinary citizens to publish blogs, tweets, podcasts, Facebook postings, and Instagram and Flickr images. Citizen journalists can crowd-source funds for important stories and not-for-profits can operate news platforms that compete with legacy media. At the same time, the financial model of traditional media is under chronic stress. Fourth Estate investigative journalism that was once funded by the 'rivers of gold' generated by classified advertising has lost much of its funding base as people have turned to alternative online sources. Investigative reporting does not come cheaply. Tighter budgets mean less funding for submissions to governments objecting to laws that would muzzle the press and fewer challenges to suppression orders or appeals to higher courts on points of law and free press principles. There is greater pressure on publishers and networks to settle out of court. Bloggers and citizen journalists may be left stranded without the resources to defend legal threats unless they can garner the support of a union, an international NGO or a pro bono (unpaid) lawyer.

A downside to the technological revolution is the level of surveillance of the journalistic enterprise, available to governments and their agencies. Anti-terror laws introduced internationally—modelled on the USA Patriot Act—give intelligence agencies unprecedented powers to monitor the communications of citizens. There is also an inordinate level of surveillance, logging and tracking technology in use in the private sector—often held in computer clouds or multinational corporate servers, in jurisdictions that may be subject to the search and seizure powers of foreign governments. Even cars and appliances now store information as the Internet of Things (IoT). These factors—including geolocational data about where and when we are using a device—have disturbing implications for journalists and their confidential sources—typically government or corporate 'whistleblowers', who may risk their reputations, jobs and even lives. While the internet can be a tool for democracy, there is a downside to the use of social media and blogs if you are working in a country that does not value free speech: web-based activities can be monitored quite easily and careless use of such media can leave you dangerously exposed. Countries with high levels of censorship maintain tight controls over expression, and take action against online writers who question their authority.

In the internet era, even the US First Amendment protections are sometimes not enough to protect citizen journalists. In 2006, Josh Wolf spent seven and a half months in prison for refusing to hand over to a court the footage of protesters he had posted to his site. The most controversial example of bold internet publishing has been the release of vision and classified documents by WikiLeaks since its 2006 launch. Its 2010 upload of classified US diplomatic cables prompted legal actions and threats, including the arrest, charging and conviction of Private Bradley (now Chelsea) Manning as the source of the leaks, demands that Twitter hand over account information, pressure on companies to refuse donations to WikiLeaks and threats of defamation suits—all of which culminated in an asylum claim by WikiLeaks director Julian Assange, who in 2018 remained effectively under house arrest in the Ecuadorian embassy in London. The timing of his document dumps detailing US presidential candidate Hillary Clinton during the 2016 elections led to allegations he was a 'tool of Russian intelligence' (Smiley, 2017).

A leak of classified US documents had international diplomatic repercussions in 2013 and 2014 when former NSA employee Edward Snowden worked with mainstream media organisations to release tranches of surveillance records showing how the phones of world leaders had been electronically monitored. When the Australian Broadcasting Corporation (ABC) joined *The Guardian* in publishing revelations that Australia had phone-tapped Indonesia's president, that country withdrew its ambassador and ceased cooperation on anti-people smuggling and military initiatives. Like Assange, Snowden sought political asylum—in his case, in Russia.

While the identities of WikiLeaks and NSA whistleblowers were revealed and they were either jailed or forced to flee, the German journalists who broke the Pulitzer Prize-winning 'Panama Papers' story via more than 100 media organisations managed to keep secret (via encryption and other techniques) their 'John Doe' confidential source who had provided them with more than eleven million financial documents linking international figures to secret bank accounts (Harding, 2017).

Some governments and legal systems put pressure on ISPs and multinational websites, or require them to disclose the origin of their content.

MEDIA FREEDOM IN AUSTRALIA

Prior to European settlement, communication and storytelling within and between Aboriginal and Torres Strait Islander peoples were navigated through a range of socio-linguistic, cultural and religious conventions related to seniority, gender, place, traditions and purpose (Klapproth, 2004: 6). In that sense, 'communication law' was markedly different from the laws we consider in this book, yet similar in that it was socially determined over thousands of years according to the various rights of the individuals communicating in the many cultures and places where that communication took place.

As a British colony, freedom of the press in Australia shadowed its development in England. Mayer (1964: 10) recorded that Australia's first newspaper, *The Sydney Gazette* (1803–42), was published 'By Authority', indicating its level of censorship by the governors of the day. Mayer (1964: 17) listed the early direct pressures on newspapers as being censorship, demands for securities, actions for libel and contempt of court or parliament.

Pullan (1994) wrote a colourful account of the early instances of censorship in nineteenth-century Australia; it is a litany of prosecutions for sedition, criminal libel and contempt as governors attempted to force their will on the fledgling press. The excerpt from the *Newspaper Acts Opinion* in 1827 (see Classic Case 2.1) captures a crucial moment in the development of press freedom in Australia: the dispute between NSW Governor Ralph Darling and Chief Justice Sir Francis Forbes over newspaper licensing. Former NSW Chief Justice James Spigelman (2002) described the episode as 'the most serious conflict between the judiciary and the executive that has ever occurred in Australian history' because there were 'fundamental principles at stake involving the rule of law, the independence of the judiciary and the freedom of the press'.

Unlike other Western democracies, Australia has no equivalent to the US First Amendment and no written law enshrining freedom of the press at a national level. (However, some state and territory charters are detailed below.) The Australian Constitution did not explicitly mention freedom of speech or of the press at Federation in 1901. Nevertheless, Australian laws affecting press freedom deviated little from the British system. It was not until the 1990s that major High Court decisions held that the Australian Constitution contained an implied, albeit limited, right to freedom of speech on topics of political discussion.

CLASSIC CASE 2.1: *NEWSPAPER ACTS OPINION*

Newspaper Acts Opinion [1827] NSWSC 23 (1 April 1827)

Governor Darling, who had taken office at the end of 1825, was offended by criticism published in the Sydney press, particularly *The Australian* and *The Monitor*. He introduced a newspaper licensing Act and a stamp duties Act, which required certification from Chief Justice Francis Forbes before they could become law. Forbes CJ refused to issue a certificate for the licensing Act. He wrote:

> *By the laws of England, the right of printing and publishing belongs of common right to all His Majesty's subjects, and may be freely exercized like any other lawful trade or occupation. So far as it becomes an instrument of communicating intelligence and expressing opinion, it is considered a constitutional right, and is now too well established to admit of question that it is one of the privileges of a British subject . . . [I]t is clear that the freedom of the press is a constitutional right of the subject, and that this freedom essentially consists in an entire exemption from previous restraint; all the statutes in force are in accordance with this first principle of law; they facilitate the means of proof; in certain cases, they increase the measure of punishment; but in no instance do they impose any previous restraint either upon the matter of publication or the person of the publisher . . . By the laws of England, then, every free man has the right of using the common trade of printing and publishing newspapers; by the proposed bill, this right is confined to such persons only as the Governor may deem proper. By the laws of England, the liberty of the press is regarded as a constitutional privilege, which liberty consists in exemption from previous restraint;*

by the proposed bill, a preliminary license is required, which is to destroy the freedom of the press, and to place it at the discretion of the government.

. . . That the press of this Colony is licentious may be readily admitted; but that does not prove the necessity of altering the laws.

– Francis Forbes, Chief Justice, New South Wales

HIGH COURT POLITICAL FREE-SPEECH DECISIONS

A series of High Court decisions had a major impact on recognition of the value of political speech in Australia, beginning in the 1990s. In further decisions in 2001–02, differences in opinion emerged among High Court justices on the extent of what was termed 'the implied freedom'. In 2012–13, the High Court restricted its involvement to reviewing whether legislation was constitutional, and refused to overturn 'reasonably adapted and appropriate' laws that impacted upon free expression. We will now consider these periods briefly in tracking the movement of Australia's highest court regarding what it has described as 'the implied constitutional freedom to communicate on matters of politics and government'.

THE GROUND-BREAKING 1992 DECISIONS

The first important decisions on the implied freedom of political communication were handed down in 1992: the *ACTV case* and *Wills' case*. The first challenged the federal government's power to prohibit political advertising on radio and television on the eve of an election (see Key Case 2.1). The second challenged federal power under the *Industrial Relations Act 1988* to punish those who write or speak words calculated to bring the Industrial Relations Commission or its members into disrepute. The High Court found that both pieces of legislation impinged on citizens' rights to communicate on matters of government—a right that is fundamental to the system of representative government and implied in the Constitution.

KEY CASE 2.1: *ACTV CASE*

Australian Capital Television (ACTV) Pty Ltd v Commonwealth (1992) 177 CLR 106 (30 September 1992)

FACTS

The Commonwealth government amended the *Broadcasting Act 1942* to restrict political commercials during election campaigns. The legislation was designed to reduce the influence of campaign donors. Advertisements were to be replaced by free election broadcasts. Australian Capital Television Pty Ltd operated a Canberra commercial television station and challenged the restrictions.

LAW

Chief Justice Mason, and the majority of the court, found there was an 'implied guarantee of freedom of communication, at least in relation to public and political discussion'. Freedom of communication was an indispensable element in the system of representative government. It was enshrined in the Constitution, although not expressly stated. Chief Justice Mason said, 'in the area of public affairs and political discussion, restrictions of the relevant kind will ordinarily amount to an unacceptable form of political censorship'. Nevertheless, a court should go through the process of weighing the benefits of any restrictive legislation against the burden on freedom of communication.

LESSONS FOR JOURNALISTS AND PROFESSIONAL COMMUNICATORS

This landmark case, along with its accompanying free speech case, *Wills' case*, represented a turning point in judicial recognition of freedom of political communication in twentieth-century Australia. We can look to this case as the recognition by our highest court that political speech is fundamental to the workings of our system of government, and should not be curtailed except in pressing circumstances.

1994: ESTABLISHING A CONSTITUTIONAL DEFENCE TO DEFAMATION

Two cases in 1994 tested the extent to which political free speech arguments could be used by the media in defending defamation actions. In *Stephens' case*, the High Court broadened a defamation defence called 'qualified privilege' (see Chapter 8) to apply to the media when the defamation occurred in the course of discussing government or politics. Three articles published in 1992 by *The West Australian* newspaper about travel by six Western Australian politicians as members of a government committee quoted an MP describing the trip as a 'mammoth junket' and a 'rort'—a waste of public funds done without parliament's knowledge. The politicians sued. The court held that a publisher need not prove the truth of a defamatory imputation published as part of political discussion, as long as it was published in good faith, the information appeared to be reliable and it had been obtained from a person who had an apparent duty or interest in making the information available to the public.

In *Theophanous's case*, the court took a slightly different path and developed a new defence to defamation, separate and distinct from the existing qualified privilege defence, based on the implied constitutional guarantee of freedom to communicate on matters of government. Victorian RSL president Bruce Ruxton had published a letter in the *Sunday Herald Sun* imputing that Labor MP Dr Andrew Theophanous was biased towards Greeks as migrants and that he was an 'idiot'. Theophanous sued. The court, in a four-to-three majority, developed a new defence based on the 1992 free speech decisions. The defence would apply if defamatory material were published in the course of discussion of political matters about members of federal parliament to do with their suitability for office, provided that the publisher acted reasonably in the circumstances, and that the publication was not made with knowledge that it was false or in reckless disregard for the truth.

These decisions shifted the balance of defamation law towards the media. They initially freed up the political debate, giving media outlets the scope to publish legitimate—though unprovable—criticisms of politicians, public officers and their performance.

THE 1997 DECISIONS: REAFFIRMING BUT REFINING FREE SPEECH

The next major test came in 1997 in *Lange's case*, in which the High Court unanimously reaffirmed a version of the political qualified privilege defence. Former New Zealand Prime Minister David Lange sued the ABC over a broadcast on *Four Corners* about political donations. The High Court said that every citizen's freedom to discuss matters of government and politics was central to our system of representative government, even though it was not stated in the Constitution. This implied freedom was not a positive right, however; rather, it was a brake on the efforts of government or legislators to limit what people might say. The question in each case was whether the particular law was a burden on communication about government and political matters; if so, the next question would be whether the law was nevertheless reasonably adapted to serve a legitimate end. With regard to defamation, this required the application of a 'reasonableness' test being applied to the publisher, which we examine in Chapter 8.

Another case heard at the same time as *Lange* had implications for free speech. *Levy's case* involved an opponent of duck shooting who was charged under Victorian law with being in a hunting area during a prohibited period without a licence. He was collecting dead and wounded ducks and drawing the media's attention to the issue. Levy contended that the regulation used to charge him was invalid because it infringed his freedom to communicate on matters of government. While the High Court agreed that political communication could involve acts, deeds, symbols or images as well as words, it rejected his argument and held that the freedom to communicate on politics was not absolute and would not override 'reasonably appropriate' laws.

2006: PRIOR RESTRAINT REVISITED

In 1966, three children from the Beaumont family, aged nine, seven and four, had disappeared in South Australia, in one of Australia's most notorious unsolved crimes. Police suspected that they had been murdered. In November 1975, James O'Neill was convicted of the murder of a young boy he had abducted in Tasmania earlier that year. In an interview with Tasmanian police, O'Neill confessed to the murder of another young boy. The Tasmanian Commissioner of Police was reported as saying O'Neill could also be responsible for the South Australian kidnapping of the Beaumont children. Three decades later, in 2005, a film dealing with the kidnapping and O'Neill's possible involvement, *The Fisherman*, was due to be screened nationally on ABC TV. O'Neill sued for defamation, and an injunction preventing the broadcast was granted in Tasmania (*Fisherman case*, 2006). The ABC appealed to the High Court. In setting aside the injunction, the High Court found the Tasmanian Supreme Court Full Court had failed to give enough weight to the significance of free speech in considering prior restraint of publication.

2012–18: RE-BALANCING THE FREEDOM

The High Court once again reaffirmed—but narrowed—the implied freedom in three important free speech appeals in 2012 and 2013. The first was the *Palm Island Parole case* in 2012. Lex Wotton was an Aboriginal man sentenced to six years' jail for taking part in a riot on Palm Island after the death of an Aboriginal man in police custody. He was eligible for parole after two years' imprisonment. The Parole Board granted him parole but stipulated 22 conditions, including prohibitions on him attending public meetings on Palm Island without permission or receiving any direct or indirect payment or benefit from the media. He appealed to the High Court, arguing that those conditions infringed his freedom of political communication. He also challenged two sections of the Queensland *Corrective Services Act 2006*—section 200(2), under which the parole conditions were set, and section 132(1)(a), which banned any unauthorised interview of a prisoner (even one on parole). A majority of the High Court dismissed Wotton's appeal, finding that while the provisions did burden his freedom of communication about government or political matters, they were reasonable and served a legitimate end. Wotton had to wait until his parole period expired in 2014 before he could attend a public meeting on the island or be interviewed by the media without permission.

The High Court considered two further non-media free speech cases in 2013 that reinforced this position. In the *Mall Preachers case* (2013), Caleb and Samuel Corneloup were evangelical members of the fundamentalist 'Street Church', who preached in Adelaide's busy Rundle Mall in a loud, animated and sometimes confronting style. Adelaide City Council tried to stop them, by using a by-law prohibiting anyone preaching or distributing printed matter on any road to any bystander or passer-by without permission. The High Court majority held that the *Local Government Acts* empowered the council to make the by-laws. They 'were a valid exercise of the Council's statutory power to make by-laws for the good rule and government of the area, and for the convenience, comfort and safety of its inhabitants'. Although they 'burdened political communication, they did not infringe the implied constitutional freedom' because they served a legitimate end in a manner compatible with our system of representative and responsible government.

In the *Afghan Letters case* judgment, handed down on the same day, the High Court split three–three over whether a law restricting the use of the postal service to distribute offensive materials was invalid because it was inconsistent with the implied constitutional freedom of political communication. An anti-war protester, Man Haron Monis, sent at least twelve letters and a recorded message to the families of Australian soldiers killed in action in Afghanistan, and to the mother of an Austrade official killed in Indonesia. The letters were critical of Australian forces being sent to Afghanistan and, while sympathetic at the start, proceeded to insult and criticise the deceased. The NSW *Crimes Act* prohibited a person using a postal or similar service 'in a way . . . that reasonable persons would regard as being . . . menacing, harassing or offensive'. The six High Court justices hearing the appeal found unanimously that the legislation did restrict political communication, but they were divided equally on whether the legislation was legitimate or implemented in a manner compatible with Australia's system of representative and responsible government. An appeal fails when the court is deadlocked. Man Monis later instigated the Lindt Café siege in Sydney in 2014, during which he and two of his hostages died during a shoot-out with police.

In *O'Shane's case*, in 2013, the NSW Supreme Court held by majority that discussion of a judicial officer's conduct in a particular case did not qualify as discussion concerning political or governmental matters, even if the person making the statements was, in effect, seeking the judicial officer's removal.

In 2017, two justices of the High Court refused an application for leave to appeal by army reservist Major Bernard Gaynor against his dismissal over ultra-conservative political comments against tolerant defence force policies on homosexuality and Islam. The court held that the regulation under which Gaynor was dismissed—on the grounds that his retention as an officer was not in the interest of the Defence Force—was valid because on its proper operation it did not burden the implied freedom of political communication. This was despite the fact that he was expressing private views about political matters (*Army Reserve case*, 2017).

Conversely, also in 2017, the High Court held in *Brown v Tasmania* that the *Workplaces (Protection from Protesters) Act 2014* (Tas), which empowered police to direct protesters to leave and stay away from business premises and business access areas under pain of arrest and criminal penalties, was invalid to the extent that it *impermissibly* burdened the implied freedom of political communication, where protesters in the vicinity of forest operations in Lapoinya Forest had been directed to leave and stay away from forestry land, then arrested and charged.

The nation's top judges and lawyers are still deciding the extent of any implied constitutional freedom to communicate on matters of politics and government, but the more recent decided cases have in general concerned the exercise of that freedom by individuals, rather than the media.

BILLS OF RIGHTS: THE ACT, VICTORIA AND A NATIONAL RECOMMENDATION

Australia has no national Bill of Rights—no document stating the fundamental rights of citizens. For several decades, civil liberties advocates have pushed for one without success, including a question in a 1988 Commonwealth referendum. The National Human Rights Consultation Committee recommended to the Commonwealth government in 2009 that it introduce a Commonwealth Human Rights Act, but this has not occurred. Independent MP Andrew Wilkie introduced an Australian Bill of Rights Bill in 2017, which proposed to give effect to various international human rights instruments, but the Bill lapsed in 2018. Victoria and the Australian Capital Territory (ACT) have their own human rights legislation, which grants rights of freedom of expression to individuals among a host of other rights. Section 16 of the Australian Capital Territory's *Human Rights Act 2004* states that everyone has the right to freedom of expression, including to impart information and ideas orally, in writing or in print, or in another way, subject only to reasonable limits set by Territory laws that can demonstrably be justified in a free and democratic society. In Victoria, Section 15 of the *Charter of Human Rights and Responsibilities Act 2006* (Vic) expresses the right in very similar terms, subject to lawful restrictions reasonably necessary to respect the rights and reputation of other persons; or for the protection of national security, public order, public health or public morality.

PRESS CENSORSHIP AND SYSTEMS REGULATION

Theorists have attempted to classify the functions of the press, within different government systems. Siebert, Peterson and Schramm's (1963) *Four Theories of the Press* categorised press systems into 'Authoritarian', 'Libertarian', 'Soviet-Communist' or 'Social Responsibility' categories. Others have criticised this approach for its simplicity and out-dated perspective, with Denis McQuail (1987) adding two further categories: the development model and the democratic-participant model.

When used to describe approaches of governments to media regulation, the libertarian model has most commonly been associated with private ownership of newspapers and their active watchdog role as the Fourth Estate. But liberal democratic societies have also adopted a 'social responsibility' approach to the regulation of broadcast media, originally based on public or collective interest in control of what was in the pre-digital era of analogue broadcasting a scarce resource, given the limited number of radio and television frequencies then available for allocation as broadcasting licences (Feintuck and Varney,

2006: 57). Proposals by inquiries into media regulation in the United Kingdom (Leveson, 2012), Australia (Finkelstein, 2012) and New Zealand (Law Commission, 2013) would have extended the social responsibility model to print and new media regulation. Rather than taking a libertarian approach and reducing the government regulation of broadcasters because scarcity and media concentration arguments are diminishing, the inquiries recommended mechanisms to bring newspaper companies under government control.

These inquiries re-examined sacrosanct principles like 'freedom of the press' and 'free expression' in the context of converged and globalised communications, and the damaged economic foundations of the so-called 'legacy' media. The Finkelstein report asserted that there was a 'gulf' between the ethical standards of the news media and those of the public, a similar perception to that which triggered the Leveson inquiry in the United Kingdom over the phone-hacking activities of the *News of the World* and other London tabloids, particularly on matters of privacy and deception (Finkelstein, 2012: 124).

Communication theories of press systems provide mechanisms to help us contextualise media regulation, and to help explain why media laws condone or prohibit certain media practices. Media regulations were generally born of an Anglo-American approach to journalism, shaped largely by the libertarian positioning of the press in those countries (truth, the public's right to know and source confidentiality) and refined somewhat by the social responsibility pressures of the late twentieth and early twenty-first centuries (concerns over broadcast licences as a public resource, privacy and discrimination).

Some countries justify their stricter regulation of the press, and limitations of media freedom, on religious, cultural or economic grounds. There has been debate about the lack of press freedom in the Asia-Pacific region: Malaysia, Singapore, Brunei and Fiji have state licensing systems in place for their newspapers, justified by a 'development' model for the media 'to support the government in its quest to promote harmony, solidarity, tolerance and prosperity' (Dutt, 2010: 90)

In addition to the laws we discuss in this book, a host of self-regulatory documents define acceptable work practices for professional communicators as they go about their daily tasks. For example, public relations consultants have to be mindful of the Public Relations Institute of Australia's (PRIA) Code of Ethics and journalists of the Media, Entertainment and Arts Alliance (MEAA) Journalist Code of Ethics and in-house and industry codes of practice. (See Appendices 1–3).

MINDFUL PRACTICE: REFLECTING UPON MEDIA LAW IN THE WORKPLACE

It is the aim of this book that those who use it will be able to apply their knowledge to work situations. Professional communicators should be able to recognise legal or ethical issues and be equipped to deal with them. The solution may be as simple as knowing when to consult a lawyer or as complex as rewriting another journalist's story or media release to avoid legal or ethical pitfalls.

The term 'mindfulness' is commonly used in modern Western societies, but has its origins in Buddhism. Smith and Novak (2003: 43) explain that the step of 'right conduct' in Buddhism involves 'a call to understand one's behaviour more objectively before trying to improve it' and 'to reflect on actions with an eye to the motives that prompted them'. This has parallels with the strategic approach developed by educationalist Donald Schön, whose research aimed to equip professionals with the ability to make crucial decisions in the midst of practice. Schön (1987: 26) coined the expression 'reflection-in-action' to describe the ability of the professional to reflect on some problem in the midst of their daily work. Such reflection is crucial to a considered review of a legal or ethical dilemma in a news-gathering or professional communication context. It is essential to have gone through such a process if a journalist or public relations practitioner is later called to account. Many ethical decisions are portrayed in terms of the 'public interest' when the core motivating factor has not been the greater public good, but rather the ambition of an individual journalist or the commercial imperative of an employer. Professional communicators should pause to reflect not only on the legal risks involved, but also on the implications of their actions upon others—the people who are the subjects of their stories, others who might be impacted, the effects upon their own reputations and the community standing of others, and the public benefits ensuing from this particular truth being told in this way at this time.

A PROCESS OF MINDFUL DECISION-MAKING IN MEDIA LAW

What steps can a professional communicator follow in developing and actioning a more mindful practice for identifying and reflecting upon a media law dilemma? The first challenge is to be able to identify a potential media law issue in the midst of researching or writing. Given that a journalist or public relations consultant might be working on numerous stories, investigations, production or communication tasks in any single day, what might indicate to them the 'red flags' that indicate a situation that is worthy of reflection or advice from supervisors or lawyers?

The answer lies in a combination of situational/emotional analysis and media law knowledge, combined with a routine system of reflection. We have identified these situations and emotions over decades of training and advising professional communicators in media law. Table 2.1 presents some key professional communication situations and emotions mapped against the areas of media law that might become relevant. We deal with the legalities of these topic areas in the ensuing chapters of the book, so you are not expected to know the details yet, but it is important here that you are aware of the situations and emotions that might trigger media law risks.

Table 2.1 Key professional communication situations and emotions

Situation	Media law risks
Going commando? You are too rushed to check or you feel you are out of your depth.	All areas of media law, including the main ones of defamation, contempt of court and breach of court reporting rules, can result from feeling rushed or pressured. Learn to recognise when you are feeling that way—then pause and reflect.

Table 2.1 Key professional communication situations and emotions *continued*

Situation	Media law risks
You are broadcasting live or have direct publishing authority without checks or editing.	A danger zone for defamation, contempt, identification restrictions and other laws. All journalism and professional communications should be checked or edited by others. Live broadcasts should be cautious and only conducted by experienced practitioners abreast of media law.
Partisan?	
You have a vested interest or strong opinion on the matter.	Defamation defences can be lost if you are biased or partisan.
The item is—or relates to—advertising or promotion.	This can lose defamation defences and news reporting protections under consumer law.
You are responding to a criticism or it is a correction or apology.	Defamation defences can be lost and new plaintiffs can be defamed through poorly worded corrections, apologies or offers of amends. Legal advice is essential. Your responses to criticisms can escalate problems, increase damages and lose defences.
Stealth?	
You are 'borrowing' images or words from the internet or social media.	You are risking a breach of copyright suit and allegations of plagiarism. Take advice.
It involves secret recordings, surveillance, tapping, hacking, disguise, deception or entry onto private property.	Be specially aware of the laws of trespass, breach of confidence, surveillance devices legislation, and of gathering evidence, which might not be admissible for a defamation defence.
Exposé?	
You are exposing wrongdoing or misconduct.	Defamation and contempt are potential issues. Seek legal advice on requirements of defences like truth, fair report and qualified privilege.

continues

Table 2.1 Key professional communication situations and emotions *continued*

Situation	Media law risks
It involves secrets, private matters or confidential sources, or the disclosure of confidential documents.	Be on the alert for breach of confidence and privacy laws, and of relying on evidence that might be unavailable as a defamation defence such as the veracity of a confidential source. 'Shield laws' might not be available or might be inadequate. Risk of jail or fine for refusing to reveal source (disobedience contempt). High risk of an injunction.
Emotional?	
You are feeling angry, exhausted, annoyed, betrayed or emotional, or you have been drinking, using substances or are mentally unwell.	This is no time to publish or use social media. Your state of mind increases legal risk, impacts your media law assessment of the situation, and can leave you exposed to allegations of malice, lack of belief in the truth of what you have published and failure to establish reasonableness, thus losing key defamation defences.
It 'feels wrong' or you get that feeling that you wouldn't want to be the person mentioned.	Deeper consideration might reveal a risk of defamation, contempt or breach of confidence/privacy.
It involves a reluctant or difficult source, client or threat of legal action.	Any threat of legal action should trigger your organisation's legal escalation procedures involving formal legal advice. Reluctant or difficult sources might sue, or later give a false account or recant what they have told you, so thorough review is necessary.
It allows unmoderated and uncivil public commentary.	This can be defamatory, contemptuous, discriminatory, vilifying and subject to some legislative protections under the *Broadcasting Services Act 1992*. Australian law can render publishers responsible for the comments of third parties on their sites and social media feeds.

Table 2.1 Key professional communication situations and emotions *continued*

Situation	Media law risks
Crime and justice?	
It involves police, crime, violence (including domestic violence), children or national security.	Defamation, contempt and various publication restrictions on victims (especially complainants in sexual assault cases, or any mention of children), terrorism, security agencies, operational matters, even in some cases perpetrators (particularly at bail or committal stages) may apply.
It relates to a current or upcoming court case.	Defamation, contempt and various reporting and identification restrictions on victims, terrorism and security agencies can apply. Reporters must attend the proceedings, be aware of suppression and non-publication orders and produce a fair and accurate report only of what happens in court without extraneous or historic information. Do not report what happens in the absence of the jury.
Sensational?	
It sounds unbelievable.	If the story seems far-fetched, it probably isn't true: unverified claims present major problems in defamation.
It uses colourful or emotional language.	Imprecise and hard to defend: often raises real problems with defamation defences, where the item may carry defamatory meanings you or the person being quoted did not realise or intend to convey. Keep fact and opinion strictly separated. Court reports should use clear and concise language to avoid a contempt or defamation risk. The only exception is if you are quoting direct from what a person actually says in evidence before the jury.

continues

Table 2.1 Key professional communication situations and emotions *continued*

Situation	Media law risks
The material concerns sex, nudity or sexuality.	This requires special care, as it can raise legal issues around defamation, breach of confidence, court reporting restrictions and indecency.
It generalises, stereotypes, or is offensive to religions or cultures.	This can be defamatory if certain individuals are identifiable, and might also breach discrimination and vilification laws.
Reputation?	
It makes you think less of someone or laugh at their expense.	Defamation defences should be thought about in advance where a reputation is going to be damaged or a person ridiculed.
It criticises someone's performance or competence.	Defamation defences—particularly the requirements of the truth and honest opinion/fair comment defence—should be checked and legal advice must be sought: the factual basis for the criticism must be set out or adequately referred to.
Its descriptors could apply to others or it hints that the audience should 'read between the lines'.	'Hidden' defamatory and contemptuous meanings are hard to defend and other plaintiffs can sue if they can prove people reasonably thought the item was referring to them—even if it was completely unintentional. Use narrow and precise identification and ensure your defences are in order rather than identifying vaguely and 'writing in code': if you can see the hidden meaning, the jury certainly will too.
It involves the rich, powerful, famous . . . or lawyers or the judiciary.	While all citizens are equal, many defamation, breach of confidence and injurious falsehood suits come from these quarters, so an extra check is required. Implying judges have some improper motive could also be contemptuous (scandalising).

Table 2.1 Key professional communication situations and emotions *continued*

Situation	Media law risks
It is about a person or company 'too far away' to sue.	Defamatory material is actionable wherever material is downloaded and the internet and social media can bring legal consequences in distant jurisdictions, particularly if your organisation has a legal presence there or if you ever travel there, or back in Australia if you are filing or blogging from overseas.
Recycling?	
It uses sourced or file footage or past images in a new context.	This not infrequently forms the basis of the most serious defamation and contempt cases, and also carries the risk of breach of copyright.
It uses material from earlier stories on the topic—from your outlet or other media.	Cutting and pasting historic material from earlier coverage can repeat earlier errors, increasing damages in defamation, constitute contempt by prejudicing a jury trial, and breach copyright if it is the work of others.
Vulnerable?	
It relates to someone's mental health or other vulnerability.	Special restrictions apply to mental health and some coroners' proceedings, and both defamation and breach of confidence could be in play.
It involves children in any way.	The mention, identification or photograph of any child requires extra legal checks and permissions. Court, crime, family law and apprehended violence order restrictions may apply and there is a fundamental ethical obligation not to cause any harm to a child.

continues

Table 2.1 Key professional communication situations and emotions *continued*

Situation	Media law risks
Vision? It uses images or footage that might misidentify, be inaccurate or reflect poorly on others, particularly if they are not closely checked against the accompanying text and captions.	Images and footage arise in a host of legal areas including defamation, contempt, court restrictions, and breach of privacy, confidentiality and copyright. Be especially careful to check it portrays who it claims to portray, that this is allowed, and that others are not inadvertently pictured—such as children or sex crime victims, or others who might be defamed by association.
Damaging? People or organisations could lose money or suffer emotional distress because of it.	The seriousness of the wrong done and emotional distress are key factors in the award of damages for a range of actions, including defamation, breach of confidence, breach of privacy, injurious falsehood and breach of copyright. Actual financial loss, or even loss of opportunity in the future, can be hugely expensive.

TIPS FOR MINDFUL PRACTICE

- Get familiar with your rights at a national and international level, but understand that free expression is often trumped by other rights and interests.
- Before planning your travel itinerary, look carefully at the censorship record of the nations you plan to visit and ensure that you have not published anything online that might put you in breach.
- Follow the international free expression groups such as the Electronic Frontier Foundation, Amnesty International, Reporters Without Borders, Freedom House and IFEX, and see whether you can do anything to help raise awareness of free internet expression.
- Try to practise a mindful approach to media law in the workplace by pausing and 'reflecting in action' about the legal ramifications of the material you are about to publish. Weigh the public interest against

the legal risks and the impact of the publication on other stakeholders. Work through the situational analysis in Table 2.1.

IN A NUTSHELL

- The origins of free speech (and censorship) can be traced back at least to the time of Socrates, though the battle for a free press was taken up by the likes of Milton, Locke, Mill and Jefferson through the seventeenth, eighteenth and nineteenth centuries.
- US government attempts to restrain publications in the national interest have often failed on First Amendment grounds.
- Other countries have taken a range of approaches to press freedom, varying markedly according to their political, cultural and historical backgrounds.
- Article 19 of the Universal Declaration of Human Rights, the key document of the United Nations, gives all world citizens the right to freedom of opinion and expression and the right to 'receive and impart information and ideas through any media and regardless of frontiers'.
- Australia's colonial history was marked by considerable censorship of its media, although an early battle between Governor Darling and the Chief Justice in 1827 prevented the licensing of newspapers.
- Australia has no equivalent to the US First Amendment enshrining freedom of the press. However, in recent decades the High Court of Australia has recognised an implied freedom to communicate on matters of politics and government, which is still being refined, and there is some limited protection in charters of rights in the ACT and Victoria.
- Press systems and ethical frameworks are on the agenda in all societies, and we are challenged to accommodate free expression and its close relative, press freedom, within new regulatory, technological and cultural contexts.
- A mindful approach to media law situations can pay dividends by improving the quality of your work and minimising legal risks.

DISCUSSION QUESTIONS

2.1 Winston Churchill once described democracy as the 'least worst' option (House of Commons, 11 November 1947). Is the libertarian model of press freedom also the 'least worst option' or can we have press freedom within some other system of regulation, implying a different ethical framework for truth-seeking and truth-telling?

2.2 Is it always best that the truth be exposed? Can you think of situations where a greater public benefit arises from the truth being withheld?

2.3 Is the notion of the media as an independent watchdog too idealistic or out-dated for the twenty-first century? Why or why not?

2.4 Why are the advocates of media freedom so opposed to the exercise of 'prior restraint'?

2.5 Think of a situation where you have encountered censorship in your own life, or would have liked to have had something censored or removed from public view. Explain how it arose and the competing interests at stake.

2.6 Governments in some developing countries argue that their people are not yet ready for press freedom. Think of arguments for and against this position.

2.7 Think about the concept of 'reflection-in-action' or 'mindful practice', and discuss how it might apply to media law in the workplace.

2.8 Think about the concept of 'fake news', both in terms of attempts to de-legitimise truth-telling and the risk posed by deliberate manipulation of the public discourse. Is the answer that truth will always defeat falsehood, and that the remedy for untrue speech is more speech? If you were the moderator or host of a website or blog, what legal, ethical or moral questions might arise in relation to a 'hands-off' approach or a more interventionist 'editorial' model?

REFERENCES

Akha Heritage Foundation 2009, 'Harry Nicolaides refused bail for third time in *lèse majesté* case in Thailand, remains in prison', <www.akha.org/content/bookreviews/verisimilitude.html>.

Amnesty International 2017, 'Thailand: *Lèse-majesté* verdict must be quashed', Amnesty International Canada, <www.amnesty.ca/news/thailand-l%C3%A8se-majest%C3%A9-verdict-must-be-quashed>.

Avalon Project, Yale Law School 2002, *Declaration of the Rights of Man 1789*, <http://avalon.law.yale.edu/18th_century/rightsof.asp>.

Blackstone, W. 1765–69, *Commentaries on the Laws of England*, The Avalon Project, Yale Law School, <http://avalon.law.yale.edu/subject_menus/blackstone.asp>.

Brasch, W.M. and Ulloth, D.R. 1986, *The Press and the State: Sociohistorical and Contemporary Interpretations*, University Press of America, Lanham, MD.

Cochrane, L. 2017, 'Thai student activist given human rights award, but kept in jail ahead of *lèse majesté* trial', *ABC News*, 18 May, <www.abc.net.au/news/2017-05-18/thai-student-activist-given-human-rights-award,-but-kept-in-jail/8536176>.

Committee to Protect Journalists (CPJ) 2017, '1258 journalists killed since 1992/Motive confirmed', Committee to Protect Journalists, 26 October, <https://cpj.org/killed>.

Dutt, R. 2010, 'The Fiji media decree: A push towards collaborative journalism', *Pacific Journalism Review*, 16(2), 81–98.

Feather, J. 1988, *A History of British Publishing*, Routledge, London.

Feintuck, M. and Varney, M. 2006, *Media Regulation, Public Interest and the Law*, 2nd edn, Edinburgh University Press, Edinburgh.

Finkelstein, R. 2012, *Report of the Independent Inquiry into the Media and Media Regulation*, Department of Broadband, Communications and the Digital Economy, Canberra, <www.dbcde.gov.au/digital_economy/independent_media_inquiry>.

Harding, L. 2017, 'Panama Papers investigation wins Pulitzer Prize', *The Guardian*, 11 April, <www.theguardian.com/world/2017/apr/11/panama-papers-investigation-wins-pulitzer-prize>.

Inglebart, L.E. 1987, *Press Freedoms: A Descriptive Calendar of Concepts, Interpretations, Events, and Court Actions, from 4000 BC to the Present*, Greenwood Press, New York.

Klapproth, D.M. 2004, *Narrative as Social Practice: Anglo-Western and Australian Aboriginal Oral Traditions*, Walter de Gruyter & Co., Berlin.

Law Commission (NZ) 2013, *The News Media Meets 'New Media': Rights, Responsibilities and Regulation in the Digital Age*, Law Commission, Wellington, <www.lawcom.govt.nz/project/review-regulatory-gaps-and-new-media/report>.

Leveson, B. 2012, *Report of an Inquiry into the Culture, Practice and Ethics of the Press*, The Stationery Office, London [Leveson Report].

Locke, J. 1690, 'Preamble' to *Essay Concerning Human Understanding*, <www.rbjones.com/rbjpub/philos/classics/locke/ctb0prea.htm>.

Mayer, H. 1964, *The Press in Australia*, Lansdowne Press, Melbourne.

McMaster, P.K. 2005, 'Patriot Act is exhibit A on the risks of secrecy', American Press Institute, <www.americanpressinstitute.org/pages/resources>.

McQuail, D. 1987, *Mass Communication Theory: An Introduction*, Sage, London.

Media Arts and Entertainment Alliance (MEAA) (2017) 'Joint Media Organisations submission on National Security Legislation Amendment (Espionage and Foreign Interference) Bill 2017', <www.meaa.org/mediaroom/joint-media-organisations-submission-on-national-security-legislation-amendment-espionage-and-foreign-interference-bill-2017>.

Mill, J.S. 1991, *On Liberty and Other Essays*, Oxford University Press, Oxford.

Office of the High Commissioner for Human Rights 1976, *International Covenant on Civil and Political Rights*, <www.ohchr.org/en/professionalinterest/pages/ccpr.aspx>.

Overbeck, W. 2001, *Major Principles of Media Law*, Harcourt, Fort Worth, TX.

Patrides, C.A. (ed.) 1985, *John Milton: Selected Prose*, rev edn, University of Missouri Press, Columbia, MO.

Pember, D.R. 2001, *Mass Media Law*, McGraw Hill, Boston.

Pullan, R. 1994, *Guilty Secrets: Free Speech and Defamation in Australia*, Pascal Press, Sydney.

Reporters Without Borders 2017, *World Press Freedom Index*, <https://rsf.org/en/ranking>.

Schön, D. 1987, *Educating the Reflective Practitioner*, Jossey-Bass, San Francisco.

Siebert, F.S., Peterson, T. and Schramm, W. 1963, *Four Theories of the Press*, University of Illinois Press, Urbana, IL.

Smiley, S. 2017, 'Assange "tool of Russian intelligence": Clinton to *Four Corners*', *The World Today*, ABC Radio, 16 October, <www.abc.net.au/radio/programs/worldtoday/assange-tool-of-russian-intelligence-clinton-to-four-corners/9054106>.

Smith, H. and Novak, P. 2003, *Buddhism: A Concise Introduction*, HarperCollins, San Francisco.

Smith, J.A. 1988, *Printers and Press Freedom: The Ideology of Early American Journalism*, Oxford University Press, New York.

Spigelman, J. 2002, 'Foundations of the freedom of the press in Australia: The inaugural Australian Press Council Address', Banco Court, Supreme Court of NSW, Sydney, 20 November, <www.lawlink.nsw.gov.au/lawlink/supreme_court/ll_sc.nsf/pages/SCO_speech_spigelman_201103>.

United Nations 1948, *Universal Declaration of Human Rights*, adapted and proclaimed by General Assembly Resolution 217A(III) of 10 December 1948, <www.un.org/en/documents/udhr>.

Whitton, E. 1998, 'High Court seeks to raise the quality of journalism', *Australian Press Council News*, 10(1), <www.presscouncil.org.au/pcsite/apcnews/feb98/evan.html>.

CASES CITED

ACTV case: Australian Capital Television Pty Ltd v Commonwealth (1992) 177 CLR 106.

Afghan Letters case: Monis v The Queen [2013] HCA 4 (27 February 2013), <www.austlii.edu.au/cgi-bin/sinodisp/au/cases/cth/HCA/2013/4.html>.

Army Reserve case: Gaynor v Chief of the Defence Force [2017] HCATrans 162 (18 August 2017), <www.austlii.edu.au/cgi-bin/viewdoc/au/cases/cth/HCATrans/2017/162.html>.

Brandenburg's case: Brandenburg v Ohio (1969) 395 US 444.

Brown v Tasmania [2017] HCA 43.

Fisherman case: ABC v O'Neill [2006] HCA 46.

Flag Burning case: Valerie Morse v The Police [2011] NZSC 45 (6 May 2011), <www.nzlii.org/cgi-bin/sinodisp/nz/cases/NZSC/2011/45.html>.

Lange's case: Lange v Australian Broadcasting Corporation (1997) 189 CLR 520.

Levy's case: Levy v Victoria (1997) 189 CLR 579.

Mall Preachers case: Attorney-General (SA) v Corporation of the City of Adelaide [2013] HCA 3 (27 February 2013), <www.austlii.edu.au/cgi-bin/sinodisp/au/cases/cth/HCA/2013/3.html>.

Minnesota case: Near v Minnesota (1931) 283 US 697.

Newspaper Acts Opinion NSWSC 23 (1 April 1827), Supreme Court of New South Wales. Forbes CJ, April 1827. Source: Forbes CJ to Governor Darling, 16 April 1827, Historical Records of Australia, Series 1, vol. 13, pp. 282–5; Mitchell Library, A 748, Reel CY 1226, pp. 24–8, 63–6, <www.austlii.edu.au/au/other/NSWSupC/1827/23.html>.

O'Shane's case: O'Shane v Harbour Radio Pty Ltd [2013] NSWCA 315 (24 September 2013), <www.austlii.edu.au/cgi-bin/sinodisp/au/cases/nsw/NSWCA/2013/315.html>.

Palm Island Parole case: Lex Patrick Wotton v The State of Queensland & Anor [2012] HCA 2, <www.austlii.edu.au/cgi-bin/sinodisp/au/cases/cth/HCA/2012/2.html>.

Pentagon Papers case: New York Times v US; US v Washington Post (1971) 713 US 403.

Stephens' case: Stephens v West Australian Newspapers Ltd (1994) 182 CLR 211.

Sullivan's case: New York Times v Sullivan (1964) 376 US 254.

Theophanous's case: Theophanous v Herald and Weekly Times Ltd (1994) 182 CLR 104.

Wills' case: Nationwide News Pty Ltd v Wills (1992) 177 CLR 1.

Yates' case: Yates v US (1957) 354 US 298.

CHAPTER 3

Legal and regulatory systems and principles

KEY CONCEPTS

Common law
The law made by judges—including both the law as it has been decided in cases in the courts over hundreds of years and the courts' interpretation of legislation.

Statute
Legislation passed by the state, territory or federal parliaments.

Separation of powers
The principle that the three arms of government—the judiciary (the courts), the legislature (the parliaments) and the executive (the government and the public service)—should remain separate and independent of each other.

Media regulation
Formal laws directly controlling the activities of the media.

Co-regulation
Laws enshrining industry complaints-handling processes that typically allow for those processes to run their course before a government authority will intervene.

Self-regulation
Rules established by an industry association or other private body to deal with complaints about the ethics of its members, without the authority of law and without statutory remedies being available.

PROFESSIONAL COMMUNICATORS, JOURNALISTS AND LAWS

An introductory account of the workings of the legal and regulatory systems allows an informed discussion of areas of media law that affect professional communicators in their work. The democratic process hinges on effective reporting of each element of the political and legislative system at work: from the point at which there are initiatives for new laws or changes to legislation, through the phase of lobbying and public debate of proposals, the drafting of the legislation, committee deliberations, and the readings and debates of the Bills in the houses of parliament, to their final assent, enactment and actual operation once enacted. Journalists need to understand these political and legal processes if they are to report on them properly, and other professional communicators also need to be familiar with them if they are to write about, or consult to, a political or legal client.

AUSTRALIAN LEGAL SYSTEM: HISTORICAL AND INTERNATIONAL CONTEXT

The Australian legal system as it operates today has evolved from four major influences:

- *The adoption of the British legal system from the time of the arrival of Captain Arthur Phillip in Australia in 1788.* Each state was established as a separate colony, with its own parliaments and courts. The legal principle of *terra nullius*—'nobody's land'—gave no recognition to thousands of years of Aboriginal and Torres Strait Islander occupation and customary law.
- *The creation of the Commonwealth of Australia in 1901.* This gave Australia its own Constitution, and positioned a federal level of government above those of the states to enact laws relating to the national interest as specified in the Constitution. It also established a High Court as the court of appeal from the state Supreme Courts and the adjudicator of constitutional questions, although there was an alternative route of appeal to the Privy Council in England, abolished in 1986.

- *High Court decisions on federal laws and constitutional matters.* Points of uncertainty in the Constitution and its interpretation have been decided by the High Court as the highest forum for appeal in such matters since 1986.
- *Legislative enactments.* These have affected the authority and operations of the lower echelons of the court system, and have allowed for the establishment of a range of commissions and tribunals.

SEPARATION OF POWERS

Central to the function of our system of government is the doctrine of the separation of powers incorporated in the Australian Constitution. It dictates that the three arms of government—the judiciary (the courts), the legislature (the parliaments) and the executive (the government and the public service)—should remain separate and independent of each other. The doctrine is crucial to the democratic process, and is meant to ensure that the judicial system and the executive administration are able to operate independently. Part of the social function of the media, as the Fourth Estate, is to ensure via thorough reportage that any breach of the separation of powers is brought to the attention of the public. At the state level, the separation of powers is not set out in state constitutions, but breaches of the principle have been exposed by the media (Polden, 2010) and it does apply indirectly to state courts, which have the power to exercise the judicial power of the Commonwealth, in particular where state laws seek to override judicial decision-making or impose non-judicial roles on the judiciary (Polden 2010; see *Totani's case*).

SOURCES OF LAW

There are two major sources of Australian law: law made by politicians (statute law), and law found in the decisions of judges, either in areas not yet covered by statute or in interpreting what any particular piece of statute law actually means (common law). Each plays a vital role in the legal process.

STATUTE LAW

Statute law is legislation passed by the state, territory or federal parliaments. The federal (Commonwealth) government has power under the Constitution to legislate in a range of areas. Section 51 of the Constitution gives the Commonwealth government power to enact laws in 40 areas, including immigration, foreign affairs, defence, telecommunications, welfare, corporations and currency. Anything not specified in the Constitution as being among these 40 heads of power is left to the states, unless a mutual agreement is reached under which the states transfer that power to the Commonwealth.

It follows that the states have much more general power with which to legislate about matters that concern their internal activities, such as the provision of health services, prisons, roads, education, consumer affairs, police and emergency services. Where a state and a Commonwealth law conflict on a matter over which the Commonwealth has power to legislate, the Commonwealth law will prevail under section 109 of the Constitution.

In the Commonwealth parliament, and in all states except Queensland, there are two houses of parliament. Legislation must pass through both houses before it becomes law. Draft Acts are known as Bills. Bills are usually introduced by the responsible minister to the lower house of parliament (known as the House of Representatives at the federal level and the Legislative Assembly at state level). Copies are distributed to all members of the lower house. (This is known as the first reading.) This is followed by the second reading, during which the Bill is discussed in the lower house. If the Bill is passed by a vote at this stage, it moves on to the committee stage, during which it is debated in detail by the lower house. It then moves on to a third reading and a final vote is taken. If it passes this vote, the Bill moves on to the upper house for assent (the Senate at the federal level and the Legislative Council at the state level). If it is passed in the upper house, it goes to the Governor (state) or Governor-General (federal) to be signed. At that point, the Bill becomes an Act of parliament and is law from the date specified in the legislation. (Bills are sometimes introduced in the upper house and must still be considered by both houses.)

COMMON LAW

Common law is the law set out in the decisions of judges—law as it has been decided in court cases over hundreds of years. The common law is premised on an important legal principle known as the 'doctrine of precedent', which asserts that courts are bound to follow the past decisions of courts superior to them in the court hierarchy.

Over the centuries, bodies of law have been developed using the doctrine of precedent. An example is the law of defamation, which continues to exist in its common law form in Australia, to the extent that it is not inconsistent with the *Uniform Defamation Acts 2005*. The doctrine of precedent underlies the common law, which operates whenever legislation is non-existent or imprecise in its language or scope, or where it specifically preserves common law rights. Where there is both clear-cut legislation and a court decision on the same matter, the legislation will take priority unless (in a very limited category of case) it has been struck down by the High Court as unconstitutional. Thus the obvious starting point when examining any area of the law is to ask: What is the relevant legislation? It is then necessary to look at how that statute has been interpreted by the courts.

Take, for example, the *Motor Accident case* (2017). There, the High Court unanimously dismissed an appeal from the Court of Appeal of the Supreme Court of Victoria concerning the test for serious injury under section 93(17) of the *Transport Accident Act 1986* (Vic) ('the narrative test') laid down in the earlier Victorian Supreme Court case of *Humphries v Poljak* (1992). The appeal centred on a woman's psychiatric treatment for post-traumatic stress disorder after an accident, and whether any compensation depended upon whether she had been admitted to a psychiatric institution. The High Court ultimately agreed with the majority of the Court of Appeal that the extent of treatment was only one among a range of considerations that needed to be taken into account. Thus the case worked its way through the varying levels of appeal to the High Court, which applied a test developed in a historic Supreme Court case—demonstrating all levels of the appeal system and the importance of common law interpretations in tandem with legislation.

CASE CITATIONS

As an indication of the adversarial context in which they are fought and decided, cases are cited according to the parties contesting them, with a 'v' (standing for versus) between their names. (While this means 'versus', in Australian usage we actually say the word 'and' or 'against'.) For example, the citation for the famous *Mabo case* on Indigenous land rights is *Mabo v Queensland (No. 2)* (1992) 175 CLR 1, spoken as 'Mabo and Queensland number two'. This indicates that Eddie Mabo was the person bringing the appeal to the High Court, the state of Queensland was the respondent, it was Mr Mabo's second case before that court, and the case was reported in 1992 in volume 175 of the *Commonwealth Law Reports*, starting at page 1. The name of the party bringing the action (or the appeal) appears first in the citation.

Sometimes cases have Latin words instead of the names of one or other of the parties. When a state government or the federal government brings an action, the letter 'R', an abbreviation for *Regina* or *Rex*, from the Latin meaning the Queen or King of the day, will often be used to represent them—as in *Hinch's case*: *R v Hinch* [2013] VSC 520.

ACCESSING LEGAL MATERIALS

Legal materials are held in a variety of locations and can be accessed in several ways. A wealth of legal material is available online. The two most extensive databases on Australian law are the Australasian Legal Information Institute <www.austlii.edu.au> and the Federal Register of Legislation <www.legislation.gov.au>, the approved, whole-of-government website for Australian government legislation and related documents. Each state and territory also has its own legislation database.

CATEGORIES OF LAW

The law can be classified in a number of ways. For our purposes, the most useful division is between the criminal and civil law, as the media law areas we examine are spread across these two primary categories. Put in the simplest terms, criminal law concerns offences against the state, for which offenders can be tried and punished. Crimes are detailed in the *Crimes Acts* or Criminal Codes of the various states, as well as federally. Crimes may also involve a breach of other legislation, such as taxation or corporations law, or laws for the control of drugs. Punishments for crimes can include prison sentences, fines, the forfeiture of property (this is normally done using proceeds of crime legislation) and court orders, including those referred to as injunctions (from the old French expression *enjoindre*, meaning 'to order'), which are orders to do something or to refrain from doing something, such as seeing a probation officer, not driving a car or—of prime importance for journalists—not to publish something. Serious crimes involving publication include deliberate breach of injunctions, sedition (now 'urging violence'), contempt of court or parliament, criminal libel, hate speech, breach of publishing restrictions, unlicensed publishing, fraud and various national security breaches. Those who commit crimes face fines and a range of other punishments, which in some countries (although not Australia) can include execution, or corporal punishments such as caning.

The other kind of law, civil law (also known as private law), concerns the rights and obligations of individuals and companies in their relationships with other individuals and companies. In this area, parties may persuade a court to order the unsuccessful party to perform or refrain from some action—such as never publishing a particular story again, making some payment in compensation for damage they have caused, and often both. Breaching, defying or ignoring such an order may be treated as a criminal matter under the law of contempt.

Both kinds of law may come into play over the one event. In 2005, paparazzo photographer Jamie Fawcett was accused of planting a listening device outside actor Nicole Kidman's Sydney property. Police dropped the criminal charges against him because they believed there was not enough evidence to satisfy a jury on the criminal 'beyond reasonable doubt' test that Fawcett had planted the bug. Fawcett later sued Fairfax, publisher of *The Sun-Herald* newspaper, in a civil action for defamation, and a Supreme Court justice found on the lower civil 'balance of probabilities' test that it was true that Fawcett had planted the bug. He lost the case. Both criminal and civil proceedings were involved in *Jane Doe's case*—see Focus Case 3.1) in 2007, which highlights several of the key concepts we address in this chapter.

In 2017, in the *Kazal case*, a defendant in a defamation action who had been ordered by a judge of the Federal Court to cease publishing certain material, but had defied that order, was sentenced to eighteen months' imprisonment, and had his conviction and imprisonment upheld (though reduced to fifteen months) on appeal by the Full Federal Court.

FOCUS CASE 3.1: *JANE DOE'S CASE*

Doe v Australian Broadcasting Corporation & Ors [2007] VCC 281 (3 April 2007)

FACTS

In March, 2001, the plaintiff 'Jane Doe' (a legal pseudonym used to protect her identity) was raped by her estranged husband, 'YZ'. He was charged with rape and other offences, and was convicted and sentenced a year later. On the afternoon of the sentence, ABC radio broadcast news stories about the matter in three bulletins. In its 4.00 pm and 6.00 pm bulletins, the reports identified YZ by his real name, described the offences as 'rapes within marriage' and named the suburb. The 5.00 pm bulletin went further and identified the victim by name. All three bulletins were in breach of section 4(1A) of the *Judicial Proceedings Reports Act 1958* (Vic), which makes it an offence to publish information identifying a victim of a sexual offence.

LAW

In subsequent criminal proceedings, the ABC reporter and sub-editor pleaded guilty to publishing the identifying material, but did not have convictions recorded against their names. A written apology to Jane Doe, signed by both journalists, was presented in court. In a separate civil action in 2006, Jane Doe sued the ABC and both journalists in the County Court, seeking damages for breach of statutory duty, negligence, breach of privacy and breach of confidence. In April 2007, Judge Felicity Hampel found for Jane Doe and awarded $234,190 in damages.

LESSONS FOR JOURNALISTS

This was the first time in Australia that a journalist or news organisation had been sued for breach of privacy in the civil courts, when the case had already been dealt with in criminal proceedings. We will look at the legal aspects of privacy in this case in Chapter 12. For the moment, these are the main lessons:

- Journalists cannot identify the victims of sexual crimes, and cannot even identify the accused if that might lead to the identification of the victim. Specific prohibitions vary between states and territories.
- The criminal and the civil courts operate in different ways, and for different purposes. Here, both the rapist—and the journalists who identified the victim—were charged, tried and (in the case of the offender) sentenced under the respective criminal laws. Later, the victim used the civil courts to win damages against the ABC and the journalists as compensation for the hurt, distress, embarrassment and financial loss she suffered as a result of being identified.
- Journalists' legal and ethical errors can have a huge impact on ordinary members of society. It is worth reading the above case in full to gain an understanding of the effect that the identification of Jane Doe in the radio bulletins had on her as she tried to recover from the trauma of rape.

COURT STRUCTURE

It is important for professional communicators to know the hierarchy of the court system so they can assess where a particular case is likely to be heard, gauge the probability of a decision being appealed and weigh the importance of a case to their media audiences and clients.

STATE AND TERRITORY COURT SYSTEMS

STATE AND TERRITORY COURTS OF SUMMARY JURISDICTION

Classified as 'inferior' courts, these are known in different states as Magistrates Courts, Local Courts and the Court of Petty Sessions. Generally referred to as courts of summary jurisdiction, these courts are at the bottom of the judicial hierarchy, yet they are vital to the system's effective operation. The courts of summary jurisdiction are the busiest, hearing minor civil matters such as disputes over small debts and breaches of contract up to a set maximum sum (for example, up to $75,000 in Western Australia), minor criminal charges and committal proceedings for major criminal matters. (In committal proceedings, the magistrate—who is a qualified legal practitioner—has to decide whether there is a *prima facie*—'at first appearance'—case on which a jury in a superior or intermediate court might convict the accused if presented with the evidence.) Magistrates also hear special matters when constituted as a Coroner's Court (inquiring into deaths and fires), Children's Court (dealing with juvenile offences) or Licensing Court (hearing applications for liquor licences). They are given the name 'courts of summary jurisdiction' because magistrates have special powers allowing them to deal with matters summarily (immediately, without the need to constitute a jury). More serious crimes requiring a jury are known as 'indictable offences'.

INTERMEDIATE COURTS

The intermediate courts are called District Courts in some states and County Courts in others. There are no such courts in Tasmania, the Australian Capital Territory or the Northern Territory. The intermediate courts have a wide jurisdiction to hear civil matters that are disputes beyond the scope of the courts of summary jurisdiction up to a set sum in some jurisdictions (e.g. $750,000 in Western Australia and New South Wales, although the limit may be increased in specified circumstances) and unlimited amounts in others (e.g. Victoria). They also have the power to hear all but the most serious criminal matters, such as murder and treason. The criminal matters heard in the intermediate courts are indictable offences, which means they usually require a jury.

SUPREME COURTS

The highest court within each state's system is the Supreme Court. It is a 'superior court of record', and can deal with any criminal matter—

including the most serious–and any civil matter that comes within its jurisdiction. It is usually organised into a number of divisions and lists reflecting the kinds of cases it hears. Categories might include probate, adoptions, professional negligence, construction, commercial, admiralty, defamation, administrative law and corporations. An important sphere of the Supreme Court's operation is the hearing of appeals. Its appeal court (both criminal and civil) can hear appeals from the magistrates or intermediate courts or from decisions of single Supreme Court justices. Appeals from the Supreme Court go to the High Court of Australia if special leave to appeal is granted.

OTHER STATE COURTS

Different states may have courts dealing with particular areas of the law, such as state industrial law, land and environment law, maritime law, intellectual property, taxation and workers' compensation. Some states also have special 'drug courts' designed to deal with non-violent cases involving people with a drug dependency. The first started in New South Wales in 1999 and such courts typically have powers to order rehabilitation treatment and supervision as part of their sentencing. Western Australia is the only state with its own Family Court at state level.

Most states and territories also have less formal Magistrates Court procedures involving the presence of families and community elders–designed primarily though not exclusively for Aboriginal and Torres Strait Islander people. They are variously called Aboriginal Sentencing Courts–'Nunga Courts' (SA), Murri Courts (Qld), the Aboriginal Community Court (WA), Circle Sentencing (NSW) and the Koori Court (Victoria). Victoria established the intermediate-level Koori County Court in 2008.

See Figure 3.1 for a diagram of Australia's court hierarchy.

FEDERAL COURT SYSTEM

Each of the Commonwealth territories has a similar court structure to that of the states, albeit without an 'intermediate' (county or district) court. Thus there is no need to repeat the court structure as it applies

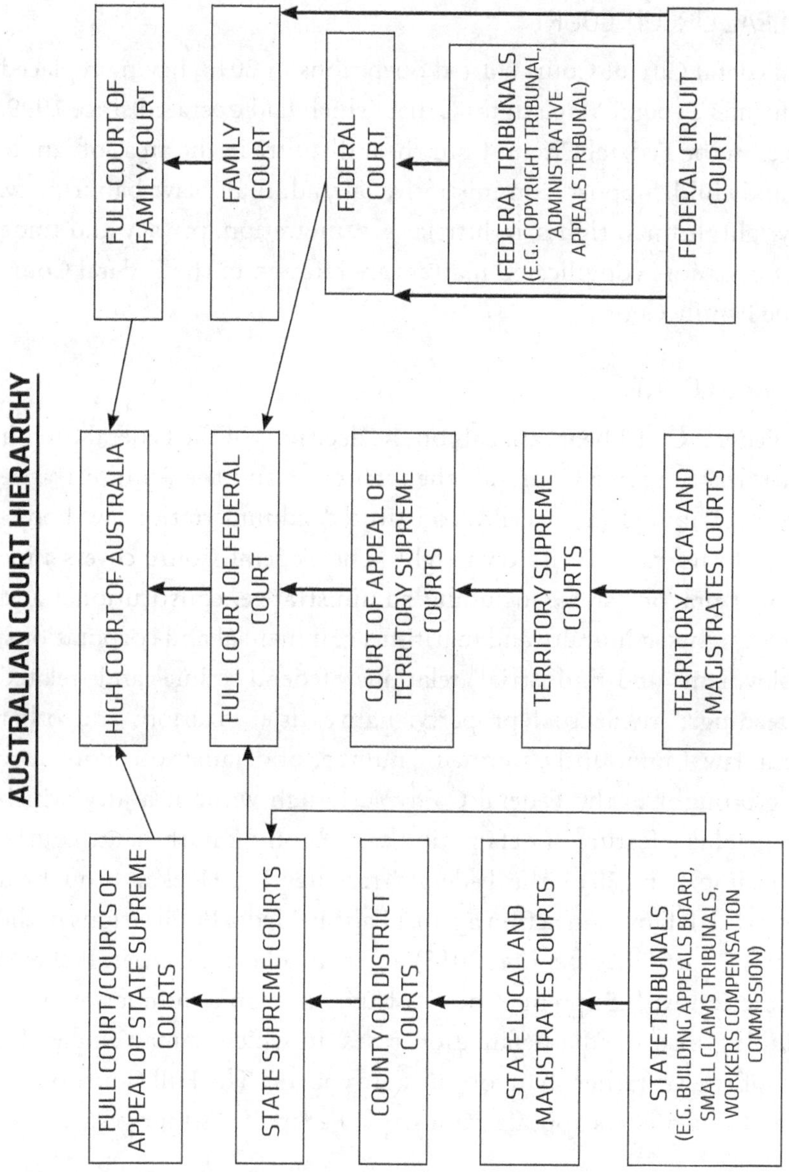

Figure 3.1 Australian court hierarchy

to them. The discussion here will centre on federal courts of appeal and specially constituted federal courts.

FEDERAL CIRCUIT COURT

The Federal Circuit Court started operations in 2013, having replaced the former Federal Magistrates Court, which had operated since 1999. Judges in the Federal Circuit Court hear disputes in the areas of family law and child support, administrative law, admiralty law, bankruptcy, copyright, human rights, industrial law, migration, privacy and trade practices. More complicated matters are referred to the Federal Court or the Family Court.

FEDERAL COURT

The Federal Court hears appeals on the decisions of the Federal Circuit Court, the Supreme Courts of the territories and the Administrative Appeals Tribunal (a specially constituted administrative law body). It also hears cases in its own right. The Federal Court covers nine national practice areas, including administrative, constitutional and human rights; admiralty and maritime; commercial and corporations; employment and industrial relations; federal crime and related proceedings; intellectual property; native title; taxation; and other federal law. Importantly, a growing number of defamation actions are being brought in the Federal Court, although without a jury, which in general is a feature of defamation cases brought in the state courts. For example, in 2015 the Federal Treasurer Joe Hockey brought a successful defamation action against Fairfax Media Publications in the Federal Court (*Treasurer case*, 2015). It sits in all capital cities. It shares jurisdiction with Supreme Courts of the states in a number of areas, including mass media defamation cases, in which it may empanel a jury (of twelve, rather than four in state courts). The Full Court of the Federal Court hears appeals from single Federal Court judges.

FAMILY COURT

The Family Court also sits throughout Australia, dealing with all matters related to marriage, such as divorce, property settlements and parenting cases. Journalists need to be mindful of the blanket ban in section 122 of the *Family Law Act 1975* on publication of any report of Family Court proceedings that contains material leading to the identification of parties.

HIGH COURT

The highest court in Australia, the High Court, deals with appeals from all state Supreme Courts, the Federal Court, the Family Court and single High Court justices. The court consists of seven justices, headed by a Chief Justice, and can sit as a full court or in combinations ranging down to a single justice. Appellants must seek leave to appeal to the High Court, a procedure that reserves the court's attention for only the most important matters. Under the Constitution, it can also hear some constitutional cases that have not previously been heard in another court (such as disputes over citizenship entitlements affecting the eligibility of several members of the Commonwealth Parliament throughout 2017 and 2018).

QUASI-JUDICIAL BODIES

At both federal and state levels, there are numerous quasi-judicial bodies—tribunals and commissions with powers similar to those given to the courts—set up to deal with specialist tasks. Some are temporary, such as Royal Commissions, while others are permanent commissions and tribunals. These can provide fruitful reporting areas for journalists. Examples are the Independent Commission Against Corruption (ICAC) in New South Wales, the Crime and Corruption Commission (CCC) in Queensland and the National Native Title Tribunal at the Commonwealth level.

ALTERNATIVE DISPUTE RESOLUTION

In recent years, there has been a trend in the legal profession to move outside the court system for the resolution of disputes. Arbitration, negotiation and mediation are different forms of dispute resolution that are popular and less expensive alternatives to the judicial system.

While this move may have distinct advantages for the parties involved, disputes resolved outside the court system cannot normally be reported as a court case might be, leaving the public very much in the dark about the workings of the process. In an important decision in this area, however, the High Court refused mining magnate Gina Rinehart leave to appeal from a decision of the NSW Court of Appeal, in which it refused to suppress information relating to court proceedings about a commercial dispute, despite the existence of a deed that said the dispute and its outcome were to be dealt with in mediation and remain confidential (*Gina's case*, 2011).

PROFESSIONAL COMMUNICATION REGULATION AND SELF-REGULATION

Professional communicators also encounter a second body of rules: those developed and enforced by independent organisations (known as 'self-regulation') or delegated under legislation to regulatory bodies (known as 'co-regulation'). In these regulatory systems, laws overlap with ethical codes, where codes of practice and ethical charters are enforced by industry groups and quasi-governmental tribunals.

In the print domain and in public relations, the trend has been towards self-regulatory mechanisms, including media organisations' in-house codes of practice, the MEAA ethics processes, the industry-funded Australian Press Council and the disciplinary powers of the Public Relations Institute of Australia (PRIA).

Broadcast media are regulated by the Australian Communications and Media Authority (ACMA), operating under the *Broadcasting Services Act 1992* in a system of 'co-regulation'. The different approaches to print and broadcast regulation were more easily explained in the pre-internet era, when the various media forms fell into tidy categories. Section 51(v) of the Constitution granted the Commonwealth parliament control over 'postal, telegraphic, telephonic, and other like services', which for more than four decades was interpreted to include broadcasting, leaving control of the print media to the states via laws such as defamation. However, since the advent of the internet, there has been a strong view in some quarters that, given the digital orientation of the modern print media, the section 51(v) powers would extend to online versions of newspapers and, further, that the Commonwealth's powers to legislate on the operations of corporations and interstate trade would strengthen its argument to regulate the press (Ruddock, 2004). Proposals for such regulatory change were raised in 2013 in the form of the Convergence Review (2012), the Independent Media Inquiry (Finkelstein, 2012) and the Gillard Labor government's failed attempt to introduce a News Media (Self-Regulation) Bill in 2013.

While most media organisations have some internal protocols for dealing with complaints, many disputes between media organisations and the public go beyond the in-house solution but do not finish up in the courts. These are the complaints dealt with by co-regulatory and self-regulatory bodies.

IN-HOUSE CODES OF PRACTICE

Internal complaints-handling protocols vary across media outlets, partly because of their own corporate policies and partly because some media sectors are obliged to have such processes, while for others it is purely voluntary. Newspapers and their new digital products operate in a voluntary self-regulatory environment, so their complaints-handling processes might range from an editor's whim through to a formal corporate policy. Some former newspaper and online news groups have established codes of practice for journalists within their own newsrooms. Such codes are in operation at News Corp and Fairfax publications, although their level of internal enforcement has been questioned. In addition to these codes, journalists at some organisations have developed 'charters of independence', seeking to establish a firewall between the media group's management and their editorial operations. Fairfax newspapers have such charters, designed as a mechanism to protect their newsrooms from interference by owners who might want to meddle with the journalistic process (Fairfax Media, 2012).

Under the *Broadcasting Services Act 1992*, all broadcast outlets, including the ABC and Special Broadcasting Service (SBS), have registered codes of practice applying to a range of programming activities, including news and current affairs. The ABC has the most comprehensive of these. Its Editorial Policies and Code of Practice were updated in 2009–16 and can be viewed on its corporate website.

AUSTRALIAN PRESS COUNCIL

The Australian Press Council (APC) was established in 1976, at a time when it appeared that the then Commonwealth government might move towards greater regulation of the press. Its history was well documented in the Independent Media Inquiry report (Finkelstein, 2012: 221–7). Its primary goal, as outlined in the first object of its constitution (APC, 2013), is to 'promote freedom of speech through responsible and independent print and digital media, and adherence to high journalistic and editorial standards'. To do so, it:

- deals with complaints about newspapers, magazines, journals and other print and digital media
- encourages print and digital media to address causes of complaints
- reviews and challenges developments threatening the dissemination of information of public interest and the public's right to know
- represents the interests of free speech and access to information in public forums
- undertakes research to these ends
- promotes better understanding of its role through consultations and forums.

The APC is a non-profit organisation funded by print and digital media publishers, but major players have sometimes not been represented. In 2017, the Council had 25 members, including an independent chair, two vice-chairs and eight other public members (not affiliated with media organisations), ten nominees of media organisations and four independent journalists (APC, 2017). Its key documents for ethical self-regulation are its Statements of Principles, covering fundamental values like accuracy, fairness, privacy and integrity (see Appendix 2); specific Standards for covering sensitive issues like suicide and interviews with hospital patients; and Advisory Guidelines on specific areas of reporting and publishing practice.

The APC outlines its complaints procedures on its website, <www.presscouncil.org.au>. Its only punitive power is to announce its findings and to ask its members to publish them. Adjudications are issued against newspapers, magazines or digital outlets themselves, rather than against particular journalists. Complaints can be upheld in full or in part or dismissed, or the APC might simply choose to express an opinion on the matter. Member publications are expected to publish the APC's adjudication on matters involving them, although from time to time they have refused to do so. Adjudications and statistics are published on the APC's website and in its annual report. The APC typically receives about 500 complaints in a given year, only 30 of which proceeded to adjudication in 2015–16 (APC, 2016: 95). Those not adjudicated by the APC were declined at first instance, withdrawn or discontinued, or a remedy was agreed without adjudication. Seven West Media established its own complaints body—the Independent Media Council—to self-regulate its print and online publications following its resignation from the APC in 2012. It operates as a three-member independent tribunal, in 2013–17 consisting of retired Supreme Court Justice Peter Blaxell as chair along with former Attorney-General Jim McGinty and former state minister Cheryl Edwardes. Only nine complaints were adjudicated in 2016.

MEAA ETHICS PANEL

Unlike the APC, the ethics panel of the MEAA has actual disciplinary powers at its disposal for use against individual journalists who breach its Code of Ethics—but it has rarely used them. Its powers extend to any journalist who is a member of the alliance. However, large numbers of journalists throughout the industry are not members. Members of the MEAA are required to abide by the Code of Ethics (see Appendix 1). This is the primary document cited by journalists, lawyers, politicians and commentators whenever an ethical issue to do with journalism arises. It is mentioned throughout this book, particularly in relation to secrets, confidentiality, intellectual property, privacy and discrimination. Its twelve items demand honesty, fairness, independence and respect for the rights of others. The MEAA's ethical complaints procedures are outlined in section 8 of the rules of the MEAA (2017), summarised on the union's website. Complaints must be in writing, stating the name of the journalist, the unethical act and the points of the code that have been breached. The judiciary committee (made up of experienced journalists elected every two years by state branch members) can then meet to consider the complaint. It can dismiss or uphold the complaint without hearing further evidence, call for further evidence and hold hearings. Hearings involve the committee, the complainant and the journalist, and follow the rules of natural justice. Lawyers are excluded. Penalties available to the committee include a censure or rebuke for the journalist, a fine of up to $1000 for each offence and expulsion from the union. Both parties have 28 days to appeal to an appeals committee of three senior journalists in each state elected every four years and then to a national appeals committee of five journalists.

AUSTRALIAN COMMUNICATIONS AND MEDIA AUTHORITY

The Australian Communications and Media Authority (ACMA) is the federal body responsible for the regulation of broadcasting, radio communications, telecommunications and online content. It regulates the operations of all broadcast media except the national broadcasters (the ABC and SBS), although it can review their handling of complaints. ACMA's powers are set out in the *Broadcasting Services Act 1992*, as amended.

Its website, <www.acma.gov.au>, explains that ACMA's powers are wide ranging, covering the planning of frequency allocations for broadcasting and narrowcasting, the licensing of services, the regulation of ownership and control of the industry, and regulation of the content of radio, television and internet services. Section 4 of the *Broadcasting Services Act* states that ACMA is supposed to regulate 'according to the degree of influence that different types of broadcasting services, datacasting services and Internet services are able to exert in shaping community views in Australia'.

While all of ACMA's functions are of some interest to journalists and other professional communicators, the one most likely to impinge directly on their work is the regulation of broadcast and internet content. Under the 1992 Act, this was partly deregulated and developed into a system of co-regulation. Under section 123, the responsibility for the development of codes of practice was devolved to the main radio and television industry groups, which include Free TV Australia and Commercial Radio Australia. Other codes of practice cover community broadcasting, narrowcasting, subscription television and internet services. Such codes are meant to cover a range of topics, including 'promoting accuracy and fairness in news and current affairs programs' and the development of complaints-handling protocols. The ABC and SBS have their own codes of practice, which are notified to ACMA.

Of special interest to journalists are the Commercial Television Industry Code of Practice (Free TV Australia, 2015) and Commercial Radio Code of Practice (Commercial Radio Australia, 2017), covering accuracy and fairness in news and current affairs programs. The guidelines are, by definition, qualitative and subjective, requiring the licensees to present news and current affairs programs that are accurate, impartial and balanced, and to correct significant factual errors. News and current affairs programs should not be simulated to mislead or alarm, and fact and opinion must be distinguishable. Issues of privacy, grief, race, gender, sexual preference and disability must be handled sensitively.

Complaints about breaches of these guidelines are directed first to the commercial station involved. If the complainant is dissatisfied with the station's response, or the station has not responded within 60 days, the complainant can take the complaint to ACMA for investigation (*Broadcasting Services Act 1992*, s 148). ACMA has a number of options available to it. Under section 141, it can direct a licence-holder to implement administrative and training systems to comply with a code of practice and, under section 142, failure to implement such remedial action can incur substantial fines. Every day they are in contravention is considered a new offence. It can dismiss the complaint as frivolous or vexatious, and proceed no further; direct the licensee to redress the breach; impose a condition on the broadcast licence that requires the licensee to comply with the code of practice; or develop its own standard if it is of the view the existing code does not safeguard the community adequately. Ultimately, failure by a licensee to comply with such directions from ACMA can result in the authority pursuing a civil remedy, reference out for prosecution as an offence, suspension or cancellation of the licence under section 143, or acceptance of an enforceable undertaking (Part 14D). Broadcast journalists are advised to read the legislation and codes applying to their particular stations very carefully.

MEDIA WATCH: THE MOST EFFECTIVE JOURNALISM REGULATOR?

Regulatory bodies vary markedly in their powers and influence over journalists and their behaviour. However, the institution that many journalists fear most, and that many quite simply despise, is the ABC's weekly program *Media Watch*, which was first screened in 1989. Its website promotes it with the tag line 'Everyone loves it until they're on it'. *Media Watch* has exposed some spectacular ethical breaches. These include blatant instances of plagiarism and privacy invasion and, most famously, an exposé of secret payments being made to talkback radio stars for their endorsement of products and services, without the knowledge of listeners. This became known as the 'cash for comment' scandal, and was the subject of a major inquiry by the ABA (now ACMA) in 2000 (ABA, 2000). While *Media Watch* itself has no sanctions available, the power of the program lies in the fact that ethical breaches and glaring errors are exposed on national television, when journalists know their colleagues are watching. In 2014, Fairfax reporter Natalie O'Brien sued the ABC over a *Media Watch* item that the ABC successfully defended as honest opinion, a decision that was upheld on appeal (*Toxic Playground case*, 2017).

AUSTRALIAN COMPETITION AND CONSUMER COMMISSION

Media corporations fall under the jurisdiction of the Australian Competition and Consumer Commission (ACCC) to the extent that they interact with consumers and are required to comply with trade practices and consumer protection laws. Professional communicators might encounter the ACCC in a range of situations, including in connection with its substantial powers to control anti-competitive behaviour by companies and to veto mergers and acquisitions because of their impact on competition in media markets.

Of most relevance to journalists and professional writers is that the ACCC is responsible, under the *Competition and Consumer Act 2010*, for policing section 18 of the Australian Consumer Law, which targets 'misleading and deceptive conduct' in trade or commerce. News organisations get a 'media safe harbour' exemption from these provisions under the 'prescribed information provider' exception (s 19), which was introduced to the legislation's predecessor, the *Trade Practices Act 1974*, after it had been in operation for almost a decade.

In 1984, in the *Global Sportsman case*, it was held that the publication of statements–including statements of opinion made in the ordinary course of news–could constitute conduct that was 'misleading or deceptive'. Successful lobbying by media companies pressured the government of the day into introducing a news media exemption, which applied unless the deceptive material related to the publication of advertisements or promotion of the information providers' own commercial interests. 'Prescribed information providers' included 'a person who carries on a business of providing information', encompassing newspapers, holders of broadcasting licences, the ABC and SBS.

The 'media safe harbour' acknowledged the fact that news organisations could not vouch for every claim made by those quoted in their news columns or stories (Applegarth, 2008). However, as soon as news material was sponsored, or run in return for some compensation in cash or kind, or was used to promote the news organisation's own operations (such as in a promo), it fell outside the exemption and left any misleading content potentially subject to an action against the media proprietor. This rendered journalists and their organisations particularly vulnerable in the realm of advertorials (now known as 'branded content'), if space was devoted to promoting a company's products or services because it happened to be an advertiser, or if some arrangement or understanding had been reached to that effect. If the advertorial was proven to be 'misleading or deceptive', the media outlet could then be held responsible, and could face an injunction preventing further publication or a damages claim from those adversely affected. The result is that if a media organisation has struck such a deal, it must be able to prove the truth of any claims it makes about the relevant products and services.

Under the 'misleading and deceptive conduct' provisions, media outlets can be sued by any of their readers, viewers or listeners who have been misled, and by any businesses affected by loss of trade as a result. In the *Horwitz Grahame Books case* (1987), Justice Wilcox noted that the 'information provider' exemption did not apply when the material related to the supply of goods or services by the information provider itself. This was highlighted in the *Mobile Phone case* (1996), when News Limited newspapers published a series of promotional advertisements offering a 'free mobile phone for every reader' with an asterisked 'conditions apply' notation. The conditions were extensive, with the offer open to only 5000 readers and with a range of fees payable on the uptake of the offer. The publisher, Nationwide News, was fined a total of $120,000 for the breaches.

The 'media safe harbour' has been narrowed down by superior courts in recent years. In the *Craftsman Homes case* (2008), the behaviour of a television reporter and colleague who pretended to be a husband and wife in order to film a surprise interview with the owner of a building company was found to be misleading and deceptive. The court held in that case that the exemption did not apply to journalists' behaviour 'pre-publication'. It resulted in awards of damages against reporter Ben Fordham and Channel Nine. On appeal, the NSW Court of Appeal held that the reporters' lies about being interested in building a home related to the building company's activities in 'trade or commerce', and therefore fell within the scope of the Act (at paras 41–9). The decision sent a loud warning to journalists using 'ambush' interview techniques or fake identities when researching stories.

The High Court upheld an appeal by the ACCC against Channel Seven (*Wildly Wealthy Women case*—see Focus Case 3.2) in 2009. A four-to-one majority ruled that, by entering an 'exclusive' arrangement with a company and then making false statements about its activities, the television program *Today Tonight* lost the right to the exemption. This decision might well make media outlets more careful in their publication of claims by those with whom they have signed exclusive deals.

We deal with the ACCC and consumer law again in Chapter 13, where we consider how these laws apply to public relations consultants, freelancers and new media entrepreneurs.

FOCUS CASE 3.2: *WILDLY WEALTHY WOMEN CASE*

Australian Competition and Consumer Commission v Channel Seven Brisbane Pty Ltd [2009] HCA 19 (30 April 2009)

FACTS

Channel Seven's evening current affairs program *Today Tonight* struck an exclusive arrangement with a company called Universal, which was selling a property investment scheme called 'Wildly Wealthy Women Millionaire Mentoring Program'. The business was owned by Dymphna Boholt and Sandra Forster, and claimed to teach women how to become wealthy through investments in real estate at a cost of $3000 each for a nine-month course. The television program's producer Howard Gipps agreed via email and phone conversations to run six stories about the scheme through 2003 and 2004, as long as *Today Tonight* held exclusive rights to coverage through to November 2004. No payment was involved. The interview made claims that the women had become millionaires through their property scheme, that one of the women had bought more than $1 million worth of property 'with no money whatsoever' and that the other owned more than 60 properties. None of those claims was true. The so-called 'millionaire' in fact had less than $115,000.

LAW

The ACCC started action against Channel Seven under the misleading and deceptive conduct provisions of the *Trade Practices Act 1974* (since replaced by similar provisions under the *Competition and Consumer Act 2010)*. Channel Seven argued that it was a 'prescribed information provider' under the Act, and should not lose that exemption, because the false statements were not related to goods or services that it supplied and were not part of an advertisement. After a successful High Court appeal, an injunction was granted, restraining the parties from making such false statements in the future, and declarations were issued to the effect that the statements were false.

Crucial to the High Court decision was the finding that media outlets ('prescribed information providers') would lose their exemption from the misleading and deceptive conduct provisions when the false claims related to their own goods and services, or when advertising others' goods and services, or in situations like this where they had struck a 'contract, arrangement or understanding' with a third party to promote their goods and services.

LESSONS FOR PROFESSIONAL COMMUNICATORS

Professional communicators—particularly journalists—should always check and double-check the factual basis of their stories. They need to be even more vigilant in checking the truthfulness of claims when they are dealing with advertorial copy, advertisements and claims made by third parties with which they have signed exclusivity deals or 'contracts, arrangements or understandings'. When the divisions between journalism, marketing and advertising become blurred—for example, when media organisations strike special coverage arrangements with sporting franchises or engage in innovative social media marketing campaigns—the onus reverts to reporters to verify the validity of the claims that their sources might be making. Public relations and marketing personnel need to be aware of this law when approaching media outlets to publish their advertorial material, which we consider in Chapter 13.

PUBLIC RELATIONS SELF-REGULATION

The Public Relations Institute of Australia (PRIA) is a self-regulatory professional body with disciplinary powers over its members for breaches of its Code of Ethics (see Appendix 3) and the organisation's Consultancy Code of Practice (applying to full professional members who are registered consultancies). These documents are detailed at <www.pria.com.au>. They require ethical practice in relation to honesty, confidentiality, conflict of interest, fee charging practices, transparency of funding, exaggerated claims, misrepresentation and injury to other practitioners. Given the lack of laws requiring the registration, licensing or accreditation of public relations personnel in Australia, there are no statutory sanctions for misconduct. Instead, PRIA has power to censure, fine, suspend and expel members who have breached the code—and to 'suitably publicise' its decisions. All members are required to agree in writing that they will adhere to the Code of Ethics upon joining PRIA. Ethics complaints are adjudicated by the national council of PRIA's College of Fellows—a committee of the industry's senior practitioners. The complaints procedure is detailed in the *Code of Ethics Administration Procedure Manual* (PRIA, 2003).

OTHER REGULATORS CONTROLLING PROFESSIONAL COMMUNICATION

Other regulatory bodies exercise powers that can impact on the research and publishing activities of professional communicators. The Australian Securities and Investment Corporation (ASIC) polices the *Corporations Act 2001*, which places strict conditions on claims made in documents associated with company floats and initial public offering (IPO) announcements. These documents often tread a fine line between marketing, sales and compliance, and ASIC has powers to pursue marketers, public relations consultants and journalists who do not ensure that statements about future outcomes are reasonably based, and to ensure that major risks are disclosed in print, broadcast, online and social media statements. ASIC identified risks in the use of social media in marketing IPOs in a 2016 report (ASIC, 2016). Other entities with powers to act against professional communicators include the various state-based anti-corruption bodies, mental and guardianship health tribunals, the Therapeutic Goods Administration (TGA) on drugs and treatments, parliamentary committees and many more.

Journalists, bloggers and public relations personnel should research the laws that apply to their specialty areas of research and writing.

DIGITAL DIMENSIONS: TERMS OF USE AND SOCIAL MEDIA POLICIES

The digital era has heralded a series of other regulatory measures that impact professional communicators. Two of the most important are the terms of use (or 'terms of service') of the major social networking platforms and the social media policies controlling use of these media in the workplace as a journalist, blogger or public relations practitioner.

TERMS OF USE

When you join social networking platforms like Facebook, Twitter, Snapchat, LinkedIn, Instagram and Flickr, you are asked to agree to abide by that company's terms of service. These vary somewhat between platforms, but cover topics like copyright in the material you post and the extent to which the organisations can share your details and material with other companies and governments. They also cover the so-called 'rules of engagement'–giving the social media company the right to suspend your account for what it deems to be misuse or misbehaviour. This can involve something as serious as cyber-bullying or posting offensive material, through to setting up an account in something other than your real name. Professional communicators need to be familiar with the terms of use of the major platforms they use, and ensure that they are compliant: it can be embarrassing and expensive if your private or professional social media presence is suddenly shut down. However, terms of service also represent a non-legal avenue of recourse for professional communicators wanting redress against trolls and troublesome users who might be damaging their brands and reputations on social media. For example, a common clause in terms of service states:

> *We may also remove or refuse to distribute any Content on the Services, suspend or terminate users, and reclaim usernames without liability to you. (Twitter, 2017)*

Platforms vary in their appeal processes for disabled or terminated accounts.

SOCIAL MEDIA POLICIES

One of the most important regulatory systems in place in the Web 2.0 workplace is the social media policy of the organisation that employs you as a professional communicator. These can vary from just a few dot points through to highly legalistic industrial regulations. Decisions by the Fair Work Commission have offered guidance to employers on what constitutes an effective social media policy. Two key decisions involved companies Linfox and The Good Guys: these established that the dismissal of an employee for insulting their employer and colleagues on social media will be ruled unfair unless the company has a clear and reasonable social media policy that it has drawn to the attention of its staff (Bunch, 2012). We return to this topic in more detail in Chapter 13, but for the moment it is important that, as a journalist or professional communicator, you become familiar with your own employer's policy to check whether your social media activities are compliant.

TIPS FOR MINDFUL PRACTICE

- Every citizen needs a working knowledge of legal and legislative processes and the court system. Professional communicators need to know them intimately. Journalists might be expected to report upon them and public relations personnel might interact with them in a range of ways, including as a communications officer for the courts or the legislature.
- Become familiar with the codes of conduct and legislation that apply to your particular medium or professional communication sector.
- Maintain and encourage the highest ethical and professional standards in your own workplace, to minimise the likelihood of complaints.
- Take special care with advertorials (branded content), infomercials and your own corporate promotional material. Remember that you do not

qualify for the publishers' exemption from the misleading and deceptive conduct provisions of the Australian Consumer Law when writing or publishing such items. Take care, too, with your investigation methods, avoiding the temptation to use false identities or to conduct so-called 'ambush' interviews.

- Get to know your social media platforms' terms of service to avoid having an account disabled over a breach. Become familiar with your organisation's social media policy and ensure you are complying with it.

IN A NUTSHELL

- The Australian legal system has four main historical influences: the English law that British settlers brought with them; the Constitution; High Court decisions; and laws made by state and federal parliaments.
- The doctrine of the separation of powers dictates that the three arms of government—the judiciary (the courts), the legislature (the parliaments) and the executive (the government and the public service, including the police)—should remain separate and independent of each other.
- There are two major sources of Australian law: that made by the legislature (statute law) and that found in decisions of judges (common law). Each plays a vital role in the legal process.
- Section 51 of the Constitution gives the Commonwealth government power to enact laws in 40 areas, including immigration, foreign affairs, defence, telecommunications, welfare, corporations and currency. The states can pass laws on all other matters.
- As an indication of the adversarial context in which they are fought and decided, cases are cited according to the parties contesting them with a 'v' (standing for 'versus' but spoken as 'and'), as in *Mabo v Queensland*.
- Criminal law is concerned with offences against the state for which offenders can be tried and punished, while civil law is concerned with the rights and obligations of individuals, corporate entities and government in their relationships with others.

- In the print and online domains, the trend has been towards self-regulatory mechanisms, including the industry-funded Australian Press Council, the Independent Media Council (WA) and in-house codes of conduct.
- Broadcast media are regulated by the Australian Communications and Media Authority (ACMA), operating under the *Broadcasting Services Act 1992*.
- Professional communicators may also fall under the jurisdiction of other regulators like the Australian Competition and Consumer Commission (ACCC) and self-regulators like the Public Relations Institute of Australia (PRIA).

DISCUSSION QUESTIONS

3.1 Why do you think it is important that the three arms of government—the judiciary, the legislature and the executive—are separate? Discuss some examples of where this relationship may have become blurred.

3.2 Devise your own system of ethical regulation that does not involve government, but that could still feature tougher sanctions for unethical behaviour than those presently in existence. Explain how it might operate.

3.3 Debate the topic 'There are already enough media laws. We don't need more regulation of free expression.'

3.4 Telephone or email a journalist, professional blogger or public relations consultant and ask them about an ethical breach they have encountered in their career. What were the consequences of their actions? To what extent did the regulators get involved? Write a 300-word report summarising your interviewee's responses or a short feature story about it.

3.5 You are editing an in-flight magazine for a major Australian airline. One of the main stories is about the special offers it is making available to its frequent flyer club members. How might you address the requirements of the Australian Consumer Law when preparing this article?

REFERENCES

Applegarth, P. 2008, 'How deep is the media safe harbour?', *Gazette of Law and Journalism*, 23, <http://archive.sclqld.org.au/judgepub/2008/How%20deep%20is%20the%20safe%20media%20harbour.pdf>.

Australian Broadcasting Authority (ABA) 2000, *Commercial Radio Inquiry: Final Report*, ABA, Sydney, <www.abc.net.au/mediawatch/transcripts/1339_aba.pdf>.

Australian Press Council (APC) 2013, *Australian Press Council Constitution*, <www.presscouncil.org.au/uploads/52321/ufiles/APC_Constitution_-_August_2013.pdf>.

—— 2016, *Australian Press Council Annual Report 2015–2016*, Australian Press Council, Sydney, <www.presscouncil.org.au/uploads/52321/ufiles/Annual_Report/APC_Annual_Report_40_2015-2016.pdf>.

—— 2017, 'Welcome to the Australian Press Council', <www.presscouncil.org.au>.

Australian Securities and Investment Commission (ASIC) 2016, *Marketing Practices in Initial Public Offerings of Securities*, <download.asic.gov.au/media/4011746/rep494-published-19-september-2016.pdf>.

Bunch, M. 2012, 'Employee sacked for Facebook comments wins reinstatement', *Aitken Legal Employment Update*, February, <www.aitkenlegal.com.au/userfiles/files/14_%20Employment%20Update%20-%20February%202012%20-%20Employee%20sacked%20for%20facebook%20comments%20wins%20reinstatement%20(AL00063971).pdf>.

Commercial Radio Australia (CRA) 2017, *Commercial Radio Code of Practice*, <http://commercialradio.com.au/CR/media/CommercialRadio/Commercial-Radio-Code-of-Practice.pdf>.

Convergence Review 2012, *Convergence Review: Final Report*, Department of Broadband, Communications and the Digital Economy, Canberra, <www.dbcde.gov.au/__data/assets/pdf_file/0007/147733/Convergence_Review_Final_Report.pdf>.

Fairfax Media 2012, *Charter of Editorial Independence*, <www.smh.com.au/national/fairfax-media-charter-of-editorial-independence-20120619-2014t.html>.

Finkelstein, R. 2012, *Report of the Independent Inquiry into the Media and Media Regulation*, Department of Broadband, Communications and the Digital Economy, Canberra, <www.dbcde.gov.au/__data/assets/pdf_file/0006/146994/Report-of-the-Independent-Inquiry-into-the-Media-and-Media-Regulation-web.pdf>.

Free TV Australia (FTA) 2015, *Commercial Television Industry Code of Practice*, <www.freetv.com.au/media/Code_of_Practice/Free_TV_Commercial_Television_Industry_Code_of_Practice_2015.pdf>.

Media, Entertainment and Arts Alliance (MEAA) 2017, *Registered Rules of the Media, Entertainment and Arts Alliance*, <www.meaa.org/resource-package/registered-rules-of-the-media-entertainment-and-arts-alliance>.

Polden, M. 2010, 'Anti-bikie laws may be fatally flawed', *Law Society Journal*, 48(9), 64–7.

Public Relations Institute of Australia (PRIA) 2003, *Code of Ethics Administration Procedure Manual*, 2nd edn, PRIA, Sydney, <www.pria.com.au/documents/item/4384>.

Ruddock, P. 2004, 'Government moves one step closer to uniform defamation law', Media Release, 29 July, <parlinfo.aph.gov.au/parlInfo/download/media/pressrel/64AD6/upload_binary/64ad63.pdf;fileType%3Dapplication%2Fpdf>.

Twitter 2017, 'Twitter terms of service', <https://twitter.com/en/tos>.

CASES CITED

Craftsman Homes case: TCN Channel Nine Pty Ltd v Ilvariy Pty Ltd [2008] NSWCA 9, <www.austlii.edu.au/cgi-bin/sinodisp/au/cases/nsw/NSWCA/2008/9.html>.

Gina's case: Rinehart v Welker [2011] NSWCA 403 (7 December 2011), <www.austlii.edu.au/cgi-bin/sinodisp/au/cases/nsw/NSWCA/2011/403.html>; *Rinehart v Welker & Ors*, HCATrans 57 (9 March 2012), <www.austlii.edu.au/cgi-bin/sinodisp/au/cases/cth/HCATrans/2012/57.html>.

Global Sportsman case: Global Sportsman v Mirror Newspapers (1984) 2 FCR 82.

Hinch's case: R v Hinch [2013] VSC 520.

Horwitz Grahame Books case: Horwitz Grahame Books v Performance Publications (1987) ATPR 40–764.

Humphries v Poljak [1992] 2 VR 129.

Jane Doe's case: Doe v Australian Broadcasting Corporation & Ors [2007] VCC 281 (3 April 2007), <www.austlii.edu.au/au/cases/vic/VCC/2007/281.pdf>.

Kazal case: Thunder Studios Inc. (California) v Kazal (No. 2) [2017] FCA 202, <www.austlii.edu.au/cgi-bin/viewdoc/au/cases/cth/FCA/2017/202.html>.

Mobile Phone case: Nationwide News Pty Ltd v Australian Competition and Consumer Commission [1996] 1120 FCA 1.

Motor Accident case: Transport Accident Commission v Maria Katanas [2017] HCA 32, <www.austlii.edu.au/cgi-bin/viewdoc/au/cases/cth/HCA/2017/32.html>.

Totani's case: South Australia v Totani [2010] HCA 39, (2010) 242 CLR 1, High Court (Australia).

Toxic Playground case: O'Brien v Australian Broadcasting Corporation [2017] NSWCA 338, <www.austlii.edu.au/cgi-bin/viewdoc/au/cases/nsw/NSWCA/2017/338.html>; *O'Brien v Australian Broadcasting Corporation* [2016] NSWSC 1289, <www.austlii.edu.au/cgi-bin/viewdoc/au/cases/nsw/NSWSC/2016/1289.html>.

Treasurer case: Hockey v Fairfax Media Publications Pty Limited [2015] FCA 652, <www.austlii.edu.au/cgi-bin/sinodisp/au/cases/cth/FCA/2015/652.html>.

Wildly Wealthy Women case: Australian Competition and Consumer Commission v Channel Seven Brisbane Pty Ltd [2009] HCA 19 (30 April 2009), <www.austlii.edu.au/au/cases/cth/HCA/2009/19.html>.

PART 2

ISSUES IN JUSTICE AND TRANSPARENCY

CHAPTER 4

Open justice and freedom of information

KEY CONCEPTS

Open justice
The principle that, wherever feasible, the courts should remain open to public and media attendance and scrutiny.

Suppression orders
Orders by a judge or magistrate to prevent disclosure or publication, including by the media, of all or part of a case. They can apply to a whole case or to certain sensitive elements of a case, such as the identification of a protected witness. Orders preventing publication—but not disclosure—are known as 'non-publication orders'. Orders against disclosure—which can sometimes include non-disclosure of the order itself—are known as 'suppression orders'.

Freedom of information
Also known as 'right to information', freedom of information refers to laws aimed at opening as much government data to public scrutiny as is reasonably possible and in the public interest. This is often backed by legislation giving citizens the right to access government information, particularly data about themselves and sometimes by positive laws requiring government departments to self-publish information.

Two centuries-old principles of transparency underscore access to information in the court system and in government. Insofar as it applies to courts, the principle of 'open justice' is based on a rationale dating back to Saxon times: that the justice system benefits when publicity is given to court proceedings. Freedom of information (FOI) legislation (also called 'right to information') was first enacted by the Swedish parliament in 1766, and operates on the premise that democracy is better served if information held by governments can readily be accessed by the public. This chapter is divided into accounts of how these two principles function, in judicial and governmental processes.

OPEN JUSTICE: HISTORICAL AND INTERNATIONAL CONTEXT

Open justice is the principle of public access to courts. It is entrenched in the legal systems of the United Kingdom, North America and Commonwealth countries including Australia through their connection with English common law, under which the judicial process has been relatively open since at least the twelfth century. Under the principle of open justice, the judicial process should be transparent and open to public examination. Ordinary people should be able to sit in court and watch cases as they unfold. The media are seen as the 'eyes and ears' of citizens who cannot be in the courtroom to witness proceedings themselves. Taken to its extreme, open justice can earn criticism for interfering with justice by tipping the balance towards 'trial by media'—where adverse publicity prevents a celebrity or the accused in a high-profile trial from getting the chance to be tried before an impartial jury. Trials in recent decades, such as those of Oscar Pistorius in South Africa and the late pop star Michael Jackson in the United States—along with the advent of Court TV—have fuelled this concern. Somewhere in between the extremes of a media free-for-all and judicial clampdown is a legitimate and vital space for journalism, in which courts can be subjected to vigorous examination and criticism in the public interest, while those accused of a crime can still receive a fair trial.

It is important that journalists and other professional communicators are aware of the principles of open justice because, as with freedom of the press, they might be called upon to defend them. Occasionally, judges and—much more frequently—magistrates are tempted to restrict the reportage of controversial or distressing cases. Unless they are reminded of the important role the media play in the administration of justice through the free and fair reporting of court cases, they may be tempted to agree to restrictions, often because the prosecution and defence have reached an agreement to consent to non-publication orders. Here a comment in the judgment of Sir Christopher Staughton in *Ex parte P* (1998) is relevant. He stated, 'When both sides agreed that information should be kept from the public that was when the court had to be most vigilant.'

English Master of the Rolls Lord Neuberger (2011) traced the history and modern application of open justice in an important lecture. It stems back to the earliest history of the English courts. Even in Saxon times (the fifth to eleventh centuries), courts were constituted by the attendance of the people who gave their verdict, and in Norman times (the eleventh and twelfth centuries), the idea of a jury of twelve neighbours continued this open tradition (*Raybos's case*, 1985 at 50). Sir William Holdsworth (1945: 156) recorded that, as early as the sixteenth century, the Star Chamber, a notorious English court, was routinely open to the public. Sir William Blackstone, in his *Commentaries on the Laws of England* (1765–69: 373), wrote that the open examination of witnesses 'in the presence of all mankind, is much more conducive to the clearing up of truth'.

A hallmark British case early last century, *Scott's case* (1913), encapsulated the notion of open justice. There the court quoted the nineteenth-century legal scholar Jeremy Bentham's (1825) treatise on the need for publicity of the judicial process (at 477):

> *In the darkness of secrecy, sinister interest and evil in every shape have full swing. Only in proportion as publicity has place can any of the checks applicable to judicial injustice operate. Where there is no publicity there is no justice . . . Publicity is the very soul of justice. It is the keenest spur to exertion and the surest of all guards against improbity.*

The open justice concept was tied closely to the notion that justice was compromised when conducted behind closed doors, because secrecy gave the impression that perhaps wrongdoing or bias was being allowed to creep into deliberations not subject to the public gaze. Such concern arose in a British case, the *Sussex Justices case*, in 1924 (at 259) when Chief Justice Lord Hewart pronounced that 'justice should not only be done, but should manifestly and undoubtedly be seen to be done'.

It is not just countries of the former British Empire that have open courtrooms. Article 14 of the International Covenant on Civil and Political Rights reads (OHCHR, 1976):

> *1 All persons shall be equal before the courts and tribunals. In the determination of any criminal charge against him, or of his rights and obligations in a suit at law, everyone shall be entitled to a fair and public hearing by a competent, independent and impartial tribunal established by law. The press and the public may be excluded from all or part of a trial for reasons of morals, public order (*ordre public*) or national security in a democratic society, or when the interest of the private lives of the parties so requires, or to the extent strictly necessary in the opinion of the court in special circumstances where publicity would prejudice the interests of justice; but any judgment rendered in a criminal case or in a suit at law shall be made public except where the interest of juvenile persons otherwise requires or the proceedings concern matrimonial disputes or the guardianship of children.*

While the requirement for a public trial appears to be eroded somewhat by the third sentence, which allows for exclusion of the media or the public, the organisation's Human Rights Committee later issued an explanation of this article that restated the importance of publicity in the judicial process (OHCHR, 1984, para. 6).

OPEN JUSTICE: AUSTRALIAN LAW

Former NSW Chief Justice Jim Spigelman (2005) said that the principle that justice must be seen to be done 'is one of the most pervasive axioms of the administration of common law systems'. The High Court has made several pronouncements on the importance of open justice, including in *Zhao's case* (2015), where it stated that 'the rationale of the open court principle is that court proceedings should be subjected to public and professional scrutiny, and courts will not act contrary to the principle save in exceptional circumstances'. Chief Justice French stated that the right to publish a report of proceedings is a corollary of the right to attend and observe them (*Sex Offenders case*, 2011, para. 22). Open justice includes the right to identify parties to court proceedings as part of a report. While the principle may be overridden by statute in certain circumstances, any provision purporting to do so must show a clear intention on the part of parliament to displace the principle. As McHugh J observed in the *Police Tribunal case* (1986 at 481, n 22):

> *some common law rights are of such importance that an intention to repeal or amend any of them will only be attributed to the legislature when the language of its statute is unmistakably clear. I think the right to publish a fair and accurate report of court proceedings is a common law right of sufficient significance to fall within this category.*

The landmark Australian case in the area of open justice and the media was *Raybos's case* (1985). The defendant, a solicitor named Bernard Patrick Jones, sought a court order suppressing the publication of his name. In refusing the application, the court traced the history of open justice and explained that there were sometimes good reasons to deviate from the rule. Nevertheless, Justice Kirby stated (at 55):

> *The principles which support and justify the open doors of our courts likewise require that what passes in court should be capable of being reported. The entitlement to report to the public at large what is seen and heard in open court is a corollary of the access to the court of those members of the public who choose to attend.*

He concluded (at 60):

> *Widespread publicity, through the modern media of communications, may do great harm. Sometimes quite unjustifiable damage can be inflicted on individuals. However that may be, a price must be paid for the open administration, particularly of criminal justice. The alternative, of secret trials, where important public rights may be in competition and individual liberty may be at risk is so unacceptable that courts of our tradition will tend to avoid the consequence.*

As two of the *Local Court cases* (2005 and 2007) demonstrated, at common law a court must be satisfied that an order restricting access or reporting is strictly necessary to ensure the administration of justice in the circumstances.

In the NSW Supreme Court, in the *Idoport case* (2001), Justice Einstein identified six limited exceptions to the open justice principle:

1. cases involving trade secrets, secret documents or communications
2. cases such as extortion (blackmail) cases, where public disclosure would undermine the whole purpose of the action
3. cases involving the need to maintain order in the court
4. some cases involving national security
5. cases involving some administrative action, which may best be dealt with in chambers
6. cases where the court sits as the guardian of wards of the state or the mentally ill.

While Justice Einstein's list reflects the position at common law, based on the interpretation of previous cases, journalists need to bear in mind the forest of statutory restrictions on publication, which differ markedly from state to state. In 2009, the Australian Law Reform Commission (ALRC) identified more than 500 secrecy provisions in

176 pieces of primary and subordinate legislation, with hundreds more at the state and territory levels (ALRC, 2009). An ALRC report into rights and freedoms in 2015 identified numerous exceptions to open justice in a host of Commonwealth statutes in the areas of court powers, national security and witness protection, along with selected provisions in family law, indigenous heritage protection, migration, child support and administrative appeals (ALRC, 2015: 234–7). The main statutory restrictions a reporter can expect to come across—and of which every reporter should be aware—concern sexual offences, children, divorce, inquests, juries, bail, national security and official secrets. These are covered in more detail in Chapters 6 (court reporting) and 10 (anti-terrorism and hate laws), while restrictions on publication after arrest and during a trial (*sub judice* contempt) are addressed in Chapter 5.

While we have established that it may be regarded as a public good that the public knows what has gone on in court, it must be stressed that this is a broad principle applying to all members of the public. Journalists have been granted a number of privileges as representatives of the ordinary citizen, some of which can be withdrawn at the discretion of the court. They include being able to take notes and use devices in court for purposes of accuracy, the provision of special seating, access to information about parties and cases, and in some courts even being able to use social media in the courtroom. Judges and magistrates will also sometimes allow journalists to remain in court when the court has been closed to the general public, on the condition that they do not report on the proceedings or do not identify some witnesses, although this practice varies between states and territories. In some instances, this special access regime is enshrined in legislation. An example is section 10 of the *Children (Criminal Proceedings) Act 1987* (NSW). Such privileges are detailed in Chapter 6.

Exactly what latitude members of the public (and the media as their representatives) are allowed under the open justice principle varies somewhat throughout the case law. The principle of the media's legitimate role in reporting court proceedings has been long held, and was reaffirmed by the Federal Court in *Davis's case* (1995), involving sexual allegations against a Canberra doctor, where the Full Court ruled (at 514):

> *In Canberra as elsewhere, the media habitually report pretrial proceedings, including evidence given in committal proceedings. Whatever their motives in reporting, their opportunity to do so arises out of a principle that is fundamental to our society and method of government: except in extraordinary circumstances, the courts of the land are open to the public. This principle arises out of the belief that exposure to public scrutiny is the surest safeguard against any risk of the courts abusing their considerable powers . . . This includes [reporting] the names of the parties to proceedings, which are ordinarily known to everyone in court.*

The court used this as its rationale in lifting a non-publication order over the name of the accused.

The common law, legislation and court procedures in all states and territories mean journalists can expect access to transcripts, charge sheets and most other documents tabled in open court. However, the courts will usually require special reasons why they should make the following kinds of documents available:

- documents such as affidavits that have not yet been tested in court
- hand-up briefs and other similar documents from committal hearings, at least until after any subsequent trial has concluded
- transcripts and other documents related to older cases.

Access will rarely, if ever, be granted to the following categories of documents:

- victim impact statements
- character references
- pre-sentence reports
- medical and psychiatric reports and certificates

- documents protected by public interest immunity—such as those that might identify a police informer or prejudice an ongoing investigation
- child protection reports
- prior criminal record (except on sentencing)
- written submissions, handed up by counsel—although the parties may be prepared to supply them.

SUPPRESSION ORDERS

Sometimes a judge or magistrate will use their power to prevent disclosure or publication, including by the media, of all or part of a case. This is known as issuing a 'suppression order'. Sometimes a slightly narrower 'non-publication order' or even a 'pseudonym order' may be made. Section 3 of the *NSW Court Suppression and Non-publication Orders Act 2010* defines a non-publication order as 'an order that prohibits or restricts the publication of information (but that does not otherwise prohibit or restrict the disclosure of information)', while a suppression order is 'an order that prohibits or restricts the disclosure of information (by publication or otherwise)'. It gives news organisations standing to appear to oppose an order (s 9), to seek a review of an order (s 13) and to appeal against an order (s 14).

Sadly, despite comments by Chief Justices in both New South Wales and Victoria that too many suppression orders were being issued (Ross, 2005), the Australia's Right to Know-commissioned Moss Report (Moss, 2007: 202) found that there were more than 1000 suppression or non-publication orders imposed by courts throughout Australia at that time. Bosland (2017) reported that Victorian courts alone had issued more than 220 suppression orders per year in 2014 and 2015—despite the introduction of the *Open Courts Act 2013* (Vic), which had aimed to reduce their numbers and ambit. Breach of a suppression order can have serious consequences for journalists. For example, broadcaster and blogger (now Senator) Derryn Hinch was sentenced to home detention in 2011 after he breached suppression orders and named sex offenders on his website <www.hinch.net> and at a public rally. The offenders had served their sentences and Hinch was warning the public of their release into the community. He failed to win a High Court appeal on the argument that the suppression orders issued under section 42 of the *Serious Sex Offenders Monitoring Act 2005* (Vic) contravened principles of open justice and the implied constitutional freedom to communicate (*Sex Offenders case*, 2011). Hinch had already served twelve days in prison in 1987 for broadcasting prejudicial material about a sex offender on the eve of his trial (*Hinch's case*, 1987). He was later fined $100,000 in 2013 for breaching another suppression order, by again revealing details of the criminal history of the man accused of raping and murdering ABC worker Jill Meagher in Melbourne (*Rape Priors case*, 2013). Hinch had reported on his 'Human Headline' blog that the accused—Adrian Bayley—was on bail and parole at the time he murdered Meagher, that Bayley's parents had alerted police to the fact that he might attack a woman again, and that the Sexual Crimes Squad had twice appealed for Bayley's parole to be revoked. Hinch had also posted tweets indicating that he was aware of the suppression orders. Hinch refused to pay the fine and was sentenced to 50 days in prison in 2014.

Suppression orders or non-publication orders can apply to a whole case or to certain sensitive elements of a case, such as the identification of a protected witness. In South Australia, a court may issue a suppression order when it considers it desirable 'to prevent prejudice to the proper administration of justice' or 'to prevent undue hardship' to victims, witnesses or children, under section 69A of the *Evidence Act 1929* (SA).

While superior courts (Supreme Courts, the Federal Court and the High Court) have an inherent power to issue a suppression order over current court proceedings purely on the grounds of possible prejudice to a forthcoming trial, even in an 'exceptional' case, the appropriate course will normally be for a court to postpone the trial date or to order a stay of proceedings. Except where a special statute has been passed (as in the NSW *Court Suppression and Non-Publication Orders Act 2010*) so-called 'inferior' courts (District, County, Magistrates and Local Courts) have an implied power to do the same, but only if it is strictly necessary. In *Apps' case* (2014), the NSW Supreme Court struck down on appeal a blanket non-publication order made by a magistrate, based on fears of prejudice to the fair trial of a woman accused of murder. But in *Obeid's case* (2016), the High Court issued a non-publication order on any information linking the identity of former NSW government minister Eddie Obeid in relation to an application which had been made on his behalf for special leave to appeal, his application to stay proceedings in his trial for misconduct in public office and his application for non-publication orders. Justice Gageler decided that the order 'was necessary to prevent prejudice to the proper administration of justice' on the grounds that to allow publicity about Obeid's appeal would undermine the effectiveness of non-publication orders issued by the NSW courts in relation to the same matter (*Obeid's case*, 2016, at para. 22). The orders had been issued to stem the tide of adverse publicity about Obeid in the lead-up to his forthcoming trial by jury, in order to encourage the so-called 'fade effect' on potential jurors' recollections about Obeid (at para. 17). No representatives of news organisations had appeared in the High Court to oppose the order. In *Bromfield's case* (1991) in Western Australia, the Supreme Court held that a newspaper publisher was entitled to be heard by a magistrate at the time he was suppressing details of a committal hearing. This was an important decision for journalists, which was followed in the *Police Commissioner's case* (2007).

In recent years, news organisations have routinely challenged the courts' attempts to suppress key information in cases, with varied success. The Snowtown murder trials (where several bodies were found in barrels in the vault of a former bank building in South Australia) began in 2000 with press appeals against suppression orders imposed by the magistrate conducting the preliminary hearing. Not only did he suppress material, but he also ordered that the reasons for his decision be suppressed. By the end of the Snowtown trial, more than 200 suppression orders had been issued (Ross, 2005). Three news organisations were fined a total of $75,000 in 2004 for breaching one of those orders, which prohibited the publication of a photograph of one of the accused (*Snowtown case*, 2004).

In the *PQR case* (2000), the Victorian County Court issued a 'pseudonym order'—a type of suppression order requiring that someone be referred to by a series of letters instead of their real name. The Herald and Weekly Times succeeded in having the order overturned in the Victorian Supreme Court as the naming did not endanger national security, prejudice the administration of justice, endanger anyone's life or cause undue stress or embarrassment (*PQR case*, 2000). The newspaper group also convinced the Full Court of the Federal Court to set aside a suppression order over the name of an Australian Football League (AFL) footballer who was alleged to have disguised some of his income as 'consultancy' payments to a company, despite the fact that he might be embarrassed and his reputation damaged (*AFL case*, 2003). Mere embarrassment for the parties to an action should never be enough to prompt a court to issue a suppression order. As Justice Kirby of the NSW Supreme Court said in one of the *Local Court cases* (1991, at 142):

> *It has often been acknowledged that an unfortunate incident of the open administration of justice is that embarrassing, damaging and even dangerous facts occasionally come to light. Such considerations have never been regarded as a reason for the closure of courts, or the issue of suppression orders in their various alternative forms.*

In the 2007 Benbrika terror trial in Victoria, one of the accused, Abdul Benbrika, made an application for total suppression of all media reporting of the trial, including the charges, the evidence, the arguments, the verdict and, if there were sentences following the trial, the sentences and the reasons for them. The basis was that Benbrika, along with three of the other accused, was facing not just one trial on terrorism charges, but a second trial on even more serious terrorism charges. The trial judge held in favour of the media, on public interest grounds given the seriousness of the alleged offences, the number of accused and the importance of terrorism as an issue (*Benbrika case*, 2007, at para. 13).

Some of the nation's leading media law cases have resulted from large newspaper and television organisations arguing or appealing against the decisions of courts to restrict access. Sometimes, however, journalists do not have the financial support of their organisations behind them when they wish to state their case for a suppression order to be lifted or not to be made. A magistrate might turn to the press bench in the courtroom after a defence counsel has asked for a suppression of their client's identity and ask, 'Do the representatives of the media have anything to say about this request?' That is when many a reporter will freeze, daunted by the authority of the courtroom, and shake their head shyly. Sadly, such a response can represent another nail in the coffin of open justice. Perhaps the next time the magistrate will not even bother to ask for a media response.

But it is not just in those jurisdictions that journalists should speak up for open justice. From time to time in most jurisdictions, a well-informed journalist will take on the role of representing the principles of free press and open justice in the courtroom. All it really requires is a basic understanding of the role of the media in the legal system and the ability to remind the magistrate in clear and simple terms of the public interest values at stake. Sometimes all it takes is a short note of request to a magistrate. That was all former *Townsville Bulletin* court reporter Melissa Ketchell needed when she wrote to the local magistrate seeking permission to report on a case involving two of the most sensitive elements of restrictive reporting: children and sex. Ketchell wrote a four-paragraph letter to the magistrate reminding him that there were legislative provisions permitting media to be present during such proceedings and explaining that she understood the non-identification requirements. Ketchell explained that the magistrate granted her application despite opposition from the defence counsel. The resulting story, 'School officer tells of "rape"', met the requirements by detailing the circumstances of the case without identifying any of the children involved (Ketchell, 1999).

On the eve of the release of the previous edition of this book, the authors were surprised to hear on the grapevine that a new suppression order had been issued by the Victorian County Court over any report linking Jill Meagher murderer Adrian Bayley with that crime. This was because he was facing new charges over other rapes. Our book discussed Bayley as the Meagher murderer in several passages explaining how, in the *Rape Priors case* (2013), blogger Derryn Hinch had been fined (and ultimately jailed) for breaching a non-publication order about Bayley's criminal record. After seeking legal advice, the publisher decided to print a revised version of the book with Bayley's name deleted and to store those already printed until the order had expired at the end of his new trial (Pearson, 2015). Bayley was convicted of two other rapes, but subsequently appealed successfully against one of those convictions (AAP, 2016).

In 2018, a particularly high degree of caution was exercised in a committal hearing involving charges based on historical claims of abuse against Cardinal George Pell. Details of the actual charges brought were suppressed (Marr, 2018) and no opening address was given in public (Wright, 2018). After the charges had been laid, Melbourne University Press voluntarily withdrew Louise Milligan's book about Cardinal Pell from Victorian bookshops.

RECORDING AUDIO AND VISION IN COURT

The extreme form of open justice is where the courts allow the media to record proceedings. Judges and magistrates have the power to allow recording of proceedings, and this has happened more often in recent years. In most jurisdictions, courts now allow the use of digital recorders with the permission of the judge or magistrate. Judicial officers have been allowing cameras and tape recorders in their courtrooms more frequently. The Federal Court has been live streaming selected cases since 1999 (see <www.fedcourt.gov.au/digital-law-library/videos>). NSW Deputy Coroner Jacqueline Milledge made the news in 2006 when she allowed television news crews to 'mike her up' for a visit to the site where a body had been found (Merritt, 2006). Public hearings at the 2009 Victorian Bushfires Royal Commission, the 2011–12 Queensland Floods Commission of Inquiry and the Royal Commission into Institutional Responses to Child Sexual Abuse in 2013 and 2014 were streamed live via the internet. From October 2013, the High Court of Australia made available its Canberra-based hearings on its website at <www.hcourt.gov.au/cases/recent-av-recordings>. Some courts now routinely allow the media to record and broadcast a judge's remarks (Supreme Court of Queensland, 2016; District Court of NSW, 2015).

Journalists can certainly seek the permission of the judge or magistrate to record proceedings, and a convincing argument might be the fact that a sound recording of proceedings can help a reporter to ensure their reports are fair and accurate—an outcome very much in the interests of the media and the legal system. But, in the absence of permission, the use of cameras or recording devices within the court precinct (the building itself, not just the courtroom) is likely to be regarded as a contempt of court.

OPEN JUSTICE: DIGITAL DIMENSIONS

The extent to which open justice applies to new media is still at issue as judges and magistrates ponder whether to allow ordinary citizens to blog or tweet from their courtrooms.

Internationally, the first reporter to tweet from a courtroom appears to have been Trish Mehaffy in Iowa in the United States in early 2008. According to the *ABA Law Journal*, she micro-blogged with the permission of Judge Mark Bennett. In 2009, Australian Federal Court judge Dennis Cowdroy allowed technology reporters to tweet from his Sydney courtroom during the landmark *iiNet case*—a copyright case attracting international interest (*iiNet case*, 2009, summary at para. 4).

Times journalist Alexi Mostrous made history in the United Kingdom with this tweet in December 2010: 'Judge just gave me explicit permission to tweet proceedings if it's quiet and doesn't disturb anything.' He was tweeting from WikiLeaks founder Julian Assange's bail hearing in London, where chief magistrate Howard Riddle had granted reporters permission to post social media updates on the sensational court appearance of the free information warrior. A few days later, the High Court banned the use of Twitter in the appeal against that decision, and later ruled that it would be at the discretion of the judge in future cases.

During the trial of Victorian police officer Simon Artz for alleged leaks to *The Australian* newspaper about a counter-terrorism operation, *Crikey* journalist and academic Margaret Simons was live tweeting proceedings from the hearing without the permission of the magistrate, and was told such behaviour would be considered contempt if it were repeated (Simons, 2011). The examples represent the variation in approaches taken by courts to the use of social media. Johnston (2011) identifies four key issues arising when judicial officers allow tweeting or blogging from the courtroom:

- interruptions to proceedings
- the brevity of the tweets restricting contents and context
- the temptation to use smartphone cameras, and
- the capacity for people to tweet without knowing the workings of defamation or contempt laws.

A further consideration can be added to this list: the security issue of people in court using devices to transmit witness testimony to other witnesses about to give evidence in the same trial. This was a key reason given by then NSW Attorney-General Greg Smith when in 2013 he amended section 9A of the *Court Security Act 2005* to prohibit the unauthorised transmission of proceedings from a courtroom using any device—even 'entries containing the sound, images or information on social media sites or any other website'—with a potential penalty of one year in prison. The government then proceeded to exempt journalists from the ban by passing a new regulation allowing journalists to use devices 'for the purposes of a media report on the proceedings concerned' (Court Security Amendment (Exemption) Regulation 2013). South Australian Supreme and District Court rules were changed in 2013 to allow instant live tweeting and texting from court of 'outcomes, such as verdicts, sentences, judgments, rulings, results of appeals in bail cases'. However, the courts imposed a fifteen-minute delay on texts being sent from the courtroom about evidence adduced or submissions made during proceedings, such as witness accounts or addresses from counsel. Queensland journalists can use social media to cover court so long as they do not interrupt proceedings. Again, judges can ban both devices and social media use at their discretion (Hemingway, 2016).

Sometimes courts will issue a notice to 'take down' certain material from a site or to shut down the whole site. Such orders are sometimes issued to the ISP or search engine host. In Australia, media organisations were ordered to remove from their searchable archives material related to the upcoming trial of drug trafficker Tony Mokbel (*Trafficker case*, 2010). The NSW Court of Appeal held in *Ibrahim's case* (2012) that a court can order an internet content host to remove material on the grounds of prejudice to a forthcoming trial, but that it must have been made aware of the suppression order and would not be subjected to orders if they were 'futile'—in other words, if the material was readily available and easily searched by prospective jurors beyond the jurisdiction where the suppression order had been issued (at para. 79).

This ruling was applied in a NSW Court of Criminal Appeal decision in 2016 when Nationwide News and the ABC appealed against orders that they remove certain stories from their websites until the end of a criminal murder trial involving Sydney gang members. The appeal court held that it would be futile to make the orders because the material would continue to be available on other sites. This was despite the fact that there was evidence that the removal of one item 'had had some effect in reducing the information available to a searcher on the internet'. This was because much of the material identified in the order was old and the appeal court had faith in juries acting responsibly if directed adequately by a trial judge to restrict their deliberations to the evidence presented in court, and not material they might find online (*Gang Murders case*, 2016, at paras 89–91).

Despite the potential for futile orders, the Law Commission of New Zealand recommended in 2017 that courts be given powers to issue take-down orders against online content hosts, but that accredited media be given standing to oppose such orders (Law Commission, 2017: 7). In the case of Cardinal Pell's committal hearing in 2018, detailed and explicit directions were given regarding the use of social media (Magistrates Court Victoria, 2018).

FREEDOM OF INFORMATION/RIGHT TO INFORMATION

While the principle of open justice is centred on the publicity of judicial process, freedom of information (FOI, also known as 'right to information') is all about maximising the transparency of, and accountability for, government decision-making processes in a modern democracy.

HISTORICAL AND INTERNATIONAL CONTEXT

According to Goldberg (2006: 35–6), the practice of FOI might well have existed as early as the Tang Dynasty in China (618–907 CE), although formal legislation can be traced back at least 200 years to the 1766 Swedish Edict of the Freedom of the Press, the *Tryckfrihetsförordningen* (TF). The Swede Peter Forsskal set the intellectual scene for the Nordic law by writing extensively about the need for free expression, lack of censorship and free knowledge in democratic society. The Finn Anders Chydenius was a key figure in crafting the law and negotiating its passage through the parliament.

The Global Network of Freedom of Information Advocates <www.freedominfo.org> listed 117 countries with FOI laws in 2017, with recent entries to the list including the Philippines, Sri Lanka, Tanzania, Togo, Vanuatu, Vietnam, Malawi and Lebanon.

The United Nations acknowledged the vital role of FOI by including it along with free expression in Article 19 of the Universal Declaration of Human Rights, adopted in 1948:

> *Everyone has the right to freedom of opinion and expression; this right includes freedom to hold opinions without interference and to seek, receive and impart information and ideas through any media and regardless of frontiers.*

In 2000, the UN Special Rapporteur on Freedom of Opinion and Expression, appointed by the UN Commission on Human Rights to monitor and report on the implementation of Article 19 of the ICCPR, proposed this set of FOI principles:

- Freedom of information legislation should be guided by the principle of maximum disclosure.
- Public bodies should be under an obligation to publish key information.
- Public bodies must actively promote open government.
- Exceptions should be clearly and narrowly drawn and subject to strict 'harm' and 'public interest' tests.
- Requests for information should be processed rapidly and fairly and an independent review of any refusals should be available.
- Individuals should not be deterred from making requests for information by excessive costs.
- Meetings of public bodies should be open to the public.
- Laws which are inconsistent with the principle of maximum disclosure should be amended or repealed.
- Individuals who release information on wrongdoing—whistle-blowers—must be protected. (McMillan, 2011: 8–9)

While we will learn that the aspirations of FOI are noble, the reality of the application of the laws can be deflating. Lidberg (2005: 31) conducted an international comparison of FOI regimes and filed similar FOI requests in five countries: Sweden, Australia, the United States, South Africa and Thailand. He found that only two of twelve requests in four countries generated any information, and found that Australia was the worst case in the study. Australia's rhetoric projected 'an image of a mature functioning FOI system', but according to Lidberg, the FOI regime was 'close to completely dysfunctional from a user's perspective'.

A more recent analysis by Lidberg (2013) positioned FOI laws internationally in the context of major releases of US defence and security documents by the WikiLeaks organisation and former National Security Agency analyst Edward Snowden in 2013. All major releases of these sensitive documents were channelled through major news enterprises, and all contained information that would never have been released under the strict FOI exemptions on such documents applying in Western nations. The irony was that Australian citizens could gain ready access to some of their nation's most sensitive information about surveillance of the leaders of neighbouring nations and their families but were being refused access to much more mundane bureaucratic data because of public service exemptions to FOI laws.

AUSTRALIAN LAW

FOI legislation was first introduced by Australia's federal government in 1982, and by 2006 there were FOI laws in all states and territories. The Commonwealth legislation is contained in the *Freedom of Information Act 1982*, while in the other jurisdictions FOI is contained in the following statutes:

- *Government Information (Public Access) Act 2009* (NSW)
- *Right to Information Act 2009* (Qld)
- *Information Act 2002* (NT)
- *Freedom of Information Act 1992* (WA)
- *Freedom of Information Act 1991* (SA)
- *Right to Information Act 2009* (Tas)
- *Freedom of Information Act 1989* (ACT)
- *Freedom of Information Act 1982* (Vic).

FOI is premised on the principle that there is a strong public interest in the administrative decisions of governments and quasi-governmental bodies being as transparent and as open as possible. The theory is that government documents about an individual should be released free to that person. Other documents should be available for payment of a fee. Nevertheless, there are recognised exceptions to such openness, particularly regarding decisions involving private and commercially sensitive matters and the protection of national security information.

Each jurisdiction varies in its FOI protocols and charges, so in the interests of space we will outline briefly the basic Commonwealth processes under its *Freedom of Information Act 1982*. Students and professional communicators should research the details of FOI laws in their own state or territory.

Government agencies hold a wealth of information about citizens. At the Commonwealth level, such information includes immigration, taxation, defence and welfare records. As we explain in Chapter 12, Australian government agencies collect, store and release information under the Information Privacy Principles (IPPs) established under the *Privacy Act 1988*. The combination of the FOI and *Privacy Acts* means that individual citizens can gain access to information about themselves much more easily and quickly than journalists are able to obtain the information that government holds about other people.

Of course, the sensible first step for a journalist is often to ask for information via the usual channels in a government agency—either directly from the bureaucrat responsible or through a media relations officer. This can be much less expensive in terms of both time and resources—and better suited to normal news deadlines for less controversial documents.

Commonwealth government agencies are also required to take a much more proactive approach to publishing key information as a result of an 'information publication scheme' introduced in 2011 (*FOI Act*, s 7A). The scheme requires agencies to publish their information publication plans, specifies types of information that must be published and provides a mechanism for agencies to publish other government information proactively. Some security and intelligence agencies are exempt from this requirement.

Section 8 of the *Freedom of Information Act* specifies nine categories of information that agencies must publish, in addition to their information publication plans, including details of the agency's structure, functions, statutory appointments, annual reports, public feedback arrangements, information routinely requested via FOI and/or provided to parliament, FOI officer details and the agency's FOI operational information. Agencies might also publish other information, such as research, reports and statistics that journalists and other professional communicators might find useful.

Those who cannot access the information by a simple request, or to whom an agency's information is not available via the information publication scheme, might make a formal FOI request. Once an FOI request has been made, the government department or responsible minister has to follow the formal processes under the Act to reach their decision on a document's release. Under Section 15, the procedure for making an FOI request to a Commonwealth agency involves the following steps:

- Make the request in writing (many agencies have forms on their websites).
- State that it is an application for the purposes of the *Freedom of Information Act.*
- Provide information about the documents required, to help the agency or minister identify them.
- Provide an email or postal address so notices can be sent.
- Send the request by hand delivery, post, email, fax or online submission.
- Importantly for journalists, the reasons for requesting the information do not have to be provided.

The agency or minister must notify the applicant of the request's receipt within fourteen days and a public servant may offer advice on refining the scope of the request to save on time and expense. Decisions on granting or refusing access to documents must be made by a designated officer within the agency.

A document that is requested must be disclosed unless:

- the document or information it contains originated in an agency that the *Freedom of Information Act* does not cover, such as ASIO
- the document is 'exempt' (including national security, defence, international relations, Cabinet, law and public safety, trade

secrets, commercial-in-confidence and a range of other documents) (Part IV)

- the document is 'conditionally exempt', and release at the time is not in the public interest (for example, a document that, if released, could prejudice an agency examination or test)
- there is already a charging process in place for that type of document (such as with an application for evidence of Australian citizenship).

The agency or minister is required to 'take all reasonable steps' to notify you of their decision within 30 days of their receipt of the FOI request. This can be extended by up to 30 days if the applicant agrees in writing, if another agency needs to be consulted, or if it relates to the business affairs or personal privacy of others. It might also be extended if the agency advises that the scope of the request is unreasonably wide, if charges are being negotiated or payment is pending, or if the Information Commissioner has granted an extension.

If a request is refused, the agency must notify the applicant in writing, stating the name and position of the decision-maker, the reasons for the decision and the facts taken into account, the public interest factors considered and the applicant's rights to review. A decision not issued within the required timeframe is classed as a 'deemed refusal', and the review processes are then available.

Applicants can request an internal review where a different officer in the agency makes a fresh decision within 30 days, or this appeal step can be bypassed by appealing directly to the Information Commissioner.

FOI requests by a person for their personal information do not incur an application fee, but other applicants such as journalists will generally incur processing charges for non-personal information. Agencies have the power to reduce or waive a charge upon the request of the applicant, with the most common reasons being financial hardship or 'public interest', although the latter is rarely granted in the case of FOI requests from the established mass media. In 2018, the basic charges for a Commonwealth agency processing an FOI request were:

- search and retrieval–$15 per hour
- decision-making–$20 per hour (after a complimentary first five hours)
- photocopy–10 cents per page
- transcript–$4.40 per page
- supervised inspection–$6.25 per half hour
- delivery–cost of postage or delivery.

There is no charge for making an FOI request to an agency or minister for access to a document, and agencies are required to send an estimate of costs and to give the applicant 30 days to agree or contest the quoted sum. The amount must be paid in full before the documents can be accessed. The documents might be withheld for a further period if a third party has the right to seek a review of their release.

FREEDOM *FROM* INFORMATION?

Given the exceptions to the release of information, the cost of filing applications and the time spent filing them and appealing against adverse decisions, some cynics have dubbed the legislation 'Freedom *from* Information' rather than 'Freedom *of* Information'. Dissatisfaction with the laws reached a high point in 2006 when, in the *Treasury case,* the High Court upheld the federal government's power to prevent Treasury documents being released to *The Australian*'s then FOI editor, Michael McKinnon. He had applied to the federal Department of the Treasury for documents related to the extent and impact of 'bracket creep' (the phenomenon where a taxpayer moves into higher tax brackets when their income rises to keep pace with inflation), and the use, abuse and impact of the First Home Owners Scheme (a government payment to purchasers of their first residential property).

The department listed 40 documents relevant to the bracket creep matter, with all but one claimed to be exempt from FOI release, and 47 related to the First Home Owners Scheme, of which most were claimed as wholly or partially exempt. McKinnon applied first for an internal review of the exemptions and then applied to the Administrative Appeals Tribunal (AAT), the next stage in the appeal process. Before the applications for review were listed for hearing, the then Treasurer, Peter Costello, used his powers to sign so-called 'conclusive certificates' stating that the disclosure of many of the documents would be 'contrary to the public interest' because of their potential to compromise confidentiality, and that the documents were only 'provisional' and their disclosure would be likely to mislead the public if released.

McKinnon appealed to the High Court, which ruled against him by a three to two majority. The majority held the Act did not allow the tribunal to undertake its own assessment of the public interest required, or to substitute its own opinion on whether the release of documents would be contrary to the public interest. Two justices argued that the tribunal should have considered other facets of the public interest. While the *Treasury case* was in many ways a technical appeal centred on the wording of the review provisions of the *Freedom of Information Act*, it sent a chilling message to journalists about the power of governments to quarantine themselves from FOI requests for information that they might find disquieting. McKinnon's familiarity with the FOI laws and the appeal processes is a lesson in itself. Any reporter wanting to work with such laws should become very familiar with the details of the legislation and the case law in the area.

This led to the federal government making major changes to the *Freedom of Information Act 1982* (Cth). While the reforms got rid of conclusive certificates, they also amended the *Freedom of Information Act 1982* by excluding from FOI all documents, no matter what their content, that had originated with, or had been received from the Australian Security Intelligence Organisation (ASIO), the Australian Secret Intelligence Service (ASIS), the Inspector-General of Intelligence and Security (IGIS), the Office of National Assessments (ONA), the

Defence Imagery and Geospatial Organisation (DIGO), the Defence Intelligence Organisation (DIO) or the Defence Signals Directorate (DSD). Such security agency documents were formerly within the scope of the Act, when in the hands of ministers. Their wholesale excision from the scope of FOI takes effect whether or not access would cause, or could reasonably be expected to cause, any damage at all to Australia's security or defence interests.

Some media organisations have used the FOI laws quite effectively despite their limitations. It is a style of reporting requiring meticulous record-keeping, precise applications, a generous budget and a hearty serve of patience. Some journalists use the legislation to avoid confidentiality binds. Rather than exposing themselves or their sources to disobedience contempt or a breach of confidence action, they find out from their anonymous sources as much detail as they can about the document in question, then file a very specific FOI application seeking its release, thus protecting their sources from exposure and protecting themselves from a possible jail term for refusing to reveal a source in court.

The Walkley Award for Investigative Journalism in 2017—the joint Fairfax-ABC investigation 'Bleed Them Dry Until They Die'—was based partly on documents obtained via freedom of information requests by an aged care resident for records about her own care and file notes by staff about her proposed eviction. The investigative team of Adele Ferguson, Sarah Danckert and Klaus Toft integrated the supportive documentation into their reportage (Ferguson and Danckert, 2017).

FOCUS CASE 4.1: *IMMIGRATION DOCUMENTS CASES 1 AND 2*

Farrell and Department of Immigration and Border Protection [2013] AICmr 81 (21 November 2013)

Paul Farrell and Department of Immigration and Border Protection (Freedom of information) [2017] AICmr 116 (15 November 2017)

FACTS

Paul Farrell was a freelance journalist in a team investigating a series of incidents in Australian immigration detention centres for the websites Detention Logs, <http://detentionlogs.com.au>, and *New Matilda*, <https://newmatilda.com>. In the first case, on 15 November 2012, he applied to the Department of Immigration and Border Protection for access to a series of incident reports about five self-harming events logged on the department's FOI disclosure log. On 14 January 2013, the department provided Mr Farrell with edited copies of five documents totalling 23 pages related to his request, citing its 'operations of agency' and 'personal privacy' exemptions under sections 47E and 47F of the Commonwealth *Freedom of Information Act 1982* as its reasons for the deletion of material. On 14 February 2013, Mr Farrell applied to the Information Commissioner for review of the information exempted by the Department under section 47E.

Farrell joined *The Guardian* in 2013 and won the Walkley Young Journalist of the Year Award for public service journalism in 2017 for his 'Nauru Files' investigation before leaving to work for *BuzzFeed*. It was while researching that story that he applied again to the department for all email correspondence related to a departmental review of the 2000 Nauru incident reports, which formed the basis of the second appeal case, this time to the Office of the Australian Information Commissioner (Case 2).

LAW

In the first case, the Privacy Commissioner ruled on 21 November 2013 that the department's decision should be set aside and the exempted information should be released to Mr Farrell. The exemption under section 47E(d) provides that, 'A document is conditionally exempt if its disclosure under this Act would, or could reasonably be expected to . . . have a substantial adverse effect on the proper and efficient conduct of the operations of an agency.' The department had argued that its operations would have been adversely affected if details had been released about an incident of self-harm while an individual was about to be deported from Australia on a scheduled commercial flight. It argued the information might help others avoid deportation by adopting the same behaviours. The Privacy Commissioner ruled (at paras 12 and 13) that much of the requested information was already in the public domain and thus would be unlikely to have a substantial adverse effect on the department's operations or require it to alter its deportation procedures.

In the second case, in 2017, Farrell's request was deemed refused when the department had not responded after a month, and this was followed a month later by the Information Commissioner demanding reasons for the refusal. The department responded that this request, combined with two others by Farrell, 'would substantially and unreasonably divert the resources of the Department from its other operations'. Farrell revised the request to limit its timeframe to just two months of emails, which the department estimated would take 130 hours to process 1550 pages of identified documents. The department maintained that the work would still be an unreasonable diversion of its resources. The Information Commissioner rejected that excuse, finding that the department had not taken reasonable steps to assist Farrell and that the revised estimate of 37 hours of departmental processing time would not represent an unreasonable diversion of its resources from other operations.

During 2017, the Information Commissioner conducted an investigation into the department's FOI processes after a leaked document revealed a separate system of consultation and delay applied to requests by journalists. The Commissioner found there were systemic delays and impediments in the protocols adopted by the department and recommended a range of measures to improve transparency and responsiveness within the statutory timeframes (Pilgrim, 2017).

LESSONS FOR JOURNALISTS AND PROFESSIONAL COMMUNICATORS

The cases hold important lessons about the workings of FOI and the exemptions that are available. On the one hand, Farrell and his colleagues were able to publish a substantial body of material about the experiences of asylum seekers in detention as a result of numerous FOI requests–information later published as stories, searchable databases and graphics on news sites including *The Guardian*, *The Global Mail*, *New Matilda* and *BuzzFeed*. However, the cases also provide an insight into the bureaucratic, technical, time-consuming and sometimes politicised side of the FOI application process. Each request took a full year to be filed, rejected and reviewed, and the department still had 28 days to appeal to have the decisions reviewed by the Administrative Appeals Tribunal. That would have opened the way to a series of court appeals over the decisions if either party chose to pursue them. Theoretically, it could take years before the release of the requested information, which might then be more of historical than news value.

TIPS FOR MINDFUL PRACTICE

- Ordinary journalists can prepare submissions to the court even if legal advice is not available. You can stand up in court and seek leave to state quite simply that the historical principles of open justice and the public's right to know are powerful reasons why access should be granted on this occasion.
- Think of some valuable social reasons that will support your 'public interest' arguments. Courts will be more convinced by some actual social good coming from your reportage than a bold argument about 'the public's right to know'.
- Use FOI/right to information laws to their best effect. Despite their obvious shortcomings for major breaking stories, the patient use of the FOI mechanism can save a great deal of angst over confidentiality issues. You may be protected from having to reveal a source if you hold the relevant document issued under an FOI request. Make your FOI requests as sharply focused as possible. Such precision saves time and money.

IN A NUTSHELL

- Journalists will have the greatest chance of success if they request documents that have been used in open court, rather than documents containing untested evidence or preliminary submissions that ultimately might be excluded from the trial.
- Judges and magistrates have the power to issue suppression and non-publication orders, which can be challenged by media organisations.
- Some of the nation's leading media law cases have resulted from large newspaper and television organisations appealing against decisions of courts to restrict access to documents or their publication.
- Judges and magistrates have the power to allow cameras, audio recorders and laptops in their courtrooms—as well as tweeting and blogging from court—and are doing so more frequently. However, to do so without permission may be deemed contempt of court.

- All states and territories and the Commonwealth government now have FOI legislation, designed to allow public access to documents held by governments and their agencies.
- Journalists can use FOI requests to reduce their exposure to source identification; however, they are faced with the obstacles of processing delays, application costs and a list of 'exempt documents' that governments are not obliged to release.

DISCUSSION QUESTIONS

4.1 How has the principle of open justice become so entrenched in our system? Comment.

4.2 Given the number of exceptions to the open justice principle, do you think it still has force, or has it become mere rhetoric? Explain.

4.3 Assume you are covering a committal hearing where a local businessman has been charged with sexual assault of an employee. The businessman denies the charge, and his lawyer asks that his identity be suppressed to protect his personal reputation and good business name. What issues arise? Would your position change if it were a fraud charge rather than a sexual charge? What arguments might you raise to oppose such a suppression order? What would you say if the basis of the proposal put forward was that disclosure of the businessman's identity would inevitably involve identifying the complainant?

4.4 Prepare a submission to a magistrate asking that you be allowed to tweet updates of proceedings in her court. Raise open justice and practical reporting reasons to support your submission, and mention any relevant legislation or court rules.

4.5 The basic procedures for an FOI application to a Commonwealth agency have been described in this chapter. Find the relevant website explaining your state or territory FOI or right to information procedures, and summarise the basic process and costs there. List their advantages and disadvantages compared with the Commonwealth system.

4.6 Download an FOI application form from either the Commonwealth government's website or your state or territory's website. Go through the process of completing the form as if you are requesting a letter dated 4 March 2017 from the Minister for Health to the Acme Pharmaceutical Company concerning the drug company's donation to Diabetes Australia. What issues arise in completing the form? How much is the application likely to cost? Reviewing the legislation and guidelines, what chance is there that you will be given the information? What appeal mechanisms are available to you if you are refused access?

4.7 Find a recent example of a court or policy decision either opening or closing the justice system to the public or the media.

REFERENCES

Australian Associated Press (AAP) 2016, 'Adrian Bayley has his sentence reduced after winning an appeal against a rape conviction', news.com.au, <www.news.com.au/national/victoria/courts-law/adrian-bayley-has-his-sentenced-reduced-after-winning-an-appeal-against-a-rape-conviction/news-story/75cfa59b4ce12d0c5376d042f279a721>.

Australian Law Reform Commission (ALRC) 2009, *Secrecy Laws and Open Government in Australia*, ALRC, Sydney.

—— 2015, *Traditional Rights and Freedoms: Encroachments by Commonwealth Laws. Final Report*, ALRC, Sydney.

Bentham, J. 1825, *Treatise on Judicial Evidence*, J.W. Paget, London.

Blackstone, W. 1765–69, *Commentaries on the Laws of England*, Clarendon Press, Oxford.

Bosland, J. 2017, 'Two years of suppression under the *Open Courts Act 2013* (Vic)', *Sydney Law Review*, 39(1), 25–57.

District Court of NSW 2015, Directions for Recording and broadcasting of judgment remarks, <www.districtcourt.justice.nsw.gov.au/Pages/practice_procedure/Media-resources.aspx>.

Ferguson, A. and Danckert, S. 2017, 'Bleed them dry until they die', *Sydney Morning Herald*, <www.smh.com.au/interactive/2017/retirement-racket/bleed-them-dry>.

Goldberg, D. 2006, 'Access to information laws in Scotland and England: Close freedom of information (FOI) encounters of the third kind', *Comparative Media Law Journal*, 8, 33–72, <www.juridicas.unam.mx/publica/librev/rev/comlawj/cont/8/arc/arc2.pdf>.

Hemingway, C. 2016, 'Journalists' use of social media and Twitter in court proceedings', *LegalVision*, <https://legalvision.com.au/can-journalists-cover-court-proceedings-via-twitter>

Holdsworth, W. 1945, *A History of English Law*, 3rd edn, Methuen, London.

Johnston, J. 2011, 'Courts' new visibility 2.0', in P. Keyzer, J. Johnston and M. Pearson, *The Courts and the Media: Challenges in the Era of Digital and Social Media*, Halstead Press, Canberra.

Ketchell, M. 1999, 'School officer tells of "rape"', *Townsville Bulletin*, 20 November.

Law Commission of New Zealand 2017, *NZLC R140—Reforming the Law of Contempt of Court: A Modern Statute*, <www.lawcom.govt.nz/sites/default/files/projectAvailableFormats/NZLC%20R140%20-%20Reforming%20The%20Law%20of%20Contempt%20of%20Court.pdf>.

Lidberg, J. 2005, 'Freedom of information: Banana republics and the Freedom of Information Index', paper presented to the Journalism Education Association Conference, Griffith University, Gold Coast, December.

—— 2013, 'From freedom to right: Where will freedom of information go in the age of WikiLeaks?', *Australian Journalism Review*, 35(2), 73–85.

Magistrates Court Victoria 2018, 'Operational update for media 5 March 2018 Committal in the matter of *Christopher Reed v George Pell*', Magistrates Court of Victoria, Melbourne.

Marr, D. 2018, 'Secrecy and security envelop George Pell's Magistrates Court show', *The Guardian*, 26 July, <www.theguardian.com/australia-news/2017/jul/26/secrecy-and-security-envelop-george-pells-magistrates-court-show-david-marr>.

McMillan, J. 2011, *Guide to the Freedom of Information Act 1982: Protecting Information Rights—Advancing Information Policy*, Office of the Australian Information Commissioner, Canberra, <www.oaic.gov.au/images/documents/migrated/oaic/repository/publications/agency_resources/guide_freedom_of_information_act_1982.pdf>.

Merritt, C. 2006, 'Wired for sound and doing her public duty', *The Australian*, 4 May.

Moss, I. 2007, *Report of the Independent Audit of the State of Free Speech in Australia: Executive Summary*, <www.smh.com.au/pdf/foIreport5.pdf>.

Neuberger, Lord of Abbotbury (Master of Rolls) 2011, 'Open justice unbound?', Judicial Studies Board Annual Lecture, 16 March, <www.judiciary.gov.uk/Resources/JCO/Documents/Speeches/mr-speech-jsb-lecture-march-2011.pdf>.

Office of the High Commissioner for Human Rights (OHCHR) 1976, *International Covenant on Civil and Political Rights*, <www.unhchr.ch/html/menu3/b/a_ccpr.htm>.

—— 1984, 'Equality before the courts and the right to a fair and public hearing by an independent court established by law' (Article 14), Twenty-first session, General Comment 13, <www.unhchr.ch>.

Pearson, M. 2015, 'You wouldn't read about it: Adrian Bayley rape trials expose flaw in suppression orders', *The Conversation*, 27 March, <https://theconversation.com/you-wouldnt-read-about-it-adrian-bayley-rape-trials-expose-flaw-in-suppression-orders-39375>.

Pilgrim, T. 2017, 'Freedom of information complaint investigation: Notice of completion', email to Mr Michael Pezzullo, Secretary, Department of Immigration and Border Protection, <www.scribd.com/document/367210421/Information-commissioner-review>.

Ross, N. 2005, 'Suppression orders double in Victoria', news.com.au, 14 December, <www.news.com.au/story/0,10117,17565077500204 0,00.html>.

Simons, M. 2011, 'Simons: To tweet or not to tweet from court', *Crikey*, 4 November, <www.crikey.com.au/2011/11/04/simons-to-tweet-or-not-to-tweet-from-court/?wpmp_switcher=mobile>.

Spigelman, J. 2005, 'The principle of open justice: A comparative perspective', address to the Media Law Resource Centre conference, London, 20 September, <www.lawlink.nsw.gov.au/lawlink/Supreme_Court/ll_sc.nsf/pages/SCO_spigelman200905>.

Supreme Court of Queensland 2016, 'Protocol for the recording and broadcasting of judgment remarks', <www.courts.qld.gov.au/about/news/news233/2016/protocol-for-the-recording-and-broadcasting-of-judgment-remarks>.

Wright, T. 2018, 'No time for trial by media as relaxed Cardinal saunters in to court', *Sydney Morning Herald*, 5 March, <www.smh.com.au/national/no-time-for-trial-by-media-as-relaxed-cardinal-saunters-in-to-court-20180305-p4z2ut.html>.

CASES CITED

AFL case: Herald & Weekly Times Ltd v Gregory D. Williams (formerly identified as VAI) [2003] FCAFC 217 (10 September 2003), <www.austlii.edu.au/au/cases/cth/FCAFC/2003/217.html>.

Apps' case: ABC v Local Court of NSW [2014] NSWSC 249, <www.austlii.edu.au/cgi-bin/sinodisp/au/cases/nsw/NSWSC/2014/239.html>.

Benbrika case: R v Benbrika & Ors (Ruling No. 13) [2007] VSC 543 (13 December 2007), <www.austlii.edu.au/cgi-bin/sinodisp/au/cases/vic/VSC/2007/543.html>.

Bromfield's case: Re Bromfield, ex parte West Australian Newspapers Ltd, SCL 8930 (21 June 1991).

Davis's case: R v Davis (1995) 57 FCR 512.

Ex parte P, reported in *The Times*, 31 March 1998, <http://swarb.co.uk/ex-parte-p-ca-31-mar-1998>.

Gang Murders case: *Nationwide News Pty Limited v Qaumi* [2016] NSWCCA 97 (27 May 2016), <www7.austlii.edu.au/cgi-bin/viewdoc/au/cases/nsw/NSWCCA/2016/97.html>.

Hinch's case: Hinch and Macquarie Broadcasting Holdings Limited v Attorney-General (Vic), HCA 56; (1987) 164 CLR 15.

Ibrahim's case: Fairfax Digital Australia & New Zealand Pty Ltd v Ibrahim [2012] NSWCCA 125, <www.austlii.edu.au/cgi-bin/sinodisp/au/cases/nsw/NSWCCA/2012/125.html>.

Idoport case: Idoport Pty Ltd v National Australia Bank [47] [2001] NSWSC 1024 (14 November 2001), <www.austlii.edu.au//cgi-bin/disp.pl/au/cases/nsw/supréme_ct/2001/1024.html>.

iiNet case: Roadshow Films Pty Ltd v iiNet Limited (No. 3) [2009] FCA 24, <www.austlii.edu.au/cgi-bin/sinodisp/au/cases/cth/FCA/2010/24.html>.

Immigration Documents cases 1 and 2: Farrell and Department of Immigration and Border Protection [2013] AICmr 81 (21 November 2013), <www.oaic.gov.au/images/documents/freedom-of-information/ic-review-decicions/2013-AICmr81.pdf>; *Paul Farrell and Department of Immigration and Border Protection (Freedom of information)* [2017] AICmr 116 (15 November 2017).

Local Court cases: John Fairfax Publications Pty Ltd v Ryde Local Court (2005) 62 NSWLR 512 (Spigelman CJ); *O'Shane v Burwood Local Court* (2007) 178 A Crim R 392; *John Fairfax Group v Local Court of NSW* (1991) 26 NSWLR 131.

Obeid's case: Obeid v The Queen [No. 2] [2016] HCA 10, <www.austlii.edu.au/cgi-bin/viewdoc/au/cases/cth/HCA/2016/10.html>.

Police Commissioner's case: New South Wales Commissioner of Police v Nationwide News Pty Ltd [2007] NSWCA 366 (8 February 2008), <www.austlii.edu.au/cgi-bin/sinodisp/au/cases/nsw/NSWCA/2007/366.html>.

Police Tribunal case: John Fairfax & Sons v Police Tribunal of NSW (1986) 5 NSWLR 465, 476–7.

PQR case: Herald & Weekly Times Ltd v PQR & Anor [2000] VSC 335 (25 August 2000), <www.austlii.edu.au//cgi-bin/disp.pl/au/cases/vic/VSC/2000/335.html>.

Rape Priors case: R v Hinch [2013] VSC 520 (2 October 2013), <www.austlii.edu.au/au/cases/vic/VSC/2013/520.html>; *R v Hinch (No. 2)* [2013]

VSC 554 (18 October 2013), <www.austlii.edu.au/cgi-bin/sinodisp/au/cases/vic/VSC/2013/554.html>.

Raybos's case: Raybos v Jones (1985) 2 NSWLR 47.

Scott's case: Scott v Scott [1913] AC 417.

Sex Offenders case: Hogan v Hinch [2011] HCA 4 (10 March 2011), <www.austlii.edu.au/cgi-bin/sinodisp/au/cases/cth/HCA/2011/4.html>.

Snowtown case: Registrar v Nationwide News Ltd & Ors [2004] SASC 223 (29 July 2004), <www.austlii.edu.au/au/cases/sa/SASC/2004/223.html>.

Sussex Justices case: R v Sussex Justices; Ex parte McCarthy [1924] 1 KB 256.

Trafficker case: News Digital Media Pty Ltd & Anor v Mokbel & Anor [2010] VSCA 51 (18 March 2010), <www.austlii.edu.au/cgi-bin/sinodisp/au/cases/vic/VSCA/2010/51.html>.

Treasury case: McKinnon v Secretary, Department of Treasury [2006] HCA 45 (6 September 2006), <www.austlii.edu.au/au/cases/cth/HCA/2006/45.html>.

Zhao's case: Commissioner of the Australian Federal Police v Zhao (2015) 316 ALR 378, [44] (French CJ, Hayne, Kiefel, Bell and Keane JJ).

CHAPTER 5

Contempt of court

KEY CONCEPTS

Contempt of court
Communications or behaviours that 'interfere with the proper administration of justice' or constitute a 'disregard for the authority of the court'.

Sub judice
From the Latin meaning 'under a judge', this area of contempt restricts the publication of material that is intended to, or has a 'real and definite tendency' to, prejudice an upcoming trial or, more generally, to interfere with the due administration of justice.

Contempt in the face of the court
Improper behaviour (usually in a courtroom) during a hearing that interferes with the administration of justice in the proceedings.

Scandalising the court
The publication of material that tends to undermine public confidence in the administration of justice.

The charging of young journalist Krystal Johnson with contempt of court and the fine of $300,000 issued against her employer Yahoo!7 in 2017 following publication of an online news story that caused a murder trial to be aborted underscored the importance of knowing the legal limits of reporting criminal cases (*Krystal's case*, 2017—see Key Case 5.2).

Despite the 'open justice' principle, explained in Chapter 4, journalists and bloggers face restrictions when reporting on crime and the justice system. Their behaviour, reportage and comments can lead to substantial fines or even prison terms if they breach the common law of contempt of court, or any of the numerous state and federal prohibitions on publication of what takes place in court—which typically include identifying children, sexual crime victims and jurors (covered in Chapter 6). This chapter examines three of the main areas of contempt of court as they apply to reporters, bloggers and other communicators.

BACKGROUND AND INTERNATIONAL CONTEXT

The *Encyclopaedic Australian Legal Dictionary* (Butt and Nygh, 2004) describes contempt as 'Words or actions which interfere with the proper administration of justice or constitute a disregard for the authority of the court'. As with most areas of media law, contempt does not just apply to journalists and bloggers. The law is there, waiting to be used against anyone who stands in the way of justice.

The reason why this area of law is of special concern to the media is that so much of a journalist's work relates in some way to the justice system: reporting crimes, covering court cases, scrutinising the workings of the courts and sometimes even appearing in court as witnesses. Public relations consultants occasionally have to navigate the judicial system when a client appears in court, and bloggers sometimes find that a court case arises in their area of specialist reportage. Infrequent contact with the court system presents special dangers because practitioners may not be abreast of current restrictions. Some professional communicators deal with the courts and contempt restrictions daily—particularly those in the role of public information officer (PIO) for the various court systems, those working in the media branch of the various police services or those engaged in traditional police rounds for a newspaper or television network.

Contempt is a sizeable body of law that deals with a range of actions with the potential to impair the administration of justice. Like most areas of media law, the laws of contempt represent an attempt to balance fundamental rights and freedoms. Where contempt laws have been applied to the behaviour of journalists and others who may publish their own blogs or online websites, legislators and judges have had to juggle wide and sometimes conflicting principles, including freedom of expression (and of the press), an individual's right to a fair trial, the public's right to be informed of the workings of the legal and political process, journalists' interests in maintaining confidentiality—particularly for protected sources—and the general community's right to be assured of the effective administration of justice. Few would argue with the legitimacy of any of these ideals. Rather, disputes tend to focus on the relative weight each should be given in a particular set of circumstances.

While the task of balancing these important rights and interests might be a delicate one in modern times, this was not always the case. The original purpose of contempt law was to establish and maintain the authority of the court by punishing those whose actions were disrespectful. Arlidge and Eady (1982) report that as early as the twelfth century, the *Treatise on the Laws and Customs of the Kingdom of England* (known as 'Glanvill') referred to 'contemptus curiae', meaning the contempt shown by a party in failing to appear before a court. Contempts recorded through the Middle Ages concerned direct physical or verbal threats to the authority of the court, such as drawing a sword or throwing a brickbat to strike a judge; assaulting clerks, jurors, witnesses or opposing parties; or writing letters deriding judges. Modern contempt law is still premised on an underlying need to preserve the dignified authority of the administration of justice.

First Amendment rights in the United States have given the media a degree of immunity in recent times, but 'trial by media' can still prompt a mistrial, and lawyers can be disciplined if they make prejudicial statements outside court during a trial. Contempt by publication has been prosecuted most often in the United Kingdom and Commonwealth countries, although some European countries like Denmark have laws against publications that might seriously damage a trial.

AUSTRALIAN LAW OF CONTEMPT

There are five main categories of contempt affecting journalists. These are (ALRC, 1987; NSWLRC, 2000):

1. *sub judice* contempt—publishing material that tends to prejudice a fair trial
2. scandalising the court—publishing allegations that tend to undermine public confidence in the administration of justice
3. revealing the deliberations of juries
4. contempt in the face of the court—improper behaviour in a courtroom during a hearing
5. disobedience contempt—failure to comply with a court order or undertaking given to a court, such as refusing to answer a question in court or to deliver notes or other materials to a court or quasi-judicial body.

We deal with the first four types of contempt in this chapter, and with disobedience contempt in Chapter 9 when looking at secrets and confidentiality, because contempt can arise when journalists refuse on ethical grounds to betray a confidence or refuse to hand over files that might reveal their sources.

Contempt law has a number of features that distinguish it from other kinds of law, particularly in the processes used to apply it. The underlying imperative here is that a court may need to act in a swift and uncomplicated fashion to check any affront to the administration of justice. Unfortunately, the structure that allows this to happen does not always sit well with some of the basic principles of natural justice that apply in other areas of the law. The special features of contempt law include a special summary mode of trial when a contempt has been committed during a court hearing, in which the judicial officer acts as prosecutor, judge and jury; unlimited sentencing powers for judges in superior courts; and a lack of the usual requirement of 'guilty intent' *(mens rea)*: there is no need to show any intention to interfere with the administration of justice—a mere intention to publish the material is enough.

These differences have led to the criticism that contempt laws themselves go against the spirit of the foundational principles of the justice system and are out of place in modern society. Such shortcomings make contempt a problematic area of media law which, at its extreme, can result in professional communicators being jailed for their actions—sometimes because of an attempt to protect someone else or to expose wrongdoing.

SUB JUDICE CONTEMPT

Every few years there is a sensational crime where media coverage is a step ahead of the justice process. In the 1980s, Australia was obsessed with the *Lindy Chamberlain case* (1984), in which a mother was jailed for what was held at the time to have been the murder of her nine-week-old daughter, Azaria, at a Northern Territory camping ground. She was exonerated in 1988 when a court decided the baby really had been taken from their tent by a dingo, as the mother had claimed all along. In September 2012, 29-year-old Irish woman Jill Meagher was raped and murdered in Melbourne while walking home from her job at the ABC late at night. Police engaged traditional and social media to try to find her. As soon as her accused killer—Adrian Ernest Bayley—was arrested, the authorities had to try to shut down public commentary and speculation about his guilt and his past. In the *Rape Priors case 2* (2013), blogger, tweeter and broadcaster Derryn Hinch was jailed for failing to pay a fine after breaching a suppression order over Bayley's criminal record. How much coverage of these sensational crimes should be allowed? At what point does media coverage jeopardise an individual's right to a fair trial? This section should assist you to make judgements about the degree of risk involved in these kinds of situations, and sensitise you to the kinds of situations in which you should seek advice.

The Latin phrase *sub judice* literally means 'under or before a judge or court' (NSWLRC, 2000: 8), and applies to the period during which there are limitations placed on what the media may report about a case. The courts have attempted to balance the competing rights and interests of those involved in court cases and those reporting on them by restricting what may be published about a case while it is before the courts. The restrictions are considered necessary to avoid 'trial by media', where free speech interferes with the usual safeguards on the fair trial of an accused person, with potentially dire consequences for the case at hand and for public confidence in the administration of justice.

The practical concern the courts have here is the potential influence such a media trial might have on current or prospective jurors (and, to a lesser degree, on witnesses or even parties to the case, or their legal representatives). The fear is that their judgement (in the case of jurors), testimony (in the case of witnesses) or frank and fearless representation of a client's interest might be tainted—or even *be seen* to be tainted—by media coverage of the case, or other publications before or during trial, and may 'poison the fountain of justice before it begins to flow', as one judge expressed it in *Parke's case* in 1903.

The courts place stringent tests on the admissibility of evidence, and respect the rules of 'natural justice' (essentially, the right to know the case against you and having a fair opportunity to answer it)—protocols that have little or no tradition in media coverage, although the MEAA Code of Ethics does counsel journalists to 'Do your utmost to give a fair opportunity for reply' (see Appendix 1). Above all, the legal system enshrines the principle that an accused person should be considered innocent until proven guilty in court on the basis of admissible evidence considered (in the case of serious indictable offences) by a jury of twelve fellow citizens. In 1811, Lord Ellenborough put it this way in *Fisher's case*:

> *If anything is more important than another in the administration of justice, it is that jurymen should come to the trial of those persons on whose guilt or innocence they are to decide, with minds pure and unprejudiced.*

Yahoo!7 and reporter Krystal Johnson learned this the hard way after publishing a story during a murder trial containing inadmissible evidence of a victim's social media posts that had not been presented to the jury (*Krystal's case*, 2017—see Key Case 5.2).

The existing law in the *sub judice* area presents two main problems to the media: it is ill-defined in many respects, leaving journalists and bloggers unsure of what can be published in particular circumstances; and its enforcement is infrequent and unpredictable, sometimes tempting publishers to take risks on the premise that prosecution for contempt is unlikely. Sometimes this seems to be a commercial decision, reached by weighing the size of the potential fine against the boost to circulation, ratings or online page views.

Proceedings are *sub judice* in Australia when they are 'pending', rather than 'imminent', as is the case in England and Wales. Civil proceedings are pending from the issue of a writ, a statement of claim or a summons. However, *sub judice* contempt charges are very rarely pressed in civil matters—the exception being where the contempt consists of publication that places improper pressure on a litigant, as in the *Thunder case* (2017) discussed below. In criminal matters, the authority is *James' case* (1963), in which the High Court held that an article published while a 'manhunt' was in progress after a double murder was not in contempt because the proceedings were not 'pending', as no warrant had been issued for the suspect's arrest. They were certainly 'imminent', however, as an arrest occurred within a day of the publication and police were on the suspect's trail.

The definition of 'pending' varies. In *James' case*, the High Court majority stated 'that curial procedures, and not merely police activity, must have commenced' (at 605). But when do 'curial procedures' start? In criminal proceedings, the crucial point has been defined in various cases at any of the following points in time: when a warrant has been issued; when a person has been arrested with a view to being charged; when a person has been arrested on warrant; or when a person has been arrested and charged. While law reform commissions continue to debate the appropriate starting point, crime reporters and bloggers are best advised to be cautious, and to consider that the restricted period starts from the moment of arrest, as it can be difficult to establish the point at which charges have been laid. That was certainly the message of the NSW Court of Appeal in *Mason's case* (1990), when it identified the moment of arrest as the starting point 'when the criminal law was set in motion'.

Once proceedings are 'pending', and until facts related to a crime are actually mentioned in open court, the media are restricted to reporting just the 'bare facts' of the crime. These were described in *Packer's case* (1912) as being 'extrinsic ascertained facts to which any eyewitness could bear testimony, such as the finding of a body and its condition, the place in which it is found, the persons by whom it was found, the arrest of a person accused, and so on' (at 588). But journalists and bloggers cannot report on any fact that might be contested in court, and certainly not on facts that might indicate guilt or innocence, most importantly including any prior criminal record or alleged confession.

Of course, the *sub judice* period ends when the proceedings are no longer considered to be 'under a judge'. This is also a grey area, particularly when cases may be subject to appeal or retrial. While criminal proceedings continue as pending until an acquittal, the expiry of time for an appeal or when all possible appeals have been completed, the prospects of a fresh trial occurring without substantial delay are generally fairly low, except in the case of an aborted hearing or hung jury.

In recent years, the broadcasting or distribution of a number of 'true crime' films and mini-series has been banned in some high-profile cases, on the basis that they are *sub judice*. The Victorian Supreme Court suppressed the broadcasting of the series *Underbelly* on the eve of its television premiere in February 2008, fearing interference with a murder trial involving the execution of gangland figure Lewis Moran. An appeal was largely unsuccessful (*Underbelly case*, 2008), with the Victorian Court of Appeal saying a serious risk of prejudice arose 'by reason of the contemporaneous and graphic nature of *Underbelly* being available to jurors immediately before and during the conduct of the trial' (at para. 73).

Civil proceedings are even less certain here, but the *sub judice* period seems to end at the time when the judgment at first instance is delivered rather than at the expiry of the opportunity to appeal (NSWLRC, 2000: 255).

By far the most concern has been about safeguarding the process of criminal trials, and this is where journalists and bloggers need to be particularly careful. If proceedings are pending, it is a contempt to:

- publish material intending to prejudice the trial, or
- publish material that has a tendency to do so.

The former requires proof of *mens rea* (guilty mind), consisting of an intention to prejudice the proceedings, while for the latter it need only be proven that the act of publication was intentional, regardless of whether the publisher intended to prejudice proceedings. It is no excuse that the material was published by mistake, or that reasonable precautions were taken to exclude prejudicial material.

The courts are particularly concerned that the media do not become a second-rate, de facto criminal investigative body, making their own inquiries to solve crimes and jeopardising the official criminal investigation. This point was established in the *Evening Standard case* in 1924, where three English newspapers were fined for publishing the results of their independent investigations into a murder when the police had already charged someone. The proceedings were already 'pending', and their sensational reports had the tendency to prejudice the trial.

In 2006, the Tasmanian Supreme Court trial judge in *ABC v O'Neill* (the *Worm Farming case*) showed disdain for 'trial by media', stating it is 'not for the *public benefit* that the media should publicly allege that a person has committed crimes of which he or she has not been convicted, whether or not there are currently proceedings afoot with respect to the crimes' (para. 84). However, when the ABC took the case on appeal, the two judges in the leading majority judgment of the High Court, including then Chief Justice Gleeson, took a different view of 'trial by media', stating:

> *if the expression 'trial by media' means any public canvassing by the media, outside the reporting of court proceedings, of the merits of topics which could become, or are, the subject of civil or criminal litigation, then we are surrounded by it. The idea that the criminal justice system ought to be the exclusive forum for canvassing matters of criminal misbehaviour is contrary to the way our society functions in practice . . . (para. 28)*

This offered some hope that Australia's highest court might tolerate reasonable discussion of criminal matters in the media and on social media, subject to the other limitations of contempt of court and defamation.

'REAL AND DEFINITE TENDENCY'

When deciding whether a publication is in contempt, the courts look to its 'tendency' to interfere with pending proceedings (NSWLRC, 2000: 106):

> *To amount to contempt, a publication must be shown to have a real and definite tendency, as a matter of practical reality, to prejudice or embarrass particular legal proceedings.*

When considering whether the publication has the 'tendency' to interfere with proceedings, the courts gauge the potential effect of the *sub judice* material, not whether the material actually caused harm, with the test applied at the time of publication rather than at some later date. Even if the accused in the publicised trial eventually pleads guilty, or dies before the trial, the publication can still be held in contempt.

Just how likely must prejudice be for the courts to deem a publication contemptuous? High Court Justices Gageler and Keane stated in the *Crime Commission case* (2013) that such a contempt occurs 'only when there is an actual interference with the administration of justice' or 'a real risk, as opposed to a remote possibility' of such an interference. They continued that 'the "essence" of contempt of that kind is a "real and definite tendency to prejudice or embarrass pending proceedings" involving "as a matter of practical reality, a tendency to interfere with the due course of justice in a particular case"'.

> *The finding of such a real risk or definite tendency necessarily requires more than abstract assertion: it requires the finding at least of some logical connection between the action that is impugned and some feared impediment to the conduct of the proceedings that are pending, which impediment can properly be characterised as an interference with the administration of justice or, more specifically in a particular case, as unfairness to an accused. (para. 320)*

The courts take into account a number of relevant factors in determining whether there is such a real possibility of prejudice, including the prominence of the item printed or broadcast; the images accompanying it; the time lapse between publication and likely trial; the social prominence of the maker of contemptuous statements; the extent of existing pre-trial publicity; and the extent or area of publication.

In the *Cop Killer case* (2007), contempt charges failed against the Herald and Weekly Times Ltd and the publication's editor over articles dealing with a committal hearing, in which police sought to use DNA, guns and bullets to link the accused to a new murder after he had already been convicted of murdering two police. One article was even headlined 'Cop Killer'. Extensive publicity prior to the laying of fresh charges had identified the accused as a police killer. On that basis, it was not established beyond reasonable doubt that the articles had the necessary tendency to interfere with a fair trial.

In the *Rape Priors case 1* (2013), Victorian Supreme Court Justice Kaye found blogger Derryn Hinch guilty of one charge of contempt for breaching a suppression order over the accused's extensive criminal record when he was facing charges over the rape and murder of Jill Meagher. The case offers an excellent summary of the relevant factors considered in deciding whether there is a real risk of prejudice to a trial, because Hinch was acquitted on a second contempt charge that his blog 'had a tendency, or was calculated, to interfere with the due administration of justice in the trial of Bayley'. Justice Kaye ruled that three factors combined to reduce the tendency of Hinch's blogging to prejudice potential jurors: the small readership of the article; the period of delay between the publication of the article and the likely trial date of Bayley; and other prejudicial material about Bayley circulating in the media and social media at the time (para. 114). While he believed Hinch's material was 'highly prejudicial', Justice Kaye had a 'reasonable doubt' in light of those three factors that the article would have prevented Bayley getting a fair trial.

There is also the possibility that prosecuting authorities will charge all media outlets that published contemptuous stories, although it may have been one particularly sensational item that prompted action. For example, in *Mason's case* (1990), the NSW Attorney-General charged two newspapers and four television stations with contempt over their coverage of an alleged murderer's 'walk through' of the crime scene after he had been charged but before his trial. The outlets with the less sensational reports attracted lower fines ($75,000 as against $200,000).

But what about a situation in which the publication does not involve the mass media, but instead is made by a private blogger, individual or operator of a website? In the *Thunder case* (which also involved criminal contempt by breach of court orders), advertisements had been placed on a fleet of four vans circulating in the Sydney CBD, inviting those who viewed them to visit a website where 'all involved will be exposed'. When the solicitor for one of the people named on the website wrote to demand that the material be removed from the vans, he was informed that his picture would be added to the vans. The Federal Court held that this threat was calculated or intended to influence in an improper way a party to proceedings (via pressure upon their lawyer), and thus was a contempt because of the real risk of interference with ongoing proceedings, even though there was no jury involved.

In *Sandy's case* (2016) the Supreme Court of Western Australia had to decide whether the Yindjibarndi Aboriginal Corporation should be punished for contempt for interfering with the due administration of justice by publishing on its website, email and Facebook page articles that were said to have placed improper pressure on the plaintiff to not proceed. In that case, the court concluded that even though the publications were *not* a fair report of what happened in court, they did not, as a matter of practical reality, have a real or definite tendency to interfere with the course of justice in the case by deterring the plaintiff from continuing the proceedings. The outcome might, however, have been very different if the case had been a criminal one, and particularly if it involved a jury and, as we will see in Chapter 8 on defamation, lack of fair report will often rob a publisher of one of its main defences.

WHO MIGHT BE INFLUENCED?

Restrictions on reporting, both before and during a trial, are directed at what may influence potential jurors and witnesses and, in rare cases, parties to the proceedings. At one extreme, it is clear that publication of some facts or opinions is clearly prohibited. For example, a statement or insinuation that an accused is guilty, or even innocent, of a crime is a clear contempt. Similarly, any mention of potentially inadmissible and seriously prejudicial evidence, such as an accused person's previous convictions or an alleged confession, is a contempt. (Mentions of previous convictions can, however, be reported in bail hearings in all states other than Tasmania—although the identity of the accused may be suppressed, particularly in cases involving allegations of child sexual assault.) Photographs or drawings of the accused cannot be published if identification may be an issue at the trial: it is often difficult to tell whether identification might become an issue, and if there is any doubt at all, identifying material should not be published. For this reason, the media routinely 'pixelate' the faces of the accused once they have been arrested, even where there has already been wide publication of identifying material during a 'manhunt' for a suspect.

The prime example occurred in the contempt trial of the publisher of *Who Weekly* magazine over its cover photograph of Ivan Milat, later convicted of the 'backpacker serial killings' in the Belanglo State Forest in New South Wales between 1989 and 1992. Unknown to the publisher, a single identification witness, Paul Onions, had been brought out from England for the trial. The magazine's publisher was fined $100,000 and its editor $10,000 for this error of judgement (*Who Weekly case*, 1994). All copies had to be withdrawn from circulation and reprinted with Milat's face masked. The publication came in a crucial time zone–after Milat had been arrested and charged, but before his trial. Identification was going to be crucial. The court ruled that publication of a picture of an accused person would normally be regarded as carrying a risk of interference with the due course of justice, unless the identification were so clear-cut that neither party would dispute it.

It is now well established that judges and magistrates are not considered susceptible to influence by what is published in the media. The courts assume judges possess legal training, which–theoretically–allows them to dismiss irrelevant considerations from their minds. Jurors–untrained lay citizens–lack such training, and are therefore thought to be more vulnerable to prejudicial coverage.

Despite that, a contempt charge can still be based upon a publication that may cause 'embarrassment' to judicial officers on the eve of a trial or verdict (NSWLRC, 2000: 8). This is not because it is assumed that the judicial officer would be influenced, but because members of the public might *think* that their decision had been affected by the publication. It would have to be severe pressure indeed to meet the test. In June 2017, for example, three federal ministers who criticised the highest court in Victoria during an active terrorism appeal narrowly escaped being charged with contempt of court by apologising for and withdrawing their remarks, despite having been warned by Victorian Chief Justice Marilyn Warren that there was a prima facie case against them (Wahlquist, 2017).

Civil proceedings such as defamation actions and personal injury cases can also involve jurors. However, while there is still a risk that media coverage might influence them, a greater amount of leeway is given in relation to civil jury trials than in criminal cases, in which a person's liberty is at stake. In 2014, for example, the then prime minister's comments on radio station 2GB that defamation proceedings involving the ABC which would inevitably involve a jury amounted to 'defending the indefensible' and were 'not a very good way to spend government money' (Davidson, 2014) were widely republished without any contempt action being taken.

A major research project conducted in 2001 found jurors appeared to be less likely to recall pre-trial publicity, and seemed to be less influenced by bias in mid-trial reportage than had been presumed previously (Chesterman, Chan and Hampton, 2001). The media's potential influence on jurors was put to the test in 2004 when John Fairfax Publications appealed against an order by a District Court judge that the media not be allowed to publish the verdict in a high-profile corporate crime case involving the director of a company exclusively devoted to gay and lesbian business because the accused would later be facing further charges and coverage might influence a future jury (*Gay and Lesbian case*, 2004). The NSW Court of Appeal overturned the District Court ban, noting that several high-profile criminals had failed in their attempts to gain a stay of proceedings because of media publicity (*Gay and Lesbian case*, 2004, at para. 59). The court noted that such cases 'have decisively rejected the previous tendency to regard jurors as exceptionally fragile and prone to prejudice' (at para. 103) and cited several superior court judgments placing greater faith in jurors' abilities to put prior coverage from their minds and focus on the matters presented at trial.

The NSW Supreme Court recognised the robustness of the jury system when it stated in the *Selim case* (2008, at para. 53):

> *In more recent times the courts generally have been less prepared to treat jurors as some kind of exotic or fragile beings who must be protected from the ravages of the outside world while performing their civic duty. The whole criminal justice system operates on the basis that jurors can put out of their minds extraneous material that has no real bearing upon the issue that they are to decide even if that material might possibly have some prejudicial aspect.*

DEFENCES TO *SUB JUDICE* CONTEMPT

There are two possible defences that can be raised against *sub judice* contempt charges. The first is clear-cut: a fair and accurate report of what has been said in open court. The second is more difficult to establish: that there was some overriding public interest at stake in continuing discussion of some larger public issue, that the *sub judice* report formed part of that discussion, and that any effect on the due administration of justice was an incidental and unintended by-product of that discussion.

Fair and accurate reports of court cases

Some immunities are offered to journalists in their reporting of court cases. The most notable is the protection attached to fair and accurate reports of what is said in open court—which also serves as a defence to defamation actions, as we will learn in Chapter 8. Although it carries a number of exceptions and qualifications, this immunity generally operates well, and is the vehicle by which the media can report court cases. It is one of the cornerstones of the principle of open justice, outlined in Chapter 4, and the primary mechanism by which the legal system is open to public criticism and scrutiny.

CLASSIC CASE 5.1: *BREAD MANUFACTURERS CASE*

Ex parte Bread Manufacturers Ltd; Re Truth and Sportsman Ltd (1937) 37 SR (NSW) 242

FACTS

In 1936, a bread carter commenced a defamation action against a company, Bread Manufacturers Ltd, which represented almost 90 per cent of Sydney's bakers. The bread carter claimed the company had defamed him in a letter. Meanwhile, the *Truth* newspaper set about publishing a series of articles accusing the bakers of acting as a cartel by trying to keep bread prices artificially high and pressuring the smaller operators. The newspaper was charged with contempt on the grounds that the articles about the bread cartel were likely to influence the administration of justice by prejudicing the jurors who would be called on to rule on the upcoming defamation case involving Bread Manufacturers Ltd.

LAW

The Full Court of the NSW Supreme Court dismissed the motion for contempt on the basis that the *Truth* had not intended influencing the jury in the defamation case, and did not even know of its existence. Chief Justice Jordan established a new defence for *sub judice* contempt with these words (at 249):

> *The discussion of public affairs and the denunciation of public abuses, actual or supposed, cannot be required to be suspended merely because the discussion or denunciation may, as an incidental but not intended by-product, cause some likelihood of prejudice to a person who happens at the time to be a litigant.*

The defence allows for the ongoing discussion of important public matters, even though they may indirectly influence a pending case.

LESSONS FOR PROFESSIONAL COMMUNICATORS

This defence was later extended to cover criminal trials, and even situations where the media knew there was some risk to an upcoming trial, but that there was an overriding public interest at stake. Nevertheless, the defence would apply only if the comments were incidental to the upcoming case—and it could not be used as a smokescreen for an actual discussion of the matters at issue in the upcoming trial.

Public interest defence

The *Bread Manufacturers case* ruling (see Classic Case 5.1) was interpreted in Australia as meaning that the protection would extend to *sub judice* discussion of upcoming court proceedings, if that element of the publication was only a minor part of the public discussion of a predominant issue. The principle did not apply if the litigation was the 'immediate occasion' for the publication of the material. For example, in *Ruse's case* (1969) in Western Australia, the judge ruled that the accused could not show to a witness the contents of a box he had brought into the courtroom. The *Daily News* published details of its contents—$20,000 in cash. Neville J held that the *Bread Manufacturers* defence did not apply, stating, 'The intention and purpose of the publication was not to call attention to a matter of great public interest . . . but rather to increase the sales of the newspaper' (at 145).

The *Bread Manufacturers* immunity was put to the test in the High Court in *Hinch's case* in 1987 (see Key Case 5.1). The case confirmed that the public interest defence could be used in a criminal trial as well as a civil one, and that some matters of extreme and fundamental public importance might outweigh the public interest in the administration of justice. However, it also established that media outlets with large audiences could have a lasting impact on jurors, and that the pre-judging of an accused person's guilt and the revelation of their previous criminal record would rarely, if ever, be entertained by the court.

Nevertheless, the public interest defence received a strong boost from the NSW Supreme Court in 1999 in the *Heroin Syndicate case*, when the scales tipped in favour of the media reporting a matter of great public interest despite there being a related trial pending at the time. This case showed that a publication could still be in the public interest and escape contempt liability, even though it was on the front page of a metropolitan daily newspaper and had a tendency to prejudice a pending criminal trial, naming an accused, labelling him the 'top heroin distributor' under his headshot, suggesting he gambled proceeds to launder the earnings and mentioning that he was facing drug charges in a trial scheduled to start in five months. However, having found the material had the tendency to interfere with the accused's fair trial, NSW Supreme Court Justice Graham Barr proceeded to uphold the newspaper's public interest defence:

> *The articles were part of a substantial series of articles dealing with subject matter of substantial broad public interest. The trial was likely to raise narrower issues which were only incidental to those canvassed in the articles.*

Legal advice should be taken on whether a story is of sufficient public interest to warrant such a risk. In 2014, the NSW Supreme Court relied upon the *Bread Manufacturers* principle in overturning blanket suppression orders made in relation to a murder trial in *Apps' case* (see Chapter 4). However, the Victorian Supreme Court made it very clear in the *Rape Priors case 1* (2013) that public interest in the safety of women and children, violence against women and the operation of the parole system would not outweigh the right of an accused to a fair trial on rape and murder charges, particularly if reference to the prior record of an accused was central to the article.

KEY CASE 5.1: *HINCH'S CASE*

Hinch v Attorney-General (Vic) (1987) 164 CLR 15

FACTS

Then Melbourne radio journalist (and more recently Senator) Derryn Hinch had made three *sub judice* broadcasts relating to an upcoming trial of a former Catholic priest, Father Michael Glennon, on child molestation charges. In the broadcasts, Hinch named the accused, detailed previous charges Glennon had faced, including some for which he had been jailed and others on which he had been acquitted. Hinch questioned why a person with such a record should continue in his role as governing director of a youth foundation, particularly when facing further charges. Parts of the broadcast either stated or implied that the priest was guilty of the new charges. The following excerpt from Hinch's first broadcast on the subject on 13 November 1985 provides an idea of the language used and the territory covered:

> *I think by now most regular listeners would know . . . my attitude . . . about poachers in the sanctuary, those who use their position to prey on the vulnerable, those who use a position of trust and authority for their own personal gain, those who use their position of trust and authority for their own sexual gratification, and I've talked about it many times on this program before . . .*

He followed these words with examples of such breaches of trust, and moved immediately to name Glennon and the charges he had faced the previous day when he appeared in court:

> *Police say Glennon was forced to resign from practising within the Catholic Church after he was charged with sexual assault and jailed in 1978.*

> *Father Michael Glennon appeared in the Melbourne County Court in 1978 charged with rape. However, when he pleaded guilty to indecent assault of a sixteen-year-old girl, police did not proceed to the rape charge.*
>
> *On the indecent assault charge, Father Glennon was found guilty and sentenced to the [sic] two years' jail with a minimum of twelve months to serve. The same priest was then charged in the Melbourne County Court in September of 1984 with two counts of rape of a twelve-year-old boy. On those charges he was acquitted.*
>
> *. . . I know the question police are asking is how many other children may have been involved, how many other children may have been too scared over the years to come forward.*
>
> *And the question I have to ask, and I'm sure you, I'm sure that every reasonable, thinking, caring adult would also ask along with me, how does a man come to be able to continue to run a youth foundation with that background? How does a man continue to be able to take children into his care and take children in his care to youth camps, when he has a criminal record, a sexual criminal record involving juveniles?*

The two subsequent broadcasts were similar. The thrust of the broadcasts was, in the words of Chief Justice Mason, 'to highlight the danger to children inherent in Father Glennon continuing to occupy his position as Governing Director of the Foundation and to question how it was that he was permitted in the circumstances to continue in that position' (at 17). Hinch had conducted an ongoing campaign against those who exploited positions of trust, particularly in their relationships with children. Importantly, though, the broadcasts went further than this. They set up the general scenario of breach of trust, introduced Glennon and reported that he had been charged, mentioned previous convictions and charges, implied his guilt on this occasion by asking, 'How many other children may have been too scared to come forward?', and called for him to be stood down from his position in charge of the youth foundation on the basis of the previous convictions.

LAW

Clearly, the reportage had been published during the sensitive period of a court case when tight restrictions applied due to the potential to influence a prospective jury. The key question was whether the *Bread Manufacturers* defence could be extended to apply to a case where discussion of a particular upcoming criminal case predominated, but was still part of a continuing debate on a matter of public interest. The trial judge and the majority of the Full Court of the Victorian Supreme Court held that the defence did not protect Hinch and the radio station. The High Court affirmed the Supreme Court majority's ruling, and ruled that Hinch had gone too far into the specific case to allow him to establish the defence. Justice Deane went so far as to suggest that, had Hinch just called for Glennon's removal from office while the charges were pending, he might have stayed within the bounds of the public interest defence. All judges found the pre-judgment of guilt the ultimate stumbling block, leading to the upholding of Hinch's conviction. He was jailed for 28 days and fined $10,000.

Two other important issues arose in *Hinch's case*. One concerned whether the *Bread Manufacturers* immunity could be extended to criminal, as well as civil, proceedings. The High Court determined that it could, although the public interest in ensuring that criminal proceedings were conducted without prejudice would attract greater weight, and would be less likely to be outweighed by the free discussion than civil proceedings might. The second concerned the period that might elapse between the contemptuous publication and the prospective trial. The court held that, while an anticipated lapse of time before the trial might diminish the likely prejudice of a publication, in this case the broadcast was so widespread (to 200,000 listeners each time), and the *sub judice* comments so serious, that an impression of guilt would live on in the minds of potential jurors, ready to be rekindled whenever the trial was held.

Glennon later appealed to the Court of Criminal Appeal and had the jury's guilty verdict against him quashed for the sexual charges on which Hinch was commenting, arguing that Hinch's broadcasts had polluted the minds of the jurors (*Glennon's case*, 1992). However, the High Court, by a narrow four-to-three majority, overturned that appeal court's acquittal, and held that the timespan between the contempt conviction and Glennon's trial made a vital difference, particularly in relation to radio broadcasts. The events came close to a situation where the actions of a journalist, espousing notions of justice, almost helped a criminal escape punishment for the very wrongs the journalist was highlighting. In fact, he committed further offences during the 1985–92 period while free pending his trial and various appeals. Glennon died in prison in 2014.

LESSONS FOR PROFESSIONAL COMMUNICATORS

The key lesson for journalists and bloggers in *Hinch's case* is that the courts will tolerate some discussion of a matter related to an upcoming trial if there is an overriding public interest at stake, as long as the reporter or commentator minimises the risk to the trial by avoiding any comment on the guilt or innocence of the accused, does not raise issues to do with past charges or convictions and does not identify the accused where this may be at issue in the trial.

Journalists whose content is broadcast or circulated at considerable distance from where the crime occurred or where the trial will be held, so that it is unlikely to reach the pool of potential jurors and witnesses, can usually report much more freely than those in the immediate vicinity; however, internet publication makes all news available wherever the trial might be scheduled. The longer the likely time period between the report and the trial, the less likely it is that the authorities will press a contempt charge. The impact of social media is still being navigated by the courts, often by better instructions to and training of empanelled jurors about inappropriate access to online information.

KEY CASE 5.2: *KRYSTAL'S CASE*

DPP v Johnson & Yahoo!7 [2016] VSC 699 (28 November 2016)

DPP v Johnson & Yahoo!7 (No. 2) [2017] VSC 45 (17 February 2017)

FACTS

Journalist Krystal Johnson uploaded to the Yahoo!7 website an article titled 'Man Paused to Take "Smoke Break" While Bashing Girlfriend to Death' on the second day of the Melbourne trial of Mataio Aleluia for the murder of Brittany Harvie. Under the sub-heading 'Brittany Harvie predicted her death on Facebook', the article presented Facebook posts in which the victim had made chilling predictions of her death at the hands of the accused, taken from media coverage after she had been killed. The social media posts suggested a history of violence against the victim by the accused. She had posted three months prior to her death, 'It won't be long and he will put me six feet under. I love him until the day he kills me. He needs a punching bag, we all do.' The Yahoo!7 article contained this and other social media posts, even though the highly prejudicial evidence had not been presented to the jury and the prosecutor did not intend to present it. The judge was alerted to the article four days after its publication and decided after submissions that the jury should be discharged.

LAW

Victorian Supreme Court Justice John Dixon was satisfied beyond reasonable doubt that the publication 'objectively and as a matter of practical reality, had a real and definite tendency to prejudice the trial of the accused' (*Krystal's case* 2, para. 1). He reached this conclusion after offering a useful summary of the fifteen key elements of *sub judice* contempt (*Krystal's case 1*, para. 24). He decided the article still had a 'real and definite tendency to prejudice the trial' despite the facts that the jury had been instructed not to access the internet and to disregard publicity about the case; that the article was only viewed by about 4000 people; and that other historic articles containing the offending material could still be accessed at the time of the trial.

Justice Dixon adjudged both Johnson and her employer Yahoo!7 guilty of contempt of court. He fined Yahoo!7 $300,000 but allowed Johnson to undertake to enter a two-year good behaviour bond which, if she complied, would lead to the dismissal of the charge.

LESSONS FOR PROFESSIONAL COMMUNICATORS

Quite apart from the useful summary of the principles of *sub judice* contempt, which we suggest all journalists read and remember, the case had very important lessons for crime and court reporters and their media organisations.

First, it underscored the fundamental principle that reports of criminal cases after a jury has been empanelled should be limited to fair and accurate coverage of the content of each day's proceedings in a trial—and only material that has been presented in open court in the presence of the jury. This demands a reporter's physical attendance at a court case and requires that they do not recycle material from earlier coverage.

Second, the judge found serious flaws in Yahoo!7's editorial checking mechanisms when dealing with such cases. Resources and deadline pressures meant the inexperienced reporter uploaded the article directly to the website when it should have been checked by a more senior editor.

It appears that this did not occur due to a lack of resources and pressure of deadlines. Legal advice had not been sought prior to publication, which the company agreed to make available in future instances when required. Justice Dixon observed, 'Time pressures inherent to the media's work must be balanced against the responsibility to ensure that the appropriate checks are in place' (*Krystal's case 2*, para. 29).

Other examples

Too often, the combination of human nature, frenzied media competition for a 'scoop', the pressure of circulation and sales and the enthusiasm or self-serving attitudes of law-enforcement agencies can lead to extensive pre-trial reports on police investigations of major crimes that fly in the face of *sub judice* restrictions. This has resulted in incidents like the pre-charge parading of an accused before reporters and cameramen—known to police reporters as 'the walk'. That happened in *Mason's case* (1990), where the hunt for a killer, Paul Mason, over a two-month period in 1989 had followed the axe murders of two women and a child. Mason eventually surrendered himself to police and confessed to the murders. The police allowed the media to film Mason being walked around the scene of the murders and issued to the media details of Mason's confession, which they then proceeded to publish. Some months later, Mason killed himself while in prison. Two newspapers and four television channels were convicted of *sub judice* contempt for their coverage of the matter. Their defence arguments—that the police case was watertight (and therefore a foregone conclusion), and that the trial would not be for a considerable period—were rejected. The court said that everyone deserved a full and fair trial, no matter how convincing the case against them, and that the impact of the coverage was so great it would risk influencing any potential juror. The six outlets were fined a total of $670,000 (NSWLRC, 2000: 509–10).

Sub judice contempt cases involving a range of media, situations and outcomes have included the following:

- *The A Current Affair case (2003).* The Nine Network was fined $80,000 and WIN Television Queensland $1000 for broadcasting a story on the national television program *A Current Affair* featuring prejudicial witness interviews on the day a hung jury verdict was returned. An 86-year-old man was standing trial for the sexual assault and murder of two girls 28 years earlier. Despite the fact that a retrial might not be held for some months after the jury was discharged, there was still 'a real and definite tendency, as a matter of practical reality, to prejudice or embarrass particular legal proceedings'.
- *The Age case (2006). The Age* newspaper was fined $75,000 for publishing an accused man's prior convictions before his trial. Justice Cummins said the convictions had not been in the public domain prior to publication, and prospective jurors were likely to remember them because they were directly related to the offences the accused was alleged to have committed.
- *The Gangland cases (2008).* The Herald and Weekly Times Ltd was fined $10,000 over a graphic that linked an accused to Melbourne's gangland wars on the second day of a criminal trial. The judge accepted that while pressure of time and high copy flow on the night were factors, where there was conflict between deadlines and legal compliance, it was the deadline that must give way. *The Age* and *The Age Online* were fined $10,000 and $2000 respectively over similar errors, involving a chronology.

MINDFUL CRIME AND COURT REPORTING: TIME ZONES AND RESTRICTIONS

What can a reporter or blogger include in a story at each stage of the criminal process? It is best to pause to reflect upon this in terms of a number of 'time zones'. Each time zone involves different limitations on the work of a journalist wanting to report on the judicial system. Some of those limitations are brought about by the application of defamation law, to be covered in Part 3. The techniques of court reporting are addressed in detail in Chapter 6. However, it is important at this early stage to get a feel for the way the pressures of *sub judice* contempt interplay with those of defamation, to affect the reportage of crime and justice. Table 5.1 provides an idea of the level of reporting allowable at each stage of the criminal process. The important point to remember is the need to be mindful of both key areas of the law when reporting on a crime and any subsequent trial. A defamation or contempt issue is often overlooked by a reporter, editor or news director, who may think they are well within their rights to publish, having focused their attention on one, but not the other.

Table 5.1 Crime reportage time zones

Time zone	Description	Restrictions on reportage
1	After crime, before arrest or charging	No restriction for contempt, but ensure a defamation defence is available. What if the suspect sues for defamation, as happened in WA in *Rayney's case* (2017) after a barrister (who was innocent) was named as the prime suspect in his wife's murder?
2	After arrest or charging, before first court appearance	Reporting limited to the 'bare facts' of the crime (*Packer's case*), with no information that might risk interfering with eyewitness identification, such as photographs or 'pen portraits' of the accused, or that might prejudice a future jury against them. Ensure a defamation defence is available. What if no charges are in fact laid, or are withdrawn? The accused could sue you for defamation and you would not have the protection of a court report defence. Do not interview potential witnesses. No mention of confessions, previous charges or convictions.

continues

Table 5.1 Crime reportage time zones *continued*

Time zone	Description	Restrictions on reportage
3	After charging, during preliminary appearances and hearings	As for zone 2; however, court appearances and committal hearings during this period can be reported with care under the principle that the public interest in open justice usually takes precedence over the public interest in an unprejudiced hearing. No photographs or sketches if identification may be an issue. Ensure a defamation defence of fair report is available. What if charges are dropped? Take special care with state-based laws banning identification of the accused at this stage, as with sex crimes in Queensland, South Australia and the NT, and banning bail hearing reportage in Tasmania (see Chapter 6). Watch for suppression orders on identification or certain evidence. Stay away from witnesses and avoid comment on guilt or innocence.
4	During trial	Restricted to fair and accurate report of trial and description of 'bare facts' of crime. No use of material from preliminary hearings, or of anything that takes place in the absence of the jury (as occurred in *Krystal's case* (2016, 2017)). No photographs or sketches if identification may be an issue. Similar defence applies to defamation. Again, no interviews with witnesses, watch for suppression orders, don't identify children or sex crime victims, and don't prejudge guilt or innocence.
5	After trial, before appeal expiry date	Report with some care, avoiding anything of an extreme or overly sensational nature that might influence a jury or witness on retrial. (Particularly avoid interviewing jurors.) Defamation may still be an issue, although fair reporting of a court case is still protected. Beyond that, reportage and comment must be covered by some other defence. Certainly don't imply an acquitted person is really guilty.
6	After appeal or acquittal	No *sub judice* restrictions. Defamation still a concern. Ensure a defence is available. Again, don't imply the guilt of someone acquitted.

DIGITAL DIMENSIONS

As we have already seen in some of these examples, new technologies have complicated *sub judice* law for the media. All news media are now digital and use social media, while journalists have Facebook pages and use Twitter, LinkedIn and other platforms. All this presents potential problems relating to both the time and place of publication of *sub judice* material. For example, if the *Whyalla News* newspaper in South Australia publishes *sub judice* material about an upcoming Tasmanian case in its printed newspaper, it will most likely escape prosecution because of its distance from the location of prospective jurors and witnesses—particularly if it is well in advance of the trial. However, if it publishes the same material on its website or social media pages, it leaves itself wide open to *sub judice* charges: potential jurors and witnesses in Tasmania have ready access to the website and, if it is archived, it could well be accessible on the eve of the trial.

Social media are placing more stresses on the jury system, and courts are being forced to turn to remedial measures such as the training of jurors, and better methods of instructing them (Johnston et al., 2013). We now have the phenomenon of the 'rogue juror'—the individual who accesses the internet and social media to seek out information on the accused, and sometimes even brags on social media about their jury experiences. Manchester mother of three Joanne Fraill, 40, was sentenced to eight months in prison by London's High Court in 2011 for exchanging Facebook messages with the accused in a drug trial while she was serving on the jury. She also searched online for information about another defendant while she and the other jurors were still deliberating. All this went against clear instructions from the judge to jurors to stay away from the internet (*Facebook Juror case*, 2011). In another British case, the *Dallas case* (2012), a female juror was sentenced to six months in prison for contempt of court for conducting research on the internet, including definitions of the word 'grievous' and a newspaper report of an earlier rape allegation against the accused, having shared this with fellow jurors. Several Australian jury trials have since miscarried because jurors have done their own research on the internet or have misused social media.

In some jurisdictions, legislation had been introduced in an effort to deal with this: under the *Jury Act 1977* (NSW), it is an offence for a juror to 'make an inquiry for the purpose of obtaining information about the accused, or any matters relevant to the trial, except in the proper exercise of his or her functions as a juror', which includes a ban on conducting any electronic search of a database for information.

In *Benbrika's case* (2010), the Victorian Court of Appeal affirmed trial judge Justice Bongiorno's handling of a situation where jurors had used internet sites, including Wikipedia and Reference.com, to seek definitions of terms related to the terrorism trial (definitions the judge said were not substantially different from those stated in court). The Appeal Court said the trial judge had found that 'it was distinctly possible that they had interpreted his directions as meaning that they should not seek information about the case, rather than using the internet for more general purposes' (at para. 199). They noted the important difference between this kind of search and searching for 'information that is both inadmissible at trial, and prejudicial to the accused', which might prompt the discharge of a jury (at para. 214).

In summary, key considerations for professional communicators in the realm of *sub judice* contempt include the following:

- A media outlet is liable for *sub judice* contempt even when it is merely reporting the contemptuous comments of others (*Wran's case*, 1987).
- Even if the publication suggests that the accused in a criminal trial is innocent, it can still interfere with the administration of justice (*Wran's case*, 1987).
- The fact that police or other official sources provided the *sub judice* material for publication is no defence.
- It is no defence to a contempt charge that other media organisations had already reported or were in the process of reporting the *sub judice* material or that it was widely circulated on social media. (This may, however, affect the court's determination of whether there was a 'tendency' to prejudice the trial.)

- Pressure of deadlines is no defence: where deadlines conflict with legal requirements, courts expect them to give way.
- Ignorance is no defence: newspapers and digital media are expected to check for themselves to see whether proceedings are pending and whether relevant orders have been made. This holds true even if there has been a failure by the court to inform the media via established channels.
- The fact that the *sub judice* material is later proved to be true is no defence. At issue is the tendency to prejudice the proceedings at the time of publication.

SCANDALISING THE COURT

A second kind of contempt of court by publication is known as 'scandalising the court'. The term 'scandalising' was described in the High Court in *Dunbabin's case* (at 442) in 1935 as applying to:

> *publications which tend to detract from the authority and influence of judicial determinations, publications calculated to impair the confidence of the people in the Court's judgments because the matter published aims at lowering the authority of the Court as a whole or that of its judges and excites misgivings as to the integrity, propriety and impartiality brought to the exercise of the judicial office.*

This type of contempt can be committed by publishing material that scandalises the courts or judges by abusing them in scurrilous terms, alleging they are corrupt or lack integrity, or that they have bowed to outside influences in reaching their decisions. Historically, the courts have been tolerant of reasonable criticism. Lord Atkin (at 335) summed the approach up well with this quote in 1936 in *Ambard's case*: 'Justice is not a cloistered virtue; she must be allowed to suffer the scrutiny and respectful, though outspoken, comments of ordinary men.'

The two best-known cases in this area in Australia are known as the *BLF cases*, as both involved trade union leaders from the Builders'

Labourers Federation (BLF)–Jack Mundey and Norm Gallagher–albeit one decade apart. In each case, the accused had made comments (which were then published) implying that judges had bowed to union pressure in reaching their decisions.

The first, *Attorney-General (NSW) v Mundey (BLF case 1)*, occurred during the heat of the anti-apartheid protests against South Africa in the early 1970s. Members of the BLF had sawn off the goalposts at the Sydney Cricket Ground in the prelude to a Rugby Union Test match between Australia and South Africa's Springboks. After their trials, union official Jack Mundey told the media that the judge should have allowed evidence of broader political material in their defence, such as UN documentation on South Africa's race policies. Mundey claimed that there had been a miscarriage of justice, and that the judge was a racist. Mundey was charged with contempt for these comments, but the charges were dismissed in the Supreme Court because Mundey's comments about the judge being a racist needed to be considered in the broader context of his comments about racism throughout Australian society. The court ruled that Mundey would have been in contempt if he had implied that the judge had been motivated by some racist bias against the accused in reaching his decision.

BLF case 2, a decade later, had a different result. There, BLF federal secretary Norm Gallagher won a Federal Court appeal against one contempt charge, but his comments about the judicial process landed him in contempt on a new charge of scandalising the court. Gallagher told the media that industrial action by his union members had exerted enough pressure to force the court to reverse the decision to jail him over the first contempt charge. He told one television channel that, 'the rank and file of the union . . . has shown such fine support of the officials of the union and I believe that by their actions in demonstrating in walking off jobs . . . I believe that has been the main reason for the court changing its mind' (*BLF case 2*, 1983, at 239). The Federal Court held that the statement was contemptuous, and sentenced Gallagher to three months' jail. The decision was appealed to the High Court, which upheld the contempt conviction. The court said Gallagher's insinuation that the Federal Court had bowed to outside pressure in reaching its decision was calculated to undermine public confidence in the Federal Court.

In the *Anissa case* (1999, at para. 19), Justice Cummins of the Supreme Court of Victoria summed up the three basic principles of contempt by scandalising the court:

> *First, proceeding for contempt of court is not and must not be in diminution of free speech. Second, proceeding for contempt of court is to preserve the administration of justice. Third, proceeding for contempt of court is not to protect the individual person of the judge.*

More recently, the NSW Court of Appeal upheld a magistrate's right to sue for defamation over criticisms of her performance in her role, rather than limiting her rights in view of the protection given by the principle of 'scandalising' contempt (*O'Shane's case*, 2013).

Of course, the risk of being charged with scandalising the court should not prevent journalists and bloggers partaking in fair, well-reasoned criticism of the courts and the judicial process. It is only when the criticism is personal, amounts to scurrilous abuse of a judge that brings the judicial system into disrepute or implies some improper motive on the part of the judiciary that it oversteps the mark.

In recent years, there have been several charges of scandalising the court, involving extreme statements about the judiciary. These include:

- *Mahaffy's case (2018).* Assertions that a NSW District Court judge tampered with the transcript of court proceedings, that the District Court was corrupt and that a judge engaged in corruption went beyond legitimate criticism, but amounted to specific accusations calculated to induce a lack of confidence in the ordered and fearless administration of justice, and resulted in conviction and a jail sentence.
- *Liberal Ministers' case (2017).* The Victorian Court of Appeal issued a public statement warning of potential *sub judice* and scandalising charges against three Commonwealth government ministers who had implied on social media that the Supreme Court would issue a lesser penalty against terrorists because they were left-wing

appointments and had an ideological agenda and that this eroded trust in the judiciary. The court asserted the statements were 'calculated to improperly undermine public confidence in the administration of justice'. The comments had been quoted in an article in *The Australian* titled 'Judiciary "Light on Terrorism"'. The charges were not pursued after the newspaper and the ministers eventually apologised.

- *Barrister's case (2017).* A Queensland barrister was fined $4000 for accusing a magistrate of being cranky and then stating, 'And that's why you don't do things according to law.'
- *Lackey's case (2013).* In this Family Court matter, a disgruntled party in a child custody case went on social media, criticising the courts and judicial officers.
- *The Talkback case (2006).* Veteran Adelaide broadcaster Bob Francis was given a nine-week suspended jail sentence and fined $20,000 over a program in which he criticised a magistrate for considering granting bail to a man accused of possessing child pornography. Francis told his audience, 'Oh, smash the judge's face in.' The magistrate also settled out of court for a reported $110,000 defamation payout (McGarry, 2006).
- *Hoser's case (2003).* The author of two books about police corruption in Victoria was fined $3000 and his publishing company was fined $2000 for making malicious and baseless allegations of bias and impropriety against two judges who had tried earlier cases involving the author. A defence that the statements were fair comment made in good faith failed.
- *The Anissa case (1999).* A Victorian solicitor, when formally asked to read a court order at the scene of a property dispute on his land, proclaimed to all present that the judge who had issued the order 'has his hand on his dick'. A different judge, presiding over the contempt case, said the words were 'gratuitous and offensive', but did not constitute contempt by scandalising. 'It may be offensive, but it is not contempt of court, for a person to describe a judge as a wanker,' the judge ruled.

Journalists, bloggers and politicians' media advisers need to ensure that any criticism of the judiciary and the legal system is carefully phrased and measured so it does not unfairly imply any wrongdoing that might erode public confidence.

DEFENCES TO SCANDALISING THE COURT

A turning point in the law of scandalising contempt was reached with one of the High Court's famous free-speech decisions in 1992–*Wills' case*. A newspaper group challenged the federal government's power to legislate against criticism of the Industrial Relations Commission or its members. The High Court held that there was an implied constitutional freedom to criticise important public institutions, and that this legislation infringed that right. However, the court also ruled that the offence of scandalising the court was not obsolete and that two defences applied to it: truth and fair comment (Chesterman, 2000: 68). In other words, it would be a defence to a charge of scandalising the court if you could prove that the substance of your criticisms was true or that your criticisms were made in good faith, were honestly held, fairly conducted and did not imply improper motives on the part of the judiciary.

REVEALING THE DELIBERATIONS OF JURIES

The inside story on jury deliberations makes for fascinating reading, but such coverage is banned in many places. Numerous statutory prohibitions on communicating with jurors exist, and legal advice should be sought before publishing any material that may have come from jurors, even if it was unsolicited. We look at this issue in more detail in Chapter 6. In New South Wales, for example, sections 68 and 68A of the *Jury Act 1977* forbid anyone seeking information from jurors, even after a trial has concluded, but do not forbid publication of a jury's deliberations (other than during the trial) if the information is volunteered by a juror who does not receive a fee or reward in return. Journalists should seek legal advice before dealing with jurors in any way at all, even if the jurors have approached them.

CONTEMPT IN THE FACE OF THE COURT

Almost any behaviour that disrupts the courtroom can be considered a 'contempt in the face of the court'. This branch of contempt law is directed at behaviour in the actual courtroom that interferes with the administration of justice. The Australian Law Reform Commission (1987: 3) defines 'contempt in the face of the court' as:

> *Improper behaviour in court. Anything done to interrupt significantly the smooth and appropriately dignified hearing of a case in a courtroom risks being treated as contempt and punished accordingly.*

Examples have included outright physical assaults in the courtroom, verbal abuse, inappropriate dress, sleeping and even attempting to release laughing gas into the court building. In recent years, people have been convicted in India, the United States and the United Kingdom because their mobile phones rang in court (Cassens Weiss, 2010).

Judges have a wide discretion in determining what is unacceptable behaviour in court. It is hardly surprising that behaviour such as undressing and lying naked in court or releasing laughing gas into the courtroom have incurred the wrath of presiding judges. However, for less extreme behaviour it is difficult to establish the degree to which it might be interfering with the administration of justice. For example, how might a court view a protester raising a clenched fist in the courtroom or making insulting or blasphemous remarks during a trial? This happened in 1970 in *Tuckerman's case*, when both actions were found to be contemptuous. So too were examples of seemingly innocuous behaviour, such as failing to stand when a magistrate entered the courtroom and reading a newspaper in court.

Many a rookie journalist has approached court reporting duties with trepidation in the light of the latter examples—worried that some minor breach of court etiquette might land them in jail for contempt at the whim of a belligerent judge or magistrate. Such concern is largely unjustified, as the chance of this happening is remote. Nevertheless, there have been several charges of contempt in the face of the court in recent years, usually committed at points when emotions were running high:

- *Lovell's case (2002).* Western Australian author Avon Lovell was fined $30,000 for contempt of the Western Australian Police Royal Commission for refusing to enter the witness box at the commission and then leaving the commission, stating that he was going to have a cup of tea.
- *Murderer's Brother case (2005).* A 22-year-old fruit marketer, upon hearing his brother being found guilty of murder in a jury trial, addressed one of the jurors by name from the back of the courtroom and 'made remarks calculated to intimidate and upset her'. He was sentenced to 250 hours of community service for contempt in the face of the court.
- *Abuse cases (2007 and 2013).* Frustrated litigants told a magistrate and a judge to 'get fucked'.
- *Bubble Gum case (2011).* The accused was jailed for one month for blowing bubble gum bubbles in the direction of the magistrate. The charge was quashed on appeal in the Supreme Court for a lack of procedural fairness by the magistrate after the accused had served half a day.
- *Snaphappy Juror case (2011).* A Sydney juror was charged with contempt in 2011 when she used a mobile phone in court to take a photo of a family friend who was sitting in a jury panel (Jacobsen, 2011). She was fingerprinted, her phone was seized and she was granted bail, but the charge was later dropped and signs were erected in the courthouse warning that no photography was allowed.
- *Camera Shy Prisoner case (2013).* A prisoner who refused to appear before a magistrate via video link was convicted of contempt 'in the face of the court' even though he was not in court and could not be seen or heard by the magistrate. His non-appearance still 'interfered with the conduct of proceedings which were in progress or imminent'.

- *Dock Assault case (2017).* Two men charged with a number of offences arising out of their involvement in the activities of a criminal organisation known as the Brothers for Life at Blacktown (BFL Blacktown) violently set upon another accused man in open court. The incident was captured on the CCTV above the dock area, where the accused sat. One man attempted to use a pen as a weapon and struck a blow towards the upper body, neck or head of one of his co-accused. After that man was removed by court officers, a second man threw two or three punches at or towards the head of the same co-accused. The incident occurred almost immediately upon the door being closed behind the jury. A barrier was subsequently erected between the co-accused and a plastic screen closed whenever the jury were absent from the courtroom. This act of violence in the dock in the presence of a judicial officer, calculated to intimidate and injure the co-accused, was held to be a serious example of contempt.
- *Indigenous Laughing case (2017).* An Aboriginal land rights activist was jailed for two hours after defying a Gympie magistrate by laughing at him in the courtroom. Gary Tomlinson (also known as 'Wit-boooka') had challenged the authority of the court to hear public nuisance and trespass offences related to a protest at Gympie Regional Council.
- *NT Homeless 'Genius' case (2017).* A homeless man, self-described genius and would-be mayoral candidate who continuously insulted court officers, interrupted the judge and disrobed in court was twice jailed for contempt in the face of the court in 2016 and 2017. His appeals failed against his total of five months' contempt sentence and alleged bias by the judge.

The Australian Law Reform Commission (1987: 71) found that the summary procedures for dealing with contempt in the face of the court contravened fundamental doctrines of criminal law and procedure, leading to the perception that justice, while perhaps being done, was not being seen to be done. That was exactly the reservation described by the Victorian Supreme Court in the *Bubble Gum case* (2011), outlined above.

Journalists and other communicators are warned to show respect in the courtroom. This extends beyond paying attention to the proceedings, remaining clothed and avoiding throwing projectiles at the magistrate.

TIPS FOR MINDFUL PRACTICE

- Court and crime reporters and bloggers should purchase a copy of the legislation that outlines the court's powers in relation to contempt in their jurisdiction. It can normally be found in the rules of the respective courts or tribunals, or the Acts under which they operate.
- Main areas of caution when reporting during the *sub judice* period include any indication of pre-judgment (whether as to guilt or innocence), publishing potentially inadmissible evidence, publishing witnesses' statements beyond their evidence in court, revealing criminal records and alleged confessions of the accused, or identification of the accused where it may be an issue in the trial (always assume it will be). Be especially careful of prejudicing the trial of an accused by reporting developments in the arrest or trial of an alleged accomplice.
- Beware of the pressures of competition. Just because your competitor appears to have overstepped the mark, it does not mean you have to do so. Seek legal advice if you fear the boundaries are being pushed. It is no defence to your *sub judice* contempt charge that others did the same thing (just as it is no defence to a speeding charge to say that you were following a car going 20 kilometres per hour faster).
- Be especially careful when the crime has occurred in your circulation or broadcast area. Remember, media from other places might get away with publishing more details because they might not attract a large audience in the area from which witnesses and jurors will be drawn.
- Avoid interviews with witnesses after charges have been laid. The courts may rule that such interviews risked prejudicing their later testimony.
- Visual identification is a particularly sensitive matter, and it can be most difficult to predict whether it will be at issue. Err on the side of caution.

- Take care when pixelating or masking an image of an accused's face. Remember, it is not just the face and the eyes that are identifying features. Other features, such as hair colour, body markings and piercings, can identify someone.
- Consider defamation. It is too easy to forget the potential for defamation when weighing up the likelihood of contempt charges. Remember, these must be considered as separate issues. You would do well to return to this after reading the defamation chapters (Chapters 7 and 8).
- Beware of information supplied by police and other official or influential sources (e.g. political leaders). Their official position offers you no protection from contempt.
- Confidence in the newsroom about *sub judice* reportage ebbs and flows with time. The news media's awareness of contempt laws and their willingness to risk prosecution for the sake of a good story seems to operate in cycles. Journalists will be cautious for a period after someone has been convicted of contempt, but will gradually increase in confidence until the point that someone else is charged and the cycle resumes. Don't be the fool who gets caught up in the wave of excessive confidence and prejudices someone's trial.
- Double-check everything: spelling of names, addresses, charges, photo captions, headline wording, stand-first or write-off, pull quotes, graphics, supers and subtitling on television news, tweets and other social media posts, and so on.
- Watch the time zones. When publishing reports about crimes and court cases, be aware of the respective time zones and the restrictions on reportage that apply to them. Photocopy the time zone chart (Table 5.1) and have it available for reference when crime stories unfold. Err on the side of caution, and assume the *sub judice* period has started from the point of arrest.
- Stick to the 'bare facts'. The period after arrest and before the first court appearance has tight restrictions on reporting. During this period, however, you can still report on the 'bare facts' of the crime, and this allows you considerable leeway to report a range of matters that do not influence the trial itself.

- Refrain from publishing anything implying the guilt or even innocence of the accused or discussing matters that will form the basis of witnesses' accounts during the trial.
- Work to the public interest defence. If there is some ongoing issue of public importance that requires coverage during the *sub judice* period and in some way relates to the trial, seek legal advice before relying on it. Keep any such references general rather than specifically mentioning matters that are at issue in the trial.
- Is there 'a real and definite tendency to influence proceedings'? The courts will examine whether your report has a 'real and definite tendency' to prejudice an upcoming or current trial.
- Ensure that any criticism of the judiciary and the legal system is carefully phrased and measured so that it does not unfairly imply any wrongdoing or improper motive that might erode public confidence and incur a scandalising the court contempt charge (or lead to a defamation action from the judge or magistrate).
- Websites and social media raise special issues to do with contempt, particularly as they are accessible beyond your normal circulation or broadcast area, and highly prejudicial material may remain on them right up to (and during) trial. If you have any doubt that material you have already posted online may be contemptuous, remove it first, then seek legal advice.
- Beware of the dangers of a summary conviction for contempt in the face of the court. Keep your mobile phone turned off during trials—or at least have it switched to silent mode. And don't attempt to take any photos or make recordings in the courtroom unless you have been given permission to do so. If you get the giggles, excuse yourself and leave the courtroom to recover. It is important to respect the authority of the court and to avoid being perceived as being disrespectful to the court or judicial officer.

IN A NUTSHELL

- Contempt is conduct impairing or threatening to impair the administration of justice.
- Contempt by publication includes:
  - material that tends to prejudice a fair trial (*sub judice* contempt)
  - allegations that tend to undermine public confidence in the administration of justice (scandalising the court)
  - an account of the deliberations of a jury in most jurisdictions.
- Other forms of contempt affecting journalists are:
  - improper behaviour in a courtroom during a hearing, which is also known as 'contempt in the face of the court'
  - failure to comply with a court order or undertaking given to a court, which is known as 'disobedience contempt' (applies to journalists who refuse to reveal a source in court, covered in Chapter 9).
- *Sub judice* means 'under a judge', and it applies to the period when proceedings are 'pending'. In criminal matters, it applies from the time someone has been arrested.
- After someone has been arrested but before they appear in court, the media are restricted to reporting the 'bare facts' of the crime: 'extrinsic ascertained facts to which any eyewitness could bear testimony'.
- Civil proceedings are pending from the issue of a writ, a statement of claim or a summons. However, *sub judice* contempt charges are rarely pressed in civil matters.
- If proceedings are pending, it is a contempt to publish material intending to prejudice them, or to publish material that has a tendency to do so.
- When considering whether the publication had the 'tendency' to interfere with proceedings, the courts look to the potential effect of the *sub judice* material, with the test applied at the time of publication rather than at some later date.
- The courts take into account a number of relevant factors in determining whether there is a real tendency to prejudice, including the prominence

of the item printed or broadcast; the images accompanying it; the time lapse between publication and likely trial; the prominence of the maker of contemptuous statements; and the extent or area of publication.

- Courts are particularly concerned with material that might influence potential jurors or witnesses, such as insinuations that an accused is guilty or even innocent, the mention of potentially inadmissible evidence, publication of an accused person's previous convictions or the publishing of photographs or drawings of the accused, if identification may be an issue at the trial.
- There are two possible defences that can be raised against *sub judice* contempt charges. The first is clear-cut: a fair and accurate report of what has been said in open court in the presence of the jury. The second is more difficult to establish: that there was some overriding public interest at stake in the discussion of some larger public issue, and the *sub judice* report was part of that ongoing discussion (known as the *Bread Manufacturers* defence).
- *Sub judice* contempt is complicated by the advent of the internet and social media. Media organisations that might otherwise have escaped on account of their limited geographical circulation or broadcast area are now susceptible because the same material carried on their associated websites may be published into a jurisdiction where witnesses or jurors might be influenced.
- Scandalising the court can be committed by publishing material about courts or judges that abuses them in scurrilous terms, alleges that they are corrupt or lack integrity, or suggests that they have bowed to outside influences in reaching their decisions.
- 'Contempt in the face of the court' is improper behaviour in court. It extends to anything that might significantly interrupt the smooth hearing of a case in a courtroom.

DISCUSSION QUESTIONS

5.1 The law positions the *sub judice* period as starting at the instant of arrest of a criminal suspect. What advantages or disadvantages are there in having the *sub judice* period starting:

(a) earlier, perhaps at the time when police are searching for a suspect or questioning a suspect

(b) later, perhaps only after a suspect has appeared in court?

5.2 In the *Who Weekly case*, the magazine challenged the court's view that witnesses might be influenced by it publishing a photograph of the accused while the trial was pending. What are the arguments for and against such a photograph being published?

5.3 The theory is that judges and magistrates are able to erase prejudicial media and internet publicity from their minds when presiding over a case, but that jurors are vulnerable to such influence. What is your view on this?

5.4 Why do judges and the legal system need to be protected by the offence of scandalising the court? Isn't it enough that judges have the right to pursue defamation actions to restore their reputations?

5.5 What kinds of actions by a professional communicator might amount to attempting to exert improper pressure on another party in legal proceedings, either directly or through their legal representatives?

5.6 Search online and find a recent example of contempt of court. Compare and contrast it with one of the cases in this chapter.

REFERENCES

Arlidge, A. and Eady, D. 1982, *The Law of Contempt*, Sweet & Maxwell, London.

Australian Law Reform Commission (ALRC) 1987, *Report No. 35—Contempt*, AGPS, Canberra, <www.austlii.edu.au/au/other/alrc/publications/reports/35>.

Butt, P. and Nygh, P. 2004, *Butterworths Encyclopaedic Australian Legal Dictionary*, LexisNexis, Sydney.

Cassens Weiss, D. 2010, 'Fla Appeals Court overturns contempt finding for ringing cell phone', *ABA Journal Online*, 2 April, <www.abajournal.com/news/article/fla._appeals_court_overturns_contempt_finding_for_ringing_cell_phone>.

Chesterman, M. 2000, *Freedom of Speech in Australian Law: A Delicate Plant*, Ashgate, Aldershot.

Chesterman, M., Chan, J. and Hampton, S. 2001, *Managing Prejudicial Publicity: An Empirical Study of Criminal Jury Trials in New South Wales*, Justice Research Centre, Law and Justice Foundation of NSW, Sydney.

Davidson, H. 2014, 'Tony Abbott warns on ABC funding over defence of Chris Kenny lawsuit,' 7 March, <www.theguardian.com/media/2014/Mar/07/tony-abbott-warns-abc-funding-chris-kenny-defamation>.

Jacobsen, G. 2011, 'A quick click or two in court lands a young woman in the nick', *Newcastle Herald*, 9 September, <www.theherald.com.au/story/936338/a-quick-click-or-two-in-court-lands-a-young-woman-in-the-nick>.

Johnston, J., Keyzer, P., Holland, G., Pearson, M., Rodrick, S. and Wallace, A. 2013, *Juries and Social Media: A Report Prepared for the Victorian Department of Justice*, Centre for Law, Governance and Public Policy, Bond University, <www.sclj.gov.au/agdbasev7wr/sclj/documents/pdf/juries%20and%20social%20media%20-%20final.pdf>.

McGarry, A. 2006, 'Jail for Bob the broadcaster?', *The Australian*, 3 August, p. 14.

NSW Law Reform Commission (NSWLRC) 2000, *Discussion Paper 43: Contempt by Publication*, NSWLRC, Sydney, <www.lawlink.nsw.gov.au/lrc.nsf/pages/dp43toc>.

Wahlquist, C. 2017, 'Coalition ministers will not face contempt charges', *The Guardian*, 22 June, <www.theguardian.com/australia-news/2017/jun/23/coalition-ministers-no-contempt-charges-court-accepts-apology>.

CASES CITED

Abuse cases: Registrar of the Supreme Court of South Australia v Moore-McQuillan [2007] SASC 447 (14 December 2007), <www.austlii.edu.au/cgi-bin/sinodisp/au/cases/sa/SASC/2007/447.html>; *Jenkins v Trigg* [2013] NTSC 4 (31 January 2013), <www.austlii.edu.au/cgi-bin/sinodisp/au/cases/nt/NTSC/2013/4.html>.

The Age case: R v The Age Company Ltd & Ors [2006] VSC 479, <https://www.austlii.edu.au/cgi-bin/viewdoc/au/cases/vic/VSC/2006/479.html>

Ambard's case: Ambard v Attorney-General of Trinidad and Tobago [1936] AC 322.

Anissa case: Anissa Pty Ltd v Simon Harry Parsons on application of the Prothonotary of the Supreme Court of Victoria [1999] VSC 430, <www.austlii.edu.au//cgi-bin/disp.pl/au/cases/vic/VSC/1999/430.html>.

Apps' case: ABC v Local Court of NSW [2014] NSWSC 249, <www.austlii.edu.au/cgi-bin/sinodisp/au/cases/nsw/NSWSC/2014/239.html>.

Barrister's case: Attorney-General for the State of Queensland v Di Carlo [2017] QSC 171, <www.austlii.edu.au/cgi-bin/viewdoc/au/cases/qld/QSC/2017/171.html>.

Benbrika's case: Benbrika v The Queen [2010] VSCA 281, <www.austlii.edu.au/cgi-bin/sinodisp/au/cases/vic/VSCA/2010/281.html>.

BLF case 1: Attorney-General NSW v Mundey [1972] 2 NSWLR 887.

BLF case 2: Gallagher v Durack (1983) 152 CLR 238.

Bread Manufacturers case: Ex parte Bread Manufacturers Ltd; Re Truth and Sportsman Ltd (1937) 37 SR (NSW) 242.

Bubble Gum case: Zukanovic v Magistrates' Court of Victoria at Moorabbin [2011] VSC 141 (20 April 2011), <www.austlii.edu.au/cgi-bin/sinodisp/au/cases/vic/VSC/2011/141.html>.

Camera Shy Prisoner case: Mansell v Mignaccarandazzo [2013] WASCA 262, <www.austlii.edu.au/au/cases/wa/WASCA/2013/262.html>.

Cop Killer case: R v Herald and Weekly Times [2007] VSC 482, No. 8683 of 2006 Supreme Court of Victoria (23 November 2007).

Crime Commission case: Lee v New South Wales Crime Commission [2013] HCA 39 9 October 2013, <www.austlii.edu.au/cgi-bin/viewdoc/au/cases/cth/HCA/2013/39.html>.

A Current Affair case: Attorney-General for State of Queensland v WIN Television Qld Pty Ltd & Anor [2003] QSC 157 (28 May 2003), <www.austlii.edu.au/au/cases/qld/QSC/2003/157.html>.

Dallas case: Attorney General v Dallas [2012] EWHC 156, <www.bailii.org/ew/cases/EWHC/Admin/2012/156.html>.

Dock Assault case: R v Farhad Qaumi, Mumtaz Qaumi & Jamil Qaumi (Sentence) [2017] NSWSC 774 (16 June 2017).

Dunbabin's case: R v Dunbabin; Ex parte Williams (1935) 53 CLR 419.

Evening Standard case: R v Evening Standard; Ex parte Director of Public Prosecutions (1924) 40 TLR 833.

Facebook Juror case: A-G v Fraill [2011] EWCA Crim 1570), <www.bailii.org/ew/cases/EWCA/Crim/2011/1570.html>.

Fisher's case: R v Fisher (1811) 2 Camp 563.

Gangland cases: R v The Herald and Weekly Times Pty Ltd & Anor [2008] VSC 251 (17 July 2008), <www.austlii.edu.au/au/cases/vic/VSC/2008/251.html>; *R v The Age Company Ltd & Ors* [2008] VSC 305 (20 August 2008), <www.austlii.edu.au/au/cases/vic/VSC/2008/305.html>; *R v The Herald and Weekly Times Ltd* [2009] VSC 85 (16 March 2009), <www.austlii.edu.au/au/cases/vic/VSC/2009/85.html>; *R v General Television Corporation Pty Ltd* [2009] VSC 84 (16 March 2009), <www.austlii.edu.au/au/cases/vic/VSC/2009/84.html>.

Gay and Lesbian case: John Fairfax Publications Pty Ltd & Anor v District Court of NSW & Ors [2004] NSWCA 324, <www.austlii.edu.au/au/cases/nsw/NSWCA/2004/324.html>.

Glennon's case: R v Glennon (1992) 173 CLR 592, <www.austlii.edu.au/au/cases/cth/HCA/1992/16.html>.

Heroin Syndicate case: Attorney-General (NSW) v John Fairfax Publications Pty Ltd [1999] NSWSC 318, <www.austlii.edu.au/au/cases/nsw/supreme_ct/1999/318.html>.

Hinch's case: Hinch v Attorney-General (Vic) (1987) 164 CLR 15.

Hoser's case: Hoser & Kotabi Pty Ltd v The Queen (ex parte The Attorney-General for the State of Victoria); The Queen (ex parte The Attorney-General for the State of Victoria) v Hoser & Kotabi Pty Ltd [2003] VSCA 194 (15 December 2003), <www.austlii.edu.au//cgi-bin/disp.pl/au/cases/vic/VSCA/2003/194.html>.

Indigenous Laughing case (2017), Gorrie, A. (18 December 2017). 'Gympie activist serves two hours for contempt'. *Gympie Times*, 18 December, <www.gympietimes.com.au/news/update-gympie-activist-serves-two-hours-for-contem/3293365>.

James' case: James v Robinson (1963) 109 CLR 593.

Krystal's case: DPP v Johnson & Yahoo!7 [2016] VSC 699 (28 November 2016), <https://www.austlii.edu.au/cgi-bin/viewdoc/au/cases/vic/VSC/2016/699.html>; *DPP v Johnson & Yahoo!7 (No. 2)* [2017] VSC 45 (17 February 2017), <www.austlii.edu.au/cgi-bin/viewdoc/au/cases/vic/VSC/2017/45.html>.

Lackey's case: Lackey & Mae [2013] FMCAfam 284 (4 April 2013), <www.austlii.edu.au/cgi-bin/sinodisp/au/cases/cth/FMCAfam/2013/284.html>.

Liberal Ministers case (2017), Supreme Court of Victoria, 16 June, 'Statement of the Court of Appeal in terrorism cases', <www.supremecourt.vic.gov.au/contact-us/news/statement-of-the-court-of-appeal-in-terrorism-cases>; Supreme Court of Victoria (23 June 2017), 'Statement of the Court of Appeal in *DPP v MHK and DPP v Besim* (23 June 2017)', <www.supremecourt.vic.gov.au/law-and-practice/judgments-and-sentences/judgment-summaries/statement-of-the-court-of-appeal-in-dpp>.

Lindy Chamberlain case: Chamberlain v R (No. 2) [1984] HCA 7 (1984) 153 CLR 521.

Lovell's case: Kennedy v Lovell [2002] WASCA 217 (5 August 2002), <www.austlii.edu.au/au/cases/waWASCA/2002/217.html>.

Mahaffy's case: Mahaffy v Mahaffy [2018] NSWCA 42 (14 March 2018), <www.austlii.edu.au/cgi-bin/viewdoc/au/cases/nsw/NSWCA/2018/42.html>.

Mason's case: Attorney-General (NSW) v TCN Channel Nine Pty Ltd (1990) 20 NSWLR 368, (1990) 5 BR 419.

Murderer's Brother case: Regina v Omar Rustom [2005] NSWSC 61, <www.austlii.edu.au/au/cases/nsw/supreme_ct/2005/61.html>.

NT Homeless 'Genius' case: Jenkins v Whittington [2017] NTSC 65, <www.austlii.edu.au/cgi-bin/viewdoc/au/cases/nt/NTSC/2017/65.html>.

O'Shane's case: O'Shane v Harbour Radio Pty Ltd [2013] NSWCA 315 (24 September 2013), <www.austlii.edu.au/cgi-bin/sinodisp/au/cases/nsw/NSWCA/2013/315.html>.

Packer's case: Packer v Peacock (1912) 13 CLR 577.

Parke's case: R v Parke [1903] 2 KB 432.

Rape Priors cases: R v Hinch [2013] VSC 520 (2 October 2013), <www.austlii.edu.au/au/cases/vic/VSC/2013/520.html>; *R v Hinch (No. 2)* [2013] VSC 554 (18 October 2013), <www.austlii.edu.au/cgi-bin/sinodisp/au/cases/vic/VSC/2013/554.html>.

Rayney's case: Rayney v The State of Western Australia [No. 9] [2017] WASC 367, <www.austlii.edu.au/cgi-bin/viewdoc/au/cases/wa/WASC/2017/367.html>.

Ruse's case: Ruse v Sullivan [1969] WAR 142.

Sandy's case: Sandy v Yindjibarndi Aboriginal Corporation RNTBC [2016] WASC 350 (2 November 2016), <classic.austlii.edu.au/cgi-bin/sinodisp/au/cases/wa/WASC/2016/350.html>.

Selim case: Director of Public Prosecutions (Cth) v Elisabeth Sexton [2008] NSWSC 152 (3 March 2008), <www.austlii.edu.au/cgi-bin/sinodisp/au/cases/nsw/NSWSC/2008/152.html>.

Snaphappy Juror case: see Jacobsen (2011).

Talkback case: DPP v Francis & Anor (No. 2) [2006] SASC 261 (25 August 2006), <www.austlii.edu.au>.

Thunder case: Thunder Studios Inc. (California) v Kazal [2016] FCA 1598 (21 December 2016); *Kazal v Thunder Studios Inc. (California)* [2017] FCAFC 111 (31 July 2017).

Tuckerman's case: Ex parte Tuckerman; re Nash [1970] 3 NSWR 23.

Underbelly case: General Television Corporation Pty Ltd v DPP & Anor [2008] VSCA 49 (26 March 2008), <www.austlii.edu.au/cgi-bin/sinodisp/au/cases/vic/VSCA/2008/49.html>.

Who Weekly case: Attorney-General (NSW) v Time Inc. Magazine Co. Pty Ltd (NSW Court of Appeal, 40331/94, unreported).

Wills' case: Nationwide News Pty Ltd v Wills (1992) 177 CLR 1.

Worm Farming case: Australian Broadcasting Corporation v O'Neill [2006] HCA 46; 80 ALJR 1672; 229 ALR 457 (28 September 2006), <www.austlii.edu.au/cgi-bin/sinodisp/au/cases/cth/HCA/2006/46.html>.

Wran's case: Director of Public Prosecutions (Cth) v Wran (1987) 7 NSWLR 616.

CHAPTER 6

Covering court

KEY CONCEPTS

Privileges

Special qualified entitlements or permissions given to individuals or a select group, as distinct from irrevocable rights held by all citizens. Thus journalists might be granted a 'privilege' to tweet from court that can be revoked by a magistrate.

Committal hearing

The preliminary proceedings in serious cases (indictable offences), where the prosecution is called upon to convince the magistrate that it has a *prima facie* (on the face of it) case against the accused to allow the matter to proceed to trial. The case is dismissed if the magistrate decides there is not enough evidence upon which a jury could convict the accused.

This chapter examines the reporting techniques required of the journalist or blogger covering court stories, and the public relations practitioner working in the justice system or whose client is suddenly in the news because of a court appearance. It profiles some of the main legislative restrictions on reporting and publishing material about court proceedings. The chapter is not meant to be a one-stop shop for court reporters, because so much vital information for court reporting is covered in other chapters on the legal system, open justice, contempt of court and defamation. Court reporters must also become intimately familiar with the related legislation in their own jurisdictions because particularities vary across states and territories.

BACKGROUND AND INTERNATIONAL CONTEXT

The news media have a responsibility to society, recognised in the principle of open justice (covered in Chapter 4), to show the community that justice is being done. Some scholars, such as Ericson, Baranek and Chan (1987), argue that the media's role in reporting on the justice system fulfils a function of social control: by reporting the consequences of deviant behaviour, it sends a message to the broader society that such behaviour is unacceptable. At the same time, it should serve to demonstrate that those falsely charged will be acquitted through the effective working of the justice system. While the media's role might be seen as such an agent of social control, there is no doubt that the legal system is also inherently newsworthy, providing both public-interest and economic reasons for reporting court. Court cases—large and small—help to sell newspapers, generate website traffic and social media sharing, and boost viewing and listening audiences. As Gregory (2005: 12) explains, court reports 'appeal to the voyeur in ordinary citizens'.

The court system itself, as it has evolved, is also full of conflict. The British-based system of law reflects the medieval justice system it replaced: the duel. This adversarial system, involving two distinct sides to any case, lends itself to a news portrayal as a battle of words and evidence, with clear winners and losers. Of course, this might not be the optimum method of coverage, but it helps to explain how the news ingredient of conflict is often highlighted. Audiences enjoy the theatre of the courtroom and the drama of people's lives that has led them there—theft, arguments, assault, deceit, vice and murder. Court reporting keeps judges under public scrutiny and also help ratings and circulation.

While in some people's eyes court reporting might be about economics and entertainment, the ethical and mindful journalist or blogger trying to report court is faced with balancing these pressures against a duty to present matters of genuine public interest both fairly and accurately. In granting the public and journalists access to the courts, society is striking a balance between the right of an accused to a fair trial, privacy and an untarnished reputation, and the right of the press to report on a case so that the public can see justice taking its course. Accurate reporting of a trial also enhances its 'fairness' by putting every important aspect of the trial on the public record.

Court reporting is also a very convenient and predictable round, which traditional media organisations assign reporting staff to cover. In an era of belt-tightening throughout the Western legacy media, editors and news directors see court reporting as an efficient use of resources. Like police and parliamentary rounds, the legal system offers enough routine, scheduled events to be relied on as a regular source of news. A chief of staff or news director can be confident that a reporter sent to a courthouse will return at the end of the day with a reasonable offering of stories, on deadline. But the decision to cover the courts can bring with it logistical difficulties: there are a great many courts, and a large number of cases decided in each of them. Editors must decide whether they can cover court comprehensively, particularly when their staff budgets are already stretched to the limit. Covering only selected cases, perhaps only in part, can lead to allegations of unfair reporting from both the public and the judiciary, and possible loss of fair report protection. It can even result in a charge of contempt, as we learned from *Krystal's case* (2017) in Chapter 5, where a news reporter tried to cover a case in another city by patching together other news items and social media snippets without attending court herself.

The daily listing of cases for any court is a great equaliser of journalists. It could be compared with two people sitting down to complete the same crossword puzzle. They are faced with the same clues, and only their individual levels of skill and judgement make the difference between how accurately and quickly they can complete the puzzle. Experience in the courtroom is certainly an advantage, because it gives the reporter the skill to judge the most newsworthy items amid all the legal terminology and processes, and the edge over their colleagues when needing to access court documents and double-check information with court officers. Like any field of reporting, the secret to a successful court report is in the quality and quantity of the information on which it is based. If there is a golden rule of court reporting, it is that the reporter must actually attend the proceedings on which they are reporting. Court reports cannot be based on interviews with those who were present or, as we learned in *Krystal's case* (2017), news reports from earlier stages of the proceedings. Journalists should report only what they have seen and heard themselves in open court in the presence of the jury where one is empanelled. (For details on the laws of access to courts, along with strategies for challenging suppression orders, review those sections of Chapter 4 on open justice.)

COVERING COURT IN AUSTRALIA

Australia's nine jurisdictions (six states, two territories and the Commonwealth) vary markedly in the privileges they allow the media in reporting court, and the restrictions they place upon them. The most we can achieve in this chapter is to direct you to some of the key points of similarity and difference. More specific detail is offered in the court rules and legislation in each jurisdiction. Given that most news and current affairs reporting is now shared and published nationally and internationally—beyond state borders—it is safest to work to the most conservative law in operation at any time. For example, a Northern Territory blogger wanting to report upon a case happening in Queensland would need to study the Queensland laws very carefully before posting the blog or commenting on social media.

Photography is allowed outside the courthouse on public property, but photographers and camera personnel should approach subjects with care, given the stress they may be going through. Many a camera person has been assaulted and their equipment damaged by violent litigants, their friends or families. You should also be aware of the legal dangers of identification detailed in Chapter 5. Courts in most jurisdictions now allow accredited media to use their digital devices to record the audio of proceedings for the sake of accuracy, although the senior reporters who still write fast shorthand notes are at a distinct advantage. All courts prohibit the use of devices to take visual images or footage in the courtroom, and courts vary on the extent to which they allow journalists to use social media during a trial. Recently, the Supreme Court (including the Court of Appeal) in Victoria has experimented with streaming selected material—mostly sentencing hearings—and maintains an archive of this material (Supreme Court of Victoria, 2018). The Supreme Court of Victoria also publishes an on-line media manual, dealing with the use of electronic devices in Court (Supreme Court of Victoria, 2016). You should check to see whether there is an online or hard copy policy or set of guidelines that apply in any jurisdiction on which you are reporting, and familiarise yourself with its contents and keep a copy, either in hard copy or digital form, for ready reference at court or when filing stories. In general, however, while this area of the law continues to develop, reporters would be wise to seek permission. Digital files and notebooks must be labelled clearly, professionally maintained and safely filed and backed up, along with accompanying copies of court documents, for ready access if challenged on the accuracy of a quote or fact.

While the law requires courts to allow a certain level of access to the public and the media, much of a court reporter's success can be attributed to the relationships the reporter has developed with court and police personnel. Key court documents are the summary and charge sheets, statements of facts, court lists (or 'cause lists' in some places) and, when available, transcripts. Courthouses in major centres usually make at least the court lists available to the press—either for collection by media representatives at the start of each day's hearings or on the court's administration website. The court lists feature the names of the individuals due to face court, the time of the session in which their matter will be heard and the exact charges they are facing. Further details are available in the charge and summary sheets, which the court or police prosecutor will usually provide as a courtesy. These include basic details such as the date and time of arrest, the date of birth, address, gender and occupation of the accused, a summary of the circumstances surrounding the charge, their bail status and the name of the arresting officer. Their contents vary between states and territories.

The police prosecutor in criminal cases will also possess a statement of facts, which will prove useful as a summary of the police case, but can only be used if it has been handed up or read out in open court. Remember, except where you hear the accused or their lawyer tell the judicial officer in open court that the 'fact sheet' (sometimes referred to as the 'police facts') is agreed, it is only ever a set of untested allegations. Be very careful that the version of the fact sheet to which you refer is identical to the one handed up in court, and that you make careful note of any concessions made by police, which not infrequently result in the 'fact sheet' being amended to drop some of the allegations. If there is an amended version, that is the one you need to ask the police prosecutor to let you see, after the matter has been dealt with.

Transcripts of superior court cases are sometimes made available to the press hours after the particular session. Normally the release of the transcripts is too late to be of use to reporters working to 24/7 digital deadlines.

Journalists' level of access to these documents will vary. The requirements are spelt out in the relevant courts and evidence legislation for the Commonwealth and state or territory. Typical is section 51 of the South Australian *Magistrates Court Act 1991*, which specifies the level of access to court documents to which 'any member of the public' is entitled. It is divided into sub-section 1, which allows the public access to court records of matters tabled in open court, and sub-section 2, which allows other materials to be accessible only with the permission of the court (material taken in closed court, subject to suppression orders, filed during preliminary examinations, audio-visual content and other prescribed materials). The courts are allowed to charge a fee for inspection or copying.

As detailed in Chapter 4, journalists have very few special privileges beyond those afforded to the general public when it comes to accessing court materials. Guidelines for dealing with the media and the level of cooperation expected are, however, stated in internal Justice Department documents or practice directions circulated to judges and magistrates. Journalists would normally at least be allowed to view documents at the end of the session, to transcribe details they have been unable to get during the hearing. The spelling of names, for example, needs to be checked against all official documents as well as ancillary sources, such as online telephone directories and electoral rolls: in some jurisdictions—for example, New South Wales—there is a policy of removing much of this identifying material, apart from names, from court transcripts. In a cooperative courtroom environment, the police prosecutor or a court official will allow a reporter immediate access to all documents for them to peruse during adjournments. Overly generous or careless provision of access can have its own dangers, however. Journalists should be sure that such documents have been accepted into evidence in court, and therefore are able to form part of a fair and accurate report of what has transpired in open court. In the case of affidavit evidence, it is common for some paragraphs not to be read, and for others to be struck out by the judicial officer. Similarly, do not confuse exhibits with documents that have been marked for identification (MFI), which do not yet form part of the evidence in the case.

Court reporters need to have a reasonable understanding of the court system and its processes in dealing with a matter, whether it is civil or criminal. Journalists reporting in a particular jurisdiction should access texts dealing with legal procedure in their state or territory, which they will find draw to varying extents from the common law, state-based legislation and court rules. In recent years, most court systems have appointed public information officers (PIOs), who have the role of liaising with the media, helping set media access policies and arranging access to documents.

IN THE COURTROOM

The actual reporting of a court case can be a stressful experience for the novice. Depending on the location and facilities, the rookie journalist, public relations consultant or blogger might be faced with a combination of scant information, confusing legalese, poor acoustics and a magistrate who mumbles at 200 words per minute. The best preparation for reporters is to 'shadow' a more experienced colleague for several days to familiarise themselves with the people and the processes.

As detailed in Chapter 4, journalists have no special rights in the courtroom, but they *may* be granted some privileges as media representatives, such as priority seating, permission to take notes, carry communication devices and tweet from court, and access to documents and court personnel. These need to be used to advantage, to ensure the accuracy and fairness of a story. Public relations consultants and bloggers might only be interested in a case because of a particular client they are representing, or for a special event they are covering, and may not be afforded the special media privileges given to journalists in the same courtroom.

Whatever the situation, you should conduct yourself professionally on the court round—both in dress and behaviour. Anyone entering or leaving a courtroom while court is in session should pause at the door, face the Bench and give a short and courteous nod of the head to show respect. Any privileges afforded to the media are not usually foremost in the minds of those working in the courthouse. Remember, they are often occupied with other matters, and you should be both patient and courteous when asking for information. Officials are usually happy to provide reporters with the charge sheets, and their weekly or monthly schedule and summaries.

Never be afraid to ask lawyers or court officials for an explanation of something you do not understand. This is best done during a break in proceedings, such as a technical adjournment or a meal break. It is better that you appear ignorant to a few court personnel than report misinformation to your audiences of thousands.

Reporters should not address the Bench unless they have been invited. If the occasion arises, you should address a judge or magistrate in court as 'Your Honour'. Judges can be approached using the right channels. Judges' associates or clerks of the court will seek clarification of matters that concern you, such as the ambit of a suppression order that has been issued during a trial. It is often wise to seek a meeting with a judge to introduce yourself and explain your role if either of you is new—perhaps even write a profile of a new judicial officer. Away from court—for example, during an interview—judges are referred to simply as 'Judge'.

WRITING THE COURT REPORT

A news report on a court case must contain certain key ingredients. Their order of presentation will depend on the medium in which a journalist is working and the particular media outlet's style of presentation. The source of the information should predominantly be what was said in the courtroom, although the details on the charges and spellings should be double-checked against the official court documents.

A basic court report should usually contain these details:

- in a criminal case, the age, occupation and full address of the accused (for example, 'Samuel David Johnston, 39, builder, of Tallow Rd, New Farm'), although in some jurisdictions the accused may not be identified in relation to a range of sex offences
- in a criminal case, the accused's plea (guilty or not guilty) if it has been entered; otherwise, state that no plea has been entered
- full details of the charge or civil action, including details of how it is alleged the crime or dispute occurred
- the outcome of the case or, if continuing, a statement to that effect, including details of the next sitting
- details of the sentence or court orders
- the name of the court where the proceedings have been held
- the date of the trial.

Longer reports may also include:

- the full names of the other parties, witnesses and victims, subject to restrictions on identification detailed below
- names and titles of the judge/magistrate, prosecutor and counsel
- extracts from the addresses of counsel and the judge/magistrate
- extracts of testimony from the parties or witnesses
- any allegations, which must be countered with balancing remarks; if one party is scheduled to present its case at a future session, this should be stated
- the judge's/magistrate's comments on sentencing
- objective observation of goings on in the courtroom (e.g. the reactions of the accused on sentencing; the time taken for certain events; the attire of individuals; and a record of who was present, subject to other restrictions).

The key to a successful court report is including as much of the above information as necessary without clogging the story with legalese. Remember, news must meet the legal requirements but also be interesting to your audience. Although there is no strict formula for the writing of a court report, a safe approach to an introduction for a report about a criminal case is to use an occupational label (rather than name) for the accused and show the punishment that has resulted from a particular crime—for example, 'An unemployed fisherman who sold undersized fish at a local wharf was fined $500 in Port Pirie Magistrates Court yesterday.' This would be followed by precise details, including the full name of the accused, as detailed above.

Be careful in reporting evidence—particularly allegations. The word 'alleged' has sometimes been over-used in court reports, but it should certainly be used whenever an allegation is being made about someone that they have not yet had the opportunity to admit or deny in court. Committal hearings and opening addresses of counsel are particularly prone to outlining all sorts of allegations, which may or may not end up being supported by the evidence that emerges.

Fair court reporting requires that the reporter's own biases do not taint the report. The report should be a fair and accurate account of what any citizen would have seen and heard in the courtroom while it was open to the public. Be particularly careful of your own adjectives and adverbs in a report. State the facts and avoid the descriptors. Of course, this does not mean the writing has to be boring. Court reports can be all the more interesting for the detailed facts they offer the reader. Journalists have the discretion to choose the aspects of the case on which to focus—as long as the report is fair. There has been some debate over whether honorifics (Mr, Mrs, Ms, Dr, Rev, etc.) should be used when referring to the accused in a criminal case, with some media outlets leaving out the honorifics as a matter of style, on the pretext that all should be equal in the eyes of the law, while others include the honorifics, using the argument that to strip someone of their title can imply their guilt.

RESTRICTIONS ON COURT REPORTING

The fair report defences to both defamation (Chapter 8) and *sub judice* contempt (Chapter 5) allow for fair and accurate reportage of what is said in open court, despite the fact that coverage might damage a person's reputation or affect a trial. Anything said in court when the jury is not present (such as procedural argument over the admissibility of evidence) cannot be published. Nor will the protection apply to reports of what is done, or the contents of documents tendered, other than in open court—for example, when the court has been closed, or when an application has been heard in a judge's chambers. The onus is on the journalist under the laws of defamation and contempt to ensure that coverage of a particular case is both fair and accurate. A further qualification applies to court reports: they must be contemporaneous (current rather than historical) when it comes to contempt. In high-profile criminal trials, editors are often tempted by the idea of a 'prequel', to set the scene for further reporting. Quoting from a police fact sheet on the eve of trial when it was in fact handed up months earlier, or referring to the fact that a list of prior offences was given on a bail application months earlier as a reason for remanding (keeping) the accused in custody may not only result in the trial date being vacated, but may lead to a charge of contempt.

The requirement that a court report be fair does not mean it must be perfectly balanced. It requires that both sides of the trial be given *appropriate* coverage. If, for example, an allegation is made by the prosecution in a criminal case, the rebuttal of that allegation by the defence must also be reported. This might happen during a single day of the trial, or it might happen some days later. The fairness requirement dictates that it must be reported, not necessarily with exactly equal prominence or weighting, although coverage of one side that is out of proportion to the other runs the risk of being unfair for the purpose of the law of defamation, just as much as for the law of contempt. Once a news organisation has committed to coverage of a case, to be deemed 'fair' it must be covered through every stage of the judicial process, through to a High Court appeal if one eventuates.

Similarly, the requirement of accuracy allows a small amount of leeway. While journalists should aim to get everything correct, the courts are more concerned with the notion of 'substantial accuracy'. A report may well have some minor errors in it but not lose a defamation defence or contempt immunity, provided the inaccuracy is not 'substantial'. A substantial inaccuracy would typically be one that misstated the evidence, or confused the identity of a party or witness, as is the situation in the *Tailor's case* (Focus case 6.1). Inaccuracies related to the guilt or innocence of an individual in a criminal trial, or the liability of a party in a civil trial, are those most likely to incur the wrath of the court, the prosecuting authorities or the person concerned. While you should always aim for complete accuracy, technical inaccuracies of a minor nature are less likely to attract attention.

FOCUS CASE 6.1: *THE TAILOR'S CASE*

Zoef v Nationwide News Pty Ltd (No. 2) [2017] NSWCA 2

Zoef v Nationwide News Pty Ltd [2016] NSWCA 283

Zoef v Nationwide News Pty Ltd [2015] NSWDC 232

FACTS

A 2013 article in Sydney's *Daily Telegraph* was headed 'Tailor's Alter Ego as a Gunrunner' and described a police raid on premises in suburban Sydney, the seizure of a cache of weapons and ammunition found in the garage on the premises, and the arrest and charging of a man named Tony Zoef with firearms-related offences and his appearance in court. The intro to the story stated: 'To Sutherland Shire locals, Tony Zoef is a friendly tailor who spends his days altering their clothes. But police allege the 43-year-old space enthusiast is the mastermind behind the haul of military-grade weapons smuggled into Australia.' Unfortunately for the newspaper, the story confused the identity of two men known as 'Tony Zoef' who lived at that same address—the 86-year-old tailor who operated his business from the back of his home and his 43-year-old son who lived independently in the garage of the same property, who was not a tailor.

LAW

The older Tony Zoef sued successfully for defamation after convincing the court that his reputation had been severely damaged and that customers and neighbours now believed he was a dangerous individual who smuggled firearms. After appeal against the newspaper's 'offer of amends' defence, he was awarded $150,000 in damages. The mistaken identity occurred because the reportage of the court case was supplemented by extraneous material sourced elsewhere by the reporter. The newspaper failed in its defence that the article was a 'fair report of proceedings of public concern' under section 29 of the *Defamation Act 2005* (NSW).

LESSONS FOR JOURNALISTS

Journalists will usually avoid these kinds of basic errors if they stick to fair and accurate reportage of the material covered in the actual courtroom. Errors like this can be costly, and they can happen when reporters have either not attended the court proceedings personally or inject extraneous material into their stories.

LEGISLATIVE RESTRICTIONS

Your alarm bells should be ringing and you should be checking for restrictions relating to any of the following:

- preliminary hearings such as bail applications and committal proceedings, and matters conducted in the absence of the jury such as a *voir dire*, which is a mini-hearing conducted to decide the admissibility of evidence
- sexual offences (identification of victim and/or accused, depending on location)
- juvenile matters (identification of juvenile offenders, child witnesses, victims, family members of accused adults, wards of the state, child custody hearings, adoptions and child protection notifications, including any that relate to children who are now deceased, or adults who were children at the time of the events alleged)
- Family Court proceedings (identification of parties)
- mental health tribunal hearings and coroners' inquests into suicides
- guardianship proceedings (may involve adults, who have mental incapacity—for example, critically ill victims of crime where another family member is involved)
- jurors (approaching them, identifying them or revealing their deliberations)
- disallowed questions (for example, there are restrictions in New South Wales on reporting a question at an inquest that is objected to on the grounds of self-incrimination)
- lapsed convictions (particularly Commonwealth offences)
- national security (for example, no identification of ASIO officers or people in preventative detention)
- investigative bodies (e.g. state crime commissions)
- interviewing prisoners.

PRELIMINARY HEARINGS RESTRICTIONS

Two of the most sensitive times for media coverage of the judicial process are the early court appearances when an accused is applying for bail and when a magistrate is presiding over committal proceedings—the essential first stage of the indictable criminal process, in which the court decides whether a jury could convict an accused on the basis of the evidence the prosecution is promising (see the Time Zones chart in Table 5.1). In a committal hearing, the prosecution is called on to convince the magistrate that it has a *prima facie* case.

Bail applications are sensitive times because the prosecution, in opposing bail, will raise aspects of the accused's behaviour and criminal past, in support of having bail refused and the accused kept in custody for the duration of the trial. Naturally, such information can be highly prejudicial to a prospective jury, which should not be aware of an individual's past when deciding whether they committed this specific crime on this particular occasion. Even details like the fact that an accused is being kept in a maximum-security wing of a prison could influence a juror.

The problem with committal hearings is that the prosecution will promise to bring all sorts of evidence that might ultimately be inadmissible in the trial itself. Documents might not be acceptable as evidence, witnesses might be challenged as untrustworthy and some evidence they are hopeful of obtaining might not in the end be able to be given at trial.

For such reasons, the courts are sometimes even more cautious about the reporting of these early stages of the criminal process than they are about the ultimate trial. Magistrates are tempted to issue suppression orders over a wide range of information. Even prosecutors might ask for a suppression order on some of the material because they do not want to risk the chance of a mistrial or a retrial on the grounds that the jury that will eventually be selected was prejudiced by the preliminary hearing coverage.

Nevertheless, in most situations both bail applications and committal hearings are reportable, subject to special regulations and court rules in each state and territory. Such regulations can get very technical and vary markedly between jurisdictions, so court reporters are advised to make an appointment with their local prosecutors and magistrates to discuss the requirements and, ideally, to get a copy of the relevant sections of the magistrates' procedures manual dealing with bail hearings, committal proceedings and suppression orders.

Bail applications cannot be covered in Tasmania. Under section 37A of the *Justices Act 1959*, you can be jailed for up to six months for publishing 'an account of the proceedings on an application in respect of bail, except an account giving the fact of the application and stating that an order has been made'. *The Advocate* newspaper in Burnie, Tasmania and its editor fell into that trap, and between them they were fined $4200. Their excuse that the reporter was inexperienced was not accepted as a mitigating factor (*PANPA Bulletin*, 2000: 9).

SEXUAL OFFENCES

Sexual offence laws in all Australian jurisdictions prohibit the identification of the complainant (victim) in a sexual offence case. This is to protect complainants from further embarrassment and trauma, to encourage others to be prepared to come forward, and in some circumstances to protect them from the fear of threat or abuse during the trial. The no-identification rule means exactly that: nothing can be published that narrows down the individual closely enough that they might be identified. Sometimes the accused cannot be identified either, as that will give away the identity of the complainant. So, for example, if there is a relationship with the accused that might identify the complainant (father–daughter, teacher–pupil, doctor–patient), that relationship cannot be mentioned along with the name of the accused, for fear of identifying the complainant. Some of the legislation specifically adds that there should be no mention of the complainant's school, address or place of work.

Breach of legislation that forbids identification of victims is considered a very serious offence, and offenders can face a hefty fine or jail. Breach can also result in an action for damages, as the ABC learned in the *Jane Doe case* (2007), in which the ABC breached the Victorian *Judicial Proceedings Reports Act 1958* by broadcasting three reports that identified by name and address a husband convicted of raping his wife, and a fourth in which the wife herself was named. The reporters involved were dealt with for breaching the Act, and the victim sued the ABC for negligence, breach of its duty not to name her, invasion of privacy and breach of confidence. The case was subsequently settled by the ABC (Applegarth, 2008).

Sometimes the legislation allows for the publication of the name of a sexual offence complainant if there is no charge pending, or if the court or victim agrees to the identification.

In Queensland, the Northern Territory and South Australia, the identification restriction is taken even further by prohibiting the identification of the accused in a sexual offence until they have been committed for trial. In South Australia, the identity restriction extends to a ban on any coverage of the preliminary proceedings of a major sexual offence until the accused person has been committed for trial or sentence (*Evidence Act 1929*, s 71A). In Queensland, the preliminary proceedings can be reported, but the identity of the accused charged with a 'prescribed sexual offence' must remain secret until after they have been committed for trial–unless a judge or magistrate orders to the contrary (*Criminal Law (Sexual Offences) Act 1978*, s 7). Identification of the accused without permission can incur a two-year jail sentence. The Northern Territory has a similar provision (*Sexual Offences (Evidence and Procedure) Act*, s 7). In Tasmania, there can be no identification of a person accused of incest, unless authorised by the courts.

Media coverage of the arrest of a prominent South Australian politician on sex charges and its political fallout in April 2011 highlighted the difficulties faced by the mainstream media in attempting to comply with the law, while their online competitors in social media and the blogosphere named and shamed the accused with gay abandon. The state's newspapers performed layout and design gymnastics as they attempted to tell their readers very different stories on different pages–one about the arrest of an anonymous politician on child pornography charges and another about the important matter of personnel changes in the South Australian parliament. Journalists faced a $10,000 fine if they identified the person and their companies could be fined up to

$120,000, the same penalties they would face if they had identified the victim (Pearson, 2011).

In the pre-digital era, Queensland media had to suppress the name of former opposition leader Keith Wright when he faced sex charges in 1993, while competing outlets in other states were able to name him if their publications were not sold in Queensland. It meant residents in the NSW border town of Tweed Heads could read about Wright and see his photo while just a minute's drive away in Coolangatta, Queenslanders could only read about 'a politician' facing the charges (Pearson, 2011).

The inherent tension between what is proscribed and the newsworthiness of the story was recognised by the NSW Supreme Court in the *Religious Leader case* in 2017):

> *Neither of the publications on its face names or would appear to otherwise identify the plaintiff to anyone who might not already know the underlying facts or what occurred at the trial . . . Although details are given in the publication, they do not appear to be more than descriptive. Were the facts stated baldly without reference to locality and context, they would hardly warrant publication. To report, without more, that a religious leader had sexually assaulted girls in his care or sphere of influence would do no more than refer, in general terms, to what Wood CJ at CL (Chief Judge at Common Law) described in* R v Markuleski *(2001) 52 NSWLR 82; [2001] NSWCCA 290 at [228] as 'the regrettable reality of paedophiliac behaviour'. This reality is manifested in countless specific instances of such conduct across religious institutions, many of which have been the subject of proceedings . . . What is newsworthy about particular instances are the details: the location; the particular religion or denomination; the position of the wrongdoer or alleged wrongdoer; the age and gender of the victim or complainant; and his or her relationship with the religious leader. There is a question whether publication of these matters . . . would infringe s 578A of the* Crimes Act *. . . (which at the time was the relevant section preventing identification of sexual assault complainants).*

Similar laws exist in many overseas jurisdictions: in 2018, a Welsh newspaper editor lost his appeal against a conviction for naming a sexual offence victim after various details about the relationship between a victim and defendant were published in the newspaper's report about a man convicted of voyeurism. He had already been convicted of identifying a youth offender in another newspaper and he was ordered to pay the equivalent of more than A$10,000 in court costs and compensation (*BBC News*, 2018).

FOCUS CASE 6.2: *THE CRICKET UMPIRE CASE*

R v The Age Company Ltd and Steven Harris and Michael Gawenda [2000] TASSC 62 (9 June 2000)

FACTS

Former Test cricket umpire Steven Grant Randell was sentenced to four years' jail by the Supreme Court of Tasmania in August 1999 on fifteen counts of indecent assault against nine schoolgirls, committed when he was a teacher in the early 1980s. The case and sentence attracted considerable publicity, given the high profile of the accused. One of the complainants, 'Z', against whom three of the assaults had been committed, agreed to be interviewed and photographed outside the court after the sentencing. The following day, *The Age* newspaper, Melbourne based but also circulating in Tasmania, ran the story naming her and showing her image. The newspaper company, its editor Michael Gawenda and its editor-in-chief Steve Harris were all charged with contempt for identifying the victim of a sexual assault.

LAW

Section 103AB of Tasmania's *Evidence Act 1910* (now *Evidence Act 2001*, s 194K) protected victims of sexual offences from the consequences that may flow from media publicity. In Tasmania, this protection is imposed regardless of whether the victim seeks out the publicity. In some jurisdictions, it is a defence to a charge of breaching such a provision if the victim has given permission for the publication. Section 4(1B) of the *Judicial Proceedings Reports Act 1958* (Vic) is an example. However, the Tasmanian legislation makes it an offence regardless of whether the victim has consented to their identity being publicised, or even whether they are alive, and a breach is treated as if it were a contempt in the face of the court (s 194K(4)). Justice Evans was highly critical of the editor, Michael Gawenda, for proceeding to publish the identifying details in Tasmania despite advice that it was illegal. Gawenda and the newspaper company were fined $20,000 each, while editor-in-chief Steve Harris escaped a fine because he was not involved in the decision.

LESSONS FOR JOURNALISTS

Journalists need to take special care with the reporting of sexual offences. Even if other media organisations appear to be covering the matter, and even if the victim is agreeable to the publicity, journalists should seek out and heed legal advice on the matter before proceeding to publication. Sometimes it is a matter of halting or restricting publication into the jurisdiction of the trial (in this case, Tasmania), which is highly problematic with internet and social media publishing.

CHILDREN IN COURT

Most states and territories ban the identification of children charged with criminal offences. Jurisdictions vary in other aspects of reporting cases involving children. Court reporters first need to know the age at which young offenders will be treated as adults under the law. People now must be eighteen to be treated as an adult in all Australian jurisdictions. (Queensland fell into line with the other states in 2018 by moving seventeen-year-olds from the adult to the youth justice system.) In some places, the court will allow (or legislation provides for) the media to be present during juvenile cases, but will restrict their reportage either totally or on the point of identification of the child. Identification of children who appear as witnesses or complainants, or who are even mentioned in trials, is usually prohibited, although this varies across jurisdictions. Some states do not allow parental consent for identification of a child, but require the permission of the court before the child can be identified.

In New South Wales, the prohibition extends to deceased children, unless the 'senior available next of kin' gives permission after consulting with other family members and ascertaining that they do not object.

The relevant law—section 11 (now repealed and replaced by Div 3A) of the *Children (Criminal Proceedings) Act 1987* (NSW)—went further than that of any other state, and was widely criticised in the *SW case*. SW died while subject to child protection reports on 3 November 2007. The first newspaper story about her death appeared on 7 November. SW was named along with her parents, as no charges had been laid. Her parents were charged ten days later, on 17 November. In the intervening period, SW's name and those of her parents had been published and broadcast frequently. Once charges were laid, no further mention could be made of her name, or those of her parents. As SW had been in the care of her parents, they were her 'senior available next of kin'. A 'senior available next of kin', once charged, cannot give or withhold consent. While NSW law would have allowed a court to authorise publication of SW's name if she were still alive, there was no matching provision dealing with a child who was deceased. In the *SW case*, there was literally no one who could give consent, although the court allowed her middle name to be reported (*SW case*, 2009). The law was subsequently changed to allow the court to give permission where it believes the public interest requires it (s 15E(5)).

It should be stressed that the states vary markedly in the extent to which children are protected under non-publication provisions. For example, under section 193 of Queensland's *Child Protection Act 1999*, details that may identify a child victim of a sexual offence or a child witness to such a crime cannot be published, extending to a ban on naming the child's school. The Act was amended in 2010 to prohibit publication of the 'name, address, school or place of employment' or photo or film of a child victim of any crime, whether that offence was committed or only alleged to have been committed (s 194). Interestingly, the names of police officers and other authorised officers cannot be mentioned in such reports, which serves to demonstrate even further the need for reporters to check the specific legislation applying to these restrictions in their own states.

In South Australia, the Youth Court is a closed court and reporting by the media is restricted. Publication of information identifying a youth is not allowed, nor is any information revealing their name, address or school. Even information that would tend to identify the victim or any other person involved in the matter, without their consent, is prohibited under section 13 of the *Young Offenders Act 1993* (SA).

From time to time, jurisdictions introduce legislation allowing the 'naming and shaming' of repeat juvenile offenders (Baskin, 2014; Caldwell, 2017).

An unusual combination of facts involving both matters of a sexual nature and a child were reported by the Hobart *Mercury* in a 2010 story about the prostitution of a 12-year-old girl by her mother and her mother's male friend. While the *Mercury* anonymised the identity of the girl and her mother, it named the accused male and listed several details that might have led readers with some knowledge of the accused or the family to identify the victim. The barrister appointed as the girl's representative in her care and protection proceedings, Craig Mackie, wanted the newspaper charged for breach of the legislation prohibiting the identification of a sex crime victim (*Evidence Act 2001*, s 194K). However, the prosecutor's office refused to act, arguing the identification was too indirect to breach the provision. Mr Mackie was also on the board of the Tasmania Law Reform Institute, and he referred the matter to that body for its review. It handed down its final report in 2013, recommending several changes to tighten the Tasmanian law, particularly as it related to 'especially vulnerable' complainants: those under 18, those with a mental impairment and those with an intellectual disability (Tasmania Law Reform Institute, 2013).

ADOPTIONS, STATE WARDS AND MENTAL HEALTH PATIENTS

Strict laws apply in all jurisdictions banning the identification of parties to adoption (children, parents, guardians and adoptive parents) and also prohibiting identification by any means of wards of the state and former wards of the state. In some jurisdictions, identification is allowed with the consent of the individuals involved and/or the permission of the court. Journalists should consult with a local lawyer before identifying anyone in these situations (see Focus Case 6.3).

There are also restrictions on the reporting of mental health cases in the courts and specially constituted mental health tribunals, and the identification of the mental health patients involved (Pearson, Morton and Bennett, 2017).

FOCUS CASE 6.3: *THE NINE-YEAR-OLD BOY CASE*

The State of Western Australia v West Australian Newspapers Ltd & Anor; ex parte James Andrew McGinty MLA, Attorney-General for Western Australia [2005] WASCA 161 (23 August 2005)

FACTS

On 18 and 19 July 2004, *The Sunday Times* newspaper and *The West Australian* published stories about a nine-year-old boy who had allegedly threatened a bedridden pensioner with a tomahawk during a home invasion. Both described the boy as a ward of the state. On 20 July, *The West Australian* ran two front-page articles on the boy and discussed his case in an editorial. The coverage included a photo of the boy on a bicycle. It gave his first name and nickname, and the first name of his grandmother. The next day, it published two more articles referring to the boy by his given name and published another photograph of him. It gave the full names of his parents and grandmother, along with a photograph of his grandmother.

LAW

The court listed the identifying factors published by *The West Australian* as his first name, nickname, age, suburb of residence, a condition from which he suffered, and the names of his parents and grandmother. The separate articles from the same publisher on consecutive days added to the identification profile, the court ruled. Section 36 of the *Children's Court of Western Australia Act 1988* (now section 237 of the *Children and Community Services Act 2004*) prohibited identification of wards of the state. The publisher—West Australian Newspapers—was fined $15,000 and the editor, Paul Armstrong, was fined $5000.

LESSONS FOR JOURNALISTS

A home invasion by a nine-year-old wielding a tomahawk is certainly a major news story, with significant public interest considerations. Nevertheless, the story could have been covered without identifying the boy (or the fact that he was a state ward) and still have complied with the legislative requirements.

FAMILY COURT

The Family Court deals with child custody and matrimonial cases. Section 121 of the *Family Law Act 1975* bans publication of a report of proceedings that identifies any party or witness involved in a family law matter. The extent to which the Commonwealth has gone to specify possible identification is evident in sub-section 3 of the Act, which prohibits mention in any 'account of proceedings' (or part of proceedings) of a person's name, title, pseudonym, alias, home or work address or locality, physical description, style of dress, occupation, official or honorary position, relationship to identified friends, relatives or business acquaintances, recreational interests, political, philosophical or religious beliefs or interests, or any property they might own that might identify them. Needless to say, images of them are banned. Given the obsession with celebrity in the modern media, professional communicators should beware that there is a high risk of breaching these provisions in places where they might least expect it, such as gossip columns, breakfast radio chat shows and on social media, where they might be tempted to mention the Family Court involvement of famous people.

In 2013, the publisher of Brisbane's *Courier-Mail* newspaper pleaded guilty to a breach of the Act after it published on its front page the names and photographs of sisters at the centre of an international custody battle in May 2012. It was fined $120,000 in 2014 (*Courier-Mail*, 2014).

IDENTIFICATION OF JURORS

Identification of jurors is prohibited in most jurisdictions in Australia. The Queensland *Jury Act 1995* is typical. Section 70 of that Act prohibits the publication of any information identifying a juror or information about what went on during a jury's deliberations. The media cannot seek a juror or former juror's disclosure of such information. Under the Queensland Act, jurors cannot disclose information about jury deliberations; however, they can identify themselves as former jurors after proceedings have ended and can be identified with their consent.

Similar provisions exist in other jurisdictions. The Western Australian legislation specifically prohibits jurors being photographed or drawn, although this is implied by the non-identification provisions of the other states' legislation. For New South Wales, see Focus Case 6.4.

FOCUS CASE 6.4: *THE JOHN LAWS CASE*

R v Laws [2000] NSWSC 885 (5 September 2000)

FACTS

A woman who was given the pseudonym 'Mrs Hansen' had sat on a jury during a murder trial. The jury had returned a verdict of 'not guilty' after deliberating for three days. Mrs Hansen was deeply upset about the verdict and felt she had been forced into it by the browbeating and stubbornness of the other jurors. After the verdict, she telephoned the murder victim's widow and told her she regretted the outcome and that she had not agreed with the verdict. A family friend contacted the wife of prominent Sydney talkback host John Laws to tell her the juror (Mrs Hansen) was actually a friend of the Laws family. Mrs Laws phoned her husband, who in turn asked his personal assistant to phone Mrs Hansen to ask her to speak on the *John Laws Program*. She agreed on the condition that it be known she was not the initiator of the interview. The interview went to air a short time later, during which Mr Laws asked the juror how long they had deliberated and what the dynamics of the jury room were. In court, Laws argued that he thought he was allowed to talk to the juror because the case had finished and she had already spoken to the victim's wife and (he mistakenly thought) a Sydney newspaper.

LAW

Mr Laws was in violation of section 68A of the *Jury Act 1977* (NSW), which states, 'A person shall not solicit information from, or harass, a juror or former juror for the purpose of obtaining information on the deliberations of a jury.' The offence carries a maximum penalty of seven years' jail. Justice James Wood pointed out (at para. 29), while former jurors can disclose details of their deliberations of their own volition after a trial, they cannot be approached by others seeking this information. Justice Wood found little benefit in fining Laws, who was already a multimillionaire. He also found it inappropriate to jail him. Instead, he convicted him and sentenced him to a suspended fifteen-month jail term, meaning that he would serve the prison sentence only if he reoffended within the fifteen-month period.

LESSONS FOR PROFESSIONAL COMMUNICATORS

As Justice Wood explained in his sentencing remarks, this story had fallen into John Laws' lap because, as it turned out, the juror was in fact a friend of the Laws family. The verdict had been the lead item in *The Daily Telegraph* newspaper that morning and on Alan Jones' talkback breakfast program. He could not resist the temptation to call the juror and interview her. The lesson for journalists and other professional communicators is that they should seek legal advice before having any contact with a juror or identifying a juror in any way. Laws vary between states, so it is wise to check the state-based law before proceeding. In New South Wales, if the former juror had taken the initiative and approached Laws independently, the broadcaster would have been free to broadcast her remarks.

WITHDRAWN QUESTIONS AND THE *VOIR DIRE*

Sometimes questions will be put to a witness in the presence of the jury and promptly withdrawn by the counsel who has asked them, either voluntarily or after an objection from the other party. The jury is asked to erase this question from their minds. It cannot be reported by the media, because the question is deleted from the record of the proceedings. Under the *Coroner's Act 2009* (NSW), you cannot report the question, or even the fact that it was objected to (let alone the answer) if a witness objects on the basis of a claim of privilege against self-incrimination. The (Bathurst) *Western Advocate* narrowly avoided a finding that it had breached an earlier version of this law by reporting that police had declined to answer questions in relation to a fatal pursuit (*Borland's case*, 2006).

Journalists are restricted to coverage of proceedings in open court in the presence of a jury, and the court can be closed or the jury can be absent for a range of reasons. A situation to be wary of is the *voir dire*—a mini-hearing where the jury is absent, so lawyers can debate the admissibility of evidence. These cannot be reported.

INTERVIEWING PRISONERS

In addition to the restrictions on reporting at the police and court end of the judicial process, there are varying restrictions on reporting at the other end of the process—when prisoners are in custody. Journalists have run foul of state- and territory-based restrictions on the interviewing of prisoners in recent years. In Queensland, section 132 of the *Corrective Services Act 2006* makes it an offence to interview, record or photograph a prisoner inside or outside a corrective services facility (or photograph a part of the prison) without the permission of the authorities. Since 1996, at least six journalists have been charged under this Queensland law or its earlier version (Johnston, 2001). Documentary-maker Anne Delaney was given a twelve-month $750 good behaviour bond under the provision in 2005 for allegedly interviewing a prisoner at the Brisbane Women's Correctional Centre (Delaney, 2006). In Chapter 2, we considered the *Palm Island Parole case* (2012), where Indigenous activist Lex Wotton appealed to the High Court, arguing that his parole conditions and the Queensland restriction on interviewing prisoners under section 132(1)(a) of the *Corrective Services Act 2006* infringed his freedom of communication about government or political matters. The court ruled the restrictions were reasonable and served a legitimate end, closing the door on that avenue of objection for free expression advocates. That was in contrast to two decisions by the New Zealand High Court in 2015 and 2016 upholding a journalist's right to interview a convicted murderer in light of the freedom of expression guarantees under section 14 of that country's New Zealand Bill of Rights Act (BORA) (*Prison Interview case*, 2016).

In 2001, the Herald and Weekly Times failed in an application to the Victorian Supreme Court for a court order instructing the Correctional Services Commissioner to allow a Melbourne *Herald Sun* investigative journalist to interview a prisoner at Barwon Prison (*Correctional Services case*, 2001). Justice Eames ruled that the commissioner's refusal of the interview should stand on the reasons given, despite the newspaper's arguments that substantial issues of public interest were at stake and that the decision limited the prisoner's rights to free expression. Again, communicators should check the wording of the law in their particular state or territory.

SUICIDE

Section 474.29A of the Commonwealth Criminal Code makes it an offence to use a 'carriage service' (the internet, a wire service or a broadcast medium) to publish material that promotes or provides instruction on a method of committing suicide, although a qualifying provision would exempt media discussion of euthanasia so long as there is no intent to provide instruction on a suicide method. Note also that, under section 75 of the *Coroner's Act 2009* (NSW), a report of an inquest may not be published where the Coroner makes a finding that death was self-inflicted, except in a form approved by the Coroner. Again, publication restrictions on Coroners' proceedings vary across jurisdictions. Section 71 of the Coroners Act 2006 (New Zealand) prohibits publication of the method, suspected method or any detail that might suggest the method of self-inflicted death, or even a description of the death as a suicide. For guidance on the reporting of suicide, journalists should consult Mindframe for Media (<www.mindframe-media.info/for-media>), a federally funded project designed to encourage responsible coverage of suicide and mental illness.

DIGITAL DIMENSIONS

The reality is that internet and social media publications defy borders, so bloggers and social media users should work to the most conservative laws applying to the situation. Courts in jurisdictions vary with regard to whether journalists can take communication devices into court and use social media without formal permission from the court, so this should be clarified by all who plan to cover court proceedings. The reality is also that internet and social media publications, content aggregators and search engines like Google defy time, so that a publication of material given at a bail hearing which discloses details or prior conviction, but might once have disappeared for all practical purposes well in advance of trial, may remain 'live' at the time a jury is empanelled. Equally, an item reporting a conviction that remains 'live' when the conviction has in fact been overturned on appeal, but is not amended to reflect that fact, could leave you exposed.

Bloggers and public relations consultants will need to deal with the courts and the justice system in the same kinds of circumstances as reporters do, but perhaps without the same privileges granted to journalists under some laws. They might want to report or comment upon trials in their area of interest, but they might not have privileged access to the courtroom and court papers or the protection of sources afforded to reporters in some jurisdictions.

Despite the existence of the 'open justice' principle, online writers face restrictions on their reporting of crimes and other matters before the court. Your behaviour, postings and comments can lead to substantial fines or even jail terms if you breach the laws of contempt of court or legislative bans on reporting, or identify certain people in the courtroom.

The temptation for the gossip or sports blogger might be to mention prohibited court material in postings about celebrities—perhaps via family or friends—without being aware of the court restrictions on identification. Heavy fines and even jail terms apply in some places if you break these prohibitions. At the very least, you need to check what bans apply in both your own jurisdiction and the place of the court proceedings before firing off those words or images.

RED-LIGHT ZONES FOR CRIME AND COURT REPORTERS

- Point of arrest—defamation and contempt dangers
- *Sub judice*—no pre-judging or publishing previous charges, recycled preliminary hearing coverage (especially trial 'previews' on eve of hearing), confessions (or police 'verbals'), media 'walks', police media releases and conferences, witness interviews or proceedings in absence of jury
- Identification evidence—no photos/video where ID may be an issue

- Announcement of inquest/objections based on self-incrimination
- No disallowed questions
- Beware of the hung jury—continue to treat everything as *sub judice*
- 'Mistrial'/jury discharge—continue to treat everything as *sub judice*
- 'Back-to-back' trials where the accused faces other charges
- Separate trials of co-accused
- Retrials
- Suppression orders
- Sexual offences—no identification of victim anywhere and further restrictions on accused ID in some jurisdictions
- Children and juveniles (no ID)
- No witness interviews
- No bail reports in Tasmania
- No Family Court ID
- No juror ID or reports of deliberations (except New South Wales, with consent)
- No prisoner interviews
- No suicide methods

TIPS FOR MINDFUL PRACTICE

- Introduce yourself to the local judges, magistrates, police prosecutors and court personnel. It is better to be dealing with officials who know you and understand your needs than with those who try to follow their regulations to the letter.
- Make yourself aware of regulations featured in the legislation applying to the particular court and in court rules and procedures manuals,

particularly on whether you can use digital devices in court for recording or communication.

- Never report on a court case unless you are there to see and hear the proceedings in person.
- Contact the public information officers for your state or territory and ask them for any information on the court system and procedures they might make available to you.
- On no account approach jurors during a trial. Professional communicators should seek legal advice before dealing with jurors in any way, even if the jurors have approached them.
- Take special care with the reporting of bail applications and committal hearings.
- Be on special alert for restrictions on reporting. Alarm bells should be ringing in cases involving sexual assault, children, family law, state wards, adoption, guardianship or the court's protective jurisdiction, mental health hearings, protected witnesses (including police informers) and national security.
- Take legal advice and refer to the legislation before attempting to interview a prisoner.

IN A NUTSHELL

- Journalists report on the courts for a range of reasons, including a duty to society, the newsworthiness of the court list, the circulation incentive and the sheer convenience of having predictable news occurring at a single location.
- Most of the media's elevated status in the courtroom is one of privilege rather than right, and much depends on the reporter's relationship with court officers, who can wield considerable power.
- If recording or live tweeting are banned in court, the notebook and any available court documents become the basic research tools of the court reporter. Both digital and paper records must be backed up and filed safely.

- Court public information officers have the role of liaising with the media, helping set media access policies and arranging access to documents.
- Defamation and contempt laws mean that journalists are restricted when reporting a court case to a fair and accurate report of the proceedings conducted in open court while the jury is present.
- A news report on a court case must contain certain key ingredients. Their order of presentation will depend on the medium in which a journalist is working and the particular media outlet's style of presentation.
- A bare minimum criminal court report must contain the name, age, occupation and address of the accused, the plea, the full charge, an account of how the crime occurred, the result, the sentence, the name of the court and the date of the trial.
- The reporter must actually attend the proceedings on which they are reporting. Court reports cannot be based on interviews with those who were present, earlier coverage, social media posts or stories posted by other media.
- Key court documents are the summary and charge sheets, statements of facts, court lists and, when available, transcripts.
- Documents must have been tendered and admitted into evidence or read out (or be taken as having been read) in open court. The level of access to these documents will vary.
- Special restrictions usually apply to reporting of sexual offences, matters involving children, family law and mental health proceedings, terrorism trials and interviews with prisoners.
- Reporters also need to beware of closed courts, mini-hearings conducted in the absence of the jury (*voir dire*), withdrawn questions during a trial and suppression orders.
- In most places, both bail applications and committal hearings are reportable, subject to the special regulations and court rules in each state and territory, such as Tasmania's ban on the coverage of bail proceedings, and in Queensland, South Australia and the NT relating to identification of those accused of sex offences, or reporting of evidence in such a case.

DISCUSSION QUESTIONS

6.1 Find three reports of the same major court case in three different media outlets. Compare and contrast the ways in which the journalists have reported the case.

6.2 Spend the day in your local court to get a feel for the types of cases being heard in the different courtrooms. Practise your reporting by taking notes and writing up a brief story on one of the cases.

6.3 Search <www.austlii.edu.au> for a short sexual assault, murder or armed robbery judgment or sentencing remarks. Write a ten-sentence story based on this judgment to practise your reporting skills.

6.4 Find the legislation for your state or territory controlling the reporting of sexual offences, children in court, jurors' deliberations or coronial inquests into suicides, and explain how their operation might affect your reporting.

6.5 Go to the Victoria Supreme Court site and read its Media and Reporting Policy, <http://assets.justice.vic.gov.au/supreme/resources/6ebfaf77-d0b8-4c35-bb9c-a78f0699d3bc/mediapoliciespractices2016_v1.pdf>. What parts are most likely to affect the day-to-day activities of reporters or bloggers? Check another jurisdiction, to see whether the courts there have a written policy available online. What similarities or differences are there between the two?

6.6 You overhear a juror in a high-profile murder trial explaining to friends at a social barbecue that the jury foreman bullied her and the other jurors into deciding on a guilty verdict. What steps will you take as a reporter or news blogger, and what issues arise?

REFERENCES

Applegarth, P. 2008, 'RIP Jane Doe: What now for invasion of privacy?', *Gazette of Law and Journalism*, 25 March, <www.glj.com.au/76-Category?cat=199&year=2008>.

Baskin, B. 2014, 'First child named by Queensland Court of Appeal under new "name and shame" legislation fails in appeal bid', *Courier-Mail*, 2 May, <www.couriermail.com.au/news/queensland/first-child-named-by-queensland-court-of-appeal-under-new-name-and-shame-legislation-fails-in-appeal-bid/story-fnihsrf2-1226903536014>.

BBC News 2018, '*Ceredigion Herald* editor Thomas Sinclair loses court appeal', 22 January, <www.bbc.com/news/uk-wales-mid-wales-42777235>.

Caldwell, F. 2017, 'LNP to "name and shame" youth offenders as young as 10', *Brisbane Times*, 18 August, <www.brisbanetimes.com.au/national/queensland/lnp-to-name-and-shame-youth-offenders-as-young-as-10-20170818-gxz2ft.html>.

Courier-Mail 2014, '*The Courier-Mail* has been fined $120,000 for illegally identifying family involved in court custody battle', 24 March, <www.couriermail.com.au/news/queensland/the-couriermail-has-been-fined-120000-for-illegally-identifying-family-involved-in-court-custody-battle/story-fnihsrf2-1226863205754>.

Delaney, A. 2006, 'An interview with a jail sentence', in *The Media Muzzled: Australia's 2006 Press Freedom Report*, Media, Entertainment and Arts Alliance, Sydney, p. 15.

Ericson, R.V., Baranek, P.M. and Chan, J.B.L. 1987, *Visualizing Deviance: A Study of News Organisations*, Open University Press, Milton Keynes.

Gregory, P. 2005, *Court Reporting in Australia*, Cambridge University Press, Melbourne.

Johnston, J. 2001, 'Public relations in the courts: A new frontier', *Australian Journal of Communication*, 28(1), 109–22.

PANPA Bulletin 2000, 'Court blunder sparks journo training', 187 (February), 9.

Pearson, M. 2011, 'South Australia's antiquated sex ID rule', *journlaw.com*, 4 May, <http://journlaw.com/2011/05/04/south-australias-antiquated-sex-id-law>.

Pearson, M., Morton, T. and Bennett, H. 2017, 'Mental health and the media: A case study in open justice', *Journal of Media Law* (UK), 9(2), 232–58.

Supreme Court of Victoria 2016, *Victoria Court Media Policy, 2016*, <www.supremecourt.vic.gov.au/contact-us/media-centre/media-policies-and-practices>.

—— 2018, 'Audio and video webcasts', <www.supremecourt.vic.gov.au/contact-us/media-centre/audio-and-video-webcasts>.

Tasmania Law Reform Institute (TLRI) 2013, *Protecting the Anonymity of Victims of Sexual Crimes*, TLRI, Hobart, <www.utas.edu.au/__data/assets/pdf_file/0011/443774/Final_Report.pdf>.

CASES CITED

Borland's case: Borland v NSW Deputy State Coroner & Ors [2006] NSWSC 982; *Attorney-General v Borland & 2 Ors* [2007] NSWCA 201 for a summary of the factual background, <www.austlii.edu.au/cgi-bin/sinodisp/au/cases/nsw/NSWSC/2006/982.html>, <www.austlii.edu.au/cgi-bin/sinodisp/au/cases/nsw/NSWCA/2007/201.html>.

Correctional Services case: The Herald and Weekly Times Ltd v Correctional Services Commissioner [2001] VSC 329 (13 September 2001), <www.austlii.edu.au/au/cases/vic/VSC/2001/329.html>.

Cricket Umpire case: R v The Age Company Ltd and Steven Harris and Michael Gawenda [2000] TASSC 62 (9 June 2000), <www.austlii.edu.au/au/cases/tas/supreme_ct/2000/62.html>.

Jane Doe case: Doe v ABC & Ors [2007] VCC 281 (3 April 2007).

John Laws case: R v Laws [2000] NSWSC 885 (5 September 2000), <www.austlii.edu.au/au/cases/nsw/supreme_ct/2000/885.html>.

Krystal's case: DPP v Johnson & Yahoo!7 [2016] VSC 699 (28 November 2016), <www.austlii.edu.au/cgi-bin/viewdoc/au/cases/vic/VSC/2016/699.html>; *DPP v Johnson & Yahoo!7 (No. 2)* [2017] VSC 45 (17 February 2017), <www.austlii.edu.au/cgi-bin/viewdoc/au/cases/vic/VSC/2017/45.html>.

Nine-year-old Boy case: The State of Western Australia v West Australian Newspapers Ltd & Anor; ex parte James Andrew McGinty MLA, Attorney-General for Western Australia [2005] WASCA 161, <www.austlii.edu.au/au/cases/wa/WASCA/2005/161.html>.

Palm Island Parole case: Lex Patrick Wotton v The State of Queensland & Anor [2012] HCA 2, <www.austlii.edu.au/cgi-bin/sinodisp/au/cases/cth/HCA/2012/2.html>.

Prison Interview case: Watson v Chief Executive of the Department of Corrections [2016] NZHC 1996, <www.austlii.edu.au/cgi-bin/viewdoc/nz/cases/NZHC/2016/1996.html>; *Watson v Chief Executive of the Department of Corrections* [2015] NZHC 1227, <www.nzlii.org/nz/cases/NZHC/2015/1227.html>.

Religious Leader case: Doe v Fairfax Media Publications Pty Limited [2017] NSWSC 1153 (30 August 2017), <www.austlii.edu.au/cgi-bin/viewdoc/au/cases/nsw/NSWSC/2017/1153.html>.

SW case: R v BW & SW (No. 3) [2009] NSWSC 1043 (2 October 2009), <www.austlii.edu.au/cgi-bin/sinodisp/au/cases/nsw/NSWSC/2009/1043.html>; *R v BW & SW (No. 2)* [2009] NSWSC 595, <www.austlii.edu.au/au/cases/nsw/supreme_ct/2009/595.html>.

Tailor's case: Zoef v Nationwide News Pty Ltd (No. 2) [2017] NSWCA 2, <www.austlii.edu.au/cgi-bin/viewdoc/au/cases/nsw/NSWCA/2017/2.html>; *Zoef v Nationwide News Pty Ltd* [2016] NSWCA 283, <www.austlii.edu.au/cgi-bin/viewdoc/au/cases/nsw/NSWCA/2016/283.html>; *Zoef v Nationwide News Pty Ltd* [2015] NSWDC 232, <www.austlii.edu.au/cgi-bin/viewdoc/au/cases/nsw/NSWDC/2015/232.html>.

PART 3

THE MEDIA AND REPUTATIONS

CHAPTER 7

Identifying defamation

KEY CONCEPTS

Defamation
The wrong of injuring another's reputation without good reason or justification.

Imputation
The defamatory meaning conveyed by the published material.

Tort
A legal term describing a civil wrong incurring a legal liability, where a person's action (for example, publishing a defamatory publication) causes someone else to suffer loss or harm.

Criminal libel
A rare version of defamation, prosecuted as a crime, with criminal penalties of jail terms or fines applying. Sometimes misused as a form of censorship.

Limitation period
The statutory period during which someone can bring a legal action. In Australia, people have one year from the time of publication to launch a defamation action.

Australian actor Rebel Wilson was the toast of Hollywood after her success with the 2015 screen hit *Pitch Perfect 2*. But the jubilation evaporated–along with potential new movie roles–after allegations in the top-selling magazine *Woman's Day* and on associated websites portraying her as a serial liar went viral. She sued for defamation over the reputational harm she had suffered and the Victorian Supreme Court compensated her in 2017 with a record $4.75 million damages, later reduced on appeal to $600,000 (*Rebel's case*, 2017 and 2018).

The case showed why defamation law is of special concern to journalists and other professional communicators who are in the business of publishing news and information about people and their activities. When stories make an audience think less of a person–damaging their reputation in the eyes of others–the person is said to have been defamed.

Defamation is the most common area of litigation for writers of all kinds across new and old media. The *Macquarie Concise Dictionary* (Butler, 2006) defines defamation as 'the wrong of injuring another's reputation without good reason or justification'. Just by using a standard dictionary, we learn two crucial things about defamation:

- It consists of injury to another person's reputation.
- In some circumstances, it may be justifiable.

In deciding whether injury to a person's reputation was 'justified' or 'with good reason', courts ask whether there is enough legally admissible evidence to establish a defence. We return to *Rebel's case* later as an example of the basic elements of defamation (Focus Case 7.1) and in the next chapter when we examine why the publisher's defences failed and why the court awarded such a large sum of damages.

This chapter is not written for lawyers: it is written for professional communicators. It is aimed at introducing you to defamation law, showing you how it affects the working practices of professional communicators and bloggers, and is intended to equip you with the ability to recognise risks and to learn when to seek legal advice.

Law school courses covering defamation as a topic emphasise legal reasoning, and students learn by extensive reading of case law. However, this book has other goals, and thus it approaches the topic differently. Only the most relevant cases will be mentioned. Some cases, like *Rebel's case*, may establish a journalistic or public relations point rather than a legal one. Through this practical approach, you should gain an effective working knowledge of this crucial area of media law.

It is important to understand that defamation is almost a daily occurrence. We defame someone whenever we say or write something that damages their reputation. Consider the following scenarios:

- You return from holiday with friends and review images on Facebook. One features a friend in an alcoholic stupor, in a state of undress. You share the image with your Facebook friends.
- You ask your former employer for a reference but miss out on the job. It turns out that in her reference she accused you of lateness, dishonesty and sexual promiscuity.
- A former public relations client of yours (with whom you parted company on bad terms) has directed a film that opens at the local cinema. You write a scathing review of the movie for a regional newspaper.
- Almost everyone in town believes the mayor is corrupt. You phone a talkback radio host and recite a petition on air, calling for her resignation on the grounds of financial malpractice.

Clearly, in each case there is real potential for someone's reputation to be damaged. Yet, depending on the circumstances, there may be a defence available. The key to navigating defamation is being able to identify both the potential for defamation (the subject of this chapter) and the most straightforward defences (covered in Chapter 8). The most any journalist or professional communicator can hope for is to know when to sound the alarm bells and call for expert legal advice.

Journalists and professional communicators need to be mindful of what they report or write about others. A person's reputation is essentially the sum of other people's perceptions of their character and integrity. Once these have been damaged, they are almost impossible to repair. The primary mechanism used by the courts when defamation is proven is to award money to compensate for damage to reputation and for the related hurt (and financial loss, as initially awarded in *Rebel's case*), but also to provide an element of vindication. Once the notion has been planted in people's minds that someone is a liar, a cheat, sexually promiscuous, unfaithful, corrupt, incompetent or otherwise disreputable, however, it is difficult to erase. Of course, sometimes hard truths need to be told about people for the greater good of society. Deciding whether to do so or not needs to involve an informed ethical and legal decision by the professional communicator.

BACKGROUND AND INTERNATIONAL CONTEXT

Defamation terminology and laws vary between countries. You will sometimes see this area of the law referred to as 'libel' (its permanently published form) or 'slander' (when the words are spoken). Mass media products, websites, blogs and social media postings fall into the 'libel' category in countries that use these terms. Australia did away with that distinction in its uniform national defamation scheme, introduced in 2005. Now we use the one term encompassing both slander and libel: 'defamation'.

Defamation is categorised by lawyers as a 'tort'—the area of the law where a citizen can file suit over a 'civil wrong' that has been done to them. If they win, the courts will usually award them a sum of damages in compensation and may sometimes make some other order—perhaps stopping further publication (an order known as a 'permanent injunction') or even ordering that posts or websites be removed or closed down (usually known as a 'take-down order').

You can still be jailed or fined in some places for 'criminal defamation'. In some countries, criminal libel or 'seditious libel' (defamation of the state) is used as a tool of censorship against the media and dissidents by corrupt politicians, business leaders and government officials. Criminal defamation still exists in many liberal democracies, including the United States and Australia, but in general prosecutions are as rare as they are unsuccessful, and are usually reserved for poisonous, malicious attacks on someone's character by someone who lacks the money to pay damages—the kind of person the courts have called a 'man of straw'.

In some countries, large corporations and government agencies can sue for libel, but in Australia only private citizens and very small companies and not-for-profit organisations can bring a defamation action. Related actions such as 'injurious falsehood' or 'trade libel' are available to corporations—with a higher burden of proof on plaintiffs (those doing the suing). Even death is no escape in some places (including Tasmania), where a deceased person's estate can sue and you can still be held liable for publications about someone who has died.

Defamation law everywhere requires proof that your publication has been made to at least one other person. It must go to this third person before anyone's reputation can be damaged, because reputation is a person's standing in the eyes of others. In other words, if you insult someone in a direct message (DM) to them alone on Twitter or Facebook, you have not defamed them. But if you repeat the slur to just one other Twitter follower or Facebook friend, your victim might then have an action in defamation.

Courts can award substantial damages to someone who has been injured in some way because of your defamatory publication (whether that is in a public forum, print, broadcast, on the internet or in social media). The fact that you did not mean to defame them will not protect you. Under the principle of 'strict liability', only your act of publication needs to be intentional, even if you did not intend to damage a person's reputation or identify an actual person.

Defamation laws throughout the United Kingdom and its former colonies, including Australia, are a mix of centuries-old case law (the 'common law') and legislation. Historically, people's reputations were considered part of their spiritual beings and defamation claims were brought in the ecclesiastical (church) courts. Over time, the role of the ecclesiastical courts diminished and defamation fell within the ambit of the King's Courts, called the courts of common law. In recent decades, the UK courts have had some of their decisions challenged via the European Convention on Human Rights (Council of Europe, 2010) and the UK's *Defamation Act 2013* reformed its laws. But the guiding principles of defamation remain similar across most places in the world formerly governed by the British. Most draw upon English case law for their definitions of defamation and offer the basic defences we cover in Chapter 8: truth, fair reporting on protected occasions, fair comment and qualified privilege (public interest). Most also still have criminal libel on their statutes.

In the United States, the key elements of a defamation action are somewhat different, and require:

- publication to one other than the person defamed
- of a false statement of fact
- that is understood as
  - being of and concerning the plaintiff, and
  - tending to harm the reputation of the plaintiff.

If the plaintiff is a public figure, they must also prove 'actual malice'.

Two important differences between the US position and British-Commonwealth law (the law in Australia) are that in the United States the plaintiff needs to prove that what was published was false (a fact which the law assumes here, in favour of the person complaining) and that US public figures have to prove that the publication was malicious.

This is because, in the United States, the concepts of free expression and a free press are embedded in law. The First Amendment to the US Constitution states that, 'Congress shall make no law . . . abridging the freedom of speech, or of the press.' The US courts have examined what this means through a series of significant decisions, the most notable being *Sullivan's case (New York Times v Sullivan)* in 1964, which established that plaintiffs who were 'public officials' had to prove a media defendant had acted with 'actual malice' if they were to win a defamation action, even if the defamatory allegation was untrue.

The test has since been expanded in the United States to apply to any 'public figure'—essentially anyone who is well known to the public, has taken on some public role or has participated voluntarily in some controversy. While the principle has some difficulties in definition and application, the media in the United States have been free to publish criticism of virtually anyone in the public domain, even if the criticism proves to be unfounded, so long as they have not acted maliciously or in 'reckless disregard' of the truth.

Australia has no such element to its Constitution. Nevertheless, as we learned in Chapter 2, the High Court handed down landmark decisions in 1992 that identified in the Constitution an implied freedom to communicate on matters of government. In 1994 and 1997, this notion was developed further in important cases (discussed in Chapters 2 and 8). While this development initially suggested a more liberal approach, it fell far short of the US defence, because the onus remained upon the media to satisfy a high standard of 'reasonableness', rather than on the plaintiff (as in the United States) to prove falsity and establish malice or 'reckless disregard'.

The European Convention on Human Rights protects free expression at Article 10, but states that it is qualified by 'the protection of the reputation or the rights of others'. The nations of Europe handle this tension in different ways. Some nations follow the British approach, while continental European countries typically offer plaintiffs a choice of criminal or civil libel actions and procedures.

Most Asian countries have defamation laws in one form or another, which is not surprising given the shame attached to a 'loss of face' in many cultures. African countries generally echo British or French defamation law, depending on their colonial origins. South Africa also has a criminal offence for the deliberate injury of another's dignity—called *crimen injuria.* Latin and South American countries roughly pattern their laws on their historical links with Spain and Portugal, while those of much of the Caribbean reflect that area's British heritage.

AUSTRALIAN LAW AND BACKGROUND

Until 2006, defamation laws differed markedly across the eight Australian states and territories. After pressure from the federal government, model national defamation laws were introduced in all states and territories in 2005 and 2006. Now professional communicators and students can deal with defamation laws that are very similar across the nation.

That legislation is known as the *Defamation Act 2005*, other than in the Australian Capital Territory (ACT), where it forms Chapter 9 of the *Civil Law (Wrongs) Act 2002* and in the Northern Territory, where it is the *Defamation Act 2006.* Sections are also numbered differently in the ACT and Northern Territory legislation, and sometimes differently in South Australia. Where the legislation is mentioned in this book, it will be referred to as the *Defamation Act* and the relevant state section that applies is provided. Only the main sections of legislation are referred to, as we are more concerned with core principles and the way they affect journalists, rather than the minutiae of individual sub-sections that professional communicators should study closely as they apply to their particular jurisdiction.

Despite the near-uniform reforms, a few notable differences remain between jurisdictions, mainly relating to the role of judge and jury. Juries are not used in civil trials in South Australia, the ACT or the Northern Territory, and generally not in cases brought in the Federal Court, as is increasingly the case. It is important to note that while all the states and territories adopted the new defamation laws, removing existing legislation, they did not do away with the common law (or 'general law'), but expressly preserved it under section 6 of the *Defamation Act* wherever it did not conflict with the legislation. This means the case law developed over centuries and existing defences available under the common law still apply in addition to the requirements and the defences the *Defamation Act* sets out in writing today. Many of the basic concepts with which we deal in this chapter are still based on historic case law. In particular, High Court decisions in defamation cases—particularly those from the 1990s relating to the implied constitutional freedom of political discussion—retain their importance.

DEFAMATION AS DEFINED IN AUSTRALIA

Some essential definitions appear in section 4 of the *Defamation Act*. The key definition describes defamatory 'matter', which includes:

> *(a) an article, report, advertisement or other thing communicated by means of a newspaper, magazine or other periodical; and*
> *(b) a program, report, advertisement or other thing communicated by means of television, radio, the internet or any other form of electronic communication; and*
> *(c) a letter, note or other writing; and*
> *(d) a picture, gesture or oral utterance; and*
> *(e) any other thing by means of which something may be communicated to a person.*

Further:

> electronic communication *includes a communication of information in the form of data, text, images or sound (or any combination of these) by means of guided or unguided electromagnetic energy, or both.*

This definition is important because it is inclusive, and covers any possible material professional communicators might produce as part of their work in traditional or new media, as does the common law. The High Court held in *Gutnick's case* (2002) that defamation occurs wherever defamatory material is downloaded and read, meaning a publisher can be sued in a jurisdiction different from that of their home or main office, or where the material was uploaded.

Journalists need to analyse material in a two-step process, just as the courts do when considering a defamation case. The key questions they need to ask are:

- Is the material I am about to publish defamatory?
- If so, is there a defence available?

This chapter will give you the tools with which to answer the first question. It examines the crucial ingredients that any lawyer or educated news producer looks for in deciding whether there is any substance in a threat of defamation action. Chapter 8 goes on to consider the second question.

The classic definitions of defamatory material are that it:

- damages a person's reputation by exposing them to 'hatred, contempt or ridicule' (*Parmiter's case*, 1840, at 342)
- 'tend[s] to lower the plaintiff in the estimation of right-thinking members of society generally' (*Sim's case*, 1936, at 671)
- 'cause[s] him [the plaintiff] to be shunned or avoided' (*Youssoupoff's case*, 1934, at 587).

The High Court summed up in simple terms the modern definition of defamation in the *2UE case* in 2009 when the majority stated:

> *A person's reputation may therefore be said to be injured when the esteem in which that person is held by the community is diminished in some respect. (at para. 3)*

In that case, it was also importantly decided that the concept of 'reputation' in defamation law included all aspects of a person's standing in the community, including someone's business or professional reputation in addition to their moral, ethical or social standing (paras 42–8).

Matter can still be defamatory if it holds someone up to 'ridicule'—that is, prompts others to make fun of them, but only if it does so in such a way that their reputation is damaged. Some cases in which this question has arisen include the following:

- *ET's case (1991).* A magazine photograph of a Rugby League player damaged his reputation and exposed him to ridicule by portraying his genitals.
- *Berkoff's case (1996).* An article in the UK *Sunday Times* called an actor 'hideous looking' and repulsive, worse looking even than

Frankenstein's monster. It was held capable of damaging his reputation by exposing him to ridicule.

- *Boyd's case (1980).* The NSW Supreme Court held that a Rugby League footballer was held up to ridicule when a newspaper described him as 'fat'.
- *Hanson-Young's case (2013). A* politician's head was superimposed on to the body of a young woman in lingerie, seen posing in the open doorway of a motel room. This was held to be capable of damaging her reputation by holding her up to ridicule.
- *Dennis Denuto case (2015).* A respected solicitor brought a claim in defamation over words which referred to him as 'Denis Denuto', a fictional solicitor from the Australian film *The Castle,* a character described by the trial judge as 'likeable and well-intentioned . . . but unprepared, lacking in knowledge and judgment, incompetent and unprofessional'. The words were found to have been defamatory, but a rare defence of triviality succeeded. An appeal failed.

Whether particular material can be characterised as merely a joke, and is incapable for that reason of being understood in a truly defamatory sense, is essentially a value judgement based on community values.

The courts tell jurors to use a 'reasonable person' test to decide whether something is defamatory. That is, they must decide whether a 'right-thinking' person of 'average intelligence' would think so. Worryingly, research in 2004 found that general social attitudes are much more liberal than jury verdicts (Bell, 2006: 138). Why? It seems people (jurors) who themselves may not think less of a person believe other 'average' people are less intelligent, and have more socially conservative views.

FOCUS CASE 7.1: *REBEL'S CASE*

Wilson v Bauer Media Pty Ltd [2017] VSC 521

Bauer Media Pty Ltd v Wilson [No.2] [2018] VSCA 154

FACTS

Australian-born actress and comedian Rebel Wilson was the star of the box office hit *Pitch Perfect* and numerous other films and television shows. A few days after the world premiere of *Pitch Perfect 2* in May 2015, the magazine *Woman's Day* published the print article 'Just Who is the REAL Rebel', asserting that Wilson was a serial liar who had lied about her name, age and other aspects of her personal life and background. The parent company Bauer Media published similar stories and follow-ups on its websites, including those of *Woman's Day*, *Woman's Weekly*, *New Weekly* and *OK Magazine*, which were available online for a further year.

LAW

Wilson sued Bauer Media in the Supreme Court of Victoria, alleging that she had suffered injury to her feelings, credit and reputation, and had been humiliated, embarrassed and suffered loss and damage, including special damages. The jury of six accepted her contention that the articles were defamatory and rejected the publisher's defences of justification, triviality and qualified privilege. They accepted that the following imputations arose from the original article and were defamatory:

> *That Ms Wilson is a serial liar who has invented fantastic stories in order to make it in Hollywood in that she has:*
>
> *(i) lied publicly about her age by claiming to be 29 years old when, in fact, she was born in 1979 and is, therefore, 36 years old;*
>
> *(ii) lied about her name by using the fake name 'Rebel Wilson' when, in fact, her real name is Melanie Elizabeth Bownds;*
>
> *(iii) lied about her background by stating publicly that she was raised by parents who trained dogs when, in fact, her parents had not trained dogs;*
>
> *(iv) lied about her background by stating publicly that, as a child, she travelled around Australia in a caravan with her family to attend dog shows when, in fact, she had not done so;*

(v) *lied about her background by stating publicly that, as a child, her family home was in a disadvantaged suburb of Sydney when, in fact, her home was in an upper-middle-class part of Sydney;*
(vi) *lied about her background by stating publicly that she had lived in Zimbabwe for a year when, in fact, she had not done so;*
(vii) *lied when stating publicly that she had been inside a cage with a leopard when, in fact, she had not;*
(viii) *lied when stating publicly that she got caught in a shoot-out when, in fact, she had not; and*
(ix) *lied when stating publicly that she had contracted malaria whilst she was in Africa when, in fact, she had not contracted the illness.*

They found similar (and other) imputations arose in the series of online articles.

Beyond the basic issues of whether the imputations were capable of being defamatory and were in fact defamatory, legal argument centred upon:

- whether the defences of justification (truth), triviality, and qualified privilege would apply—which we return to in the next chapter, and
- whether aggravated damages should be awarded beyond the statutory cap for non-economic loss (which was $389,500 at the time of the judgment) because the publisher:
  - failed to investigate properly allegations made by a source who demanded anonymity and payment,
  - knew the imputations were false, and
  - repeated them in the various online publications.
- the extent to which Wilson should be compensated for economic loss given the court accepted that she had lost the chance to win new screen roles throughout the balance of 2015 and 2016.

Wilson was awarded $650,000 in general (including aggravated) damages and $3,917,472 in special damages for those lost opportunities (plus interest of $182,448.61). In 2018 the Court of Appeal found there was no basis in the evidence for making any award of damages for economic loss and substituted damages of $600,000 for non-economic loss. As this book was going to press, Wilson had suggested she might appeal against the Court of Appeal's reduction of her damages award.

LESSONS FOR JOURNALISTS

As an introductory case in defamation, *Rebel's case* serves to illustrate several aspects of this law:

- The court looks at the defamatory meaning (imputation) that comes from the publication. Several meanings damaging someone's reputation may emanate from a single publication, while similar publications might contain different imputations.
- Courts can award very high damages in defamation cases, despite the fact that non-economic damages generally are now limited to amounts of less than $400,000 in 2018 under the uniform laws, increasing with the rate of inflation.
- The amount of damages awarded can be affected by evidence of how the defamation impacted upon the victim, in particular what people said to the victim after reading or hearing it, and the extent to which the victim's feelings were injured.
- Further damage, including that caused by the failure of a publisher to apologise and economic losses suffered by a plaintiff, can be considered by the court when awarding damages.
- Appeal courts can sometimes disagree with a trial judge's reasoning in defamation cases, resulting in major changes to the damages awarded, in this case a variation of more than $4 million.

To summarise: a statement can be the subject of a defamation claim if it does three things:

- It conveys a defamatory meaning (or imputation, as defined above).
- It can reasonably be interpreted as referring to the plaintiff.
- It is published to at least one person other than the plaintiff.

We now look at each of these requirements to see how defamation is established in practice.

THE DEFAMATORY IMPUTATION

Defamation is all to do with the meaning or 'sting' of words. To establish this element, a plaintiff must prove that the published words conveyed a meaning (in defamation, called the 'imputation') that would make others think less of them, or shun and avoid them. On their own, it is not enough that the words portray the plaintiff in some negative or ridiculous light, although it is not necessary that they convey something blameworthy or morally shameful. It can be enough, for example, to say that a person is suffering from a gross sexual deformity, as in the *Steeplechaser case* (1936), where a photograph of a jockey made his hanging saddle girth appear as if it was an intimate part of his anatomy, purportedly enhanced by his habit of smoking a particular brand of cigarettes.

It is vitally important to recognise that, at this stage, what the communicator intended to say is entirely irrelevant: jurors are required to judge the meaning of the defamatory material on its own, without any evidence of its intended meaning, the question becoming, 'What do you think an ordinary person would understand this to mean?'

An imputation can be conveyed by:

- the natural and ordinary meaning of the words (or material)
- a 'false innuendo'—a secondary meaning derived from 'reading between the lines'
- a 'true innuendo'—relying on other facts known to whoever is receiving the publication (background knowledge).

While in some cases the words or images might state the 'sting' quite explicitly, in others the reader may need to 'read between the lines' to glean it. For example, an article might say that money has gone missing from the local bank, and that the chief teller has not been seen for a week: the reader infers that the chief teller is a thief. This is a 'false innuendo'. The standard instruction that a judge gives the jury in this regard is that the average person is apt to read between the lines. It is a mistake for any journalist or blogger to fall for the comforting illusion that readers, viewers or listeners will infer the unstated meaning, but that a judge or jury will fail to notice that it is there.

There is another category of case in which an additional meaning is conveyed to readers, viewers or listeners, but only to those who already know a particular fact beyond ('extrinsic to') the material sued on—for example, a personal characteristic. This is known as a 'true innuendo', meaning the imputation arises because of some special background knowledge that some of the recipients of the material might have. For example, in *Van Riet's case* the plaintiff relied on the fact that she had told others that she had done the interior design on her home. *Australian House and Garden* magazine had published an article suggesting Mrs Van Riet had employed someone else to design it. While no mention was made in the article of Mrs Van Riet's claim (to have designed the interiors herself), she relied on the fact of at least some readers having knowledge of that fact. When they read the suggestion that someone else had in fact designed the interiors, they thought less of her for lying.

The fact that someone has been upset or offended by a publication does not mean they have been defamed. Media organisations often publish things that upset, offend or inconvenience individuals; what they publish may sometimes also be wrong, but that does not make it defamatory. Take, for example, an incorrect item in a real estate gossip column, saying that a property is no longer for sale. Such inaccuracies, although they may cause inconvenience or embarrassment, are only defamatory if they also damage a person's reputation.

A single publication often contains several different defamatory imputations about the one person. Section 8 of the *Defamation Act* limits a plaintiff to a single claim—called a 'cause of action'—per publication, even though there may be multiple imputations conveyed. So why would a plaintiff claim that more than one imputation is conveyed? The short answer is that a number of defences—in particular, the defence of truth—require the defendant to defend separately each imputation that the plaintiff is able to wring out of a single piece of writing.

REFERENCE TO THE PLAINTIFF

To establish the second essential element of a defamation action, plaintiffs must prove that the publication referred to them (or could reasonably be interpreted as referring to them). If the publication does not name them, they need to prove that at least one person understood it as referring to them.

In some cases, professional communicators have not taken enough care to identify carefully the individual who is targeted, and 'hidden plaintiffs' have come out of the woodwork. In other cases, the writers or their editors have done nothing wrong, but unexpected people have been identified through coincidental identifiers:

- *A person has been named. Another person (or more than one other person) with the same name has sued.* In *Lee's case* in 1934, a Melbourne newspaper reported a magistrate's inquiry in which a 'Detective Lee' was said to be corrupt. In fact it was a Constable Lee to whom the allegation referred. Two Detective Lees sued successfully, after demonstrating that acquaintances thought the article referred to them. And in the *Tailor's case* (2017), featured in Chapter 6, an elderly tailor named Tony Zoef sued over an imputation that he was a dangerous gun-runner when the article confused him with his son, also named Tony Zoef, who lived at the same address.
- *No one has been named, but someone meets the description of the defamed person.* This happened in *Butler's case* in 1994. *The Sun-Herald* newspaper published an article titled 'Backpack Murders: Police Quiz Socialite', which described a suspect police were questioning in relation to the Belanglo State Forest backpacker serial murders. A 33-year-old man sued the newspaper, claiming friends and relatives had identified him (incorrectly) as the suspect on the basis of identifying factors listed in the article. (Ivan Milat later received a life sentence for those murders.)
- *No individual has been named, but the defamatory article refers to a small group of people.* Consider the *John Fairfax case* in 1994. In an article in *The Australian Financial Review*, defamatory references were made

to 'officials of the National and Victorian Farmers' Federation' and 'NFF and VFF officials and their lawyers and consultant mates'. Although they were not named, six individuals sued, claiming that readers thought the article referred to them. As a rule of thumb, courts decide such cases by looking at the size of the group being defamed, the generality of the charge made and the extravagance of the accusation. The test is whether ordinary, reasonable individuals would believe the defamatory statements referred to the plaintiffs. The whole Year 12 class of 1996 at Mount Druitt High School in Sydney was defamed by a front-page photograph and story in *The Daily Telegraph* headed 'Class We Failed'. Twenty-eight members of the class—who were not identified beyond the class photograph and the mention of their school year group—won the defamation action and a confidential damages settlement (*Mount Druitt case*, 1999). In 2012, one of three sacked casino employees sued over an article that said they had all misused the company's email system, because it also said that one of them had used the system to distribute pornography (*Casino case*, 2012).

- *A fictitious character has been named.* A real person meeting the fictitious person's description sues, claiming the publication has been taken to refer to them. See, for example, the *Artemus Jones case* (see Classic Case 7.1), where an individual sued successfully after showing that people thought a fictitious character by the same name was him. In a high-profile example, a former police officer claimed to have been identified in the TV series *Underbelly* as the lover of an organised crime figure: advertising billboards lining the M4 motorway showed the actress who played 'Constable Wendy' in her police uniform embracing the actor playing John Ibrahim (*Constable Wendy case*, 2010)
- *The wrong person has been named or depicted.* Unfortunately, this is by far the most common identity error. Mistaken identity cases have happened often where a photograph of a different individual is added to a defamatory story. Brisbane's *Courier-Mail* newspaper was ordered to pay $12,500 in damages to a John Finn,

whose photograph was published accidentally next to a story about a conman who shared his name (see *Finn's case,* 2002). Judge Pack blamed the error on the newspaper's lack of an effective checking system. In the *Bondage case* (2003), a middle-aged married solicitor sued after being confused by *The Sun-Herald* with a man of the same name, who had submitted a press release about his piano-top bondage display for the Gay and Lesbian Mardi Gras, and whose blurry photograph was published in the paper alongside the remarks that he 'accepts a brief on bondage' and 'lays down the law'. Sometimes the names differ, but the wrong photograph has been used by accident.

CLASSIC CASE 7.1: *ARTEMUS JONES CASE*

E. Hulton & Co v Jones [1910] AC 20

FACTS

This is one of the most famous historic defamation cases. A London newspaper published a fictitious article about the gallivanting escapades of a lawyer, given the unlikely name of 'Artemus Jones'. It described him partying on the continent 'with a woman who is not his wife, who must be, you know—the other thing!' A real Artemus Jones, a barrister, sued successfully after establishing that people thought the article referred to him.

LAW

The court does not regard the publisher's intention as relevant when deciding whether a defamatory publication identifies a person. Whether or not the defendant intended to identify the plaintiff is irrelevant: all that plaintiffs need to show is that people reasonably thought the article or broadcast referred to them.

LESSONS FOR JOURNALISTS

Beware of creating fictitious names: people who actually have those names may be defamed unintentionally. Make identification in every story as full as possible, so it is absolutely clear to whom you are referring. In other words, if you're going to *defame* them, *name* them. *And ensure your defence is in order.*

Defamation cannot be avoided by allusion: you cannot write something and expect your audience to 'read between the lines' to get the message you are trying to convey, but expect a judge or jury won't do exactly the same thing. If some people understand what you mean, it is defamatory. If no one understands what you mean, you have failed to communicate or, worse still, you may have defamed someone else by mistake.

PUBLICATION TO A THIRD PERSON

The third element the plaintiff has to show is that the defamatory material was published to at least one person other than the plaintiff. In other words, you can write a message to a person criticising them, or say whatever you like about them to their face, but they cannot establish a case in defamation. If you write a defamatory note to them and they show it to a friend, you still cannot be sued: in such a case, it is they who are doing the publishing. But if you copy your defamatory email to just one other person you have then defamed the plaintiff to that person. Bear in mind, however, that an internet publication does not necessarily always reach a third person. The *HotCopper case* (2016) was dismissed when a plaintiff failed to establish that anyone other than he had ever actually seen the defamatory imputations that he had engaged in 'criminal conduct in the management of a corporation' and had shown 'reckless disregard' for shareholders' interests, posted to the internet forum HotCopper. The WA Court of Appeal ruled that the notion of defamatory publication was 'bilateral'—a plaintiff must prove that the defendant published the material and also that it had been viewed by a third party. West Australian Chief Justice Wayne Martin observed, 'There is a real prospect that many of the billions of web pages accessible via the internet have never been seen by anyone other than the person who posted the page on an internet site' (para. 19).

LIMITATION PERIOD

Under the uniform Australian laws, plaintiffs have only one year from the date of publication within which to launch their defamation action. If they can convince the court that it was not 'reasonable in the circumstances' that they should have been expected to do so, that time limit can be extended by up to three years. In 2018, a Queensland man failed to convince the court to extend the time limit due to his almost three-year delay in suing the Seven Network over a report he claimed imputed he was a child molester or murderer or complicit in such a crime—partly because he learned about the broadcast soon after it was aired in 2014 and he had made inquiries with solicitors about a possible defamation suit within the one year limitation period (*Cain's case*, 2018).

Unfortunately for web publishers, the clock restarts for the one-year limitation period every time the material is downloaded and read.

PLACE OF PUBLICATION

A major complexity of defamation law has been that a plaintiff can sue wherever the defamatory material had been published. Where publications and programs transcend state and national borders, defamation writs can be issued in more than one jurisdiction.

With the advent of the internet, the question arose as to whether online publications were to be judged by the defamation laws in the jurisdictions where people downloaded the material, or in the jurisdictions where the publisher uploaded the material onto a server. This point was decided in favour of the place of downloading by Australia's High Court in *Gutnick's case* (see Key Case 7.1). It followed that a plaintiff could sue for publication in multiple jurisdictions, governed by entirely different laws.

The *Defamation Act* addresses 'choice of law' issues in section 11. If defamatory matter is published wholly within a particular jurisdiction, the law of that state or territory applies. If it is published across jurisdictions, the court will apply the law of the state or territory where the harm 'has its closest connection', meaning that it will look primarily at where the plaintiff lived or had their principal place of business, and the extent of publication and harm in each jurisdiction.

KEY CASE 7.1: *GUTNICK'S CASE*

Dow Jones & Company Inc. v Gutnick [2002] HCA 56 (10 December 2002)

FACTS

The High Court had to decide whether Melbourne businessman Joseph Gutnick could bring a defamation action in the Victorian Supreme Court over an article published in the online edition of the weekly financial magazine *Barron's*, based in New Jersey in the United States.

It was proven that five copies of the print edition of the magazine were circulated in Victoria, but the key issue was whether Gutnick could sue over the internet version, which had 550,000 subscribers internationally, of whom 1700 had Australian-based credit cards.

LAW

At issue was whether the online edition was 'published from' New Jersey where it was 'uploaded', or alternatively at any location throughout the world where it was 'downloaded' by subscribers—in this case, Victoria, Australia.

The High Court justices decided unanimously that Gutnick had the right to sue in Victoria, his place of primary residence and the location where he was best known, despite the fact that the article emanated from the United States, where most of the magazine's subscribers were based.

Publication occurred not where the material was uploaded, but where a third party downloaded and read it.

LESSONS FOR JOURNALISTS

Publishers and news directors might bear in mind the locations where individuals have a significant reputation when they are assessing the defamation implications of a web-based story. Of course, there will be some individuals who have substantial reputations in a number of jurisdictions, such as prominent politicians or sportspeople. The courts will, however, be reluctant to entertain a defamation action in a place where an individual is not resident unless they can show some major impact on their reputation.

In general, there is little real risk that you will be sued for publication in an obscure foreign country over material downloaded there. The real risk lies in journalists and publishers failing to exercise the same degree of care with internet material that they would when dealing with 'old' media: in the *Taxi case* (2009), the plaintiff sued over an internet version of the hard-copy edition of *The Sydney Morning Herald*, and separately over a video presentation to which it linked, which he said accused him of improperly obtaining windfall profits from the issue of free taxi plates. Of course, some international celebrities will sometimes sue over defamatory material about them published from Australia, as West Indian cricketer Chris Gayle did successfully against Fairfax Media in 2017 (*Cricketer's case*, 2017).

WHO CAN SUE OR BE SUED?

Any living person or legal entity (except large corporations and government bodies) can bring an action for defamation.

Section 9 of the Act states that corporations cannot sue for defamation unless they are non-profit, or have fewer than ten employees and are not related to another corporation. Corporations can (and do), however, choose other actions, such as injurious (malicious) falsehood or breach of confidence (both of which we consider later), and their directors and officers can still sue in defamation if the story affects their reputation, as well as that of the company. Section 9 of the Act also prevents 'public bodies'—government authorities and local councils—from suing for defamation, although (as in the case of companies) their officers can still sue if they can prove the publication defames them as individuals. Non-profit bodies, such as unions, have to show that the defamation caused them financial harm.

People must in general be alive in order to sue or be sued for defamation, and actions by the deceased are ruled out by the *Defamation Act* everywhere but Tasmania (section 10). However, journalists should be cautious in their reportage of people after their death: aspersions about the dead can sometimes reflect on the living—for example, a suggestion that a deceased celebrity 'built the family fortune on corruption' might enable other family members to sue.

It is a common misconception that you are protected from defamation action if you are just quoting someone else. If you quote someone who is making a defamatory statement or if you publish a letter or online comment from someone that contains defamatory material, your re-publication of the material leaves you and your media outlet, often as well as the person you have quoted, liable for defamation.

While getting the other side of the story is good ethical journalism, it does not necessarily protect you from a defamation action. Unless you can perfectly balance the sting or 'bane' of the article with its antidote, the best it is likely to do is prevent you from losing one of your defences, which we consider in Chapter 8. A formulaic combination of an allegation and a denial risks being perceived—even if it reflects the response you have received—as no more than an attempt to avoid responsibility. If you need to go very far at all into the balancing detail, you should ask whether the initial angle stands up to scrutiny. In attempting to 'balance the story up', you may also end up defaming someone else. In the *Bank Sex case* (2009), the plaintiff sued over an article that outlined her allegations of sexual harassment and workplace bullying in the Commonwealth Bank, which included a balancing statement by the bank, refuting her claim.

Most people could not afford to bring a defamation action if they had to pay for it themselves. Plaintiffs do not have to show they have the necessary assets to pay a costs order if they lose, and many lawyers are prepared to act on a 'no win, no fee' basis. As there is no prospect of recovering court costs in the case of a successful defence, there is a strong temptation for the media to settle these cases, which risks encouraging this kind of litigation. One consequence is that a surprisingly large number of claims are brought by 'Ninja' ('no income, no job') plaintiffs, who have no assets to lose. In recent years, a number of high-profile cases have been won by media defendants against plaintiffs who have either gone bankrupt (*Snapper case*, 2008; *Twitter case*, 2013), or indeed were already bankrupt when they began their action (*Barrister case*, 2006). The present rules on costs create three problems. First, the majority of people with a job and some assets cannot risk using this avenue, for fear of losing everything. Second, journalists and smaller media organisations without the resources to fund expensive court action can be intimidated by wealthy plaintiffs. Third, even the larger media groups need to balance the 'cost of winning', where they know the plaintiff cannot pay up. Such an attitude creates a 'chilling' effect in the media. That said, the large media organisations have also been accused of portraying their own role in defamation actions as that of the 'underdog': lonely defenders of press freedom 'doing battle with powerful, cynical lawyers and the law' (Bell, 2006: 134).

Anyone involved in the publication can be sued, including the person who wrote the story, the editor and the official publisher. But in the *Website case* (2016, para. 45), the Supreme Court of Western Australia ruled that personal liability would not extend to a director—or even managing director—of a company unless they had played an active role in the publication process.

The only individuals who have an excuse by arguing 'innocent dissemination' under section 32 of the Act are distributors, such as newsagents, librarians, booksellers and, in some circumstances, ISPs and content hosts like Google and Facebook, who lose the defence if it is shown that they knew the publication contained the defamatory material. That happened in the *Search Engine cases* (2012–18), when Melbourne man Michael Trkulja won $200,000 in damages from Google and $225,000 from Yahoo! after his image and name appeared in search results for underworld criminal figures and the multinational outlets refused to remove them when asked. After a separate action over further instances of search results for Melbourne underworld figures showing images of him, and autocomplete predictions on a search for his name prompting an association with criminal identities, in 2018 Mr Trkulja won a High Court appeal against a Victorian Court of Appeal ruling that he had no real prospect of success proving any of the imputations were capable of being conveyed by the search engine results. The case was expected to be re-heard in a lower court as this edition went to press.

DIGITAL DIMENSIONS

Research published in 2018 by the UTS Centre for Media Transition found that more than half of defamation cases over the previous five years involved reputational damage in a digital medium, up from 17 per cent in 2007 when social media was in its infancy (Centre for Media Transition, 2018). The common perception that defamation cases typically involve celebrities suing the media for millions of dollars—such as actors Rebel Wilson and Geoffrey Rush—is a myth. The study showed that among the 189 decided cases from 2013 to 2017, only one-third of defendants were media companies, and only about one-fifth of those bringing the action were celebrities or public figures. When you read the detail on the cases, it becomes clear that most defamation cases are contests between ordinary citizens over negative remarks they have made about each other on social media, websites, emails and other means of digital communication.

The *Search Engine cases* (2012–18) in Australia raised a host of issues related to the defamation of people on the internet and in social media, and demonstrated how defamation can be a legal minefield for bloggers and other online writers. While the essential ingredients are similar the world over, there are major variations in the defences available and the constitutional frameworks underpinning them. This means trouble for internet writers and social media users because every online posting leaves you exposed everywhere your target has a reputation, the instant it is downloaded there.

A case in Western Australia was one of the world's first instances of defamation over the internet. The 1994 *Rindos v Hardwick* case involved allegations transmitted on a computer bulletin board of sexual misconduct, racist attitudes and incompetence against an anthropology academic. The plaintiff won $40,000 in damages. Of course, the High Court of Australia also became the world's first senior judicial body to rule on the time and place of international web publication in *Gutnick's case* in 2002 (see Key Case 7.1).

Eleven years later, Australia's first defamation case over material on Twitter to go through a full trial was decided by the NSW District Court in late 2013 (*Twitter case*, 2013). A high school music teacher won a damages award of $105,000 from a former student over social media comments the student had made about her—but the student declared himself bankrupt soon after. This was followed by the *Treasurer case* in 2015 where former federal treasurer Joe Hockey won $200,000 in damages over imputations conveyed in newspaper posters and tweets stating, 'Treasurer for Sale' and 'Treasurer Hockey for Sale', published by *The Sydney Morning Herald* and *The Age*. The stories explained that Hockey had provided 'privileged access' to a 'select group' in return for donations to the Liberals via 'secretive' fundraising body, the North Sydney Forum—but the court held that some readers might deduce an imputation of corruption from the phrases used in the tweets without the deeper context of the full articles, which they might not proceed to read.

Publishers and hosts of internet and social media sites engage with their content and audiences in a range of ways in the modern era—ranging from the hands-on moderation of comments posted to their sites, through providing opportunities for people to comment without moderation, eventually through to simply providing a platform or internet service that millions of people might be using at any time without the provider having particular knowledge of the material being published.

Australian and international courts have examined the issue of the responsibility for publishers of these various kinds for the comments or postings of third parties. In *Douglas's case* (2016), the Western Australian Supreme Court presented a useful list of recent influential decisions in the area, including:

- *Sims v Jooste (No. 2)* [2016] WASCA 83
- *Von Marburg v Aldred (No. 2)* [2016] VSC 36
- *Trkulja v Google Inc.* [2015] VSC 635
- *Von Marburg v Aldred* [2015] VSC 467
- *Duffy v Google Inc.* [2015] SASC 170
- *Bleyer v Google Inc.* [2014] NSWSC 897; (2014) 88 NSWLR 670
- *Murray v Wishart* [2014] NZCA 461; [2014] 3 NZLR 722
- *Tamiz v Google Inc.* [2013] EWCA Civ 68; [2013] 1 WLR 2151
- *Rana v Google Australia Pty Ltd* [2013] FCA 60

- *Trkulja v Google Inc. LLC (No. 5)* [2012] VSC 533
- *Metropolitan International Schools Ltd v Designtechnica Corp* [2009] EWHC 1765 (QB); [2011] 1 WLR 1743
- *Bunt v Tilley* [2006] EWHC 407 (QB); [2007] 1 WLR 1243
- *Dow Jones & Co Inc. v Gutnick* [2002] HCA 56; (2002) 210 CLR 575
- *Godfrey v Demon Internet Ltd* [2001] QB 201.

Justice Kenneth Martin noted the view of the New Zealand Court of Appeal in *Murray v Wishart* that the courts should focus on the particular factual situation of the role taken by an alleged publisher in an internet context because so many different types of publication can occur (para. 4).

In the *Facebook Page case* (2015), Justice John Dixon presented five key principles determining the role of the publisher in defamation via the internet:

> (a) *To allege that a defendant is a primary publisher of defamatory material on a Facebook page when that defendant is neither the author nor the originating publisher of the communication, two matters may need to be alleged. First, the pleading could allege that the defendant was instrumental in the act of publication, when it occurred, in that he intentionally was, in any degree and by whatever means, complicit in the acts of making or authorising the communication or failed to take reasonable care to prevent its publication. It is sufficient if the defendant knew of the content of the communication without actually appreciating its defamatory nature. (Knowledge factor)*
>
> (b) *Second, in the absence of complicity in the conduct of the author and/or originating publisher of the communication or an employment/agency relationship, the pleading could allege that the defendant had the ability to control whether publication occurred. A person who exercised control over publication, or the published content, of the communication independently of the author or originator, at the time of publication, is a primary publisher. (Control factor)*

(c) *To allege a subordinate publication, a plaintiff should allege that the defendant acquired knowledge of the existence of the impugned publication. An awareness of the existence of the impugned material is a precondition before an internet intermediary such as an administrator or sponsor of a Facebook page will be held to be a publisher . . . When a relevant party communicates a defamatory statement by the use of an internet platform, such as Facebook, through a medium such as a comment button or other invitation to post a communication to the platform, the internet [intermediary] is not the publisher of it if not aware of its existence. (Knowledge factor)*

(d) *When considering subordinate publication, the second limb of the test for primary publication, namely the control factor, gives way to a test of ratification in which control is an element. The internet intermediary must have sufficient responsibility for the content on the Facebook page, whether as owner, sponsor, lessee, administrator or moderator to exert control over its content. The applicable rule is that a defendant will be liable as a subordinate publisher when, aware of a communication posted by another on a Facebook page (or internet platform) within its control whether by actual personal observation or by being informed of its existence, the defendant fails to remove or terminate the communication, but only if circumstances are present that permit the conclusion that the defendant is responsible for, or has ratified, the continuing publication of that communication. The question of fact will usually be whether the defendant has acquiesced in or authorised or ratified the communication. (Ratification factor)*

(e) *Whether that ratification inference be adopted is a question of fact in all of the circumstances, which will include the manner in which the internet platform is structured, referring to the architecture of its software, how it is operated or controlled by its sponsor, and the role of the defendant in such matters. The later issue may require attention to the circumstances of the presence of the communication on the medium before the defendant knew of it, the nature of the defendant's awareness of the communication, the requirements for removing or expunging it, and the circumstances of the continued presence of the communication after he or she knew of it. (para. 37)*

In the United States, ISPs have a strong defence to defamation actions under section 230 of the *Communication Decency Act*, which gives full protection to 'interactive computer services', even protecting blog hosts from liability for comments by users. But those commenting can themselves be sued if they are identifiable.

While the First Amendment offers strong defamation protections to publishers in the United States, some users of new media have still managed to fall foul of the law. David Milum was a pioneer in defamation for all the wrong reasons. He ran a political website in Forsyth County, Georgia, and became the first US blogger to lose a libel case when in 2004 he wrote that an attorney had delivered bribes from drug dealers to a judge. The attorney won $50,000 in damages and the appeal court held in 2007 that bloggers and podcasters were just as liable for defamation action as other publishers. In another high-profile US defamation action detailed in Chapter 1, the *Courtney Love case*, up-and-coming fashion designer Dawn Simorangkir won $430,000 from celebrity rocker Courtney Love in 2011 after the star's Twitter tirade against her.

Each social medium brings its own defamation dangers. Tweeting from an event, such as a conference or a court case, as it unfolds can be risky because your tweets might contain errors in the quotes of others or might be taken out of context by someone just reading a single tweet rather than the overall coverage. Of course, you tweet with the full expectation that your work will be spread far and wide, meaning any libellous material can cause considerable damage.

Publication on Facebook, however, might be restricted to just a few friends, particularly if your privacy settings are adjusted so that your comments are not viewable to the friends of your friends. The open blog has a potentially wide distribution network, but you should take advantage of opportunities to save drafts and proofread your material in preview mode before proceeding to publication.

Anyone with direct responsibility for a publication is legally liable for it, so if your blog is on the website of another organisation, both you as the writer and the corporation hosting your work can be targeted in a defamation suit. If someone edits your work before it is published, they too share the burden of legal liability. And if anyone republishes your work, through syndication or perhaps even through re-tweeting or forwarding your defamatory material, they are also liable. Even someone who inserts a hyperlink to libellous material can be sued for defamation.

Plaintiffs will sue any of these people or organisations for a range of reasons. Sometimes they just want to gag the discussion, so they issue a defamation writ to chill the criticism. This is known as a 'SLAPP' writ—'Strategic Lawsuits Against Public Participation'—and in some countries they are simply thrown out of court as an affront to free expression. Others allow them. Plaintiffs often want to get the highest possible damages award from someone who can afford to pay it, so they might bypass the original impoverished blogger and sue the wealthier company that republished the material. Sometimes they join all of them in their action, although this adds to their legal costs if they lose.

It is also important to appreciate that defamatory material can be almost anything you publish—words, images, sounds or gestures. In a German case, where Daimler employees insulted their boss on a social media protest page, a court found even a Facebook 'like' thumbs-up symbol was enough to qualify as a defamatory statement (Oberwetter, 2011). A Swiss court reached a similar conclusion about a man who 'liked' comments that another man was anti-Semitic and fined him 4000 Swiss francs ($A5500) (BBC, 2017).

There have been many digital defamation cases throughout Asia in recent years. In China, private citizens can push for prosecution of defamation under the criminal law, and the government can pursue charges if 'the state' or 'public order' has been dealt serious harm. In late 2009, two Chinese bloggers were ordered to pay the equivalent of about US$40,000 in compensation to the widow of film director Xie Jin for claiming he died in the arms of a prostitute (*The Age*, 2009). A Malaysian activist agreed to post an apology 100 times over three days on Twitter as part of a settlement over an allegation that a magazine company had treated a pregnant employee poorly. He could not afford to apologise in newspaper advertisements (*New Zealand Herald*, 2011). In Vietnam, prominent gossip columnist Le Nguyen Huong Tra served three months in jail for alleging the son of a senior security official had affairs with beauty queens and dancers (*Journalism Now*, 2011). Indonesia's *Electronic Information and Transaction Law Act 2008* allows for up to six years in jail for criminal libel. Mother of two Prita Mulyasari was arrested under the provision in 2010 after complaining on internet mailing lists about the poor treatment she had received at a private hospital. She was held for three weeks awaiting trial, but media coverage and a Facebook support site prompted her release on bail and she won her Supreme Court appeal against damages, only to be jailed under another provision (*Jakarta Post*, 2011). Free speech groups pressed for the law to be abolished, but by 2017 at least 35 activists had been charged with online defamation in the decade of its operation (SAFENet, 2017a). A similar law in Myanmar saw 43 prosecutions for defamation against political leaders on social media in the year to March 2017 (SAFENet, 2017b).

Defamation arises for professional communicators and bloggers internationally and locally, in print and online, in a broadcast or in a social media chat, but the real key in any jurisdiction is in learning how to operate safely within the available defamation defences, to which we turn in Chapter 8.

TIPS FOR MINDFUL PRACTICE

- If you are going to imply something negative or amusing about a person or company, state it openly and identify them fully, but make sure you have a defence available (see Chapter 8). Take legal advice if you are not absolutely certain.
- Don't try to imply something defamatory by asking the reader to 'read between the lines', to detect your hidden meaning ('false innuendo').
- If a meaning slipped by under deadline pressure, say so early—when the case is likely to be able to be settled—rather than when it is due for trial.
- Quoting another person does not protect you from defamation action, no matter how accurately attributed. If it is defamatory, you can both be sued.
- Internet and social media material involves some additional legal risks, and needs to be treated even more cautiously.

IN A NUTSHELL

- Damaging someone's reputation can trigger lawsuits for defamation, and even fines and jail in some places, as 'criminal libel'.
- Defamation is a published statement that damages someone's reputation or holds them up to ridicule.
- To establish a case, plaintiffs need to show that the material was published to at least one other person, that it was defamatory (made others think less of them) and that they were identified.
- The defamatory content of a publication is known as an 'imputation'. A publication may convey one or more imputations.
- Someone can sue for defamation if they are identifiable, even if you haven't named them.
- Blogs, tweets, Facebook entries, hyperlinks, email messages and even re-tweets or 'likes' can make you liable for defamation action.
- Defamation law in Australia is a combination of legislation in the states and territories and the case law built up over centuries.
- Anyone involved in publication can be sued, including the professional communicator who writes or edits the material.
- Any living person, small company (fewer than ten employees) or non-profit corporation can sue for defamation, and even deceased estates can sue in Tasmania.
- The imputation can come from the natural ordinary meaning of published material, reading a hidden meaning 'between the lines' ('false innuendo') or from its combination with other facts known to at least some of its audience ('true innuendo').
- The internet and social media present special dangers for defamation. An important feature of the internet is that publication occurs wherever someone downloads defamatory material.
- Much more defamatory material can be published by media organisations in the United States because of First Amendment protections and a very liberal 'public figure' test.

DISCUSSION QUESTIONS

7.1 Think of some situations where defamation might not be established because:

(a) someone is upset, but there is no defamatory imputation (meaning)

(b) the plaintiff has not been identified adequately

(c) the material has not yet been 'published'.

7.2 What is the nastiest thing you have heard said about someone on social media? Talk through the implications of publishing this in Australia and defending it.

7.3 If someone wins $400,000 in defamation damages, to what extent will that be likely to restore their reputation?

7.4 Are defamation laws and free expression compatible? Explain.

7.5 To what extent should professional communicators be personally liable for their work and exposed to defamation action over their material? Aren't they just agents for their employers—just 'doing their job'?

7.6 Think about the facts of the following real-life case. A news bulletin publishes film of a man being rescued from a crash, with the words, 'Hours later, rescuers were told the man is HIV positive.'

(a) List the various meanings conveyed by this simple statement.

(b) What would change if it turned out that the victim was not HIV positive, was married and was a senior member of a conservative church?

7.7 Reread *Gutnick's case* in Key Case 7.1 (or, better still, the full High Court decision) and note three ways in which the internet has complicated defamation.

7.8 Take the top ten stories on a major news website and identify how many of them defame someone. (There should be several because much defamation is defensible.)

7.9 You want to satirise the medical system by writing a blog about a fictitious 'Doctor Yes'. What dangers might be inherent in this approach? Explain a safer way of approaching the topic.

7.10 Search online and find a recent example of defamation on social media. Compare and contrast it with one of the cases in this chapter.

REFERENCES

The Age 2009, 'Crime bloggers fined for defamation: Report', 26 December, <http://news.theage.com.au/breaking-news-technology/china-bloggers-fined-for-defamation-report-20091226-lfni.html>.

BBC 2017, 'Swiss court convicts man over "defamatory" Facebook likes', *BBC News*, 30 May, <www.bbc.com/news/world-europe-40097792>.

Bell, P. 2006, 'Defamation and reputation in the Australian press', *Australian Journalism Review*, 28(1), 125–41.

Butler, S. (ed.) 2006, *Macquarie Concise Dictionary*, 4th edn, Macquarie Dictionary, Sydney.

Centre for Media Transition 2018, *Trends in Digital Defamation: Defendants, Plaintiffs, Platforms*, UTS, Sydney.

Council of Europe 2010, *European Convention on Human Rights*, <www.echr.coe.int/documents/convention_ENG.pdf>.

Jakarta Post 2011, 'Lawyer says Prita's sentence insults Indonesian Law', 9 July, <www.thejakartapost.com/news/2011/07/09/lawyer-says-prita%E2%80%99s-sentence-insults-indonesian-law.html>.

Journalism Now 2011, 'Vietnam police release gossip blogger on bail', 21 January, <www.washingtonpost.com/wp-dyn/content/article/2010/10/28/AR2010102801501.html>.

New Zealand Herald 2011, 'Malaysian to tweet apology 100 times', 3 June, <www.nzherald.co.nz/world/news/article.cfm?c_id=2&objectid=10730019>.

Oberwetter, C. 2011, 'Gefahrliches Netzweken bei Daimler', *Legal Tribune Online*, 28 May, <www.lto.de/recht/hintergruende/h/illoyale-arbeinehner-gefahrliches-netzweken-bei-daimler>.

SAFENet 2017a, 'An Indonesian journalist Dandhy Dwi Laksono was reported to the police after comparing former president with Aung San Suu Kyi', 7 September, <http://safenetvoice.org/2017/09/an-indonesian-journalist-dandhy-dwi-laksono-was-reported-to-the-police-after-comparing-former-president-with-aung-san-suu-kyi>.

—— 2017b, 'More Myanmar Facebook users jailed for defaming Aung San Suu Kyi', 9 March, <http://safenetvoice.org/2017/03/more-myanmar-facebook-users-jailed-for-defaming-aung-suu-kyi>.

CASES CITED

2UE case: Radio 2UE Sydney Pty Ltd v Chesterton [2009] HCA 16 (22 April 2009), <www.austlii.edu.au/cgi-bin/viewdoc/au/cases/cth/HCA/2009/16.html#fnB82>.

Artemus Jones case: E. Hulton & Co. v Jones [1910] AC 20.

Bank Sex case: Blomfield v Nationwide News Pty Ltd (No. 2) [2009] NSWSC 978 (15 September 2009), <www.austlii.edu.au/cgi-bin/sinodisp/au/cases/nsw/NSWSC/2009/978.html>.

Barrister case: Stephen Archer v Newcastle Newspapers Pty Ltd [2006] NSWDC No. 5033/03, NSW District Court, Gibson J., unreported, 27 April 2006.

Berkoff's case: Berkoff v Burchill [1996] 4 All ER 1008.

Bondage case: Kelly v John Fairfax Publications Pty Ltd [2003] NSWSC 586, no. 20062/03 Supreme Court of New South Wales, Levine J., unreported, 27 June 2003.

Boyd's case: Boyd v Mirror Newspapers Ltd [1980] 2 NSWLR 449.

Butler's case: Butler v John Fairfax Pty Ltd (1994) 1 MLR 106.

Cain's case: Cain v Seven Network (Operations) Limited [2018] QDC 2, <www8.austlii.edu.au/cgi-bin/viewdoc/au/cases/qld/QDC/2018/2.html>.

Casino case: Morten Christiansen v Fairfax Media Publications Pty Ltd [2012] NSWSC 1258 (19 October 2012), <www.austlii.edu.au/cgi-in/sinodisp/au/cases/nsw/NSWSC/2012/1258.html>.

Constable Wendy case: Hatfield v TCN Channel Nine Pty Ltd [2010] NSWCA 69 (8 April 2010), <www.austlii.edu.au/cgi-bin/sinodisp/au/cases/nsw/NSWCA/2010/69.html>.

Courtney Love case: Simorangkir v Love (2009) Superior Court of the State of California for the County of Los Angeles, BC 410593, <www.dmlp.org/sites/citmedialaw.org/files/2009-03-26-Simorangkir%20Complaint_0.pdf>.

Cricketer's case: Gayle v Fairfax Media Publications Pty Ltd; Gayle v The Age Company Pty Ltd; Gayle v The Federal Capital Press of Australia Pty Ltd [2017] NSWSC 1261 (18 August 2017).

Dennis Denuto case: Smith v Lucht [2015] QDC 289, <www9.austlii.edu.au/cgi-bin/viewdoc/au/cases/qld/QDC/2015/289.html>. *Smith v Lucht* [2016] QCA 267, <www8.austlii.edu.au/cgi-bin/viewdoc/au/cases/qld/QCA/2016/267.html>.

Douglas's case: Douglas v McLernon [No. 3] [2016] WASC 319, <http://classic.austlii.edu.au/cgi-bin/sinodisp/au/cases/wa/WASC/2016/319.html>.

ET's case: Ettingshausen v Australian Consolidated Press Ltd (1991) 23 NSWLR 443.

Facebook Page case: Von Marburg v Aldred & Anor [2015] VSC 467, <http://classic.austlii.edu.au/cgi-bin/sinodisp/au/cases/vic/VSC/2015/467.html>.

Finn's case: Finn v Queensland Newspapers Pty Ltd, Qld District Court (Townsville), 20 May 2002, no. D63 of 2000, unreported.

Gutnick's case: Dow Jones & Company Inc. v Gutnick [2002] HCA 56 (10 December 2002), <www.austlii.edu.au//cgi-bin/disp.pl/au/cases/cth/HCA/2002/56.html>.

Hanson-Young's case: Hanson-Young v Bauer Media Limited [2013] NSWSC 1306 (11 September 2013), <www.austlii.edu.au/cgi-bin/sinodisp/au/cases/nsw/NSWSC/2013/1306.html>.

HotCopper case: Sims v Jooste [No. 2] [2016] WASCA 83, <www.austlii.edu.au/cgi-bin/viewdoc/au/cases/wa/WASCA/2016/83.html#fnB14>; *Sims v Jooste [No. 2]* [2014] WASC 373, <www.austlii.edu.au/cgi-bin/viewdoc/au/cases/wa/WASC/2014/373.html>.

John Fairfax case: John Fairfax Group v Farley (1994) 1 MLR 108, <www.austlii.edu.au/au/other/media/MLWS%20Commentary/Contempt%20of%20Court%20Commentary/8800.htm>.

Lee's case: Lee v Wilson & Mackinnon (1934) 51 CLR 276, <www.austlii.edu.au/au/cases/cth/high_ct/51clr276.html>.

Mount Druitt case: Bryant & Ors v Nationwide News Pty Limited [1999] NSWSC 360, <www.austlii.edu.au/cgi-bin/sinodisp/au/cases/nsw/NSWSC/1999/360.html>; *Carroll v Nationwide News Pty Limited* [1999] NSWSC 856, <www.austlii.edu.au/cgi-bin/sinodisp/au/cases/nsw/NSWSC/1999/856.html>.

Parmiter's case: Parmiter v Coupland (1840) 151 ER 340.

Rebel's case: Wilson v Bauer Media Pty Ltd [2017] VSC 521, <www.austlii.edu.au/cgi-bin/viewdoc/au/cases/vic/VSC/2017/521.html>; *Bauer Media Pty Ltd v Wilson [No. 2]* [2018] VSCA 154, <www.austlii.edu.au/cgi-bin/viewdoc/au/cases/vic/VSCA//2018/154.html>.

Rindos' case: Rindos v Hardwick, Supreme Court of Western Australia, No. 1994 of 1993. (Unreported judgment 940164), <anthropology.buffalo.edu/Rindos/Law/judgement.html>.

Search Engine cases: Trkulja v Yahoo! Inc & Anor [2012] VSC 88, <www.austlii.edu.au/au/cases/vic/VSC/2012/88.html>; *Trkulja v Google Inc. LLC & Anor (No. 5)* [2012] VSC 533 (12 November 2012), <www.austlii.edu.au/cgi-bin/sinodisp/au/cases/vic/VSC/2012/533.html>; *Trkulja v Google LLC* [2018] HCA 25 (13 June 2018), <http://eresources.hcourt.gov.au/showCase/2018/HCA/25>.

Sim's case: Sim v Stretch (1936) 52 TLR 669.

Snapper case: Fawcett v John Fairfax Publications Pty Ltd [2008] NSWSC 139 (27 February 2008), <www.austlii.edu.au/cgi-bin/sinodisp/au/cases/nsw/NSWSC/2008/139.html>.

Steeplechaser case: Burton v Crowell Publishing Company, 82 F2d 154 (CA 2, NY, 10 February 1936), <https://casetext.com/case/burton-v-crowell-pub-co#.U4l_zq21Zlc>.

Sullivan's case: New York Times v Sullivan 376 US 254 (1964), <www.access.gpo.gov/su_docs/supcrt/index.html>.

Tailor's case: Zoef v Nationwide News Pty Ltd (No. 2) [2017] NSWCA 2, <www.austlii.edu.au/cgi-bin/viewdoc/au/cases/nsw/NSWCA/2017/2.html>; *Zoef v Nationwide News Pty Ltd* [2016] NSWCA 283, <www.austlii.edu.au/cgi-bin/viewdoc/au/cases/nsw/NSWCA/2016/283.html>; *Zoef v Nationwide News Pty Ltd* [2015] NSWDC 232, <www.austlii.edu.au/cgi-bin/viewdoc/au/cases/nsw/NSWDC/2015/232.html>.

Taxi case: Kermode v Fairfax Media Publications Pty Ltd [2009] NSWSC 1263 (23 November 2009), <www.austlii.edu.au/cgi-bin/sinodisp/au/cases/nsw/NSWSC/2009/1263.html>.

Treasurer case: Hockey v Fairfax Media Publications Pty Limited [2015] FCA 652, <www.austlii.edu.au/cgi-bin/sinodisp/au/cases/cth/FCA/2015/652.html>.

Twitter case: Mickle v Farley [2013] NSWDC 295 (29 November 2013), <www.caselaw.nsw.gov.au/action/PJUDG?jgmtid=169992>.

Van Riet's case: Merle Ellen Van Riet & Jack Van Riet v ACP Publishing Pty Ltd, 1237/99. District Court of Queensland (Brisbane), 20–26 March 2002. Reported in *Gazette of Law and Journalism*, 8 May 2002, <www.glj.com.au/420-article>. See also *Van Riet v ACP Publishing Pty Ltd* [2003] QCA 37 (14 February 2003), Supreme Court of Qld—Court of Appeal, <www.austlii.edu.au/cgi-bin/sinodisp/au/cases/qld/QCA/2003/37.html>.

Website case: Douglas v McLernon (No. 3) [2016] WASC 319, <http://classic.austlii.edu.au/cgi-bin/sinodisp/au/cases/wa/WASC/2016/319.html>.

Youssoupoff's case: Youssoupoff v Metro-Goldwyn Mayer Pictures Ltd (1934) 50 TLR 581.

CHAPTER 8

Defending defamation

KEY CONCEPTS

Justification
An alternative term used to describe the defence requiring proof that a defamatory imputation or meaning is substantially true.

Honest opinion
Also known as 'fair comment' in its common law version, the main defence for expressions of opinion and comment published on a matter of public interest, and based on true facts.

Public interest
A matter of genuine public concern related to something of importance in the public domain, such as the performance of a public official or the quality of a work or product paraded for public consumption.

Fair and accurate report
A reasonably balanced and substantially accurate report of a public proceeding like court or parliament, or a summary of an official public document.

Qualified privilege
A defence available for communication of defamatory material that may not even be true, but where the damage done to reputation is excused, because in some circumstances it is outweighed by the public interest in communication of information. A special court-developed and constitutionally based version applies to political discussion.

Offer of amends
A defence for those who have made a reasonable, speedy and carefully worded offer to remedy a defamatory publication (requiring technical legal advice).

Triviality
A defence where even though the publication may fail to attract any other defence, the circumstances of its publication are that it is unlikely to do real harm.

Malice
An ulterior purpose in publishing defamatory material. A crucial factor that can defeat a defence of qualified privilege or honest opinion.

Despite there being a large amount of material that satisfies the basic test for defamation, the reality is that considerable defamatory material is published every day without any legal consequences. Some of it is published safely because the publisher cannot be identified or is beyond the legal reach of the victim. Sometimes it is because the plaintiff already has such a damaged reputation that the publication does no additional harm. Sometimes the potential plaintiff lacks the resources or emotional resilience for a court battle. And sometimes there is a rock-solid defence available to the publisher. Defences are the key to working with defamation. The professional communicator needs to know how to make otherwise defamatory material publishable by ensuring—so far as possible—that a defence is available. The question 'Is there a defence available?' is at least as crucial to the practice of journalism and professional writing as the question 'Is this material defamatory?'

BACKGROUND AND INTERNATIONAL CONTEXT

The defences to defamation vary considerably between nations and jurisdictions within them. Much depends on the level of free expression in a particular country. Regions with strong constitutional protections of free speech and press freedom, like North America and Scandinavia, offer generous defamation defences—often aligned with a Bill of Rights or other human rights document enshrining free expression or a free media. Countries with strong censorship regimes lack even the basic defences, politicise the court process or place a strong burden of proof on defendants to justify their publications—often without even the basic entitlements of natural justice.

DEFAMATION DEFENCES IN AUSTRALIA

One of the main challenges of defamation law in Australia is that the plaintiff does not have to prove that what a professional communicator wrote is false: what you wrote is assumed to be false, and it is necessary for the journalist or publisher to prove, on the basis of evidence admissible in a court of law, that it is true. Some defamation defences—in particular, qualified privilege—are rarely available to the media, or are especially difficult to establish. Those that are available require publishers to have been scrupulously accurate, thorough and fair. This chapter focuses on the defences of greatest benefit to the media.

The uniform defamation laws that came into force throughout Australia in 2005 and 2006 standardised the defences, although there are still some minor differences between some states and territories. The most important are mentioned in this chapter. One important aspect is that not only the defences set out in the *Defamation Act*, but also (in general, and subject to other state rules of court procedure) their old common law equivalents are available, in accordance with section 6 (section 118 in the ACT and section 5 in the Northern Territory) and section 24 (section 134 in the ACT, section 21 in the Northern Territory and section 22 in South Australia) of the *Defamation Act*. We will address the main defences affecting journalists in the order in which they appear in the Act, and associated common law defences as they arise within that structure.

OFFERS OF AMENDS AND APOLOGIES

Sometimes we just make a serious mistake and want to make up for it immediately. You should get legal advice the instant someone threatens you with a defamation suit—or even if they make a complaint, whether on the phone, via email or in a lawyer's letter. Before we consider other defences, we need to deal with the situation in which you need to resolve a dispute without litigation, covered in Part 3 of the *Defamation*

Act (Part 9.3 in the ACT), which establishes under sections 12–19 (ss 124–31 ACT; ss 11–18 NT) a mechanism for a publisher to make an offer of amends to an aggrieved person. The offer must meet requirements related to timing (generally, within 28 days of the complaint), content and form, all of which would normally be handled by lawyers and management. If an offer of amends was reasonable, made promptly and complied with all of those requirements, the *Defamation Act*, section 18 (s 130 ACT; s 17 NT) makes it a complete defence to any future defamation action, provided you are prepared to perform it at any time up to trial. Section 20 (s 132 ACT; s 19 NT) encourages apologies by preventing their use as an admission of fault or liability. Section 38 (s 139I ACT; s 35 NT; s 36 SA) allows evidence of corrections and apologies to be used by defendants to reduce damages. Such offers must meet technical requirements and are best handled by a lawyer. Rash or poorly worded apologies can sometimes go wrong and escalate a matter further, or erode your chance of arguing one of the defences. While we might feel the moral urge to apologise, it is best to run the wording past a lawyer first. In the *Tailor's case* (2017), the trial judge at first instance allowed an offer of amends defence to *The Daily Telegraph*, which published a story confusing an elderly tailor with his gun-running son who shared his name. However, the Court of Appeal overturned that decision, stating that the newspaper's offer had been unreasonable considering the hurt caused, the damage to the tailor's business, the unequal prominence of the correction and apology, and the modest sum offered.

CATEGORIES OF DEFENCES

The main defences available to the media are best understood by considering them under umbrella headings. The categories describe the different foundations on which the different defences are based. They are available because the defamatory matter is either:

- justified because it is true (substantially or contextually), or
- protected for some overriding reason of public importance—under this category come the other main defences of:

   - fair report
   - honest opinion or 'fair comment',
   - qualified privilege and
   - political discussion ('Lange qualified privilege') or
- excused because the material was either disseminated innocently or was too trivial to be of concern.

TRUTH AS A DEFENCE

> *Truth . . . ne'er comes into the world but like a Bastard, to the ignominy of him that brought her forth.*
>
> –*John Milton,* Doctrine and Discipline in Divorce *(1643)*

Four centuries later, this statement remains all too true for journalists and bloggers, who may suffer disgrace, dishonour and heavy financial blows for speaking the truth. The person least likely to want to hear or read the inconvenient truth is the person about whom it is spoken or written. Truth as a defence is based on the foundational premise in *Rofe's case* (1924, at 21–2) that 'by telling the truth about a man, his reputation is not lowered beyond its proper level, but is merely brought down to it'.

Truth (also called 'justification') is shackled by two conditions:

- The publication is presumed to be false, and its truth must be proven in court, through evidence which is relevant and which complies with strict rules. A genuine belief in the truth is not enough; nor is the fact that a well-placed confidential source assures you it is true.
- Proving truth is only half the battle: a defendant is required to prove the truth of the imputations (defamatory meanings) that a jury finds arise. To say that an employee was one of three sacked, and that one of the three had distributed pornography at work, may be easy to prove; however, to prove the imputation said to

> arise—that there are reasonable grounds to suspect that each of the three possessed pornography and forwarded it to others—is quite a different proposition (*Casino case*, 2012).

The Act deals with the defence of justification in section 25 (s 135 ACT; s 22 NT; s 23 SA):

> *It is a defence to the publication of defamatory matter if the defendant proves that the defamatory imputations carried by the matter of which the plaintiff complains are substantially true.*

If a media organisation has enough legally admissible evidence to prove the substantial truth of the imputations that the jury finds were conveyed, it has the best of all possible defences. This can, of course, be extremely difficult to prove in cases that rely, to a greater or lesser extent, on confidential sources. In general, the laws of evidence do not allow 'hearsay': a witness may not give evidence about what they were told by another person who is not going to give evidence, in an attempt to rely upon the supposed truth of what they were told.

While there are important discretions available to judges—for example, under the *Evidence Acts* that apply in the Commonwealth and some states and territories to excuse journalists from disclosing protected sources—it is unrealistic and unconvincing for journalists to claim that anonymous others gave them important information as the foundation stone of their truth defence.

Other complications about the admissibility of evidence include recordings (for example, audio files that may have been illegally recorded), photocopied or scanned documents (which themselves may contain hearsay, and may have been 'doctored'), journalists' notebooks (which may not have been filed efficiently, and may contain illegible notes or identify sources), digital video tapes (which may contain balancing material that was edited out before broadcast), previous drafts of articles, email and social media communications with sources, witnesses who disappear overseas or die and contested signatures. Many a defamation defendant has been left high and dry, convinced of the truth of what they wrote but unable to produce enough evidence to convince a judge or jury.

If these difficulties can be overcome, the defendant will succeed on a truth defence, so long as the evidence establishes that all the imputations that the jury accepts an ordinary reasonable reader would draw from the publication were true on the 'balance of probabilities'. That means you only need enough evidence (witnesses, documents, etc.) to convince the judge or jury that the story is more likely than not to be substantially true, although as the High Court held in 1938, the *quality* of the evidence required will vary according to the *seriousness* of the matter: see *Briginshaw's case*, in which the court held:

> *The seriousness of an allegation made, the inherent unlikelihood of an occurrence of a given description, or the gravity of the consequences flowing from a particular finding are considerations which must affect the answer to the question whether the issue has been proved to the reasonable satisfaction of the tribunal. In such matters 'reasonable satisfaction' should not be produced by inexact proofs, indefinite testimony, or indirect inferences.*

While journalists should strive to ensure every aspect of every story is true, the 'substantially true' element excuses minor errors. The distinction was explained by Lord Shaw in the 1925 *Stable case* (at 79):

> *If I write that the defendant on March 6 took a saddle from my stable and sold it the next day and pocketed the money all without notice to me, and that in my opinion he stole the saddle, and if the facts truly are found to be that the defendant did not take the saddle from my stable but from the harness room, and that he did, without my knowledge or consent, sell my saddle, so taken and pocketed the proceeds, then the whole sting of the libel may be justifiably affirmed by a jury notwithstanding these errors in detail.*

The substantial truth defence is a better situation for the media than the one that applied before the 2005 reforms. Four jurisdictions had extra requirements: in Queensland, Tasmania, the ACT and New South Wales, the publication had to be both true and 'in the public interest' or 'to the public benefit', effectively adding a privacy rider to the justification defence (*ET's case*, 1991).

Media outlets rarely use truth alone as a defence. It usually accompanies other defences, as was the situation in the *Real Estate case* (2004), where the judge found the newspaper defendant's witnesses' evidence was more plausible 'on the balance of probabilities' than the real estate agent plaintiffs' evidence and the extent to which the reporter attempted to obtain and record the other side of the story. More recently, in the *Vocational Education case* (2018—see Key Case 8.1), the Victorian Supreme Court upheld *The Australian* newspaper's use of the substantial truth defence in a story alleging unscrupulous conduct and non-compliance with quality standards by an education businessman.

In contrast, in the *Actor case* (2018—see Key Case 8.2), the Federal Court struck out the entire truth defence relied upon by Sydney's *Daily Telegraph* on the basis that it was hopelessly bad and imprecise.

An important example of 'substantial truth' relates to people who have been convicted in Australia. Section 42 of the *Defamation Act* (s 139M ACT; s 39 NT; s 40 SA) allows proof that a person was convicted of an offence in an Australian court as *conclusive* evidence that the person committed that offence. A conviction in a foreign court is allowed as evidence that the person committed the offence, but is not conclusive. However, importantly, an allegation made by a senior investigating detective that someone had behaved so that they might reasonably be suspected of being a murderer is not protected. West Australian barrister Lloyd Rayney won $2.623 million in damages from the state government after Detective Senior Sergeant Jack Lee described him as the 'prime' and 'only' suspect in widely broadcast press conferences about the investigation into his wife's 2007 death (*Barrister's Wife case*, 2017).

KEY CASE 8.1: *THE VOCATIONAL EDUCATION CASE*

Charan v Nationwide News Pty Ltd [2018] VSC 3

FACTS

In late 2015, *The Australian* newspaper published a print article ('Watchdog Takes Peak Training College to Court') and a similar online version ('ACCC to Take Top Training College Phoenix Institute to Court'). The story was about proposed court action by the Australian Competition and Consumer Commission (ACCC) against a vocational training college called Phoenix Institute owned by the publicly listed Australian Careers Network. The article mentioned earlier media reports that alleged Phoenix had sent sales staff into housing commission estates, pressuring potential students to join up, and stated that the parent company was under investigation by both the federal Department of Education and the Australian Skills Quality Authority (ASQA) and that its shares had been suspended from trading on the stock exchange for the previous month. The article identified the plaintiff, Atkinson Prakash Charan, as one of the company's heads and stated that he had amassed a $35 million fortune from the vocational education business. In short, it suggested that, 'whilst under his management, VET organisations acted unscrupulously, in breach of regulatory standards, and that he made a large amount of money as a result of that conduct' (para. 2). Mr Charan had in fact left the company about a year earlier and the next day *The Australian* published a correction to that effect in its print edition and later an online apology for the error.

LAW

The plaintiff pleaded that eight imputations arose from the article, which the judge grouped into four headings (para. 27):

1. Mr Charan was head of ACN, a company that engaged in unscrupulous business practices that took advantage of vulnerable consumers.
2. Mr Charan was head of ACN, a company that engaged in misleading and deceptive conduct.
3. Mr Charan was head of ACN, which engaged in unscrupulous door-to-door marketing practices to vulnerable consumers.

4. Mr Charan [as head of] ACN carried on a business which was significantly non-compliant with quality standards.

The defendant, Nationwide News—publisher of *The Australian*—argued successfully that imputations 2 and 3 did not arise in the articles and defended the imputations of unscrupulous business practices and significant non-compliance with quality standards using the justification (truth) defence by proving that the imputations were substantially true as required under section 25 of the *Defamation Act 2005*. To prove the substantial truth of the unscrupulous conduct allegations, it had to convince the court under the civil burden of proof—the 'balance of probabilities'—that there was 'clear and cogent proof'. To do so, it drew upon a host of material obtained after the publication, including:

- the oral testimony of a number of witnesses who had worked in the CTI group
- the oral testimony of three 'students' allegedly enrolled in CTI courses conducted by CTI companies
- the contents of a series of audit reports, student interviews and file reviews (with associated documentation) of CTT and AMA, carried out in 2015 under the instructions of DET
- a large number of emails and associated documents flowing to and from Mr Charan and other officers or employees of the CTI companies (para. 77).

The latter included records of phone calls and messages subpoenaed from Mr Charan's telephone service provider, Telstra.

Justice Forrest found that the plaintiff 'was an entirely unreliable witness, not only on this issue but as to all matters relevant to his claim'.(para. 111). He concluded with a concise summary of his 768-paragraph judgment:

> *(a) Mr Charan was defamed in both the written and online versions of the article;*
> *(b) the article defamed him by conveying imputations that:*
> *(1) Mr Charan managed a VET organisation which engaged in unscrupulous business practices which took advantage of vulnerable consumers which resulted in him making a large amount of money; and*

> *(2) Mr Charan managed a VET organisation which was significantly non-compliant with quality standards*
>
> *I am satisfied that Nationwide has established the substantial truth of both imputations. (paras. 762–3)*

LESSONS FOR PROFESSIONAL COMMUNICATORS

Several lessons arise from this rare successful use of the justification (substantial truth) defence by a publisher:

- Considerable evidence can be needed to prove the truth of imputations stemming from an article, and sometimes this has to be located after publication and before trial, although as much evidence as possible should be available at the time of publication.
- A publisher defendant can still win a case on the pleaded imputations even if there is a basic error in the story—in this case, the fact that Mr Charan had not been formally involved with the management of the company for a year. (Of course, such errors should normally be avoided.)
- Defamation cases can be enormously expensive. In this case, the 35-day trial was reported to have cost both sides more than $3.5 million in legal fees (Duke and Vedelago, 2018).

KEY CASE 8.2: *THE ACTOR CASE*

Rush v Nationwide News Pty Ltd [2018] FCA 357 (20 March 2018)

FACTS

Nationwide News, the publisher of *The Daily Telegraph* and its associated website, published material concerning the actor Geoffrey Rush. The first publication was on a billboard; while the second and third were a series of articles that appeared in the *Telegraph* and on the *Telegraph*'s website. The articles concerned a complaint that had been made to the Sydney Theatre Company alleging that Mr Rush had engaged in 'inappropriate behaviour' during performances of the Shakespeare play *King Lear*.

LAW

The defence was struck out because the scant details provided did not give Mr Rush fair or reasonable notice of the case made against him and were likely to prejudice his preparation and presentation of his case at trial. The trial judge put it in this way (at paragraphs [64] and [65]):

> *The central allegation is that contained in paragraph 18. The allegation is that Mr Rush 'touched' the actress who was playing Cordelia 'in a manner that made [her] feel uncomfortable'. Paragraphs 18A and 19 provide some further contextual detail about the circumstances in which the 'touch' occurred. It occurred during the performance of* King Lear *when Mr Rush was carrying the actress across the stage as she simulated the lifeless body of Cordelia. The 'touch' therefore occurred in circumstances where the actions of Mr Rush and the actress were being observed by the hundreds of patrons who were no doubt intently watching the performance. And, given that Mr Rush had to carry the actress during that scene, he obviously was required to be in contact with, and therefore touch, her. The alleged 'touch' must, therefore, have been something more than the contact that must have been necessary for Mr Rush to carry the actress across the stage. The final detail is said to be that the 'touch' was not 'directed or scripted' by anyone and was not 'necessary for the purpose of the performance'.*
>
> *But what exactly was the 'touch'? What part of Mr Rush relevantly touched the actress? Was it one or both of his hands or some other part of his body? And what part of the actress's body was touched? What was the nature and duration of the 'touch'? As has already been noted, plainly if Mr Rush was required to carry the actress, his arms and hands were likely to, and likely to be required to, touch parts of the actress's body. What exactly distinguished the alleged 'touch' from the contact that must otherwise have been made between Mr Rush and the actress during the scene?*

The judge concluded the particulars of the justification (truth) defence were deficient and that the defence should be struck out (at paragraph 175).

LESSONS FOR PROFESSIONAL COMMUNICATORS

Several lessons arise from this complete loss of the justification (substantial truth) defence by a publisher:

- You need to know in advance, with precision, the exact evidence you will call to prove truth.

- The court will not allow you to try to prove your case by fishing for evidence by subpoena (as News Limited tried to do): you need to know first what your case is before a subpoena will issue—you cannot put the cart before the horse, or rely on promises from sources that evidence will be available later on; any professional communicator will have marshalled their evidence *before* publication, not afterwards.
- Headlines containing plays on words and double meanings, while they are a tabloid tradition and might attract readers, need to be considered carefully: they might seem funny when you write them, but they will inevitably come under close scrutiny, so ask yourself whether it is worth mocking the plaintiff, as opposed to telling the story straight. In this case, the *Telegraph* published a photograph of Mr Rush above a large headline that read 'King Leer'. The main article appeared under the large headline 'Star's Bard Behaviour'. The judge's comments were scathing:

> *It would seem that the sub-editors, or whoever it was who was responsible for the headlines and sub-headlines, simply could not help themselves (at paragraph [17]).*

CONTEXTUAL TRUTH

A story will often contain several defamatory imputations, but sometimes the plaintiff only complains of one. They may ignore other more serious meanings because they know that the newspaper or media defendant can prove them true. The defence of 'contextual truth' in section 26 of the *Defamation Act* (s 136 ACT; s 23 NT; s 24 SA) provides for this by allowing the defence to point to the missing meanings, prove their truth and argue that their seriousness 'swamps' or outweighs anything about which the plaintiff has complained.

For this reason, lawyers sometimes advise journalists to include additional, and provable, defamatory material in a story to take advantage of the defence. This succeeded in the *Snapper case* (2008), in which the defence could not prove that a 'paparazzo' photographer placed a bug to intercept actress Nicole Kidman's private conversations, but was able to prove that he was a 'cowboy' who created havoc in Ms Kidman's private life. Contextual truth is almost always only a partial defence: in the *Toxic Playground case* (2017), the majority of the NSW Court of Appeal held that an ABC *Media Watch* item about a *Sun-Herald* journalist's claims of toxic chemicals being found in a children's playground in Sydney implied a level of 'trickery' that impacted her 'honesty'. The ABC's contextual truth defence only applied, however, to her perceived 'competence' as a journalist, a different 'sector' of her reputation to honesty. (The court did, however, uphold the ABC's fair comment/honest opinion defence for its criticism of her story.)

THE NON-TRUTH DEFENCES

Even if journalists cannot prove the truth of the defamatory imputations conveyed, or of the article itself, other defences may still be available under legislation or common law. Each involves some notion of the social importance of matters being made public, even if they cannot be proven true.

ABSOLUTE PRIVILEGE

Journalists will not qualify for this defence unless they personally appear as a witness in court or before a parliamentary body. Nevertheless, it is important to understand this defence, because it underpins the defence of 'fair report' covered below. Absolute privilege is covered by section 27 of the Act (s 137 ACT; s 24 NT; s 25 SA). It gives a complete defence to defamation action to anyone speaking during court or parliamentary proceedings, to documents tabled there, and to publications made under the order or authority of such a body. In some jurisdictions, a schedule has been added to the Act extending absolute privilege to other related bodies.

PUBLICATION OF PUBLIC DOCUMENTS

Section 28 of the Act (s 138 ACT; s 25 NT; s 26 SA) allows a defence for the publication of public documents. This can be the actual document itself or a 'fair summary of, or a fair extract', which is the avenue of most use to journalists. The section includes a wide range of documents as 'public document' and provides for extra schedules to the Act extending the list. Professional communicators should check their individual state or territory legislation to see whether such a schedule has been added in their jurisdiction, and what it contains.

The basic list includes parliamentary reports and papers; judgments and orders of civil courts; documents issued by councils and governments 'for the information of the public'; and records of governments, courts and statutory authorities open to inspection by the public. The defence is defeated if 'the plaintiff proves that the defamatory matter was not published honestly for the information of the public or the advancement of education'. The High Court adopted a narrow interpretation of an earlier defence in the *Eye Surgeon case*. In that case, *The Daily Telegraph* was denied the defence when it relied on a judge's short and incomplete summary of the previous case, where he had said simply that a patient had been operated upon by the surgeon 'and ultimately lost her sight in both eyes' and had mentioned her 'damages for a personal injury . . . suffered at the hands of [the surgeon]'. The High Court held the report was not protected because the journalist should have made further inquiries beyond the judge's summary of the earlier case to ensure the accuracy of its report. The wording of the reformed 2005 'fair report' sections was designed to get around this problem. In the *Racehorse Cruelty case* (2017—see Key Case 8.3), the defence was used more effectively.

KEY CASE 8.3: *RACEHORSE CRUELTY CASE*

Cummings v Fairfax Digital Australia & New Zealand Pty Limited; Cummings v Fairfax Media Publications Pty Limited [2017] NSWSC 657

FACTS

Sydney Morning Herald business journalist Kate Lahey was trawling through the court lists and noticed a civil case involving the name 'Cummings'—a prominent Australian horse racing family. She requested access to key court documents and was allowed to take notes from the Statement of Claim, the Defence, the Cross-Claim and the Defence to the Cross-Claim. The documents revealed that horse trainer Anthony

Cummings—son of the late legendary trainer Bart Cummings—and his companies were in a $6.4 million court dispute with a racing and breeding company owned by prominent businessman Nathan Tinkler. The parties were at odds over the non-payment of training fees totalling $173,000 and allegations of breach of duty and cruelty. Fairfax published five articles in its newspapers, *The Sydney Morning Herald* and *The Age*, and their digital versions as well as a newspaper 'poster' about the dispute—a headline summary for newsagency and public display.

LAW

Cummings and his companies sued first in the ACT for defamation, claiming more than 60 imputations about them in the Fairfax articles and poster, including allegations of cruelty to the horses in their care, negligence, incompetence, over-training, dishonesty, taking secret commissions at horse sales, paying too high a price for horses and not buying horses of a competitive quality. The actions were eventually heard in the NSW Supreme Court before Justice Stephen Rothman.

Justice Rothman held that all of the publications except the newspaper poster qualified for the defence as a fair summary of a public document under section 28 of the *Defamation Act*. However, the poster—'CUMMINGS FIGHTING CRUELTY CLAIMS'—failed to earn that defence and carried the imputation that Mr Cummings, as a racehorse trainer, was cruel to horses he trained. The poster, if read alone, did not qualify because it did not refer to court proceedings and did not purport to be a summary of court proceedings (para. 191). But the damage was limited to those people who would identify the poster as referring to Mr Anthony Cummings as a horse trainer and not his more famous father Bart, and who did not read the article to which the poster referred (para. 197).

Justice Rothman praised the evidence and reporting of the journalist Kate Lahey, stating:

> *She was a witness of truth and her evidence was reliable. I consider that Ms Lahey honestly and in good faith sought to summarise the nature of the proceedings that were before the court, being the issues between the parties as defined by the pleadings, and wrote the article honestly and in good faith to provide that information to the public and for its information. (paras 211 and 212)*

LESSONS FOR PROFESSIONAL COMMUNICATORS

The key lesson stemming from this case is that defamatory imputations contained in fair reports of public documents will be protected under section 28 of the *Defamation Act* 'as long as the summary is substantially accurate'. Even errors are excusable as long as there is not 'a substantial misrepresentation of material fact prejudicial to the plaintiff's reputation' (para. 102). A further lesson is that truncated publications like posters–and tweets, as we learned in the *Treasurer case* (2015)–will not earn such defences because they do not contain the detail, balance and context of the larger articles to which they refer.

FAIR REPORT

Journalists and others are free to report upon certain public proceedings (regardless of the truth of the statements made in those proceedings) as long as any defamatory matter 'was contained in a fair report of any proceedings of public concern' (*Defamation Act 2005*, s 29; s 139 ACT; s 26 NT; s 27 SA). This protection stems from the notion that there are certain social institutions that are so important to the democratic or judicial process that the public deserves to be told of their proceedings—regardless of whether people happened to be defamed in the process, and that reporting of such occasions encourages public confidence in the integrity of public institutions.

As we learned earlier, those speaking in court or parliament, or reported in documents tabled there, are granted an 'absolute privilege'. A witness in court or a member of parliament engaged in a parliamentary debate can say what they like about people without fear of being sued for defamation. Journalists and bloggers cannot claim absolute privilege for a news story or report, but they are entitled to a lesser, derivative protection for their reports of such proceedings, known as 'fair report'. The report must be both 'fair' and 'accurate', as Chief Justice Gleeson and Justice Gummow noted in the *Eye Surgeon case* (2003, at para. 15):

> *[I]t is in the public interest that there should be open administration of justice. That interest is served by protecting persons who publish*

> *fair and accurate reports of court proceedings so that a reader of the report will see a substantially correct record of what was said and done in court.*

To qualify for the defence, coverage must be reasonably balanced and accurate. A report of a court case must present both the defence and prosecution arguments. Names, and other important identifying details must be correct. While mistakes inevitably occur, the court's concern is that these mistakes are not important ones, that contribute to the defamatory imputation (see Chakravarti's case, 1998). The expression used is that the report must be 'substantially accurate'.

In *Thom's case* (1964, at 380), the court stated:

> *The report need not be verbatim, but to be privileged it must accurately express what took place. Errors may occur; but if they are such as not substantially to alter the impression that the reader would have received had he been present at the trial, the protection is not lost.*

Channel Seven used the defence successfully in the Supreme Court of South Australia after it broadcast a story on its tabloid-style Today Tonight program about a High Court case that had endorsed setting aside the conviction of a woman who had pleaded guilty to defrauding Centrelink of more than $20,000 in single parent payments because of a loophole in the rules (Centrelink Fraud case, 2016). The website version was headed 'The Centrelink cheat who got away'. The court held the defence of fair report at common law and the statutory defence under section 27 of the Defamation Act (SA) had been made out by Channel 7 as the story provided information that explained in a 'simplified but readily comprehensible fashion the nature of the legal proceedings that were ultimately decided by the High Court and was a fair report of proceedings of public concern' (Summary para. 9). This was despite the report drawing upon earlier court proceedings and other material not presented in the High Court case. However, an attempt to argue that the defence should apply to a fair report of a coroner's inquest in just 26 pages of a 306-page creative non-fiction book was struck out by the Supreme Court of Western Australian because the pleaded imputations—essentially that the plaintiff was a murderer—were against the book as a whole (Unsolved Murder case, 2015, paras 32–6), not just that part of it that might have amounted to a protected report.

Aside from court and parliament, public proceedings of local government bodies and public meetings offer a rich source of protected material to working journalists (but note that there is an additional 'public interest' requirement for protection of defamatory matter arising from public meetings).

HONEST OPINION AND FAIR COMMENT

The defence now known as 'honest opinion' (similar to, but a little broader than, the common law defence of 'fair comment') is the bread-and-butter defence for all opinion and commentary in the news media. It is the defence under which quite harsh criticism can be published in the form of editorials, columns and reviews of everything from sports and theatre performances through to restaurant meals and films.

Sometimes online reviewers find themselves at the wrong end of a defamation suit. That happened to two travellers who wrote a review on the popular TripAdvisor travel site, claiming an Illinois hotel had bed bugs (*Bed Bug case,* 2011). The hotel insisted that the allegation was false, and claimed $30,000 in damages. In the United States, the Supreme Court has ruled that opinions on public matters are totally protected from defamation because opinions cannot be proven false. A TripAdvisor review suggesting a NSW motel had been used to house sex offenders was considered evidence of the extent of republication of an earlier defamatory Facebook post (*Motel case*, 2016).

Of course, criticism is the opinion of the commentator or reviewer. And everyone knows that it is impossible to prove the truth of your opinion—only that it was fairly based. The defence will succeed in Australia only where the opinion clearly is an opinion rather than a statement of fact. It must be based on true (provable) facts, or privileged material (for example, a protected court report), which is either set out or adequately referred to in the publication. It must be honestly held, the subject to which it relates must be in the public domain or a matter of public interest, and the comment must be fair (not necessarily balanced, but an opinion that could reasonably be held, based on the stated facts). Finally, the opinion held must be congruent with the imputations conveyed. The defence best suits cartoonists, whose drawings are interpreted very widely as expressions of opinion rather than statements of fact.

Let's look at the honest opinion defence as detailed in section 31 of the Act (s 139B ACT; s 28 NT; s 29 SA) and consider how each of its elements applies to a work of journalism, such as a review.

First, sub-section 1 offers the three basic planks of the honest opinion defence:

> *(a) the matter was an expression of opinion of the defendant rather than a statement of fact, and*
> *(b) the opinion related to a matter of public interest, and*
> *(c) the opinion is based on proper material.*

The defamatory statement must be one of opinion, not fact

Fact dressed up as opinion will not satisfy the defence. The test is how others would interpret the material. If a sports blogger wrote: 'Memo to Referees Association: Fred Whistleblower is unfit to umpire first grade', that would almost certainly be held to convey that the referee was incompetent and unfit to be a first-grade referee, as a statement of fact. If the writer referred to previous errors, and then said: 'Based on yet another sorry performance last night, surely it's time someone showed Whistleblower the red card', the item conveys much the same defamatory meanings, but this time as an expression of opinion, covered by the defence. Importantly, under this strand of the defence, it is the form of the 'defamatory matter'—rather than the form in which a pleaded imputation is expressed—that must be expressed as opinion rather than fact. In the *Motel case* (2016), a man had posted to Facebook an allegation that motels and flats owned by the plaintiff—a former teacher—were being used by authorities as a half-way house for convicted paedophiles. The post was shared by at least 322 others and republished on other sites, and the plaintiff was seriously assaulted by people who he believed thought he must be a child molester. While the plaintiff had not been named, he had been clearly identified as the sole owner of the motels. The defendant–a self-represented electrician–failed in his honest opinion defence because the material conveyed his defamatory imputations as statements of fact rather than opinion and no 'proper material' for the opinion had been provided (paras 121–2). The plaintiff was awarded more than $150,000 in damages. A similar quantum of damages was awarded in the *Archbishop's case* (2017), after a parishioner defamed the Archbishop of the Assyrian Church of the East on his publicly open Facebook page (in Arabic) where he had more than 260 'friends'. His defence of honest opinion failed because the parishioner's opinion alleging hypocrisy and incompetence on the part of the archbishop was 'indistinguishably mixed up with the (alleged) facts upon which it might be based' (at para. 80). To reinforce this requirement, NSW Supreme Court Justice McCallum quoted High Court Chief Justice Gleeson's judgment in *Manock's case* (2007, at 245):

> *The distinction between a comment (such as an expression of an opinion, or inference, or evaluation, or judgment) and the factual basis of the comment, blurred though it may be in many communications, affects the application of the defence in a number of ways. So long as a reader (or viewer, or listener) is able to identify a communication as a comment rather than a statement of fact, and is able sufficiently to identify the facts upon which the comment is based, then such a person is aware that all that he or she has read, viewed or heard is someone else's opinion (or inference, or evaluation, or judgment). The relationship between the two conditions mentioned in the previous sentence is that a statement is more likely to be recognisable as a statement of opinion if the facts on which it is based are identified or identifiable. (at para. 74)*

In 2017, claims on Facebook that a South Australian fruit shop owner had been issuing rape and death threats against farmers' market operators and their families were ruled ineligible for the defence because they were statements of fact rather than opinion (*Fruiterers' case*, 2017 at para. 53).

The opinion must relate to a matter of public interest

In the *ZGeek case* (2015, at [101]), the Supreme Court of the ACT found defamatory comments about a lawyer on an internet forum that related to the existing legal proceedings between the lawyer and the publisher of the website not to be on a matter of broader public interest, and defences of comments and qualified privilege were lost on that (and other) grounds.

The kinds of topics the courts have found to be matters of public interest, about which a defamatory opinion might be expressed, have included:

- the same kinds of matters on which a fair report can be based (court, parliament, public meetings, etc.)
- the public conduct of anyone involved in public affairs
- the conduct of any public officer or public servant in the discharge of public functions
- the merits of any court case or of any person involved in the case
- any book or other literary work
- a composition or work of art or performance exhibited publicly
- public entertainment or sports.

The opinion must be based on proper material

Sub-section 5 defines 'proper material' as material that:

> *(a) is substantially true, or*
> *(b) was published on an occasion of absolute or qualified privilege (whether under this Act or at general law), or*
> *(c) was published on an occasion that attracted the protection of a defence under this section or ss. 28 or 29 (the public documents or proceedings of public concern provisions—ss 138–9 ACT; ss 25–6 NT; ss 26–7 SA).*

If the facts on which the opinion is based cannot be proven (and if they are not protected in some other way—for example, as a fair report), the law regards the opinion as being of no value and so does not protect it. When an article headed 'Extreme Views from the Bench' criticised a magistrate, stating that she was 'frequently angry', the defence failed: the publisher could only point to two occasions when this had occurred (*Magistrate case*, 2005). It only stands to reason that all the facts or privileged material on which the opinion is based need to appear—or be adequately referred to—in the publication, so that the audience can clearly see the basis for the opinion and judge for themselves whether they agree or disagree. While it is true that in some cases opinion can be based on matters of such notoriety that it is not necessary to set them out chapter and verse in the publication, it is usually much safer to include them. In the *Football Hormone case* (2016), the NSW Supreme Court held there was an impermissible blur between fact and opinion in the way defamatory matter was presented in a Fairfax online publication suggesting a personal trainer had injected players from a leading Rugby League team with banned human growth hormone, even though it was part of an obviously opinionated column (paras 108–9). Further, the court held there was not sufficient 'proper material'—provable fact—available to support the opinion (para. 117). In the *ZGeek case*, the comment defence failed, as there was no evidence as to the facts upon which the comments contained in various posts were supposedly based, so it was impossible to find that the comments contained in the posts were based upon, or were a fair and accurate account of, facts that were substantially true or sufficiently identified.

Whose opinion?

Sub-sections 2 and 3 allow for situations where the published opinion is not that of the actual defendant, but of someone else. Sub-section 2 covers the situation where it is the opinion of an employee or an agent of the defendant, while sub-section 3 covers circumstances where it is the opinion of a third party (previously called the 'comment of a stranger'), which covers opinion contained in quotes from sources, letters to the editor and unsolicited contributions such as comments on websites and social media pages.

The opinion must be 'honestly held'

A defendant will lose the defence if the professional communicator (or the company) did not honestly hold the opinion at the time it was published. If the opinion was that of an employee or agent, then the plaintiff has difficulties: they have to prove the defendant did not believe that employee or agent honestly held the opinion at the time it was published. To get around this problem, journalists are now often joined as parties to the proceedings. Finally, if the opinion was that of a stranger, such as a letter-writer or a website commentator, the plaintiff has to prove that the defendant had reasonable grounds to believe that the opinion was not honestly held by the commentator at the time the defamatory matter was published. A problem when checking the identity of a letter writer or web commenter might constitute such a ground.

None of this requires the opinion to be perfectly balanced. The common law allows a commentator wide latitude to take a particular view. The test is whether a person, looking at the facts set out, could form the opinion expressed–or, to put it another way, if the opinion does not bear any rational relationship at all to the facts on which it purports to be based, it cannot be comment.

The comment is not fair if it is actuated by malice. In the case of mass-media publications where honest opinion is relied upon, it can be expected that the bona fides of the journalist will be called into question. In the *Coco Roco case* (2007 and 2013), for example, it was unsuccessfully alleged that the journalist had conspired with a former employee to ruin the plaintiffs' restaurant.

The opinion must fit the imputation

As the defence is designed to protect fairly held opinions, it fails if it can be shown that the writer (or broadcaster) did not truly hold those opinions at the time of publication. There is a trap here: in the 1980s, *The Age* ran a column by David Thorpe alleging the West Indies cricket team had 'thrown' the second match in a World Series final (*Lloyd's case*, 1985). West Indies captain Clive Lloyd sued for defamation, and the newspaper lost its fair comment defence because the writer, Thorpe, had stated on oath that he did not intend to convey the imputations that were claimed to arise. Lloyd's team argued successfully that if Thorpe did not intend to convey this meaning, then it could not be his 'honest opinion' for the purposes of the fair comment defence. A similar thing happened in the *Yuk case* (1993), in which Edmund Capon, the director of the Art Gallery of New South Wales, said under cross-examination that he did not intend to convey an imputation of incompetence about painter Vladas Meskenas, who had painted a portrait of the late stockbroker Rene Rivkin. Capon said that, in his remarks (which included the word 'yuk'), he intended to criticise the painting, not the painter. To satisfy this aspect of the defence, the commentator must foresee the imputation claimed by the plaintiff to be conveyed by the defamatory material, and found by the jury to arise. For this reason, comment pieces—especially highly contentious ones—should be referred for legal advice.

Letters to the editor and comments by third parties on media websites raise special issues if they are to qualify for the honest opinion/fair comment defence. Media outlets need very careful checking systems if they are to publish letters and comments protected by the defence. They need to ensure that:

- all facts on which the comments are based are provable or privileged facts, and are stated in the material unless they are matters of notoriety
- the letter writer genuinely wrote the letter and lives at the address stated
- all amendments are checked with the writer and the approval has been signed or diarised (deletion of facts can erode the defence, and amendments can render the letter no longer the honest opinion of the writer)
- anyone defamed in such a letter or comment is afforded a reasonable right of reply
- all protocols for letters to the editor and comment moderation have been checked with the media outlet's lawyers to ensure they comply with the laws of that jurisdiction.

The advent of new communication technologies has complicated the protection for letter writers. Emailed and SMS letters to the editor, along with people's comments on social media sites, present difficulties in checking the bona fides of writers, and online chat sessions hosted on media outlets' websites can leave the publisher (and many other organisations hosting their own websites and social media sites) exposed as a result of the defamatory comments of participants.

While cartoonists appear to enjoy a great deal of freedom to satirise and comment, the courts have taken a less favourable view of other forms of satire. In 1999, the High Court refused the ABC leave to appeal against a Queensland Court of Appeal decision to uphold an injunction against the broadcast of a satirical song about the politician Pauline Hanson, titled 'I'm a Backdoor Man'. The song was created by the artist Simon Hunt—aka 'Pauline Pantsdown'—and consisted of voice grabs from Ms Hanson taken out of context and set to music so it sounded as though she was singing quite sexually explicit lyrics and advocating political views opposed to those she publicly espoused. The fact that the High Court declined leave to appeal against the prior restraint of such a satirical publication is worrying (*Hanson's case*, 1999), as is the fact that it was subsequently cited in the High Court's later *Worm Farming case* (2006) on prior restraint.

It should be noted that nothing in the uniform *Defamation Acts* does away with the previous common law defences, one of which was the defence of 'fair comment', which has a long body of established case law. Publishers frequently rely upon common law fair comment as an alternative defence. The ABC's *Media Watch* program successfully used the fair comment defence and its newer honest opinion version to defeat defamation suits by two journalists in successive decades. In *Carleton's case* (2002), Media Watch accused *60 Minutes* reporter Richard Carleton of plagiarising a BBC documentary in order to create a report titled 'The Evil that Men Do'. (Carleton later died of a heart attack at the scene of the Beaconsfield mining rescue in Tasmania in 2006.) ACT Supreme Court Justice Higgins found that the *Media Watch* program contained imputations of 'plagiarism' and 'lazy journalism', but not of theft of materials from the other programs, or deceit or dishonesty.

He upheld the defence of fair comment when all other defences failed. Seventeen years later, in the *Toxic Playground case* (2017), the NSW Court of Appeal upheld both the fair comment and honest opinion defences run by the ABC to defend *Media Watch*'s criticism of *Sun-Herald* journalist Natalie O'Brien's story about the alleged discovery by testing conducted by the Environmental Protection Authority (EPA) of toxic substances on land near an industrial site and a children's playground. The court held the imputations of irresponsible journalism and trickery were expressions of opinion, which were based on facts truly stated or sufficiently identified within the *Media Watch* program, that the opinions were expressed on a matter of public interest and that they were objectively fair. Trial Justice Lucy McCallum described it as 'a textbook illustration of the operation of the defence of fair comment' (2016, para. 61).

CLASSIC CASE 8.1: *LOBSTER CASE*

Blue Angel Restaurant v John Fairfax and Sons Ltd (1989) 11 *Gazette of Law and Journalism* 13

FACTS

This classic case demonstrates the workings of the fair comment defence. It resulted from a review by *The Sydney Morning Herald*'s then food critic, Leo Schofield. The review was headed 'High Drama Where Lobsters Have No Privacy', and started this way:

> *I have never really understood about live fish in tanks in restaurants. If they are seen as a way to guarantee freshness, then surely we ought also to have live pigs in pens in the middle of restaurants, ready for slaughter to ensure the freshest possible loin of pork and the odd steer waiting patiently to be zapped by the electric hammer before transformation.*

Schofield explained that the restaurant broiled ('grilled') its lobsters. The menu warned that there was a 45-minute wait for lobster:

> *That should really have sent the balloon up for us. Even Godzilla boiled for 45 minutes would be appallingly overcooked. Which is what our grilled*

> *lobster most certainly was, cooked until every drop of juice and joy in the thing had been successfully eliminated, leaving a charred husk of a shell containing meat that might have been albino walrus.*

He continued, stating that the 'carbonised claws contained only a kind of white powder', describing the handling of 'excellent fresh lobster at $25 a kilo' as 'close to culinary crime'.

LAW

The restaurant sued. The main imputations claimed were that the plaintiff:

- was a cruel and inhumane restaurateur in that it, by its employees, killed live lobsters by broiling them alive
- was an incompetent restaurateur in that it, by its employees, broiled lobsters for 45 minutes contrary to accepted culinary methods
- was a restaurateur that charged a price for excellent fresh lobster that, when later cooked incompetently by its employees, did not then represent good value for money
- was an incompetent restaurateur in that it, by its employees, served lobsters with charred husks of shell, meat destroyed as to quality and claws containing white powder.

The *Herald* and Schofield failed in their defence of fair comment. Most importantly, they were unable to prove the truth of the facts on which the opinion had been based, many of which appeared to have been exaggerated for effect. They had also eaten the evidence. The restaurant was awarded $100,000 in damages.

LESSONS FOR REVIEWERS, BLOGGERS AND OPINION WRITERS

The verdict was greeted with a hail of protest from the media, with many claiming it marked the end of the fair comment defence. The case was followed more recently by an initial win for the media in the *Coco Roco case* (2007), only to be overturned on appeal (2013). The first lesson is that journalists must be able to prove every fact on which they base their comments: in the *Coco Roco case*, reviewer Matthew Evans was able to produce his contemporaneous notes and there was additional evidence from his dining companion and back-up evidence (obtained after the defamation claim was received) from former restaurant employees.

The second lesson is that even the most careful work can be undone by a stray headline or fact box: the piece was headlined 'Matthew Evans fails Coco Roco', and the fact box identified each of the proprietors, who were named. The problem was that there were two separate restaurants, Coco (an expensive restaurant) and Roco (a separate, cheaper, incarnation). Matthew Evans had only dined at one of them (Coco), while the court held that the defamatory imputations referred to each of the plaintiffs in connection with their management of both.

QUALIFIED PRIVILEGE

Just as in Australia, many other jurisdictions offer a 'public-interest' or 'qualified privilege' defence for defamatory material about extremely important public issues, even though the publisher might not have enough evidence available to prove truth, and other defences might not apply. It is important to distinguish here between matters of legitimate 'public interest' and other matters such as celebrity gossip, which might be just 'interesting to the public'. Even so, under First Amendment protections in the United States, writers can get away with false publications about celebrities and other public figures as long as they are not being malicious in their attacks. The Supreme Court of Canada developed a whole new defence of 'responsible communication' in 2009. It stemmed from a *Toronto Star* article claiming property developer Peter Grant was pulling political strings in his efforts to get a golf course approved (*Golf Course case*, 2009). He sued for libel over the allegation, and the court decided that there should be a defence for publications on matters of public interest that are properly researched, even if the publication is false. Importantly, it extended the defence to non-journalist bloggers. The Canadian defence was a development of law over a decade in the United Kingdom and Australia, where cases and legislative changes had introduced guidelines for publishers wanting to take advantage of the statutory qualified privilege (public-interest) defence when the material proved to be false. These were outlined by the House of Lords in *Reynolds' case* (2001) and in section 30 of the uniform *Defamation Act* in Australian states and territories in 2005–06.

Sadly, experience suggests that the defence will rarely if ever succeed in Australia in the case of a mass media publication, because the bar for what amounts to 'reasonable' conduct has been set impossibly high.

Qualified privilege as a defence in Australia takes three forms:

- qualified privilege at common law
- qualified privilege as it was incorporated into section 30 of the *Defamation Act 2005* (s 139A ACT; s 27 NT; s 28 SA)
- the extended political qualified privilege (the *Lange* defence).

Common law defence of qualified privilege

The common law defence of qualified privilege survives in addition to the statutory defence in all jurisdictions. It protects people who are legally, socially or morally obliged to give defamatory information to others, even if they cannot prove the truth of the material, provided those to whom they publish have a corresponding interest in receiving that information. Such protection is necessary for the normal working of society, particularly in the corporate and professional spheres. The common law defence hinges on there being a reciprocal duty–interest relationship between the publisher of the defamatory material and the person receiving it: the publisher must have a legal, social or moral duty to publish the defamatory material and the recipient must have a corresponding legal, social or moral interest in receiving it. For example, teachers need to be able to discuss frankly with other teachers (and perhaps write reports about) students' attitudes, performance and perhaps very private details that might be affecting their studies.

In the *ZGeek case* (2015), the defendant was unable to persuade the court that they were under a social or moral duty to publish defamatory matter about a lawyer who reported juror misconduct to a court, nor did the recipients of the forum have a reciprocal interest in receiving the information contained in the post. Further, the allegations were poorly researched, and the defendant had not taken any reasonable steps to verify the information or approach the plaintiff for her 'side of the story' prior to publication (at para. 97).

The defence has not usually been available to mass-media publishers, because the courts do not regard the media as having a duty to publish defamatory material to the world at large: not every member of the audience would have a legitimate stake in receiving the defamatory material. The common law defence has been extended to the media for defamation that occurs during discussion of political matters (treated below as a separate defence of extended *Lange* qualified privilege) and also when it publishes a reply to a public attack directed at it (or someone else's reply to an attack upon them), when the first attack was also itself published in the media.

Qualified privilege is defeated by proof of malice. In this context, 'malice' has a wider meaning than its ordinary meaning of 'spite' or 'ill-will', but extends to any attempt to use an otherwise privileged occasion (for example, the giving of a job reference) for an improper, ulterior or 'collateral' purpose.

The statutory qualified privilege defence

Under section 30 of the Act (s 139A ACT; s 27 NT; s 28 SA), a publisher will be protected for publishing defamatory material if the publisher can prove three things:

- that the recipient has an interest or apparent interest in having information on some subject, and
- that the matter is published to the recipient in the course of giving to the recipient information on that subject, and
- that the conduct of the defendant in publishing that matter is reasonable in the circumstances (at sub-section 1).

At first glance, this offers a wonderful defence to the media publishing on important public matters, even when they cannot prove the truth of the defamatory allegations they make. The sticking point has been the requirement that the publisher's conduct be 'reasonable in the circumstances'. The courts interpreted this narrowly after *Austin's case* (1986), where Rugby League commentator Ron Casey criticised the performance of the trainer of a first-grade team, calling him a 'fitness fanatic' and giving examples of the rigorous training regimens he demanded. But he could not prove the truth of some of the allegations, so tried the earlier NSW version of the qualified privilege defence. The highest court of appeal at the time, the Privy Council, decided that while readers of a metropolitan daily newspaper did have an interest in knowing about the performance of a first-grade Rugby League team, Casey's actions were not 'reasonable in the circumstances', and he had not tried hard enough to check his facts. To this day it remains all too easy for a court to reason backwards from proven factual error: the journalist must not have taken reasonable steps. Why? Because the error would have been discovered if they had.

At sub-section 30(3), the *Defamation Act 2005* now sets out a number of factors that the court may take into account in deciding whether a publisher's behaviour was reasonable in the circumstances. It states the court may take the following factors into account:

> *(a) the extent to which the matter published is of public interest, and*
> *(b) the extent to which the matter published relates to the performance of the public functions or activities of the person, and*
> *(c) the seriousness of any defamatory imputation carried by the matter published, and*
> *(d) the extent to which the matter published distinguishes between suspicions, allegations and proven facts, and*
> *(e) whether it was in the public interest in the circumstances for the matter published to be published expeditiously, and*
> *(f) the nature of the business environment in which the defendant operates, and*
> *(g) the sources of the information in the matter published and the integrity of those sources, and*
> *(h) whether the matter published contained the substance of the person's side of the story and, if not, whether a reasonable attempt was made by the defendant to obtain and publish a response from the person, and*
> *(i) any other steps taken to verify the information in the matter published, and*
> *(j) any other circumstances that the court considers relevant.*

This list provides guidelines to reporters and editors on the amount of research they need to do, short of proving the actual truth of the allegations, in order to have a chance of establishing the defence. The fact that the list focuses, among other things, on the sources for the story 'and the integrity of those sources' does not, however, augur well for any reporter wanting to run with this defence on the basis of confidential sources: their identity is likely to be crucial to establishing the defence. In the *Club Rawhide case* (2015), *Herald Sun* reporter Andrew Rule had relied on confidential police sources to assert in an article that a strip club was used as a venue for meetings between corrupt police and members of the Outlaws motorcycle gang. The court held that this was defamatory of the club owner and was not protected by qualified privilege because it was 'not reasonable in the circumstances'. Justice Whelan said the issue was not so much the identity of Rule's sources as the fact that the imputation went further than his confidential sources had suggested:

> *What was written went beyond what Mr Rule's sources had told him about Club Rawhide. What was written did not distinguish between suspicions, allegations and proven facts. What was written about Club Rawhide was not important in relation to the significant public interest aspects of the story. It was unreasonable for Mr Rule not to contact Mrs Hardie before publishing the story. If he had contacted Mrs Hardie he may have discovered, as was revealed during the trial, that there is no evidence whatsoever of corrupt police, or indeed any police, ever meeting members of the Outlaws at Club Rawhide. (at para. 188)*

The defence is defeated—just as in the case of the common law version of qualified privilege—if the plaintiff can show that the publisher was actuated by malice (a lack of good faith, an improper motive or some other purpose).

Search engine Google failed to establish the statutory qualified privilege defence in the *Psychic Stalker case* (2017). There, Google had been notified that its search engine results on a search of the plaintiff's name, Dr Janice Duffy, generated excerpts of various websites where the medical researcher was described as a 'Psychic Stalker' after she had posted negative reviews of psychics' predictions. A majority of the Full Court of the Supreme Court of South Australia held it could not claim the statutory qualified privilege defence because not all readers who used the search engine had a legitimate 'interest' in seeing the defamatory material when they made the searches for 'curiosity alone'. There must be a 'sufficient connection' between the defamatory words and the subject of interest and it could not be established for all people searching for the terms that the defamatory results were provided 'in the course of giving them information on the subject'. Google's conduct had not been 'reasonable in the circumstances', considering its communications with Dr Duffy over the sixteen months for which she was trying to have the material removed. It upheld the award of $115,000 in damages.

Bauer Media failed on several of these grounds in its attempts to use both versions of the qualified privilege defence in *Rebel's case* (2017). The court held that the publisher had an improper motive in publishing the defamatory matter about actor Rebel Wilson and it did not establish its reasonable belief in its readers' interest in receiving the information. Interesting in the era of 'fake news', often published about celebrities, Justice Dixon stated:

> *The law does not recognise a social or moral duty in a publisher to protect the interest of readers in not being misled in their curiosity about celebrities when it was threatened by journalistic error. The interest of readers of the* Women's Weekly *website in receiving correcting information about the relatively inconsequential circumstances of a celebrity published in a different medium is not of a nature that engenders a social or moral duty. (at para. 51)*

Extended 'political' qualified privilege (*Lange* privilege)

International moves to reform defamation laws in some Western democracies in order to allow more criticism of political figures and discussion of important public issues came four decades after the US Supreme Court had decided the First Amendment should offer better defamation defences. Basic principles in US law generally followed the British common law until the 1960s, and they still share many common principles. In *Sullivan's case* (1964), an elected Alabama official claimed *The New York Times* had defamed him by publishing an advertisement that alleged police under his supervision had been violent and intimidating in their treatment of African-American civil rights protesters. However, the Supreme Court invoked the First Amendment to rule that public officials had to meet tough new tests before they could succeed in a defamation action, even if the allegations in the article were proven false. This is one reason US defamation law allows for much more vigorous public criticism and debate. Throughout the 1990s, several countries—including Australia, New Zealand, South Africa and India—followed suit to some degree and extended their defamation defences to allow a greater freedom to communicate on political and government matters.

In a series of decisions through the 1990s, the High Court of Australia held that common law qualified privilege applied to defamatory material published in the course of political discussion. It began with two important decisions handed down in 1992: the *ACTV case* and *Wills' case*. The first was a challenge to the federal government's power to prohibit political advertising on the eve of an election. The second was a challenge to the power to punish those who wrote or spoke words calculated to bring the Industrial Relations Commission into disrepute. Both pieces of legislation placed a burden on citizens' right to communicate on matters of government—a right that was fundamental to the system of representative government set out in the Constitution.

In 1994, in *Stephens' case*, the High Court held that the common law qualified privilege defence applied to media publications when they discussed political matters, but in *Theophanous's case* the court went in a different direction, developing a completely new defence: it required the media to prove, among other things, that publication was reasonable in the circumstances—the same requirement that had proven so elusive for the media under previous NSW law and that now forms part of the *Defamation Act*, at section 30.

In 1997, the High Court reaffirmed the existence of the implied guarantee of political free speech in *Lange's case*, but again held that the defence required the publisher to demonstrate that it had acted reasonably, which meant proving that:

- it had reasonable grounds for believing each of the imputations was true
- there was an absence of belief that they were untrue
- proper steps were taken to verify the material, and
- normally a response had been sought and published from the person defamed.

It is certainly not a defence that journalists should rely upon without legal advice. Defamation expert and Supreme Court of Queensland Justice Peter Applegarth summed it up by stating that 'the legacy of Lange for the law of defamation is an uncertain and unstable defence that provides little practical protection for communications about matters of public interest' (Applegarth, 2011: 99).

In *Obeid's case* (2006), the NSW Supreme Court applied the 'reasonableness' test in a political discussion case suggesting corruption. Following existing NSW decisions, it held that the defence failed because the journalists did not intend the imputations that the court found were conveyed; failed to conduct adequate research; and had included material known to be untrue. When confronted with the allegations, the government minister against whom the allegations were made—Eddie Obeid—had done no more than give a blanket denial, which the newspaper had included. The court held that his denial was outweighed by the balance of the article. (Nevertheless, ten years after he won $162,173 in damages in this case, Obeid was sentenced to five years' imprisonment for misconduct in public office and lost an appeal in 2017.)

In the *WorkCover case* (2016), the Full Court of the South Australian Supreme Court rejected the *Sunday Mail*'s attempt to use the qualified privilege defence. While there was general public interest in dishonest election practices, the defamatory matter related to narrower issues of whether one individual on the WorkCover Board of Directors lacked integrity or had breached the Code of Conduct of the Australian Institute of Company Directors. Further, the newspaper had not taken reasonable steps to verify the integrity imputation because the plaintiff had since been absolved of those allegations by independent inquiries. The newspaper had also failed to make a reasonable attempt to obtain a response from the plaintiff as to the imputations pleaded and had only interviewed her about other matters. The court awarded $75,000 in damages.

However, Channel 7 had success using the extended *Lange* qualified privilege in the *Centrelink Fraud case* in 2016. There it argued successfully that its *Today Tonight* story, 'The Centrelink Cheat Who Got Away', met three of the four requirements: it had reasonable grounds for believing the imputations were true; it took proper steps to verify their accuracy; and it did not believe they were untrue. It was excused from meeting the fourth requirement: seeking a response from the person defamed (at para. 460).

The broader lesson that reporters, bloggers and media advisers should take away from these cases is that if they rely upon qualified privilege—whether under the *Defamation Act* or the common law—their inquiries will be subjected to minute analysis. They should offer individuals a right of reply to any criticism about them, and assess the way it is presented in the story. Be wary of saying that the person who has been accused 'claims' the allegations are false, or of simply reporting an allegation and saying a person 'denies' it. A more evenly balanced treatment will not create a defence in itself, but thorough and fair reporting will minimise the chances of the defence being destroyed.

MALICE AND LACK OF GOOD FAITH

All common law qualified privilege and fair comment defences will be defeated if the plaintiff can prove that the defendant acted out of malice in publishing the material. Malice can be established if the plaintiff can prove that the defendant had an improper or collateral motive in publishing the material. That happened in the *Treasurer case* (2015), where the court considered that an editor's email stating 'launch our dirt on Hockey' and 'This one ain't over yet' combined with other discussions and events to provide enough evidence of malice towards the then federal Treasurer to defeat a defence of qualified privilege if that had been available to Fairfax Media (paras 414–15).

TWO OTHER DEFENCES

The Act mentions two other defences that would not normally affect the work of journalists. However, it is important that you at least know they exist.

INNOCENT DISSEMINATION

Section 32 (s 139C ACT; s 29 NT; s 30 SA) provides a defence of 'innocent dissemination', which excuses publication by 'subordinate distributors' who did not know the defamatory material was there, did not write or produce it, and did not have the capacity to exercise editorial control.

The only individuals who have an excuse by arguing 'innocent dissemination' are distributors, such as newsagents, librarians, booksellers and, in some circumstances, ISPs and internet content hosts, who lose the defence if it is shown that they knew the publication contained the defamatory material. In the *Psychic Stalker case* (2017), the majority of the South Australian Court of Appeal held that a delay of sixteen months after notification of defamatory material to a search engine was unreasonable, meaning Google lost any claim to an innocent dissemination defence.

TRIVIALITY

Section 33 (s 139D ACT; s 30 NT; s 31 SA) provides a defence of triviality that is short enough to repeat in full: 'It is a defence to the publication of defamatory matter if the defendant proves that the circumstances of publication were such that the plaintiff was unlikely to sustain any harm.' However, as with most apparently simple matters, it requires a publisher to be able to predict at the point of publication that the matter would be so trivial as to not impact upon the plaintiff's reputation, an assessment that would normally require legal expertise. One case in which the triviality defence succeeded is the *Dennis Denuto case*.

REMEDIES

While Division 3 of the Act (Division 9.4.3 ACT) deals with the damages available to a plaintiff if they win, the vast majority of defamation cases are settled out of court. Many are resolved without even entering the court system. Out-of-court settlements might include financial compensation and correction notices, and even agreements to desist from covering certain issues (which, of course, might be highly unethical) and, increasingly, agreement to take the offending material down.

KINDS OF REMEDIES

There are two main remedies available to the courts in defamation cases: damages and injunctions. The Act only addresses damages, but the courts also have the power to order injunctions restraining publication, although these are rarely available in defamation cases on an interim basis—at least against the mass media—before a full trial of all of the issues.

Damages

The most common remedy for defamation is an award of damages to compensate your victim for their emotional hurt and any financial loss they might have suffered from your publication. This can range from a pittance ($100 in the *Yuk case*) through to millions of dollars in the case of proven financial loss. Large damages awards have included $4.75 million in *Rebel's case* (2017) in Victoria (reduced on appeal) and $2.6 million in the *Barrister's Wife case* (2017) in Western Australia. Just as damaging can be the lawyers' fees and court costs, which can escalate immeasurably with appeals and delays. Many have criticised the system of awarding damages for defamation because in many cases it is hard to see that they actually do anything to repair a person's shattered reputation.

Section 34 of the *Defamation Act* (s 139E ACT; s 31 NT; s 32 SA) requires the court to ensure that 'there is an appropriate and rational relationship between the harm sustained by the plaintiff and the amount of damages awarded'.

Section 35 (s 139F ACT; s 32 NT; s 33 SA) sets the range for non-economic loss (hurt feelings, shock, embarrassment, etc.), subject to a formula, to be increased from time to time. In New South Wales, for example, at the time of publication this stood at $389,500 (*NSW Gazette*, 2017). On the other hand, proven economic loss has no upper limit, explaining the record extra $3.9 million component to actor Rebel Wilson in 2017 because of likely lost movie opportunities stemming from the defamatory material (*Rebel's case*, 2017), later stripped away from her in the publisher's 2018 appeal.

Section 37 (s 139H ACT; s 34 NT; s 35 SA) does away with exemplary and punitive damages, which used to be awarded as a punishment or deterrent and were not related to the amount of harm suffered. However, the category of 'aggravated damages' remains, which courts can still award if the defendant has, either during or subsequent to the defamatory publication, made the damage worse in a way that was lacking in good faith, or if its conduct was improper or unjustifiable. At common law, failure to make proper inquiries about allegations before publishing can justify the award of aggravated damages, which are unlimited in amount.

Section 38 (s 139I ACT; s 35 NT; s 36 SA) allows evidence in mitigation of damages, including apologies, corrections and previous awards of damages over publications with the same meaning.

Division 4 of the Act (Division 9.4.4 ACT) deals with costs and guides courts on taking settlement offers into account. Crucial to this is the fact that costs (court costs and legal fees) invariably outweigh the amount of damages awarded, by a wide margin. In the *Yuk case* (1993), the defendant had to pay $60,000 in costs despite the fact that the jury awarded the plaintiff only $100 in damages. Even a publisher who wins will often not have their costs paid: the plaintiff often has no money, or simply goes bankrupt, as occurred in the *Snapper case* (2008) and the *Twitter case* (2013). Sometimes defamation cases–and resulting damages–are pursued and awarded on a 'tit for tat' basis, as appeared to be the situation in the *Councillor's case* (2017). There, a property developer won $15,000 in defamation damages against a Tweed Shire councillor who had sent emails to journalists calling for an independent review of his developments and alleging he had a scandalous association with a violent murder victim (*Councillor's case*, 2017, paras 6 and 7). But after that first judgment was issued in 2014, the developer told the *Gold Coast Bulletin* that the councillor was not a 'fit and proper person' to hold her position, and these comments featured in the newspaper's story. The councillor sued both the developer and the newspaper but withdrew her suit against the *Bulletin* after it apologised. The NSW Supreme Court awarded her $45,000 in damages against the developer, mainly on the basis that he had given the quote to the newspaper on the understanding that it would be republished widely in print and online (paras 63–5).

Injunctions

Judges also have the power to issue injunctions–court orders–preventing the publication of defamatory material or insisting that already published items be removed. Courts are generally slow to issue injunctions because of a centuries-old principle against 'prior restraint' (see Chapter 2). Instead, they prefer a system where defamatory material can be dealt with by court action after it has been published, so there is minimal censorship prior to publication. While judges have generally followed this principle, there have been many exceptions where they have previewed defamatory material and issued injunctions to stop media organisations going ahead with its release. Courts will issue interim–or 'interlocutory'–injunctions only if they are satisfied a jury would certainly find the material was defamatory, and there could be no defence of truth or privilege available. They are known as 'gag orders'. Rare examples were *Chappell's case* (1988), *Hanson's case* (1998) and more recently (but later overturned) the *AAMAC case* (2009). In 2016, the NSW Supreme Court issued an interlocutory injunction for a short period in a defamation case which had its origin in a commercial dispute between competitors (rather than a media case) and it did not foresee the injunction limiting the free discussion of matters of public interest (*Security case*, 2016, para. 16).

CRIMINAL DEFAMATION

All the above discussion concerns civil defamation–the bringing of a private action against an individual or a company for some remedy, usually damages. A second body of defamation law, criminal defamation, is based on the notion that if someone has been seriously defamed, they should have some means under the criminal law by which they can secure punishment of the publisher. As Lord Denning said in the 1977 *Goldsmith case* (at 485), 'A criminal libel is so serious that the offender should be punished for it by the state itself. He should either be sent to prison or made to pay a fine to the state itself.'

Claims of criminal defamation usually arise between ordinary citizens rather than in the media. Examples include the *Wineries case* (1998), where a disgruntled businessman penned a letter, purportedly from his business partner's wife, in which she described her husband as someone who 'engages in adultery, deception, taxation fraud and is a confidence trickster' who could be 'compared to the worst, most infectious, bacterial parasite which can only be found at the bottom of the most unhygienic sewage scum swamp'. The man sent the letter to at least one South Australian winery and pleaded guilty to criminal defamation.

In 2001, a quadriplegic woman and her mother were charged with six counts of criminal defamation after they allegedly posted notices accusing townsfolk of perjuring themselves in her compensation claim against the local council and its swimming pool operators (*Quadriplegic case*, 2001). Police later dropped the charges. In another case, horse racing identities Robert and William Waterhouse prosecuted the producer and reporter of an ABC *Four Corners* program. The NSW Director of Public Prosecutions eventually stepped in to prevent the defamation prosecutions from proceeding because the defence of qualified privilege was going to be available (*Waterhouse case*, 1988).

While prosecutions for criminal defamation are rare, it is important for professional communicators to know of its existence. However, there is not sufficient space in this text to deal with it in detail. Professional communicators are advised to refer to the legislation in their jurisdiction. Victoria still has sections 10 and 11 of its *Wrongs Act 1958*, which criminalise libel if the defendant knows the publication is false. Its truth defence requires proof of both truth and public benefit, and it carries a two-year jail sentence as its maximum penalty. In most jurisdictions, the basic civil defamation defences now apply to criminal defamation.

INJURIOUS FALSEHOOD

Included in any study of defamation must be a brief account of the civil action for injurious falsehood (also known as 'malicious falsehood'), which since the 2005 defamation reforms has been used more frequently. The plaintiff needs to prove the statement:

- was false
- caused actual financial loss
- was actuated by malice.

While this onus to prove that the material is false shifts to the plaintiff (the opposite of defamation), injurious falsehood will sometimes be available when defamation is not. For example, larger corporations and local government bodies can avail themselves of this action. Unlike defamation, injurious falsehood is not concerned with reputation, but rather with false, malicious statements causing loss. A false statement—for example, that a commercial operator had ceased business—might well cause financial loss, and will sometimes be made with malice—perhaps by a competitor or vengeful former employee. A classic example was the *Go Daddy case* (2005), in which a disgruntled customer set up a blog website making unsubstantiated claims of fraud and theft, with the domain name 'hunterholdensucks'. The motor dealer franchise owner sued successfully. The reforms to defamation laws in 2005 appeared to prompt more injurious falsehood actions, because corporations with more than ten employees could no longer sue for defamation. They are also sometimes used in an effort to get around the principle against prior restraint.

In the *Toll Uniform case* (2017), the Federal Court found the behaviour of a former employee who wore items of the corporate uniform in videos and social media posts espousing his white supremacist views prima facie fulfilled the elements of the injurious falsehood action and justified interlocutory orders restraining him from doing so. In reaching its decision the court followed the reasoning in the *ReGroup case* (2016), where the court had found a prima facie case for injunctions restraining the two respondents from creating public posters and messages on mobile vans featuring injurious falsehoods about the business practices of the plaintiff and his company. A more recent example of a similar injunction, again (at least initially) restraining material displayed on vans, was the *Thunder case* (2017), discussed in Chapter 5.

TIPS FOR MINDFUL PRACTICE

To minimise the risk of defamation, professional communicators should do the following:

- Double-check everything. This includes spelling of names, addresses, charges, photo captions, headline wording, graphics, supers and subtitling on television news. Many defamation cases result from basic errors that could have been avoided. Mistakes are hard to defend.
- Give them their say. Give individuals and company representatives the opportunity to respond to allegations against them or their organisations.
- You must be able to account for every word in a quotation and every fact in your story, so ensure you keep accurate notes and store all notebooks and digital recordings safely. Remember that these are legal evidence and must be treated with respect: interview dates, times and subjects should be noted carefully and direct quotes identified at the time of note-taking or recording.
- File notes. Your notebook and digital recordings are legal documents, usually discoverable (i.e. open to the plaintiff's inspection). They may end up being tendered as evidence. Notebooks and digital recordings

need to be dated carefully and should be filed for three years—the extended limitation period for defamation actions.

- Make sure you have the evidence. Something someone told you is not enough. Truth needs to be verified and the substance of all allegations proved. Remember, you must also prove the truth of any imputations that arise.
- Work to the defences. Learn the criteria for the honest opinion defence and satisfy them when writing a review or comment piece. Make sure you clearly separate fact from comment. Ensure that your court, parliamentary and meeting reports are fair and accurate. Try not to rely on the qualified privilege defence unless the matter is of overwhelming public importance and you have sound legal advice giving the go-ahead. In the end, it usually comes down to being able to prove in court that what you wrote was true.
- Get legal advice and follow it. Familiarise yourself with your news organisation's 'escalation' or 'upward referral' policy. Trust your lawyers and level with them: they are on your side.
- Diarise. Take diary notes or send yourself an email detailing all developments in defamation actions, starting from the moment you advise your supervisor of your concern. This can be important in both a legal and an industrial sense. An accurate record of the decisions made during the reporting and verifying stage can protect you against false accusations that you were negligent or reckless.
- Avoid innuendo. Don't try to write so that the reader can understand a defamatory meaning even though it is not explicitly stated. In other words, don't ask your reader to 'read between the lines'. If you are going to defame someone intentionally (in other words, if you are sure your defences are rock-solid on sound legal advice), then do it properly within the available defences: identify them fully so that there is no confusing them with someone else.
- Take care with apologies. Once a threat of defamation has been received, notify your editor, news director or supervisor immediately. Never enter into negotiations with complainants or their representatives. Leave this to your supervisors and their lawyers. Of course, be polite. Courteously refer the person to your superior.

Apologies, corrections or offers of amends must be worded carefully and handled in accordance with the legislation.

- Be very careful of pursuits, arrests, re-enactments, police media conferences, 'ride-alongs' and 'media walks'. Remember, just because the police have told you something, that does not mean it is true. Too often, people are defamed because their questioning, arrest or charging has been wrongly reported, or because police have arrested or charged the wrong person or given out the wrong name or photograph. You are not protected against defamation action unless the material can be sourced to the person's appearance in court. You are also at risk of *sub judice* contempt by reporting at this crucial stage. (A detailed account of the various risk zones of reporting arrests and trials appears in Chapter 5.)
- Be aware of, but not cowed by, the rich and powerful. While bold journalism is important if the defences are assured, it is worth remembering that the most common professions among the lists of plaintiffs are prominent sports and entertainment 'personalities', politicians, business people, doctors and other professionals.
- Take care with humour. Remember, it can be enough that you hold someone up to ridicule for your material to be defamatory. Get it legalled.

IN A NUTSHELL

- Lawyers will advise you on defences you might be able to argue, such as truth, fair comment or privilege.
- The defamation laws introduced in all Australian jurisdictions in 2005–06 offered uniform defences to defamation, making it easier for those publishing across state and territory borders.
- If the plaintiff has established that the material is defamatory, a media outlet has five main defences available to it: truth (or 'justification'); fair report (of a public document or proceedings); honest opinion (or 'fair comment'); qualified privilege; and its political discussion ('Lange') version.

- Truth (justification) as a defence requires the publisher to prove that the defamatory imputation was substantially true.
- Absolute privilege allows complete protection for those speaking in court or parliament, and for documents that become part of the evidence, or are formally tabled or read there.
- Fair report protects accurate reports of public documents and proceedings such as court, parliament, council and public meetings. It is a vital defence—probably the most important and useful one for day-to-day reporting.
- Honest opinion or fair comment requires proof that the defamatory material was conveyed as comment rather than fact, was honestly held on a matter of public interest and was based on facts stated in the material that are provable or privileged, as well as being in line with the defamatory imputations conveyed by the material. Slightly different versions apply to a publisher's employees and to contributors, such as letter writers.
- Qualified privilege rarely applies in journalism, because it requires the publisher to prove there is a reciprocal duty–interest relationship that excuses a defamatory publication. It is a useful defence for public relations consultants and news managers for the derogatory references they might write about former staff, as long as they are written in good faith. The statutory version requires that publishers acted 'reasonably'. It is very hard to satisfy.
- The extended political qualified privilege defence for publications relating to matters of politics or government requires that the publisher prove that its conduct was reasonable in practice, and is equally hard to satisfy.
- Less common defences exist, such as triviality and innocent dissemination.
- Most defamation actions are settled out of court, and this is encouraged in the legislation with provisions for offers of amends, corrections and apologies.
- The remedies available to courts include the award of damages (compensatory and aggravated) and injunctions.

- Damages in recent years have varied in scale from $100 to more than $2 million, although the cap on damages for non-economic loss sits at just under $400,000.
- This is a complicated field, so seek legal advice.

DISCUSSION QUESTIONS

8.1 Take the position of a media advocate and explain your three main points in an argument that defamation defences are too tough on press freedom.

8.2 What are the advantages and disadvantages of a publisher making a quick offer of amends?

8.3 Search <www.austlii.edu.au> for a recent defamation case. Write a case note about it following the format of the case notes in this chapter.

8.4 Go to a law library and find out more about injurious falsehood. Write a two-page summary and present it to your colleagues or fellow students.

8.5 Research the elements of the honest opinion (fair comment) defence and then write a highly critical review of a song by your least-favourite artist. Explain how you would defend the review.

8.6 If you cannot prove a story is true, how can you possibly argue that you acted 'reasonably'? Search Austlii <www.austlii.edu.au> cases for explanations of what 'reasonable' behaviour by a journalist might require.

8.7 Think of a matter that is of such overwhelming public importance that the media might be able to argue the common law duty-interest qualified privilege defence—that is, a situation where every single member of the audience had a legal or moral interest in hearing this defamation and the media outlet had a legal or moral duty to break this news. Explain how you would defend it and the steps you would need to take in your journalism to establish it.

8.8 Go to <www.austlii.edu.au> and find a recent example of a media outlet using a defence successfully. Compare and contrast it with one of the cases in this chapter.

8.9 Find one state or territory's legislation on criminal defamation. (It might be in the Crimes Act.) Write a two-page summary and analysis of criminal defamation and explain how it might affect professional communicators.

REFERENCES

Applegarth, P. 2011, 'Distorting the law of defamation', *University of Queensland Law Journal*, 30(1), 99–117, <www.austlii.edu.au/cgi-bin/viewdoc/au/journals/QldJSchol/2011/55.html>.

Duke, J. and Vedelago, C. 2018, 'Education boss found to be dishonest in losing defamation case', *Sydney Morning Herald*, 25 January, <www.smh.com.au/business/media-and-marketing/education-boss-found-to-be-dishonest-in-losing-defamation-case-20180125-p4yyvb.html>.

T. Keim and R. Heffernan 2001, 'Defiant pool victim, mum jailed', *Courier-Mail*, 17 January, p. 5.

NSW Gazette 2017, No. 56 of 26 May.

CASES CITED

AAMAC case: AAMAC Warehousing & Transport Pty Ltd & Ors v Fairfax Media Publications Pty Ltd & Ors [2009] NSWSC 970 (21 September 2009), <www.austlii.edu.au/cgi-bin/sinodisp/au/cases/nsw/NSWSC/2009/970.html>.

Actor case: Rush v Nationwide News Pty Ltd [2018] FCA 357 (20 March 2018), <www.austlii.edu.au/cgi-bin/viewdoc/au/cases/cth/FCA/2018/357.html>.

ACTV case: Australian Capital Television Pty Ltd v Commonwealth (1992) 177 CLR 106.

Archbishop's case: Zaia v Eshow [2017] NSWSC 1540, <www.austlii.edu.au/cgi-bin/viewdoc/au/cases/nsw/NSWSC/2017/1540.html>.

Austin's case: Austin v Mirror Newspapers [1986] 1 AC 299.

Barrister's Wife case: Rayney v the State of Western Australia [No. 9] [2017] WASC 367, <www.austlii.edu.au/cgi-bin/viewdoc/au/cases/wa/WASC/2017/367.html>.

Bed Bug case: Carleton Hotel LLC v Gladstone & Braun [2011] Circuit Court of Cook County Illinois, IL006256, USA.

Briginshaw's case: Briginshaw v Briginshaw [1938] HCA 34; [1938] 60 CLR 336.

Carleton's case: Carleton v ABC [2002] ACTSC 127 (18 December 2002), <www.austlii.edu.au/au/cases/act/ACTSC/2002/127.html> [18 September 2006]; *Carleton v ABC* [2003] ACTSC 28 (2 May 2003), <www.austlii.edu.au/au/cases/act/ACTSC/2003/28.html> [18 September 2006].

Casino case: Morten Christiansen v Fairfax Media Publications Pty Ltd [2012] NSWSC 1258 (19 October 2012), <www.austlii.edu.au/cgi-in/sinodisp/au/cases/nsw/NSWSC/2012/1258.html>.

Centrelink Fraud case: Poniatowska v Channel Seven Sydney Pty Ltd & Anor (No. 4) [2016] SASC 137, <www.austlii.edu.au/cgi-bin/viewdoc/au/cases/sa/SASC/2016/137.html>.

Chakravarti's case: Chakravarti v Advertiser Newspapers Pty Ltd (1998) 193 CLR 519, <www.austlii.edu.au/au/cases/cth/high_ct/1998/37.html>.

Chappell's case: Chappell v TCN Channel Nine Pty Ltd (1988) 14 NSWLR 153.

Club Rawhide case: Hardie v The Herald and Weekly Times Pty Ltd [2015] VSC 364, <www.austlii.edu.au/cgi-bin/viewdoc/au/cases/vic/VSC/2015/364.html>.

Coco Roco case: John Fairfax Publications Pty Ltd v Gacic [2007] HCA 28; 235 ALR 402 (14 June 2007), <www.austlii.edu.au/cgi-bin/sinodisp/au/cases/cth/HCA/2007/28>; *Gacic v John Fairfax Publications Pty Ltd* [2013] NSWSC 1920 (19 December 2013), <www.austlii.edu.au/cgi-bin/sinodisp/au/cases/nsw/NSWSC/2013/1920.html>.

Councillor's case: Milne v Ell [2017] NSWSC 555, <www.austlii.edu.au/cgi-bin/viewdoc/au/cases/nsw/NSWSC/2017/555.html>.

ET's case: Ettingshausen v Australian Consolidated Press Ltd (1991) 23 NSWLR 443.

Eye Surgeon case: Rogers v Nationwide News Pty Ltd [2003] HCA 52 (11 September 2003).

Football Hormone case: Carolan v Fairfax Media Publications Pty Ltd (No. 6) [2016] NSWSC 1091, <www.austlii.edu.au/cgi-bin/viewdoc/au/cases/nsw/NSWSC/2016/1091.html>.

Fruiterers' case: Johnston v Aldridge [2017] SADC 70, <www.austlii.edu.au/cgi-bin/viewdoc/au/cases/sa/SADC/2017/70.html>.

Go Daddy case: Kaplan v Go Daddy Group & 2 Ors [2005] NSWSC 636 (24 June 2005), <www.austlii.edu.au/cgi-bin/sinodisp/au/cases/nsw/NSWSC/2005/636.html>.

Goldsmith case: Goldsmith v Sperrings [1977] 1 WLR 478 at 485.

Golf Course case: Grant v Torstar Corp (2009) SCC 61.

Hanson's case: ABC v Hanson [1998] QCA 306. Appeal no. 8716 of 1997 (28 September 1998), <www.courts.qld.gov.au/qjudgment/QCA%201998/QCA98-306.pdf>; *Australian Broadcasting Corporation v Hanson*, B40/1998 [1999] HCATrans 211 (24 June 1999), <www.austlii.edu.au/cgi-bin/viewdoc/au/cases/cth/HCATrans/1999/211.html>.

Lange's case: Lange v Australian Broadcasting Corporation (1997) 189 CLR 520, <www.austlii.edu.au/cgi-bin/sinodisp/au/cases/cth/HCA/1997/25.html>.

Lloyd's case: Lloyd v David Syme and Company Ltd (1985) 3 NSWLR 728.

Lobster case: Blue Angel Restaurant v John Fairfax and Sons Ltd (1989) 11 *Gazette of Law and Journalism* 13.

Magistrate case: John Fairfax Publications Pty Ltd v O'Shane [2005] NSWCA 164, <www.austlii.edu.au/cgi-bin/sinodisp/au/cases/nsw/NSWCA/2005/164.html?&nocontext=1>.

Manock's case: Channel Seven Adelaide Pty Ltd v Manock (2007) 232 CLR 245; [2007] HCA 60.

Motel case: Rothe v Scott (No. 4) [2016] NSWDC 160, <www.austlii.edu.au/cgi-bin/viewdoc/au/cases/nsw/NSWDC/2016/160.html>.

Obeid's case: Edward Obeid v John Fairfax Publications Pty Ltd [2006] NSWSC 1059, <www.austlii.edu.au/cgi-bin/sinodisp/au/cases/nsw/NSWSC/2006/1059.html>.

Psychic Stalker case: Google Inc. v Duffy [2017] SASCFC 130, <www.austlii.edu.au/cgi-bin/viewdoc/au/cases/sa/SASCFC/2017/130.html>.

Quadriplegic case: R v Hornberg, Roma Magistrates Court, 16 January 2001, unreported. *Source:* Keim and Heffernan (2001), in T. Keim and R. Heffernan 2001, 'Defiant pool victim, mum jailed', *Courier-Mail*, 17 January, p. 5.

Racehorse Cruelty case: Cummings v Fairfax Digital Australia & New Zealand Pty Limited; Cummings v Fairfax Media Publications Pty Ltd [2017] NSWSC 657.

Real Estate case: Millane & Ors v Nationwide News Pty Ltd t/as Cumberland Newspaper Group [2004] NSWSC 853, <www.austlii.edu.au/au/cases/nsw/supreme_ct/2004/853.html>.

Rebel's case: Wilson v Bauer Media Pty Ltd [2017] VSC 521, <www.austlii.edu.au/cgi-bin/viewdoc/au/cases/vic/VSC/2017/521.html>; *Bauer Media Pty Ltd v Wilson [No. 2]* [2018] VSCA 154, <www.austlii.edu.au/cgi-bin/viewdoc/au/cases/vic/VSCA//2018/154.html>.

ReGroup case: ReGroup Pty Ltd v Kazal [2016] FCA 1485, <www.austlii.edu.au/cgi-bin/viewdoc/au/cases/cth/FCA/2016/1485.html>.

Reynolds' case: Reynolds v Times Newspapers Ltd (2001) 2 AC 127, <www.publications.parliament.uk/pa/ld199899/ldjudgmt/jd991028/rey01.htm>.

Rofe's case: Rofe v Smith's Newspapers Ltd [1924] SR (NSW) 4.

Security case: Sydney Security Services Pty Ltd v iGuard Australia Pty Ltd [2016] NSWSC 1808, <www.austlii.edu.au/cgi-bin/viewdoc/au/cases/nsw/NSWSC/2016/1808.html>.

Snapper case: Fawcett v John Fairfax Publications Pty Ltd [2008] NSWSC 139 (27 February 2008), <www.austlii.edu.au/cgi-bin/sinodisp/au/cases/nsw/NSWSC/2008/139.html>.

Stable case: Sutherland v Stopes [1925] AC 47.

Stephens' case: Stephens v West Australian Newspapers (1994) 182 CLR 211.

Sullivan's case: New York Times v Sullivan 376 US 254 (1964), <www.access.gpo.gov/su_docs/supcrt/index.html>.

Tailor's case: Zoef v Nationwide News Pty Ltd (No. 2) [2017] NSWCA 2, <www.austlii.edu.au/cgi-bin/viewdoc/au/cases/nsw/NSWCA/2017/2.html>; *Zoef v Nationwide News Pty Ltd* [2016] NSWCA 283, <www.austlii.edu.au/cgi-bin/viewdoc/au/cases/nsw/NSWCA/2016/283.html>; *Zoef v Nationwide News Pty Ltd* [2015] NSWDC 232, <www.austlii.edu.au/cgi-bin/viewdoc/au/cases/nsw/NSWDC/2015/232.html>.

Theophanous's case: Theophanous v The Herald and Weekly Times Ltd (1994) 182 CLR 104.

Thom's case: Thom v Associated Newspapers Ltd (1964) 64 SR (NSW) 376.

Thunder case: Thunder Studios Inc. (California) v Kazal [2016] FCA 1598 (21 December 2016); *Kazal v Thunder Studios Inc. (California)* [2017] FCAFC 111 (31 July 2017).

Toll Uniform case: Toll Transport Pty Ltd & Ors v Erikson [2017] FCCA 3120, <www.austlii.edu.au/cgi-bin/viewdoc/au/cases/cth/FCCA/2017/3120.html>.

Toxic Playground case: O'Brien v Australian Broadcasting Corporation [2017] NSWCA 338, <www.austlii.edu.au/cgi-bin/viewdoc/au/cases/nsw/NSWCA/2017/338.html>; *O'Brien v Australian Broadcasting Corporation* [2016] NSWSC 1289, <www.austlii.edu.au/cgi-bin/viewdoc/au/cases/nsw/NSWSC/2016/1289.html>.

Treasurer case: Hockey v Fairfax Media Publications Pty Limited [2015] FCA 652, <www.austlii.edu.au/cgi-bin/sinodisp/au/cases/cth/FCA/2015/652.html>.

Twitter case: Mickle v Farley [2013] NSWDC 295 (29 November 2013), <www.caselaw.nsw.gov.au/action/PJUDG?jgmtid=169992>.

Unsolved Murder case: Moran v Schwartz Publishing Pty Ltd [No. 3] [2015] WASC 215, <www.austlii.edu.au/cgi-bin/viewdoc/au/cases/wa/WASC/2015/215.html>.

Vocational Education case: Charan v Nationwide News Pty Ltd [2018] VSC 3, <www.austlii.edu.au/cgi-bin/viewdoc/au/cases/vic/VSC/2018/3.html>.

Waterhouse case: Waterhouse v Gilmore (1988) 12 NSWLR 270.

Wills' case: Nationwide News Pty Ltd v Wills (1992) 108 ALR 681.

Wineries case: Rogers v State of South Australia and Benham (No. 2), No. CICD 96-922, judgment no. D3812 [1998] SADC (21 May 1998), <www.austlii.edu.au/cases/sa/SADC/1998/3812.html>.

Workcover case: De Poi v Advertiser-News Weekend Publishing Company Pty Ltd [2016] SASCFC 25, <www.austlii.edu.au/cgi-bin/viewdoc/au/cases/sa/SASCFC/2016/25.html>.

Worm Farming case: Australian Broadcasting Corporation v O'Neill [2006] HCA 46; 80 ALJR 1672; 229 ALR 457 (28 September 2006), <www.austlii.edu.au/cgi-bin/sinodisp/au/cases/cth/HCA/2006/46.html>.

Yuk case: Meskenas v Capon [1993] 1 MLR 6.

ZGeek case: Piscioneri v Brisciani [2015] ACTSC 106, <www.austlii.edu.au/cgi-bin/viewdoc/au/cases/act/ACTSC/2015/106.html>.

PART 4

SECRETS, TERROR AND DISCRIMINATION

CHAPTER 9

Keeping secrets: Confidentiality and sources

KEY CONCEPTS

Off the record
An ill-defined term used to describe a negotiated level of confidentiality about material imparted from a source ('whistleblower') to a communicator, usually a journalist.

Disobedience contempt
Interference with the administration of justice by refusing to obey an order of a court—in this chapter, a court order to a journalist or blogger to answer a question or to hand over confidential information.

Shield laws
A term used to describe an array of laws that offer varying levels of protection to journalists or other communicators who would otherwise face a disobedience contempt charge for refusing to reveal a confidential source or hand over confidential materials to government agencies or courts.

Breach of confidence
A legal cause of action at common law: a litigant can sue to protect private information that has been conveyed in confidence and seek damages by way of remedy for its wrongful release.

Newspaper rule
A rule of defamation court procedure, which provides that a defendant will not generally be compelled to reveal a source—at least in the pre-trial stages of proceedings.

Investigative journalists and political reporters have always been reliant on leaks from confidential sources, and have developed protocols for dealing with them. Over the past three decades, three Australian journalists have been jailed, another was given a suspended sentence and others were fined for refusing to reveal their sources. Several public servants ('whistleblowers') have lost their jobs for revealing confidential information to reporters or via social media (Massola, 2010). While the law recognises a public interest in relationships and information being kept confidential, it normally insists that there is a greater public interest in them being revealed in court where necessary. These competing interests are central to two important topic areas: contempt and breach of confidence. Both can involve keeping or revealing secrets. Under the law of contempt, a journalist who keeps the identity of a source secret against an order of a court or parliament can be fined or jailed. Under the law of breach of confidence, a journalist who aims to publish secret information can face an injunction and an order for the return of leaked material, which may identify its source.

In some places, including some Australian jurisdictions, legislators have helped out by introducing 'shield' laws for journalists or publishers to assist in protecting the identity of sources.

Bloggers and other professional communicators like PR consultants, however, approach the issue of confidentiality with a different background and role. Unless you are a former journalist, you are unlikely to have the training or experience in handling off-the-record information and covering your trail so that your 'whistle-blower'—confidential source—is protected. Furthermore, only some of the shield laws designed for journalists have been extended by legislators or the courts to others, like bloggers or citizen journalists. Sometimes communicators themselves take on the role of whistleblower rather than the person gathering material, as is the case with a PR source giving a journalist some background information. As we have already learned, many areas of media law overlap. Here we see the topics of contempt of court, confidentiality, defamation and privacy intersect in the contested terrain of 'off-the-record' information.

BACKGROUND AND INTERNATIONAL CONTEXT

Courts throughout the world have long insisted on witnesses answering relevant questions, whether or not they are bound by some professional or ethical obligation to maintain silence. Lawyers are an exception. Throughout North America and the United Kingdom and its former colonies, including Australia, a legal professional (attorney-client) privilege protects lawyers from having to reveal to the court prejudicial statements a client might have confided in them. In some places, the privilege has been extended to doctor–patient relationships and sometimes to priests whose parishioners might confess criminal sins to them. Witnesses are excused from answering incriminating questions in court. Sometimes judges are given the discretion to weigh up all professional confidences against the interests of justice in deciding whether a question must be answered.

Several Western democratic nations have also introduced so-called 'shield laws' specifically designed to excuse journalists from having to identify their confidential sources in court and sometimes allowing them to refuse to hand up their interview records or other documents. According to the Reporters Committee for Freedom of the Press (2018), only thirteen US states do not have shield laws protecting journalists' confidential relationships with their sources, although several have quite serious limitations. Britain offered a limited protection for journalists in its *Contempt of Court Act 1981*. New Zealand's *Evidence Act* protects journalists' sources, but gives the discretion to a judge to override this on public interest grounds. In the *Kiwi Blogger's case* (2014), New Zealand's High Court included a blogger in the definition of 'journalist' for the purposes of its shield law.

Journalists have been jailed for refusing to reveal their sources in courts or to hand over documents that might break confidences. Between 1984 and 2018, 22 US journalists were jailed under such laws, including video blogger Josh Wolf, who was released in 2007 after serving 226 days for refusing to hand over a tape of protesters damaging a police car. *New York Times* journalist Judith Miller served 86 days in prison in 2005 for refusing to tell a grand jury who leaked the identity of CIA operative Valerie Plame to the media.

It is one thing for a journalist or blogger to be allowed to keep a source confidential, but what about the sources themselves? Countries vary widely in terms of whether whistleblowers can win protection from prosecution for revealing wrongdoing within their organisations or government departments. Sometimes this is the very reason someone sets up a blog or social media account: to blow the whistle on misbehaviour within a company or the bureaucracy.

In some places, there are broad 'public-interest' protections for whistleblowing about crime and corruption, just as there is the 'disclosure of iniquity' defence to breach of confidence. In jurisdictions where anti-corruption agencies have been established, there is usually complete immunity for witnesses who come forward to reveal wrongdoing. By the turn of this century, such laws were common in the United States, Canada, the United Kingdom, South Africa, Australia and New Zealand, as Elaine Kaplan (2011) explains.

Few of these laws, however, offer protection to whistleblowers who bypass the official channels and go directly to the media with their allegations or who use online methods to leak confidential information. Lancashire detective constable Richard Horton operated a blog under the pseudonym 'Night Jack' (now inactive), giving an insider's view on police work and his opinions on political issues. He went all the way to the High Court in an attempt to stop *The Times* newspaper from revealing his real identity. But Justice Eady ruled that the blog was a 'public activity' and that citizens also had a public interest in knowing that a police officer was making these sorts of communications (*Night Jack case*, 2009). If approaches to official channels are not available or have not worked, some jurisdictions allow whistleblowers to go to the media with their allegations and retain immunity.

Despite such whistleblower protection laws, confidential sources face lengthy jail terms in most countries if they reveal state secrets because courts may not agree that there is a sufficient ethical or public interest in the material being revealed. A case in which such an interest was recognised by the courts involved one of the most famous whistleblowers of the modern era, the military analyst Daniel Ellsberg, who leaked the sensitive 'Pentagon Papers', which revealed the true story of the US involvement in Vietnam to the press in 1971 (*New York Times*, 1971). Despite government efforts to stop the publication of the material, the Supreme Court allowed *The New York Times* and *The Washington Post* to go ahead with its release. Ellsberg and a co-accused later faced charges of conspiracy, theft of government property and espionage, which were dismissed, among allegations of FBI wiretapping (see Cooper and Roberts, 2011). The 2017 political thriller *The Post*—the movie directed and produced by Steven Spielberg and based on these events—is essential viewing for any journalist or media law student.

In the modern era, it is even harder to protect communications against detection by the authorities, so you need to take extraordinary steps if you hope to keep your sources truly confidential. Geolocation technologies, phone and internet records, security cameras and metadata access laws are just some of the mechanisms agencies can use to determine who has been talking to the investigative journalist or blogger.

The international whistleblowing organisation WikiLeaks became famous for revealing the twenty-first century equivalent of the Pentagon Papers when it released thousands of secret US government files on the Middle East conflicts and broader diplomatic relations throughout 2010 and 2011. It reassured sources that its high security, encrypted submission system using an electronic dropbox protected their identity. US soldier Bradley (Chelsea) Manning was arrested in 2010 and held in solitary confinement pending trial—and ultimate conviction—over the release of the classified material (*The Australian*, 2010). WikiLeaks founder Julian Assange took refuge for several years in the Ecuadorian embassy in London in fear of being extradited to the United States over his publication of the leaks. When CNN interviewed experts about the spate of sites similar to WikiLeaks, they warned whistleblowers to examine their protocols very carefully if they wanted their identities to remain secret after the authorities discovered the leaks. Some sites reserved the right to disclose leakers' identities if subpoenaed to do so. Similar questions arose in 2013 when another whistleblower, former US National Security Agency employee

Edward Snowden, worked with mainstream media organisations to release tranches of classified documents, showing how the phones of world leaders had been electronically monitored. Snowden fled to Russia, where he sought political asylum (*RT.Live*, 2014). The 2016 film *Snowden* is also essential viewing for media law and Fourth Estate journalism geeks.

Whistleblowers also need to be aware of the law of breach of confidence that exists in the former British colonies, including Australia, under the common law, although most jurisdictions have not merged it with a right to privacy as UK judges have done (as we explain in Chapter 12). We examine the elements of the breach of confidence action later in this chapter.

AUSTRALIAN LAW: DISOBEDIENCE CONTEMPT

Our discussion of disobedience contempt was held over from our earlier outline of contempt of court in Chapter 5, so that it could be dealt with here, in the context of the law and ethics of confidentiality. We now examine that final area of contempt, which arises when an individual does not comply with an order of the court. We are especially concerned with orders that conflict with an agreement a journalist has with a source—typically that the source's identity will not be disclosed.

Disobedience of a court order can take many forms—from the blatant disregard of a suppression order through to a journalist's polite refusal to answer a question in court that might identify a source the journalist is required to keep confidential for ethical reasons. The former occurred in 2017 when blogger Shane Dowling was jailed for four months for refusing to obey court orders to take down from his website the names of women who had allegedly had sexual relationships with a high-profile media executive (*Kangaroo Court case*, 2017).

A witness who refuses to comply with a judge's order to identify a source is generally at jeopardy of 'disobedience contempt' rather than 'contempt in the face of the court' (considered in Chapter 5). For the purposes of this chapter, we treat a journalist's refusal to identify a source as disobedience contempt: a journalist's refusal to answer a question when ordered to do so is usually the result of an ethical conflict, as opposed to blatant defiance. The refusal does not need to occur in the courtroom: it can–and often does–occur outside court, by refusing to produce documents or answer questions in writing.

Since 1989, three Australian journalists have been jailed, a fourth sentenced to community service and others fined, while yet others remain at risk of such consequences for obeying the section of their ethical code which requires them to respect confidences (MEAA, 2001). In 2017, three Fairfax journalists and *The Age* newspaper lost a second application for special leave to appeal to the High Court over a decision upholding orders that they disclose their sources. Their 2010 story–predating a Victorian 'shield law' partially protecting journalists' confidences–accused a Chinese businesswoman of having bribed former Defence Minister Joel Fitzgibbon (*Chinese Businesswoman case*, 2010–16), but it was based on copies of allegedly forged documents provided by confidential sources. The eight-year wrangle had still not been resolved as this book went to press, leaving the journalists potentially facing disobedience contempt charges for refusing to reveal their sources. The decision in their case was in line with an earlier judgment against the *Herald Sun*, in which journalists Michael Harvey and Gerard McManus lost a Victorian Supreme Court appeal against being forced to name the source of leaked government information. That appeal–the *War Veterans case* (2006)–is featured as Key Case 9.1.

But perhaps the tide is turning. In 2013, orders obtained by executives accused of bribery, forcing disclosure from Fairfax journalists Nick McKenzie and Richard Baker in a case involving a Reserve Bank subsidiary, were overturned on appeal (*Reserve Bank case*, 2013) and, in a test of Western Australian shield laws, source disclosure actions against journalists Steve Pennells and Adele Ferguson by Australia's richest woman, Gina Rinehart, failed (*Rinehart cases*, 2013–14). This was followed in 2015 with a successful application of Victoria's shield laws against an attempt by a plaintiff to force journalist Nick McKenzie to reveal his sources in the interlocutory stages of a case over a story alleging the plaintiff was the head of the Calabrian mafia in Melbourne and involved in violent criminal conduct, including murder, extortion and drug trafficking (*Mafia case*, 2015). Victorian

Supreme Court Justice John Dixon refused an application by the plaintiff for an order for preliminary discovery—essentially a demand that McKenzie reveal his sources for the story. Justice Dixon ruled the shield law protection offered by section 126K of the *Evidence Act* would operate because the plaintiff could not demonstrate 'compelling public interest in disclosure of the defendants' sources which is capable of being balanced against the public interest in protection of the sources', and this would apply to preliminary proceedings in both defamation and breach of confidence (at para. 170).

The first part of this section examines the laws that led to the jailing of the three journalists, comparing the obligations of journalists with those of other professionals. It goes on to examine state and territory laws introduced in the wake of their jailing, and to assess the level of protection they provide—particularly to bloggers and those who are not employed by the mainstream media.

A journalist's obligation to preserve the confidentiality of a source, when they have agreed to do so, is clear and unequivocal under Clause 3 of the MEAA Journalist Code of Ethics (see Appendix 1):

> *Aim to attribute information to its source. Where a source seeks anonymity, do not agree without first considering the source's motives and any alternative attributable source. Where confidences are accepted, respect them in all circumstances. (MEAA, 2001)*

In obliging journalists to respect confidences 'in all circumstances', the code allows no room for manoeuvre. The ethical rationale is simple: where the only way to obtain the information is to guarantee confidentiality, the source has relied upon the journalist's promise, and to betray that promise may expose the source to disadvantage, danger or legal action. There is also a practical reason for upholding such promises: if journalists make a habit of outing confidential sources, their sources will soon dry up.

The journalists' code is unusual: it offers no escape, unless the source waives their right not to be identified. Doctors and accountants have 'escape clauses': accountants are not allowed to betray a professional confidence 'unless there is a legal or professional right or duty to disclose' (APESB, 2010: s 140.1a) and, while the Australian Medical Association's (AMA) Code of Ethics instructs doctors to 'maintain your patient's confidentiality', exceptions may include 'where required by law' (AMA, 2006). The journalist's code is as absolute as the priest's.

The courts have long insisted that a question must be answered if it is 'relevant and necessary in the interests of justice'. Except in the case of the lawyer–client relationship, which confers a privilege at common law, the courts have been reluctant to accord an evidentiary privilege (an exemption from having to answer a question in court) to professional relationships. It was expressed this way in *Buchanan's case* in 1964: 'Litigants cannot be constrained by the private codes of strangers.'

While there is a public interest served by journalists protecting sources, to aid the exposure of public wrongdoing, other factors enter the equation in the courtroom. The journalist's obligation to a source is only one consideration. Others weighing heavily on the judge are the accused person's right to a fair trial, the plaintiff's right to a remedy and the community's expectation that justice will be done. As stated in *McGuinness's case* (1940), the leading case in the area: 'No such privilege exists according to law. Apart from statutory provisions, the press, in courts of law, has no greater and no less privilege than every subject of the King' (at 91).

Australian courts have granted no special privilege to journalists seeking to protect sources, but generally have demonstrated a reluctance to press the issue, at least prior to 1989. One approach was that a judge would exercise moral pressure in favour of the journalist by intervening and asking counsel whether he or she wished to press the question. Another reason why refusal was not a major issue was that proprietors would amend their defamation defences so a journalist would not be pressed to reveal a confidential source. Essentially, the media and the courts tried separately to avoid a conflict over confidential sources in the courtroom. This happened in 2006 in a defamation case involving former NSW Fisheries Minister Eddie Obeid and *The Sydney Morning Herald* (Kux, 2006). The court refused to make a preliminary ruling on Fairfax's application for a confidential source privilege. Counsel for the confidential source appeared, explaining his client's anxiety.

Eventually, counsel for the plaintiff agreed he would not probe on the identity of the source, but pointed out that protecting the source would damage the newspaper's qualified privilege defence. In the end, most of the testimony from the journalist, Anne Davies, revolved around three other sources whose identities were able to be revealed.

Until the mid-twentieth century, disobedience contempt based on a refusal to answer questions or reveal a source was often dealt with instantly by the presiding judge. Since then, decisions of superior courts have insisted upon procedural safeguards, with the charge needing to be stated clearly, the accused allowed a reasonable opportunity to be heard in their own defence and an adjournment to permit preparation of the defence case.

While courts formerly drew a sharp line between criminal contempt (e.g. contempt in the face of the court) and so-called 'civil contempt' (e.g. disobedience contempt), the High Court did away with any suggestion that 'civil' contempt does not need to be proven on the criminal standard in *Witham's case* (1995):

> *The differences upon which the distinction between civil and criminal contempt is based are, in significant respects, illusory. They certainly do not justify the allocation of different standards of proof for civil and criminal contempt. Rather, the illusory nature of those differences and the fact that the usual outcome of successful proceedings is punishment . . . make it clear as Deane J said in* Hinch, *that all proceedings for contempt 'must realistically be seen as criminal in nature'. The consequence is that all charges of contempt must be proved beyond reasonable doubt.*

Sentencing powers of inferior courts (Magistrates, Local, District and County) are often limited by statute. At common law, sentencing powers of superior courts are unlimited.

Cases in which Australian journalists have received prison sentences for refusing to reveal their sources in recent decades have included the following:

- *Barrass's case (1989).* Perth journalist Tony Barrass served five days of a seven-day sentence in 1989 and was later fined a further

$10,000 for again refusing to reveal the same source in a higher court. Barrass was jailed for refusing to tell a Perth magistrate the name of the person who had given him printouts of two tax files. He was subpoenaed at a preliminary hearing involving a suspended tax department clerk, accused of disclosing information to *The Sunday Times* about former merchant banker the late Laurie Connell. Barrass wrote an article alleging tax officers were selling confidential information for as little as $20, but did not reveal the Connells' tax details.

- *Budd's case (1992).* Brisbane journalist Joe Budd served seven days in prison in 1992 for refusing to reveal his source in a defamation trial. *The Courier-Mail* published statements about a barrister who prosecuted in a case involving assault charges against a police officer. Budd's article contained statements about the prosecutor's treatment of witnesses and his handling of the case. When he refused to reveal his source, Justice John Dowsett suggested Budd write it on a piece of paper and hand it to the Bar table. Budd refused. The court adjourned to allow him to telephone his source to seek permission, but Budd was unable to make contact. Justice Dowsett called Budd's views 'misguided', but accepted that Budd held them.
- *Nicholls' case (1993).* South Australian television journalist Chris Nicholls was released at the end of June 1993, after serving a three-month sentence, for refusing to reveal a source during his own District Court criminal trial for impersonation, forgery and false pretences. It was alleged that he obtained bank statements and documents by impersonating the de facto husband of the state Tourism Minister in an attempt to show improper dealings during debates on gaming machines. Nicholls maintained that a confidential source had done the impersonating and forgery. When pressed to name the source, he refused. After a four-week trial, the jury took eight hours to acquit Nicholls. He was then charged with contempt and convicted over his refusal to name the source.

- *Cornwall's case (1993).* Deborah Cornwall was reporting crime for *The Sydney Morning Herald* when she was ordered to give evidence to the NSW Independent Commission Against Corruption (ICAC) about an unnamed police officer who told her that underworld figure Neddy Smith had been a police informer. Commissioner Ian Temby claimed he had information that proved the source had misled her, and that any obligation of confidence was thus rendered void. Cornwall insisted the information from her source was correct, and refused to reveal their identity. Temby cited her for contempt. The case was heard in the Supreme Court, where Justice Abadee rejected the claim that Cornwall should be exempted from answering the question because of the journalists' Code of Ethics. He also refused to allow a defence based on the argument that the law of contempt breached the implied constitutional guarantee of freedom of political communication. He found Cornwall guilty of contempt and imposed a two-month suspended sentence, including an order to complete 90 hours of community service at Redfern Legal Centre.

Judicial inquiries are a minefield for journalists. They have investigative powers that may lead them to the filing cabinets, digital data and notebooks of reporters. In defamation cases, the risk can usually be avoided if the publisher is prepared to settle or relinquish some of its defences. But a public inquiry can be as all-encompassing as a government is willing to make it. A lesson here is to ensure that any notes or digital data based on information from confidential sources are prepared in such a way that they do not disclose the identity of the source: a carelessly recorded telephone number can be enough to identify a source, as can email chains (see *WARU [West Australian Rugby Union] case*, 2008).

Our key case for this chapter is the *War Veterans case* (2006), where journalists Michael Harvey and Gerard McManus received criminal convictions and were fined while their alleged source—whistleblower Desmond Kelly—was acquitted on charges linked to the leaks.

KEY CASE 9.1: *WAR VETERANS CASE* (2006)

Harvey & Anor v County Court of Victoria & Ors [2006] VSC 293 (23 August 2006)

R v Kelly [2006] VSCA 221 (17 October 2006)

FACTS

The *Herald Sun* published an article in early 2004 by reporters Michael Harvey and Gerard McManus about federal government cuts to war veterans' entitlements. The journalists refused to reveal their source to federal police investigating alleged leaks by a public servant. In mid-2004, Desmond Patrick Kelly was charged under section 70(1) of the *Crimes Act 1958* for having communicated confidential information to an unauthorised person. The journalists appeared in the Victorian County Court on 23 August 2005 and answered questions about the documents and a phone number, but refused to answer questions about the source. Steps were taken to charge them with contempt of court, but in the meantime the journalists sought an order in the Supreme Court quashing the orders made by the County Court on the grounds that the judge had made several errors of law, including the possibility that the journalists would be exposed to 'double jeopardy' (being twice tried for the same offence).

LAW

Justice Elizabeth Hollingworth rejected the notion that the reporters would be exposed to 'double jeopardy', stating that every refusal by the journalists to answer questions would constitute a separate act of contempt for each occasion they had been directed to answer. She said (at para. 90):

> *Although the journalists' code of ethics may preclude them from naming a source, that code has no legal status. The law does not currently recognise any 'journalists' privilege'. If a journalist chooses not to reveal a source and thereby to commit an act of contempt, that is a matter of personal choice. But the possibility that a journalist might choose to disobey the law is not a relevant consideration for a judge considering whether to make an order . . . to ensure that the accused receives a fair trial. I am not satisfied that any relevant error has been demonstrated.*

In a footnote to her decision, she wrote:

> *The Commonwealth Attorney-General has said that he intends to seek leave to appear at the hearing of any contempt charges, to bring to the judge's attention the proposed changes to the uniform evidence law. But, even if such a provision is enacted in Victoria in its proposed form, the new 'confidential relationship privilege' would only create a qualified privilege. In deciding whether to order journalists to reveal their sources, the courts would be required to balance the likely harm to the source if the evidence is adduced against the desirability of the evidence being given (for example, because of its probative value or importance). (note 34)*

Public servant Desmond Kelly was convicted of the offence on the basis of telephone records showing calls to the press gallery and Mr Harvey's mobile phone number, along with some admissions of fact and circumstantial evidence. He was given a non-custodial sentence and appealed against his conviction to the Victorian Court of Appeal. There, a majority overturned the jury's conviction on the basis that it could not have been satisfied of his guilt beyond reasonable doubt and entered a verdict of acquittal. The majority justices said: 'The Crown case was plainly hindered by the journalists' refusal to testify' (at para. 26).

LESSONS FOR JOURNALISTS

Harvey and McManus each pleaded guilty to contempt. In the subsequent hearing on penalty (the offence carried a maximum of two years' imprisonment), the Chief Judge of the County Court cited the following passage from *Nicholls' case* (1993):

> *No doubt, if the appellant had a genuine but misguided belief that the undertaking obliged him to conceal the identity of his source, that is a matter to which regard could be had in fixing penalty. But when the contempt is so serious, and when it has clearly been brought home to the appellant that such a stand cannot in law be maintained against the requirements of justice, thereafter to persist in defying the law makes it difficult to give much weight to any such consideration.*

Largely because the contempts were committed during a preliminary inquiry, and not during the trial itself, each journalist received a fine rather than a sentence 'in the unique and exceptional circumstances of the case'. Clear lessons of the episode include the following:

- Journalists can be charged with contempt even if the trial in which they refuse to give evidence proceeds without their evidence, regardless of outcome.
- Journalists who refuse to answer questions in a series of proceedings related to the same matter can face separate charges for each refusal.
- Journalists who use confidential sources in their work should be aware that their communication records—mobile phone, laptop and internet access—can be monitored or recovered.
- Even under the new journalists' privilege introduced in several jurisdictions, it is entirely possible that judges and magistrates will still force the issue with journalists after weighing up the relative public interests involved—particularly in criminal trials, where the freedom of an accused may be at stake.

SHIELD LAWS IN AUSTRALIA

Pressure from media outlets, the journalists' union and press freedom organisations mounted through the 1990s and early 2000s, as these sentences were handed down, for the granting of special protection for journalists wanting to protect their confidential sources in the form of 'shield laws'. By 2014, protections of various kinds had been introduced in six of Australia's nine jurisdictions—at the federal level and in New South Wales, Victoria, Western Australia, the ACT and Tasmania (although the Tasmanian version is more general and does not specify 'journalists'). Fernandez (2013) produced a helpful comparative chart of the shield laws and their limitations. In 2018, shield laws did not yet exist in South Australia, Queensland or the Northern Territory.

As Bartlett and Jolson (2014) explain, both journalists and their media employers can take advantage of the shield laws as they have been drafted. They note the definitions of 'journalist' vary across jurisdictions, with the Commonwealth and ACT versions covering anyone who 'is engaged and active in the publication of news and who may be given information by an informant in the expectation that the information may be published in a news medium'. However, the laws in New South Wales, Victoria and Western Australia are narrower in their scope and require the shielded journalist to be 'engaged in the profession or occupation of journalism'. This rules out amateur bloggers. Importantly for bloggers, the protection is quite limited in Victoria, where courts must have regard to whether a significant part of the person's professional activity is involved in publishing news or comment, whether they are regularly published and whether they are subject to ethical standards (*Evidence Act 2008* (Vic), s 126J).

A journalist must have guaranteed anonymity to the source for the shield laws to apply. It follows that the shield laws do not offer automatic protection to all sources. Courts have a discretion to rule against shield law protection if they decide that the public interest in overruling it (usually on the grounds of the importance of the evidence to justice being done in the case at hand) outweighs any adverse impact on the informant and on the public interest in news media being able to communicate facts and opinion to the public (and the media's need to access sources of these facts and opinions) (Bartlett and Jolson, 2014).

New South Wales was the first state to introduce a general confidential disclosure provision in 1997, with section 126B of the *Evidence Act 1995*. The courts were obliged to protect the source if they were satisfied they might be harmed, and that the extent of that harm outweighed the desirability of the evidence being given. In 2002, the NSW Supreme Court applied section 126B in a case involving *The Sydney Morning Herald*, AAP and three journalists (*NRMA case*, 2002). The NRMA sought the identity of those who provided the journalists with confidential information about board meetings. The court held that the occupation of journalist fell within the 'professional capacity' required by the Act, but concluded:

> *the interests of justice in giving the plaintiff an effective remedy outweighs the possible harm which might be caused to the reputation of journalists and their ability to obtain information if they are forced to give details of their sources.*

Thus, despite the weighing-up process, the test reverted to the traditional question of whether the revelation of the source was 'in the interests of justice'.

In 2011, the NSW Act was changed to introduce a new section 126K, specific to journalists. It starts from the position that where a journalist promises an informant not to reveal their identity, neither the journalist nor their employer can be compelled to disclose it. A court may, however, still order disclosure if the public interest in it outweighs any likely adverse effect on the informant or any other person, as well as the public interest in the free flow of information to the media.

The West Australian *Evidence Act 1906* starts out with a similar approach, but goes on in section 20K (introduced in 2012) to focus on 'misconduct': any disclosure that involves an offence; any unauthorised disclosure by public servants; any information that could have been lawfully provided to another person (e.g. the police); or disclosures involving unwarranted breaches of privacy, breaches of Cabinet confidentiality or public-interest immunity (e.g. police investigations, national security or child abuse notifications) will not generally be covered.

State-based shield provisions also vary with regard to the extent to which the privilege extends beyond the courtroom, to regimes such as pre-trial discovery processes, subpoenas, search warrants and notices to produce, or to statutory investigative bodies and arms of government, such as the NSW Police Integrity Commission or ASIO.

Professional communicators should check the *Evidence Act* in their respective states or territories on <www.austlii.edu.au>—refer to Fernandez's (2013) comparative chart—and debate the precise wording and the implications for journalists and whistleblowers in that particular jurisdiction.

THE NEWSPAPER RULE

Until reforms in New South Wales in 1997, and in most of the other states and territories in 2011, the closest Australian journalists had come to being accorded a privilege like a shield law was the so-called 'newspaper rule' in preliminary defamation proceedings. It provides that a defendant in a defamation case might not be compelled to reveal a source (at the judge's discretion), at least in the pre-trial stages of proceedings. Under the rule–which judges need not follow in 'special circumstances'–a defendant will not be compelled during preliminary proceedings for defamation to disclose the sources on which the article was based. This may be used by journalists (on legal advice) to mask notebook entries that would identify confidential sources. It is not, however, an iron-clad protection, and may be over-ridden where the court considers disclosure to be 'necessary in the interests of justice'.

Dixon J in *McGuinness's case* (1940, at 104) said the rule was founded on:

> *the special position of those publishing and conducting newspapers, who accept responsibility for and are liable in respect of the matter contained in their journals, and the desirability of protecting those who contribute to their columns from the consequences of unnecessary disclosure of their identity.*

The rule may nevertheless fail to protect publishers from plaintiffs who attempt to find the source of material to seek out other defendants to sue. This happened to journalist Peter Harvey in *Cojuangco's case* (1988). He was ordered to produce his notebook so that the plaintiff–a 'coconut king' accused of corruption and cronyism with the corrupt regime of the late Philippines President Ferdinand Marcos–could identify the confidential source for Harvey's story and sue them. Fairfax got around the problem by dropping its defence of statutory qualified privilege (which we discussed in Chapter 8). *Cojuangco's case* (at 3) featured High Court comments on the ambit of privilege at common law:

> *No doubt the free flow of information is a vital ingredient in the investigative journalism which is such an important feature of our society. Information is more readily supplied to journalists when they undertake to preserve confidentiality in relation to their sources of information. It stands to reason that the free flow of information*

> *would be reinforced, to some extent at least, if the courts were to confer absolute protection on that confidentiality. But this would set such a high value on a free press and on freedom of information as to leave the individual without an effective remedy in respect of defamatory imputations published in the media.*

The court went on to say that the disclosure of a source would not be required 'unless it is necessary in the interests of justice' (at 9). It extended this principle to apply at trial, but stressed the court could compel disclosure if it were 'necessary to do justice between the parties' and said that the compellability power operated as a 'valuable sanction' that encouraged the media to act responsibly. The situation repeated itself in 2013 and 2016, in the *Chinese Businesswoman case* (2013 and 2016) mentioned above, in which three Fairfax journalists were ordered to identify a source so that the source could be sued by the plaintiff. In that case, the NSW Court of Appeal described the newspaper rule as

> *a rule of practice, not of evidence, which guides or informs the exercise of the judicial discretion in interlocutory proceedings in defamation (and related) actions. Thus, discovery of a source's identity can be required prior to trial if special circumstances justify such an order. Disclosure can also be obtained at the trial of the action if it is necessary to do justice between the parties. (2016, at para. 125)*

As in *Cojuangco's case*, *The Sydney Morning Herald* and *The Age* proposed to deal with the order by dropping their qualified privilege defences, but wanted to reinstate them when seeking leave to appeal to the High Court a second time, which was rejected in 2016.

Other cases in which courts throughout Australia have recently considered the newspaper rule include the following:

- *New Idea case (2009)*. A photo spread headlined 'Bec's Other Man' falsely claimed Rebecca Hewitt (wife of champion tennis player Lleyton Hewitt) had an extra-marital affair with a male nanny called 'Minder Mark', and purported to quote from unidentified sources. (The 'other man' she had been photographed with proved to be her brother, innocently visiting his sister.) Judge Lunn said that he was not prepared to infer the existence of any sources outside *New Idea*, but that if they were in fact the paparazzi who surreptitiously took the photographs, it would be contrary to the rationale for the newspaper rule for them to shelter behind it.

- *Bond's case (2009).* The West Australian Court of Appeal refused to order production on the basis that a substantial injustice would occur if *The West Australian* newspaper was ordered, in effect, to divulge the identity of a source at a preliminary stage. The late entrepreneur Alan Bond claimed that *The West Australian* obtained copies of confidential documents from used fax rolls, kept at his private residence. Importantly, it was *assumed* in this case that the newspaper rule applied to actions for breach of confidence.

CONTEMPT OF PARLIAMENT

Another field of contempt stems from the powers of parliaments, both state and federal. Just as contempt of court protects the administration of justice, contempt of parliament is aimed at preserving the smooth and fair operation of parliament. *Butterworths Concise Australian Legal Dictionary* (Nygh and Butt, 1998) defines it as:

> *Any act or omission which obstructs or impedes either House of Parliament in the performance of its duty, including misconduct in the House, defiance of the orders or rules of the parliament and deception of the parliament.*

There are a number of ways in which journalists and media advisers might find themselves in contempt of parliament. Walker (2000: 717–18) lists them as including disobedience to rules or orders of a House or a committee. That category operates in much the same way as disobedience contempt: a parliamentary committee may call a journalist as a witness and insist that a confidential source be revealed. If the journalist refuses, they can be found in contempt.

More commonly, contempt of parliament involves revealing the confidential inner discussions of a parliamentary committee that is bound to secrecy. Journalists who 'leak' recommendations of such a committee have found themselves facing a contempt charge. That happened in 2001, when the Senate Committee of Privileges recommended that Nationwide News receive a 'serious reprimand' for *The Australian* publishing stories that quoted from an ASIC report given *in camera* (Macfarlane, 2001).

When a similar scenario arose in June 2002 concerning *Age* journalist Annabel Crabb and editor Michael Gawenda, the Senate Privileges Committee 'reluctantly' found no contempt, because the breach had not substantially obstructed the committee's work (Beverley, 2003: 32), although the newspaper's publication of the main content of a report the day before it was due for release offended the committee's chairman. The decision prompted moves to amend the rules of parliamentary contempt (2003: 32).

The Senate adopted new guidelines in October 2005 for deciding which breaches should be pressed as contempt references. Most situations of early release or leaks should not be classed as contempt unless they involve 'actual or potential substantial interference with the work of a committee or of the Senate' or documents or information that the committee has deliberately decided to deal with *in camera* for the protection of witnesses or others, or because disclosure would otherwise be harmful to the public interest or significantly impedes the committee's freedom to deliberate (APH, 2005b). The Privileges Committee suggested the new policies would 'stem the flow of irresolvable inquiries and result in committees taking greater responsibility for their own internal discipline', given that many of the leaks seemed to come from the offices of the senators themselves (APH, 2005b). There had been 124 references to the Privileges Committee between 1971 and 2005, including several involving journalists who published leaked information.

The guidelines only apply to contempt of Senate committees in the federal parliament. Each state and territory has its own contempt of parliament protocols, outlined in an earlier report of the Senate

Privileges Committee (APH, 2005a). For example, in 2016 two Queensland members of parliament were found in contempt of parliament by that state's Legislative Assembly Ethics Committee for unauthorised disclosure of committee proceedings (Legislative Assembly of Queensland 2016a, 2016b). Press gallery reporters and media advisers in the state or federal parliaments should read both of the 2005 Senate Privileges Committee reports and their relevant local parliamentary regulations.

The Commonwealth *Parliamentary Privileges Act 1987* (s 6) recorded the abolition of parliamentary contempts because of defamation, stating that

> *Words or acts shall not be taken to be an offence against a House by reason only that those words or acts are defamatory or critical of the Parliament, a House, a committee or a member.*

AUSTRALIAN LAW: BREACH OF CONFIDENCE

A separate area of the law protects secrets via the action for breach of confidence. A journalist deciding whether confidential information can be revealed faces a heavy burden to establish a public interest that overrides any legal obligation the journalist, or anyone else, may have to keep the information confidential.

The courts apply a three-point test:

1. *The information must have a 'quality of confidence' about it.* There must be something inherent in the nature of the information itself that makes it confidential. Merely designating something as 'confidential' does not make it so. The 'quality of confidence' may have been lost by being disclosed to the public, or entering the 'public domain'.

2. *The circumstances in which the information was imparted are relevant.* The courts look to whether the person who received the information knew, or ought to have known, it was confidential. This may be inferred from the nature of the material itself (e.g. information about a person's private discussions with their doctor) or from the circumstances in which the information was

disclosed (e.g. in the course of a job interview). This principle also binds secondary recipients, such as journalists, if they ought to know from the nature of the information or the circumstances in which the source received it that it is confidential.

3. *The recipient must disclose or use the information (or threaten to), to the detriment of someone entitled to maintain its confidentiality.* It does not matter if that happens accidentally: the person who discloses the material is still liable.

TYPES OF CONFIDENTIAL INFORMATION

Confidential information is commonly of a sensitive financial, legal or private nature. The High Court ruled in the *Lenah Game Meats case* in 2001 that a photograph 'illegally or improperly or surreptitiously obtained, where what is depicted is private, may constitute confidential information'. The same conclusion was reached by the Victorian Court of Appeal in the *Sex Tapes case* (2008) (discussed in further detail in Chapter 12), which involved a jilted lover's threat to distribute secretly filmed DVDs. The Victorian County Court applied that line of thinking in a case where a woman had rifled through another woman's rubbish bins on a regular basis over a nine-year period and had extracted invoices, accounts, medical and welfare information, computer disks and legal documents–and had then distributed them to other people to the disadvantage of the plaintiff. The court held that 'a person may place confidential documents as waste in the expectation that they will be destroyed or dealt with in some other manner so that they do not become public' (*Rubbish Bin case*, 2014, para. 14). The ruling sounds a warning to gossip journalists who might be tempted to trawl through the garbage of celebrities looking for saucy information about them.

Those covering court cases need to be aware that the breach of confidence action is available to anyone who might inadvertently identify sexual assault victims in breach of the special publishing restrictions applying in all jurisdictions, and perhaps other situations like family law cases. We learned in Chapter 6 about the *Jane Doe case* (2007), where ABC broadcasts identified the victim of a rape by her former husband. She successfully sued for breach of confidence among other actions. In a similar case, breach of confidence was pursued by another Jane Doe litigant in the *Exclusive Brethren case* (2017). The plaintiff claimed she had been illegally identified as a sexual assault victim in *Sydney Morning Herald* articles about her treatment by a church member in a regional NSW city. She also claimed damages over the media company and the journalist's breach of the statutory duty not to identify her as a sexual assault complainant under the law. The case was in its preliminary stages when this edition went to press.

The obligation of confidence

The obligation of confidence can arise from situations including a contract, the employer–employee relationship, the professional–client relationship, the transfer of a secret to a third party if the third party knows (or should know) it is confidential, or under legislation—in particular laws concerning government information such as tax files. It applies equally to unsolicited information, such as the bundle of documents that 'falls off the back of a truck' and onto a journalist's desk, as it does to information a journalist has actively sought out. The test is whether its nature and/or the circumstances in which it was received mean that it should be treated as confidential.

Government information

If the information relates to government or its operations, there is an extra requirement that needs to be met before breach of confidence can be established: disclosure must be contrary to the public interest. This additional test is known as the 'Fairfax test', as it was developed by High Court Justice Anthony Mason in the *Defence Papers case* (1980) involving that newspaper company. He ruled (at para. 28): 'Unless disclosure is likely to injure the public interest, it will not be protected.' It applies to information about government and its own workings, but not to information that government holds on private individuals or companies. The test was used in the *Maleny Towers case* (2016), where an environmental engineer had applied under Queensland Right to Information (RTI) laws to the Sunshine Coast

Regional Council for correspondence between the council and the NBN (National Broadband Network) about the proposed construction of communications towers in the Maleny area. Under section 47 of the Queensland *Right to Information Act 2009*, information is exempt if its disclosure would establish an action for breach of confidence. After working through the elements of the action, and considering the Fairfax test, the Information Commissioner decided that the general rollout information in the requested material would not constitute a breach of confidence action and should be released by the council, but negotiation details about potential sites for a fixed wireless tower in Maleny would found an action for breach of confidence and were thus exempt from disclosure (paras 156–62).

DEFENCES TO BREACH OF CONFIDENCE

Legal compulsion

The law provides a defence to breach of confidence if you are ordered by a court to disclose it. As we have seen, this does not always suit the working journalist, who feels ethically bound to keep the confidence. What about the journalist who wants to publish information that is confidential, but believes some greater public interest is served by disclosing it? The defence of 'just cause or excuse' or 'exposure of iniquity' addresses this.

Just cause or excuse: the 'iniquity' defence

Unauthorised disclosure of confidential information can be defended if there is a 'just cause or excuse'. At its narrowest, a confidence can be broken if it relates to crime or fraud. Secrets may be also broken in the interests of community safety or health. The rationale behind the phrase 'there is no confidence as to the exposure of iniquity' (*Gartside's case*, 1856) was explained in the *Defence Papers case* (1980, para. 57) on the basis of protecting the community from destruction, damage or harm and in *Corrs' case* (1987) on the basis that the information lacks the necessary attribute of confidence if its subject-matter is the existence or real likelihood of the existence of a crime, civil wrong or serious misdeed of public importance. In the *Allied Mills case* (1981), it was held that breach of the consumer protection provisions in part IV or V of the *Trade Practices Act 1974* (now the Australian Consumer Law) was an 'iniquity' that justified breach of confidence. A similar argument—that exposure of recreational drug use fell within the 'iniquity' defence—was tried but failed in the *AFL case* (2006—see Key Case 9.2).

Fair report

The fact that otherwise confidential matter has been disclosed in parliament will normally be a defence to a breach of confidence action. The issue arose in both the Westpac letters case (see Classic Case 9.1) and in the AMI case (2009), in which *The Sydney Morning Herald* overturned an injunction restraining publication of a proposed story about impotence clinics, based on information provided by a doctor who had worked at one, when information was disclosed to the House of Representatives Standing Committee on Health and Ageing.

Protected disclosure

Disclosure to a narrow class of people may sometimes be considered to be in the public interest, while disclosure to a broader class may not. Disclosure to or by the media of wrongdoing may not be considered in the public interest if there are other authorities to whom the disclosure should have been made, such as the police, ombudsman or an anti-corruption body. An example is the NSW 'whistleblowers' legislation, the *Protected Disclosures Act 1994* (NSW). Public officials are protected against any action that might result from their disclosure of corruption, maladministration or a major waste of public money, but must first take their complaint to an investigating authority. Under section 19, if the authority fails to investigate or recommends against investigation, the official can take the complaint to a member of parliament or a journalist and still retain the protection (as long as the disclosure is substantially true). Other states and territories have similar legislation: the *Whistleblowers Protection Act* in Victoria and South Australia, and the *Public Interest Disclosure(s) Act* in the ACT, Northern Territory, Tasmania, Queensland, Western Australia and at the Commonwealth level.

KEY CASE 9.2: *AFL CASE*

Australian Football League (AFL) & Anor v The Age Company Ltd & Ors [2006] VSC 308 (30 August 2006)

FACTS

The AFL had an anti-doping code banning performance-enhancing drugs. In 2005, it struck a deal with the players' association for a second drugs policy, covering illicit drugs such as narcotics, aimed at education and rehabilitation: a player's first and second positive test would be kept confidential. In 2006, two newspapers received information identifying three AFL players as testing positive for illicit drugs. The AFL and the players' association sought injunctions to stop publication of the players' names.

LAW

All parties agreed the information had originally been confidential: the newspapers argued it had passed into the public domain; that an injunction would serve no purpose and was futile; that the information disclosed 'iniquitous behaviour'; and that protection of the confidential information must give way to the public interest in the identity of the three AFL players being disclosed.

Justice Kellam found the names of the players had been publicised to a limited extent, but not sufficiently to destroy confidentiality: the names had been posted to an internet discussion forum (one contributor said a player 'knows a lot about ice' and another referred to a 'nostril related hamstring' injury). They were named in a *Sydney Morning Herald* article, removed from the newspaper before publication but sent to the news excerpts service Media Monitors, which made it available to government subscribers for a five-hour period. One player was named by a telephone caller on the *Fox Footy* TV show. Club officials and friends and family of the players knew.

The judge did not accept the 'circumstances of iniquity' argument based on players having committed criminal offences:

> *[E]ven if the information can be said to disclose an iniquity, there is no suggestion that it is the intention of the defendants to disclose such matters to a third party with a real interest in redressing any such possible crime. The defendants seek to disclose the information for the purposes of what might be described as an 'interesting story' for football fans and for other readers, and for no other purpose.*

Finally, he could see no real 'public interest' being demonstrated by allowing the names to be revealed, as drug testing policies could be debated publicly without identifying the particular players:

> *[T]here is nothing other than the satisfaction of public curiosity in having the confidentiality of the names of those who have tested positive breached by being released . . . Accordingly, even if there is a public interest defence to the claim of confidentiality made by the plaintiffs I do not conclude that it outweighs the public interest in having the information remain confidential.*

Permanent injunctions were granted, restraining the newspapers from identifying any player who had tested positive on one or two occasions under the AFL's Illicit Drugs Policy.

LESSONS FOR PROFESSIONAL COMMUNICATORS

- Even if confidential material is circulated to hundreds or thousands of people, it might still be a breach of confidence to reveal it in the mass media.
- Publication is not excusable just because it reveals a crime. It needs to be a crime affecting the community as a whole, and the person disclosing it needs to have a 'real and direct interest in redressing the alleged crime', not just in building their audience.

CLASSIC CASE 9.1: *WESTPAC LETTERS CASE*

Westpac Banking Corp. v John Fairfax Group Pty Ltd (1991) 19 IPR 513

FACTS

Westpac's solicitors wrote to the bank advising it on very serious breaches of banking regulations and dubious methods being used by its merchant banking subsidiary, Partnership Pacific, in dealing with customers' foreign exchange investments. *The Sydney Morning Herald* and *The Age* obtained copies of the letters and published articles referring to them. Westpac sought injunctions, arguing that publication was a breach of confidence. Further injunctions were sought against the ABC and *The Canberra Times*.

LAW

Although there had been extensive publication of the general content of the letters, their actual detailed content had not been revealed. The injunction remained in place, even after the contents of the letters had been read in the ACT House of Assembly and the South Australian Upper House. The result was that some publishers in New South Wales and Victoria could not publish material that formed the official record in other jurisdictions' parliaments. The matter ended when Westpac's chief executive provided the letters to a Commonwealth Parliamentary Banking Inquiry and the bank consented to the discharge of the injunctions.

LESSONS FOR PROFESSIONAL COMMUNICATORS

The best tactic might have been for the newspapers to publish the letters in full, without warning, leaving themselves open to an action for breach of confidence but avoiding an anticipatory injunction restraining publication. Such an approach would only be taken after taking advice on both the legal and commercial consequences.

REMEDIES FOR BREACH OF CONFIDENCE

If the disclosure has not yet happened, the plaintiff might seek an injunction. While courts are reluctant when the injunction is sought against the media on the basis of a possible defamation, they show far less restraint where breach of confidence is alleged.

If unauthorised disclosure has already occurred, a plaintiff may seek compensation or an 'account of profits', in addition to an injunction to prevent further publication. An account of profits is a reimbursement to the plaintiff of profits the defendant has made through the use of the confidential information. Compensation is a more common remedy, with the courts attempting to restore the plaintiff to the position he or she would have been in had the disclosure not occurred.

Journalists should be alert that documents or data may have been unlawfully obtained—even stolen. They may face an injunction, together with orders compelling them to deliver up documents and reveal their sources. In the hands of a well-resourced plaintiff, such action almost invariably prevents or substantially delays publication. This throws up a dilemma: how much to telegraph the story. On the one hand, attempting to get a pre-publication response to the allegations is good, ethical journalism. On the other hand, as in the *AMI case* (2009), it is often an email or call from a journalist that prompts the seeking and issue of an injunction. In the case of confidential government information or documents, journalists may find themselves caught up in a police investigation into possible breaches of the Commonwealth *Crimes Act 1914*, particularly when dealing with defence or national security matters.

DIGITAL DIMENSIONS

There is a bewildering interplay of identity, anonymity, security and deception in the online world. The limited protections offered to journalists trying to keep their sources confidential, even in the United States, are even more restricted when it comes to internet publishers, bloggers and social media users. The shield laws vary widely in their scope, sometimes only applying to material that has already been 'published' and sometimes specifically naming 'journalists' and 'news media' as those protected. New federal shield laws introduced in Australia in 2011 extend to bloggers and tweeters—but only to those 'engaged and active in the publication of news'.

Some US state shield laws can be interpreted to cover new media users, while others are narrowly construed to apply to journalists in the mainstream media. Montana's shield laws were held to apply to anonymous internet commentators in 2008 when a former political candidate launched a defamation action over material on the *Billings Gazette* site.

Yet a blogger who was sued for defamation over comments on a message board failed to win protection under the New Jersey shield law in 2011 (Reuters, 2011). The application of Californian shield laws to bloggers was questioned in 2010 when *Gizmodo* gadget blog editor Jason Chen appeared in a video on the site displaying a prototype of an Apple iPhone 4G which had been lost then purchased by an intermediary for about $5000. Police seized six computers and other items from Chen's home. The matter was not tested when charges against Chen were not pursued (Arthur, 2010; Sarno, 2011).

There is no doubt that social media have implications for the law of confidentiality. For example, if you receive a direct message (DM) via Twitter from a contact in WikiLeaks directing you to certain information, you would likely be on notice that it is confidential. It also casts the lifting of people's Facebook photos in a new light, particularly if you have worked via friends of friends or have hacked your way through their privacy settings to get them. If someone has their privacy settings on maximum restriction, or just emails a very private image to a small circle of people, then the re-sending or posting of that image might be classified as a 'breach of confidence' or the 'disclosure of embarrassing private facts'.

There are many sound reasons why people choose to use a pseudonym or a 'handle' for their blogging and social media activities:

- It allows you to contribute to public debate while reducing the risk of verbal or physical attacks by people or governments who disagree with your opinions.
- It helps distance your personal views from those of your employer or your professional role.
- It lets you engage with others without the 'baggage' of your real life interfering with your message.

Before you can be prosecuted or sued, you need to be identifiable as a legal entity—a person or a corporation. Yet even if you operate under a pseudonym—which millions of bloggers and tweeters do—you are likely to be much more identifiable than you might first have thought. ISPs and social media enterprises like Twitter and Facebook have been ordered to reveal the identities of their anonymous clients in numerous court actions.

Courts throughout the world have taken different approaches regarding whether they will order the 'outing' of the identity of an anonymous internet user. Legal case citations have traditionally used the names 'John Doe' or 'Jane Doe' for anonymous or confidential parties. (Some jurisdictions use 'Joe Bloggs'.) In May 2011, a Utah court ruled in favour of 25 John Does known as 'Youth for Climate Truth' who had set up a fake website and issued press releases claiming the powerful Koch Industries would stop funding climate change deniers. Until 2018, the group was owned by the politically conservative Charles and David Koch who were listed among America's top ten wealthiest people. They were angered by the spoof site and its announcement so went to court to find out the identity of the protesters. But Judge Dale Kimball dismissed their motion for disclosure on the grounds that it did not meet the strict tests required to reveal the pranksters' identities (*John Does case*, 2011).

However, the High Court in England ruled in favour of another billionaire, Louis Bacon, who was attempting to force Wikipedia, the *Denver Post* and WordPress to reveal the identities of bloggers who had allegedly defamed him using pseudonyms. In 2010 it also ordered the revelation of another of Bacon's critics, who had created a website under his name.

Lawyers for Welsh footballer Ryan Giggs were not successful in discovering the anonymous tweeters who had revealed the celebrity sportsman's name in breach of a UK injunction issued to protect his privacy. They had gone to London's High Court and won an order that Twitter reveal the details, but the US microblogging company seems to have disregarded it because it was not obliged to comply with court orders from outside its jurisdiction (see Gray and Green, 2011).

The UK courts draw on a decision made by the House of Lords almost two decades before mainstream use of the internet. The 1973 *Norwich Pharmacal case* centred on a company seeking the identity of those importing goods that infringed their patents. The customs commissioners were ordered to reveal the identity of the importers. The House of Lords ruled that where a third party had become engaged in unlawful conduct, it was under a duty to help whoever had suffered damage by disclosing the identity of any wrongdoers and providing them with full information about the matter. In contrast to the United States, disclosure becomes the starting point in Britain. The High Court of Justice applied the *Norwich Pharmacal* test in the *Wikipedia case* in 2009, when it ordered Wikipedia to reveal the IP address of an anonymous party who had amended an article about a woman and her young child to include sensitive private information about them. The judge suppressed their names on confidentiality grounds because he believed the entries were part of a blackmail threat against the mother. Even though the owner of Wikipedia (Wikimedia) was based in Florida, the court issued the disclosure order. Wikimedia complied, but insisted it was not legally bound to do so because it was in a different jurisdiction and had immunity under section 230 of the US Communications Decency Act (1996) as a third-party publisher of the comments of others.

The NSW Supreme Court issued a '*Norwich* order' against the social media platform Twitter in 2017 after an anonymous tweeter had created false 'handles' in the name of the CEO of a company and another senior officer (plus another) and proceeded to release confidential financial information to the detriment of the corporation (*Financial Tweets case*, 2017). Twitter–based in the United States and Ireland–did not appear to defend the matter. The court issued injunctions preventing Twitter allowing further publications by the account holders, and further orders disclosing the identity of those account holders. Justice Pembroke stated (at para. 48):

> *I have concluded that the exercise of the discretion to make a* Norwich *order is amply justified in this case for the following reasons:*
>
> 1. *The offending tweets contained the plaintiff's confidential information. That information is highly commercially sensitive and was required to be kept confidential by the partners and employees of the plaintiff. The disclosure of the information would provide the plaintiff's competitors with a substantial commercial or competitive advantage over the plaintiff.*
> 2. *The plaintiff's confidential information has been published through at least four accounts on the Twitter platform and websites. Those publications were made without the knowledge, consent or authorisation of the plaintiff. An inference is available that the user or users of the four accounts is the same.*

3. *The plaintiff does not know the identity of the person or persons responsible for the offending tweets and therefore cannot yet restrain them from further publishing its confidential information. It is unable to commence proceedings against that person or those persons for breach of confidence.*
4. *The defendants will have, at least, the name, contact details and IP address of the person or persons who established or held the accounts from which the offending tweets emanated; and*
5. *If the person or persons responsible are not themselves restrained from further publishing the plaintiff's confidential information, there is a foreseeable risk that the plaintiff may suffer significant and irreparable damage.*

Australia's national daily newspaper *The Australian*, long an advocate of protections for confidential sources, controversially outed a government worker in 2010 who blogged anonymous political commentary as 'Grog's Gamut'. The newspaper's media editor claimed it was his duty to 'out' public servants like Greg Jericho, who secretly pushed a party-political line via their blogs and tweets. In the wake of the controversy, Jericho continued to write his blog along with the economics column 'Grogonomics' for *The Guardian*.

TIPS FOR MINDFUL PRACTICE

- You should only enter into a confidential arrangement if you have done everything within your power to get the information on the record, and then you should publish it only after weighing up the public interest against the risks to you, your organisation, your source and perhaps even other stakeholders. It is vital that you and your source discuss terms like 'off the record' and 'background' so that you each understand what the other means.
- If you are about to publish using a confidential source, let your editor and news director know. They are responsible for the publication, and deserve to have the opportunity to weigh up the risks. Similarly, you should brief your lawyers fully if legal action is threatened over any story relying on

confidential sources. It may not be too late to verify the information in some other way. Your lawyers will be keen to avoid a situation where you are standing in the witness box refusing to answer, and perhaps forgoing a useful defence that otherwise might be available.

- If you truly want to preserve the confidentiality of your source, you should not write the information (or at least identifying aspects of it) in your devices or notebook. The identity of a source is fairly obvious if the 'off-the-record' comments can be found in the middle of your otherwise 'on-the-record' notes or if you have left a digital trail.
- Orders may be made requiring the publisher to recover deleted messages from back-up files: this is a serious concern, and journalists need to consider conducting sensitive email exchanges with sources as discreetly as possible, using internet cafes and anonymised email addresses, and avoiding identifying internal references in the emails themselves. Mobile phone records, laptops and even sim cards may risk being subpoenaed or subject to an order for production. (Your metadata are also available to authorities from the major telcos under national security laws we examine in Chapter 10.) The most secure method of dealing with sources is also the oldest: face to face.
- If you genuinely don't know where information has come from, question its credibility and the motives of those who supplied it. Consult editorial executives and lawyers. The 'fell off the back of a truck' line might work when discussing it privately, but it is unacceptable in court. It is as much an ethical breach to lie in court as it is to break a confidence (and perjury is a serious offence).
- Information that is confidential today may be on the record tomorrow, after it is mentioned in court or parliament. While the exclusive story or 'scoop' is an important commercial and professional imperative, sometimes it is wiser to wait.
- There are both advantages and disadvantages to remaining anonymous when blogging or using social media. Be aware that others are doing the same thing. Always verify someone's real identity before relying on their information.
- Your anonymity can never be guaranteed, so don't publish anything under a pen name that you would not be willing to defend in real life. You might just have to do so.

- Remember that website hosts, ISPs and social media operators like Facebook and Twitter will act to take down fake accounts under their own rules after complaints.
- Be extra careful if you are operating in this area. Surveillance and monitoring are so prevalent and sophisticated today that it is very hard to keep any source confidential or secret.
- If it seems to be confidential information, then it probably is. Public relations consultants and media relations officers should talk to a lawyer before leaking information.

IN A NUTSHELL

- Courts and parliaments can punish journalists and other witnesses for contempt. Professional communicators may be charged with contempt for refusing to reveal a source or notes to a court or parliamentary committee, or for pre-empting the release of a committee's report.
- Journalists get the protection of 'shield laws' in many places, meaning they might not have to reveal their confidential source of information to the court. Only a few jurisdictions have opened this privilege up to bloggers.
- Under shield laws introduced in most Australian jurisdictions, the courts must direct that evidence not be given if it would disclose a journalist's protected source. The courts still have a discretion to order disclosure if the need for it outweighs any harm, including harm to the free flow of information to the media.
- Public servants get protection for 'blowing the whistle' on corruption and wrongdoing when they go through the appropriate channels, but will usually not earn this immunity if they run to the media or go online with their secrets.
- Under the 'newspaper rule' in defamation proceedings, a publisher defendant might not be compelled to disclose sources. Judges can choose not to exercise this discretion in special circumstances.

- The courts apply a three-point test to determine whether there has been a breach of confidence. The information must have a 'quality of confidence' about it; the circumstances in which the information was imparted must have given rise to an obligation of confidentiality; and the recipient must disclose the information (or threaten to disclose it), or use it to the detriment of someone entitled to prevent its use.
- Confidential information can include documents, ideas, words and objects. It is most commonly information of a sensitive financial, security or private nature.
- If the information relates to government or its operations, it must also be proven that its disclosure would be contrary to the public interest to amount to a breach.
- The rules on protection of bloggers' and social media users' identities vary markedly between countries.

DISCUSSION QUESTIONS

9.1 Journalists and bloggers in several countries have been jailed or fined for refusing to reveal their sources in recent years. Find an example from another country and write a short report.

9.2 Why would a journalist refuse to reveal a source in court when they could lie to the court and say, 'There is no source'? What moral and legal issues arise?

9.3 If a member of parliament on a parliamentary committee leaks you an advance draft of the committee's report, how free are you to break this news? What might be the consequences?

9.4 A music critic has never been seen without his hat. You receive a photograph in the mail (taken with a high-powered telephoto lens) of him standing in his bedroom in his underwear, without his hat. He is completely bald. What issues arise?

9.5 The newspaper rule gives reporters some protection in a pre-trial situation. Why should media publishers be protected in this way? Should it apply to other professional communicators like bloggers?

9.6 You are a public relations officer for a major pharmaceutical company and you have email evidence that the company has covered up important tests that reveal a new drug could cause cancer. You want to leak the information to a friend who is a health reporter. What issues arise and how would you handle them?

REFERENCES

Accounting Professional and Ethical Standards Board (APESB) 2010, *Code of Ethics for Professional Accountants*, <www.apesb.org.au/uploads/standards/apesb_standards/standard1.pdf>.

Arthur, C. 2010, 'Police search home of *Gizmodo* editor Jason Chen over lost iPhone 4G', *The Guardian*, 27 April, <www.theguardian.com/technology/pda/2010/apr/26/iphone-gizmodo-police-search-apple>.

The Australian 2010, 'US soldier Bradley Manning arrested over WikiLeaks video', 8 June, <www.theaustralian.com.au/news/world/us-soldier-arrested-over-wikileaks-video/story-e6frg6so-1225876791191>.

Australian Medical Association (AMA) 2006, *Australian Medical Association Code of Ethics 2004, Editorially Revised 2006*, <https://ama.com.au/tas/ama-code-ethics-2004-editorially-revised-2006>.

Australian Parliament House (APH) 2005a, *122nd Report—Parliamentary Privilege: Unauthorised Disclosure of Committee Proceedings*, 12 June, Australian Parliament Senate Privileges Committee, Canberra, <www.aph.gov.au/SEnate/committee/priv_ctte/report_122/report/index.htm>.

—— 2005b, *125th Report—Parliamentary Privilege: Precedents, Procedure and Practice in the Australian Senate 1966–2005*, 19 December, Australian Parliament, Senate Privileges Committee, Canberra, <www.aph.gov.au/SEnate/committee/priv_ctte/report_125/index.htm>.

Bartlett, P. and Jolson, A. 2014, 'Protecting journalist–source privilege in Australia', *Media Law Northern Ireland* blog, 21 March, <http://medialawnorthernireland.blogspot.co.uk/2014/03/protecting-journalist-source-privilege.html?m=1>.

Beverley, J. 2003, 'Senate may move to stop leaks', *PANPA Bulletin*, March.

Cooper, M. and Roberts, S. 2011, 'After 40 years, the complete Pentagon Papers', *New York Times*, 7 June, <www.nytimes.com/2011/06/08/us/08pentagon.html?_r=3&pagewanted=1&>.

Fernandez, J. 2013, 'States create a maze of shield laws', in *Power, Protection and Principles: The State of Press Freedom in Australia 2013*, <www.pressfreedom.org.au/2013-report/protection-and-principles/states-create-a-maze-of-shield-laws>.

Gray, R. & Green, N. 2011, 'Twitter reveals secrets: Details of British users handed over in landmark case that could help Ryan Giggs', *The Telegraph*, 28 May, <www.telegraph.co.uk/technology/twitter/8544350/Twitter-reveals-secrets-Details-of-British-users-handed-over-in-landmark-case-that-could-help-Ryan-Giggs.html>.

Kaplan, E. 2011, 'The international emergence of legal protections for whistleblowers', *The Journal of Public Inquiry*, Fall/Winter, 37–42.

Kux, Y.C. 2006, 'Obeid gave limited response to Herald questions', *Gazette of Law and Journalism*, 18 August, <www.lawpress.com.au/genews/ge172_Obeid_Fairfax_trial2_180806.html>.

Legislative Assembly of Queensland 2016a, *Legislative Assembly of Queensland Ethics Committee Report Number 168: Matter of Privilege Referred by the Agriculture and Environment Committee on 20 April 2016 Relating to an Alleged Unauthorised Disclosure of Committee Proceedings and an Alleged Deliberate Misleading of a Committee*, June 2016, <www.parliament.qld.gov.au/documents/tableOffice/TabledPapers/2016/5516T992.pdf>.

—— 2016b, *Legislative Assembly of Queensland Ethics Committee Report Number 162, Inquiry into Matter of Privilege referred by the Parliamentary Crime and Corruption Committee on 17 August 2015 relating to alleged unauthorised disclosure of committee proceedings, February 2016*, <www.parliament.qld.gov.au/documents/committees/ETHICS/2015/Matterofprivilege17Aug2015/rpt-162-17Feb2016.pdf>.

Macfarlane, D. 2001, 'Rebuke for contempt', *The Australian*, 31 August.

Massola, J. 2010, 'Controversial political blogger unmasked as a federal public servant', *The Australian*, 27 September, <www.theaustralian.com.au/media/controversial-political-blogger-unmasked-as-a-federal-public-servant/story-e6frg996-1225929679443>.

Media, Entertainment and Arts Alliance (MEAA) 2001, *MEAA Journalist Code of Ethics*, <www.alliance.org.au/hot/ethics code.htm>.

New York Times 1971, 'Supreme Court, 6–3, upholds newspapers on publication of Pentagon Report', 1 July, <www.nytimes.com/book/97/13/review/papers-final.html>.

Nygh, P. and Butt, P. (eds) 1998, *Butterworths Concise Australian Legal Dictionary*, 2nd edn, Butterworths, Sydney.

Reporters Committee for Freedom of the Press 2018, 'Shield laws and protection of sources by state', <www.rcfp.org/browse-media-law-resources/guides/reporters-privilege/shield-laws>.

Reuters 2011, 'New Jersey court denies blogger shield protection', 17 June, <www.reuters.com/article/2011/06/07/us-newjersey-shield-idUSTRE7565Q520110607>.

RT.Live 2014, 'Snowden can extend his asylum every year—lawyer', 25 January, <http://rt.com/news/snowden-extend-asylum-lawyer-176>.

Sarno, D. 2011, 'Gizmodo not motivated by financial greed in iPhone case, DA says', *Los Angeles Times*, 10 August, <http://latimesblogs.latimes.com/technology/2011/08/gizmodo-not-motivated-by-financial-greed-in-iphone-case-da-says.html>.

Walker, S. 2000, *Media Law: Commentary and Materials*, Law Book Company, Sydney.

CASES CITED

AFL case: Australian Football League & Anor v The Age Company Ltd & Ors [2006] VSC 308 (30 August 2006), <www.austlii.edu.au/cgi-bin/viewdoc/au/cases/vic/VSC/2006/308.html>.

Allied Mills case: Allied Mills Industries Pty Ltd v Trade Practices Commission (1981) 34 ALR 105.

AMI case: AMI Australia Holdings Pty Ltd v Fairfax Media Publications Pty Ltd [2009] NSWSC 863. [See *AMI Australia Holdings Pty Limited v Fairfax Media Publications Pty Limited* [2009] NSWSC 612 for judgment on the original email.]

Barrass's case: DPP v Luders, unreported, Court of Petty Sessions of Western Australia, no. 27602 of 1989; *R v Barrass*, unreported, District Court of Western Australia, 7 August 1990, per Kennedy DCJ.

Bond case: West Australian Newspapers Limited v Bond [2009] WASCA 127 (24 July 2009).

Buchanan's case: Buchanan, Re (1964) 65 SR (NSW) 9.

Budd's case: R v Budd, unreported, Supreme Court of Queensland, no. 36188 of 1992, Brisbane, 20 March 1992.

Chinese Businesswoman case: Liu v The Age Company [2010] NSWSC 1176; *Liu v The Age Company Ltd* [2011] NSWSC 53; *Liu v The Age Company Limited* [2012] NSWSC 12; *Age Company Limited and Others v Liu and Another* [2013] NSWCA 26; *The Age Company Ltd and Ors v Liu and Anor* [2013] HCATrans 205; *Liu v The Age Company Limited (No. 2)* [2015] NSWSC 276; *Liu v The Age Company Limited* [2016] NSWCA 115, <www.austlii.edu.au/cgi-bin/viewdoc/au/cases/nsw/NSWCA/2016/115.html>; *The Age Company Pty Ltd and Ors v Liu* [2016] HCATrans 306, <www.austlii.edu.au/cgi-bin/viewdoc/au/cases/cth/HCATrans/2016/306.html>.

Cojuangco's case: John Fairfax and Sons Ltd v Cojuangco (1988) 82 ALR 1.

Cornwall's case: ICAC v Cornwall (1993) 116 ALR 97.

Corrs' case: Corrs Pavey Whiting & Byrne v Collector of Customs (Vic) (1987) 14 FCR 343.

Defence Papers case: Commonwealth v John Fairfax & Sons Ltd [1980] HCA 44; (1980) 147 CLR 39 (1 December 1980), <www.austlii.edu.au/cgi-bin/sinodisp/au/cases/cth/HCA/1980/44.html>.

Exclusive Brethren case: Doe v Fairfax Media Publications Pty Limited [2017] NSWSC 1153, <www.austlii.edu.au/cgi-bin/viewdoc/au/cases/nsw/NSWSC/2017/1153.html>.

Financial Tweets case: X v Twitter Inc. [2017] NSWSC 1300, <www.caselaw.nsw.gov.au/decision/59cadc2be4b074a7c6e18fa3>.

Gartside's case: Gartside v Outrim (1856) 26 LJ 113.

Jane Doe case: Doe v ABC & Ors [2007] VCC 281 (3 April 2007), <www.austlii.edu.au/cgi-bin/viewdoc/au/cases/vic/VCC/2007/281.html>.

John Does case: Koch Industries, Inc. v John Does, 1–25, 2011 WL 1775765 *10 (D. Utah May 9, 2011) [Case No. 2:10CV1275DAK, per Judge Dale A. Kimball], <www.citizen.org/documents/Koch-v-Does-District-Court-Opinion.pdf>.

Kangaroo Court case: Doe v Dowling [2017] NSWSC 1037, <www.caselaw.nsw.gov.au/decision/5989110be4b058596cba915c>.

Kiwi Blogger's case: Slater v Blomfield [2014] NZHC 2221; [2014] 3 NZLR 835, <www.nzlii.org/nz/cases/NZHC/2014/2221.html>.

Lenah Game Meats case: ABC v Lenah Game Meats Pty Ltd [2001] HCA 63; 208 CLR 199; 185 ALR 1; 76 ALJR 1 (15 November 2001), <www.austlii.edu.au/au/cases/cth/high_ct/2001/63.html>.

Mafia case: Madafferi v The Age [2015] VSC 687, <www.austlii.edu.au/cgi-bin/viewdoc/au/cases/vic/VSC/2016/103.html>.

Maleny Towers case: Straker and Sunshine Coast Regional Council; NBN Co Limited (Third Party) [2016] QICmr 44, <www.oic.qld.gov.au/__data/assets/pdf_file/0003/31890/decision-312519-external-review-28-10-16.pdf>.

McGuinness's case: McGuinness v Attorney-General of Victoria (1940) 63 CLR 73.

New Idea case: Hewitt v Pacific Magazines Pty Ltd [2009] SASC 323, Judge Lunn (15 October 2008), <www.austlii.edu.au/au/cases/sa/SASC/2009323.html>.

Nicholls' case: Nicholls v DPP (SA) (1993) 170 LSJS 362.

Night Jack case: Anon v Times Newspapers Ltd (2009) EWHC 1358 (QB) HQ09X02293 (UK).

Norwich Pharmacal case: Norwich Pharmacal Company & Ors v Commissioners of Customs and Excise (1973) U4HL6 (UK).

NRMA case: NRMA v John Fairfax [2002] NSWSC 563 (26 June 2002).

Reserve Bank case: McKenzie & Anor v Magistrates' Court of Victoria & Anor [2013] VSCA 81 (18 April 2013).

Rinehart cases: Hancock Prospecting Pty Ltd v Hancock [2013] WASC 290, <www.austlii.edu.au/cgi-bin/viewdoc/au/cases/wa/WASC/2013/290.html> [Pennell's case]; *Hancock Prospecting Pty Ltd v Hancock [No. 2]* [2014] WASC 85, <www.austlii.edu.au/cgi-bin/viewdoc/au/cases/wa/WASC/2014/85.html> [Ferguson's case].

Rubbish Bin case: Owens v Barnett [2014] VCC 2038, <www.austlii.edu.au/cgi-bin/viewdoc/au/cases/vic/VCC/2014/2038.html>.

Sex Tapes case: Giller v Procopets [2008] VSCA 236 (10 December 2008).

War Veterans case: Harvey & Anor v County Court of Victoria & Ors [2006] VSC 293 (23 August 2006). See also *R v Gerard Thomas McManus and Michael Harvey* [2007] VCC 619 (for decision on penalty) and *R v Kelly* [2006] VSCA 221 (17 October 2006).

WARU case: Fairfax Media Publications Pty Ltd v Western Australian Rugby Union Inc. [2008] WASCA 123, <www.austlii.edu.au/cgi-bin/viewdoc/au/cases/wa/WASCA/2008/123.html>.

Westpac Letters case: Westpac Banking Corporation v John Fairfax Group Pty Ltd (1991) 19 IPR 513.

Wikipedia case: G & G v Wikimedia Foundation Inc. (2009) EWHC 3148HQ09X (UK).

Witham's case: Witham v Holloway (1995) FC 95/035 [1995] HCA 3; (1995) 131 ALR 401, (1995) 69 ALJR 847 (10 February 1995).

CHAPTER 10

Anti-terrorism and hate laws

KEY CONCEPTS

National security laws
A range of laws—many of which were introduced in the wake of the 9/11 attacks on the United States—designed to counter terrorism but often impinging on other rights and liberties expected in a democratic society.

Discrimination
Unfair treatment that happens to someone because of their personal characteristics or beliefs—such as race, age, gender or religion.

Racial vilification
The incitement of hatred, serious contempt or severe ridicule of a person or groups of people on the grounds of race, via a public act.

Cyber-bullying
Bullying—insults, demeaning comments, harassment and intimidation—using digital communication platforms such as blogs, websites and social media, and devices like mobile phones, tablets and computers.

Social and political developments over the past half-century have exposed professional communicators to two expanded restrictions upon their work: enhanced national security laws, particularly those enacted following the September 2001 terrorist attacks on the United States; and anti-discrimination and racial vilification laws designed to discourage intolerance in our increasingly multicultural societies. This chapter looks at each of these areas of the law and considers how they might affect journalists and bloggers trying to report and comment upon national security issues and cultural tensions, and other professional communicators like media advisers whose clients may want to engage in public debate about such matters.

ANTI-TERROR LAWS: BACKGROUND AND INTERNATIONAL CONTEXT

Media restrictions in the name of national security were in existence long before the attacks on New York's World Trade Center on September 11, 2001. As the Australian Law Reform Commission noted in its 2006 discussion paper on sedition laws (ALRC, 2006: 51), sedition and treason laws date back to feudal times when governments attempted to enforce allegiance to lords and monarchs. Section 80.1 of the *Criminal Code Act 1995* defines 'treason' as a range of offences relating to violent acts against the 'Sovereign, the Governor-General or the Prime Minister', levying war against the Commonwealth or assisting an enemy at war with Australia. Section 80.2 (formerly 'sedition'), and its sub-sections (80.2A–D) outline a range of crimes related to 'urging violence' and advocating terrorism or genocide. Throughout the nineteenth and twentieth centuries, nations in the Australasia-Pacific region maintained sedition and treason laws, and used them occasionally against journalists. Anti-terrorism laws were also used in Western democracies well before 2001. The United Kingdom passed special laws to respond to Irish Republican Army (IRA) terrorism throughout the twentieth century, while New Zealand introduced new restrictions after the French spy agency's bombing of the Greenpeace boat *Rainbow Warrior* in 1985, in which a photographer drowned.

Governments throughout the world ramped up their national security laws in the wake of the terrorist attacks on the United States in September 2001. Even in countries with a high regard for civil liberties and free expression, new powers were handed to security agencies and police to aid in the detection and arrest of suspected terrorists. Pressure mounted in Western democracies like Australia for even tougher laws after the Bali bombings in 2002 and 2005 and the 7/7 London attacks in 2005.

America led the way with its USA Patriot Act of 2001, in which the letters stood for: 'Uniting (and) Strengthening America (by) Providing Appropriate Tools Required (to) Intercept (and) Obstruct Terrorism'. President Barack Obama extended the legislation for a further four years from 2011 (Abrams, 2011), although in 2015 it was retired and replaced in a modified form by the USA Freedom Act (HR 2048, Pub.L. 114–23), an acronym for 'Uniting and Strengthening America by Fulfilling Rights and Ending Eavesdropping, Dragnet-collection and Online Monitoring Act'. Other countries, including the United Kingdom, Canada, Australia and New Zealand, followed by introducing their own anti-terror laws.

Between December 2014 and March 2018, 84 charges were laid in Australia against 51 people for preparatory terrorism offences. Of these, 41 charges resulted in conviction, a further 36 were the subject of ongoing prosecution and seven were withdrawn for a range of reasons, including a lack of admissible evidence (Renwick, 2017). The figures indicate that terrorism is indeed an ongoing threat in this millennium, but the key question for our societies is whether impositions upon journalism and publishing are truly necessary to reduce national security threats.

Too many anti-terror laws have been introduced internationally to detail here, but some can impact upon you if you are a journalist or blogger, or another professional communicator publishing across borders using the internet or social media. Their impacts include:

- increased surveillance powers for spy agencies and police
- new detention and questioning regimes

- seizure of notes and computer archives
- exposing confidential sources to identification
- closing certain court proceedings so they are unreportable
- exposing bloggers to fines and jail if they report on some anti-terror operations
- making it an offence to merely 'associate' or 'communicate' with those suspected of national security crimes
- exposing journalists, bloggers and social media users to criminal charges if they publish anything seen as inciting terrorism; and
- narrowing the range of material which can be accessed under freedom of information laws.

As Ewart, Pearson and Lessing (2013) explain, the broad competing policies behind anti-terror laws are usually expressed as the public's interest in national security and the public's interest in a free and fully informed press, along with the individual's right to a fair and open trial (open justice), the right to privacy and related rights against reputational damage and discrimination.

ANTI-TERROR LAWS: DIGITAL DIMENSIONS

In recent years, this media law issue has been front-page news with the emergence of major transparency enterprises like WikiLeaks—headed by Australian Julian Assange—and the data releases of former US National Security Agency (NSA) worker Edward Snowden. The alleged source of the most controversial WikiLeaks documents and vision (released in collaboration with international media outlets *The New York Times* and *The Guardian*) was US Army private Chelsea (formerly Bradley) Manning, who was sentenced to 35 years in prison in 2013 for the leak. That is the highest price a whistleblower has paid in a Western democracy, and underscores the gravity of the offence and the dangers of compromising security operations on an international level. Some high-level US politicians called for an even worse fate for

Snowden if he was captured and tried over his release of confidential diplomatic documents: a death sentence. (Manning was released from jail in 2017 after former US President Barack Obama commuted her sentence.)

Social media can also present serious risks for journalists and professional communicators letting their guard down by exercising their wit on the serious subject of national security. Twitter and Facebook are great outlets for one-liners and satire, but police and security agencies are not known for their sense of humour. Trainee accountant Paul Chambers, 27, learned this the hard way when he was arrested on UK terrorism charges for jokingly tweeting a threat to blow up a British airport. Air traffic was delayed by a heavy snowfall and Chambers was desperate to visit a female friend in Northern Ireland, so he light-heartedly tweeted to her and his 650 followers: 'C***! Robin Hood Airport closed. You have got a week to get your s*** together, otherwise I'm blowing the airport sky high!' Police swooped a week later and he was questioned over potential terrorism charges before being convicted and fined £1000 on a lesser charge of causing nuisance. He eventually won his appeal—after considerable inconvenience and heartache (Bowcott, 2012). There is a simple lesson here: do not joke about national security matters.

Governments also go straight to search engines and ISPs, demanding that they remove material. As Google's (2018) Transparency Report documents, they often comply. For example, in the first six months of 2017 the Australian government made more than 1400 requests to Google for user data, while the US government made 23,730 requests, including court orders, search warrants and subpoenas. Some governments have complained that Google and YouTube have not responded quickly enough when asked to take down terrorism-related material.

AUSTRALIAN ANTI-TERROR LAWS AND THEIR IMPACT

Pullan (1994) chronicles the use of sedition and seditious libel by governments against editors throughout colonial times and Pacific Media Watch (2018) has reported sedition charges being brought against journalists and political activists throughout the Asia-Pacific region even over recent years, when they have published what governments interpret as subversive material.

In Australia, Hocking (2004) describes the post-2001 counter-terrorism initiatives as 'the second wave', given the substantial activity in developing national security measures from the late 1960s, largely in response to isolated terrorist incidents throughout the 1970s and political reviews of the operations of the Australian Security Intelligence Organisation (ASIO). The media operated under what Hocking calls a system of 'voluntary restraint' (2004: 82), such as the 'D-notice' system involving major newspapers and the Australian government by which the news media agreed not to report on sensitive security issues in the post-war era through until the mid-1990s.

Many security provisions pre-date the 9/11 era. An example is section 92 of the *Australian Security Intelligence Organisation (ASIO) Act 1979*, providing one year's imprisonment for anyone who identifies an officer of the national security organisation other than its director-general. The legislation survives today, and sits as a warning to journalists covering national security issues, particularly those wanting to seek out a former spy for quotes.

Since 2001, the Australian government has introduced new legislation containing provisions for the arrest and detention of citizens (including journalists) who might have information on terrorists and terrorism activity, and which in certain circumstances makes communication with detainees a criminal offence. The Australian parliament passed approximately 70 laws and regulations related to national security and counter-terrorism in the 2001–18 period, with some having potential implications for open justice and news reporting. These included nine tranches of national security laws, including 273 government amendments to various Bills (Porter, 2018). In recent years, a number of suspected terrorist plots have been foiled in their planning stages. These events and the ensuing court cases have raised serious questions about the balance between national security and human rights, like free expression and the principle of open justice (Renwick, 2017: 16–25).

McGarrity (2011) argues that three key factors have limited the media's ability to effectively hold the executive to account on national security issues: the limited provision of and access to information about terrorism-related investigations and court cases; a chilling effect on freedom of speech; and media manipulation by the federal government. She states that a crucial factor is that the media are being deprived of intelligence about counter-terror operations and judicial proceedings.

McNamara (2009) examined the 'actual and potential effects' of Australia's counter-terrorism laws on journalists, public debate and circulation of information. He found through interviews with journalists and media lawyers working for major news organisations that they had minimal understanding of the anti-terrorism laws and their operation. He found journalists were worried by the potential effects of security laws on their rights and reportage (2009: 41).

KEY ANTI-TERROR LAWS POST-9/11

The key national security laws with potential impacts on the media—most of which have been introduced or amended since 2001—include the following.

AUSTRALIAN SECURITY INTELLIGENCE ORGANISATION ACT 1979

Section 25A focuses on ASIO powers and access to computer networks, with one warrant now able to apply to an entire computer network using third party computers to access target systems. Amendments were passed in 2003, making it an offence to disclose information about 'questioning' warrants and 'questioning and detention' warrants (and related operational information) for up to two years, 'even if the operation is in violation of international human rights conventions' (MEAA, 2005). There are no public-interest or media exemptions to the requirement, although disclosures of operational information by anyone other than the subject of a warrant or their lawyer requires the discloser to have shown 'recklessness' in doing so (s 34ZS (3)).

Section 35P provides for up to five years in jail for 'unauthorised' disclosure of information related to a 'special intelligence operation'—and up to ten years if the disclosure 'endangers the health or safety' of anyone or will 'prejudice the effective conduct of a special intelligence operation'. Amendments partially exempting 'outsiders' (journalists) were enacted in 2016, but grave concerns remained over the impacts on journalists for 'reckless' disclosure that might endanger safety and jeopardise an operation and the implications for their sources who faced stricter liability and more serious penalties as 'entrusted persons'.

Section 92 provides for 10 years' imprisonment for anyone who identifies an ASIO officer or affiliate (or anyone connected with them), other than any who have been identified in parliament (such as the director-general). Former ASIO employees and affiliates can be identified if they have consented in writing or have generally made that fact be known.

NATIONAL SECURITY INFORMATION (CRIMINAL AND CIVIL PROCEEDINGS) ACT 2004 (CTH)

This legislation and its subsequent amendments impacted on media coverage of court cases involving national security or terrorism matters. Division 3 of the Act authorises prosecutors and courts to use national security information in criminal proceedings while preventing the broader disclosure of such information, sometimes even to the defendant. Section 29 allows the closure of courts for national security reasons, with the potential delays to the release of the record of those proceedings (29A).

CRIMES ACT 1914 (CTH)

Amendments in 2005 defined terrorist organisations, detailed new offences and penalties for financing such organisations, and gave federal agencies new powers to impose 'control orders' and preventative detention orders on suspects as well as powers to stop, search, question and obtain information and documents as part of an investigation. Section 3ZQT makes it an offence to disclose the fact that someone has been given notice by the Australian Federal Police (AFP) to produce documents related to a serious terrorism offence under section 3ZQN. Journalists could face up to two years in prison for reporting that they have been issued with such a notice related to a story they are covering–perhaps involving their communications with, or contact details for, sources (s 3ZQP).

TELECOMMUNICATIONS (INTERCEPTION AND ACCESS) ACT 1979

After amendments in 2015 introducing 'Part 5-1A Data retention' to the Act, telecommunications providers are required to retain customers' phone and computer metadata for two years so they can be accessed by criminal law enforcement agencies (state and Commonwealth) on the issue of a warrant. Information required to be stored includes: subscriber/account information, the source and destination of a communication, and the date, time and duration of a communication or connection to a service. A 'journalist information warrant' scheme was designed to prohibit the disclosure of journalists' confidential sources without special precautions (Division 4C–Journalist information warrants). These require approval of the minister, who may act on the advice of an appointed 'Public Interest Advocate' (s 180X), although the processes are secret and disclosure of the details of any warrant for telecommunications data can incur imprisonment for two years (s 182A and B). The protocols were breached in 2017 when the Australian Federal Police admitted a journalist's call records had been accessed without following the procedures (Royes, 2017).

CRIMINAL CODE ACT 1995

Amendments in 2010 removed the term 'sedition' from Division 80 of the Criminal Code and replaced it with references to a range of 'urging violence' offences against the Constitution or Government (s 80.2), groups (s 80.2A), members of groups (s 80.2B), advocating terrorism (s 80.3) and advocating genocide (s 80.4). The Act would include words urging violence published on the internet or social media by those holding extreme views; however, alarm among the mainstream media was moderated by the inclusion of a 'good faith' defence at section 80.3, covering anyone who urges violence at the time if that person '(f) publishes in good faith a report or commentary about a matter of public interest'.

'Control orders' were introduced, banning terror suspects' communications with 'specified individuals' under section 104.5(3)(e) of the *Criminal Code Act 1995*, which could impact journalist–source communications. A ban on 'associating' at least twice with a person who is a member of, or promotes or directs the activities of, a terrorist organisation under section 102.8(1), potentially impacts journalists' coverage of national and international security issues, although required elements of knowledge and intent on the part of the journalist would minimise that likelihood.

In 2017, the Turnbull government introduced the National Security Legislation Amendment (Espionage and Foreign Interference) Bill to amend the *Criminal Code Act 1995* to (along with a range of other measures):

- amend existing, and introduce new, espionage offences relating to a broad range of dealings with information, including solicitation and preparation and planning offences
- introduce new offences relating to foreign interference with Australia's political, governmental or democratic processes
- amend existing, and introduce new, offences relating to treason and other threats to national security, such as interference with Australian democratic or political rights by conduct involving the use of force, violence or intimidation
- replace certain existing, and introduce new, offences relating to secrecy of information.

After considerable lobbying from media organisations and the journalists' union (the MEAA) over serious concerns about impacts on various media freedoms and source vulnerabilities, the government announced in 2018 that it would introduce amendments to offer at least the following media protections:

- the creation of separate offences that apply to non-Commonwealth officers that are narrower in scope than those applying to Commonwealth officers and only apply to most dangerous and serious conduct
- narrowing the definitions of 'inherently harmful information' and 'causes harm to Australia's interests', which will form part of the offences applying to Commonwealth officers
- strengthening the defence for journalists by:
  - removing any requirement for journalists to demonstrate that their reporting was 'fair and accurate'
  - ensuring the defence is available where a journalist reasonably believes that their conduct was in the public interest, and
  - clarifying that the defence is available for editorial and support staff as well as journalists themselves (Porter, 2018).

The legislation was passed in June 2018.

A host of other laws have been introduced by states and territories since 9/11 as part of their counter-terror enforcement regimes and as security measures for special events they were hosting. Of course, not all counter-terrorism legislation affects the work of journalists and media organisations. However, many of the changes have the potential to affect journalists in their reporting of terrorism-related stories.

The MEAA has detailed most of the major issues of concern to journalists in its annual press freedom reports (MEAA, 2005–17). In its 2006 report, the MEAA suggested that journalists needed to assume their conversations with sources on terrorism stories would be intercepted, as one of the 2006 amendments allowed phone tapping of third parties in connection with suspected terrorist plots. Some of the cases we highlight below prove that this has been happening. In 2011, the federal government and major news groups held discussions and reached agreement on a set of 'principles' for major news coverage of national security issues (MEAA, 2012).

KEY AUSTRALIAN CASES INVOLVING ANTI-TERROR LAWS AND THE MEDIA

Examples of the impact of federal anti-terrorism laws upon the media and others include the following.

MOHAMED HANEEF, THE GOLD COAST DOCTOR

The potential for the misuse of anti-terrorism laws by federal agencies was highlighted by the Haneef episode in 2007. Gold Coast Hospital registrar (and Indian citizen) Dr Mohamed Haneef was arrested over suspected UK terrorism connections on 2 July 2007 and became the first suspect to undergo special extended detention for investigation purposes under the amended Division 2 of Part 1C of the *Crimes Act 1914* (Clarke, 2008: viii). The charges against Dr Haneef—that he recklessly provided resources to a terrorist organisation under section 102.7(1) of the *Criminal Code Act 1995* (by providing his cousins in the United Kingdom with a telephone SIM card)—were withdrawn on 27 July 2007 due to 'no reasonable prospect of conviction'. The Federal Court even quashed the Minister for Immigration and Citizenship's cancellation of Dr Haneef's visa because the minister had not properly applied the character test under the *Migration Act 1958* (*Haneef case*, 2007). A 2008 inquiry found the AFP had managed the case poorly. Dr Haneef was awarded compensation by the Australian government, reported by some Indian media as amounting to around A$1 million (AAP, 2010).

While the case only involved the media in its reporting role, the whole episode was sadly symptomatic of how governments can enforce their newly acquired extra powers when dealing with terrorism suspects. The hearings extending Dr Haneef's detention were closed to the media. As Ewart, Pearson and Lessing (2013) explain, other lessons from the media for this case included the assumption the accused was guilty of the charges because they were so reliant on official sources for their information; the fact that only a leak of court documents to the journalists freed up the facts for the media to verify, and holes in the case then started to appear; and that anti-terror laws restricted journalists' (and Haneef's lawyers') access to some preliminary hearings.

FOCUS CASE 10.1: *THE 'JIHAD' JACK CASES*

R v Thomas (No. 3) [2006] VSCA 300 (20 December 2006)

Thomas v Mowbray [2007] HCA 33 (2 August 2007)

R v Thomas (No. 4) [2008] VSCA 107 (16 June 2008)

R v Thomas [2008] VSC 620 (29 October 2008)

FACTS

Alleged terrorist 'sleeper' 'Jihad' Jack Thomas became the first Australian to be convicted using the anti-terrorism laws introduced into Australia after 2001. Thomas had travelled to Afghanistan in March 2001–prior to the 9/11 terror attacks on the United States–to train at a Taliban training camp, and served for a week on the front line for the Taliban, then the Afghanistan government, against the Northern Alliance in a civil war. Over the following months, the 9/11 attacks, the first of the Bali terrorist bombings and an earthquake prevented Thomas returning to Australia. In early 2003, he was detained by Pakistan authorities when trying to leave the country with a falsified passport. After returning to Australia, he was convicted under section 102.6 of the Criminal Code 1995 (amended in 2002–03) for receiving funds from a terrorist organisation. The Appeal Court quashed the conviction on the basis of the inadmissibility of the police record of interview.

On 27 August 2006, a federal magistrate issued the nation's first 'control order' over Thomas under section 104.4 of the Criminal Code, restricting his movements, requiring him to report to police and banning his contact with a long list of organisations. The High Court upheld the validity of the relevant legislation in a challenge (*'Jihad' Jack case*, 2007).

On 20 December 2006, the Director of Public Prosecutions obtained an order for a retrial, based partly on admissions Thomas had made in interviews with the ABC's *Four Corners* reporter Sally Neighbour (*Four Corners*, 2006) and to *The Age*'s Ian Munro–admissions similar to those he had made in the excluded police interview. Despite this evidence, Thomas was eventually found not guilty of terrorism charges, but on 23 October 2008 he was found guilty of having falsified an Australian passport, and sentenced to nine months' imprisonment, which he had already served (*'Jihad' Jack case*, 2008).

LAW

Both *Four Corners* and *The Age* cooperated with the police, defusing a situation where police would have been tempted to use seizure powers. In *R v Thomas (No. 4)* (2008), the appeal court detailed the extent to which telephone conversations between ABC reporter Sally Neighbour and Thomas had been monitored by an ASIO agent—up to 20 times throughout 2005 on his mobile phone or landline.

The telephone conversations were generally short, and concerned practical arrangements. They did not involve any discussion of substance. The journalist was aware of the possibility of surveillance by ASIO and she was honouring an agreement with Thomas to keep the interviews secret until after the trial (para. 19).

LESSONS FOR JOURNALISTS AND PROFESSIONAL COMMUNICATORS

Anti-terrorism laws introduced since 2001 give national security agencies and the police wide powers to monitor and subpoena communications between journalists and their sources. The level of surveillance by ASIO—including the monitoring of telephone calls between an ABC journalist and a source—indicates that investigative journalists should work on the assumption that all their communications are being monitored, and factor that into their source protection. A further lesson is that records of journalists' interviews with sources might be sought as evidence in a major trial, and they will face the difficult ethical decision of whether to release them to prosecuting authorities. As Ewart, Pearson and Lessing (2013) point out, the *Jihad Jack case* raised the question of whether Commonwealth shield laws (not introduced until 2011) would have excused the journalists from providing their materials if they had existed at the time. They suggested it was likely a court would rule that a national security or counter-terror issue would constitute a situation where the public interest would outweigh a journalist's obligation to a source. This would leave a journalist exposed to a potential fine or jail term, in the event of non-compliance.

OPERATION PENDENNIS

Eight men were arrested in Melbourne and nine men in Sydney in 2005 on terrorism charges after a sixteen-month surveillance operation involving the AFP, ASIO and the Victoria Police (Ewart, Pearson and Lessing, 2013). Eventually twelve men faced trial in February 2008, of whom seven were found guilty of one or more of the charges (Kissane, 2008). Special suppression order provisions under counter-terror laws led to the imposition of more than 30 suppression orders during the Victorian Supreme Court trial, with many lifted after the verdict (Ewart, Pearson and Lessing, 2013). Despite these restrictions, the presiding judge, Justice Bernard Bongiorno, in the Melbourne case (*Benbrika's case*), as well as the magistrate at the committal hearing, Paul Smith, took several steps to accommodate the media's interest in the case. As Ewart, Pearson and Lessing (2013) note, the court officer established several communication channels to keep the media up to date with the case. Justice Bongiorno also arranged a pre-trial briefing for journalists and media organisations' lawyers. He stressed that his preference was for the media to report the proceedings of the open court, but warned against reportage while the jury was absent. He detailed procedures to avoid prejudicial publicity, including provision of transcripts of each day's proceedings. He allowed the release of trial exhibits to the media, embargoed until after the verdict.

Journalists were restricted in what they could report because of the suppression orders, some of which were not lifted for three years. Some indication of the detail of those orders can be seen by viewing the *Operation Pendennis cases* (2008) in Melbourne and Sydney. The Melbourne trial (*Benbrika's case*) demonstrated how a judiciary appreciative of the principle of open justice could manage a trial to maximise reportage despite the impositions of anti-terror laws. The Sydney trial (*Baladjam's case*) even involved the issuing of a 'super injunction', where the judge ordered suppression of 'the details of the present application, the arguments that surrounded it and, for the moment, suppress publication of the decision itself' (at para. 70).

THE DORLING RAID

In September 2008, AFP agents searched the home of Philip Dorling, national affairs correspondent with *The Canberra Times*, for documents relating to a story on the Defence Intelligence Organisation that appeared on 14 June 2008, removing the hard drive from his computer, a laptop, a mobile phone and files and paper material, including a copy of the article, which referred to classified briefing papers prepared for then Defence Minister Joel Fitzgibbon (*Law Report*, 2008). The raid related to possible breaches of the Commonwealth *Crimes Act 1914*. Under section 79 of the *Crimes Act*, a journalist is guilty of an offence if they receive anything that they know or ought to know is classified as an official secret. They are liable to seven years' imprisonment, unless they prove that it was communicated to them against their wishes.

HOLSWORTHY ARMY BARRACKS BOMB PLOT: TWEETS, LEAKS AND QUESTIONED DEALS

Several issues related to media freedom stemmed from the arrests in 2009 of five men on charges over a plot to attack the Holsworthy Army Barracks in the south-west of Sydney. The men sought a fatwa from a Somali-based terrorism group to shoot and kill as many army personnel as possible. Three of the men were eventually sentenced to eighteen years in prison following the AFP's 'Operation Neath' for conspiring with others to undertake the attack. The appeal court summarised their aim as being 'to advance Islam by violence for the purposes of coercing or influencing the Australian Government by intimidation, or alternatively to intimidate the public or a section of the public' (*Holsworthy Barracks cases*, 2013).

As Ewart, Pearson and Lessing (2013) detail, the case involved the news media at a range of levels, including police leaks to the media (which resulted in a further case against the police source, *Artz's case*, in 2013), a media outlet's exclusive arrangements with the police, a media outlet's unauthorised photography of a military base and a journalist's unauthorised tweeting of the proceedings of Artz's trial.

The Australian newspaper used a police source—later proven to be Victorian detective Simon Artz—to get details of Operation Neath prior to the arrests of the suspects. It even published some copies of the newspaper including a story about the raids in the hours prior to them occurring. The editor, Paul Whittaker, had struck an agreement with the AFP over the timing of the story, but this was at odds with the understanding of Victoria Police, also involved in the operation, who felt the stories risked tipping off the suspects prior to the arrests. In 2011, the deal between *The Australian* and the AFP was made public and called into question on ethical grounds (Simons, 2011a). *The Australian*'s reporter, Cameron Stewart, reluctantly revealed the name of a police source of his leak (after the source had signed a document formally releasing Stewart from his ethical obligation), raising further debate over the ethics of dealing with confidential sources. Detective Artz pleaded guilty to a charge of unauthorised disclosure of information and was given a four-month suspended sentence in the Victorian County Court (*Artz's case*, 2013).

The case attracted further attention when *Crikey* journalist Margaret Simons tweeted from the courtroom without having sought permission and was ordered by the magistrate to stop tweeting because of the national security nature of the material and the risk that suppression orders would be rendered useless if the material had been already tweeted before the order was imposed (Simons, 2011b). In another episode, a reporter and photographer from Sydney's *Daily Telegraph* entered and photographed the Holsworthy Army Barracks without permission, resulting in them being issued with good behaviour bonds but having no convictions recorded against them (Kontominas, 2009). In all, the *Holsworthy Barracks case* and associated legal actions highlighted journalists' difficulties in operating in the context of sensitive national security litigation. It signalled a need for better understanding of the various restrictions such as those on photographing military installations, the permissions needed before live tweeting from the courtroom and the vulnerability of sources of information in national security matters.

Ewart, Pearson and Lessing (2013) argue that these cases showed anti-terror laws introduced since 9/11 had already had the following demonstrable impacts on the reportage of national security matters:

- the willingness of judges to take advantage of new powers to issue suppression orders in national security cases, limiting public knowledge of aspects of cases as they proceed through the courts
- arrest, questioning and detention restrictions, increasing media reliance on official spokespeople once a suspect has been arrested, as evidenced by the controls of information flows by the Federal Police in the arrest and charging of Haneef
- demands by judges for journalists to reveal their sources of counter-terror stories, exemplified by the making of such demands upon *The Australian*'s Cameron Stewart regarding leaks from the AFP over the Holsworthy Barracks raids
- related to this, the freezing of information about counter-terror operations by government agencies after the above incident where *The Australian* published an account of one operation before it had commenced
- readiness of counter-terrorism agencies and prosecutors to make use of raw footage and interview material captured by journalists as prosecution evidence in their cases against terror suspects (Ewart, Pearson and Lessing, 2013).

REVIEWS OF NATIONAL SECURITY AND ANTI-TERROR LAWS

National security and anti-terror laws are in a constant state of review—at the levels of the Council of Australian Governments (COAG), the Independent National Security Legislation Monitor (INSLM) (see Renwick, 2017) and via various parliamentary committees, particularly the Parliamentary Joint Committee on Intelligence and Security (PJCIS). Students and professional communicators should search for each of these for the latest updates on changes to counter-terror and security legislation, some of which impact free expression, particularly for journalists and their sources.

RACE HATE, ETHICS AND LAW INTERNATIONALLY

There are numerous ethical codes, international conventions, national constitutions and bills of rights underpinning anti-discrimination and vilification laws protecting citizens throughout the world. As professional communicators using the internet and social media, they may provide you with some defence against spiteful attacks, but are also the reference points for those who may feel insulted by your blogs or tweets.

At the highest level, Article 2 of the Universal Declaration of Human Rights (United Nations, 2011) counsels against the withdrawal of rights based on citizens' views or backgrounds:

> *Everyone is entitled to all the rights and freedoms set forth in this Declaration, without distinction of any kind, such as race, colour, sex, language, religion, political or other opinion, national or social origin, property, birth or other status.*

Article 7 warns against discrimination:

> *All are equal before the law and are entitled without any discrimination to equal protection of the law. All are entitled to equal protection against any discrimination in violation of this Declaration and against any incitement to such discrimination.*

Article 18 confers the right to 'freedom of thought, conscience and religion'. As we have found with other areas of media law, all these rights need to be balanced against the Article 19 'right to freedom of opinion and expression . . . (including) freedom to hold opinions without interference'.

The challenge facing courts and legislators developing anti-discrimination, cyber-bullying and hate speech laws throughout the world is that countries have found different points of balance for these rights. In the United States, for example, there is a strong First Amendment protection even for hateful speech, and the Supreme Court has struck down lower court decisions and state legislation attempting to gag free expression. By contrast, Germany and several other European countries have Holocaust denial laws under which several revisionist historians and neo-Nazis have been jailed for expressing their views.

In February 2018, Poland's Senate passed, and Polish President Andrzej Duda signed into law, an amendment to existing anti-defamation laws, the Amended Act on the Institute of National Remembrance. This makes it illegal to attribute responsibility for or complicity during the Holocaust to the Polish nation or state. The law imposes up to three years in prison or a fine for accusing the Polish state or people of involvement or responsibility for the Nazi occupation during World War II. The original law, enacted in 1998, imposed fines or up to three years in prison for those who denied or belittled German or Soviet crimes during the Holocaust and subsequent Soviet invasion. The amendment does the same for those who then attribute Holocaust crimes to the 'Polish Nation or the Polish State' (Tobias, 2018).

DIGITAL DIMENSIONS OF DISCRIMINATION

Hatred features in the International Covenant on Civil and Political Rights at Article 20, which prohibits 'Any advocacy of national, racial or religious hatred that constitutes incitement to discrimination, hostility or violence' (OHCHR, 1976). Despite these words, dedicated 'hate sites' on the internet number in their thousands. Social media have helped far right extremists connect with each other, fuelling intolerance and outright hatred against any ethnic, religious or political group in their sights.

When the Danish newspaper *Jyllands-Posten* printed twelve cartoons depicting the Prophet Mohammed in 2005, its journalists knew there would be a reaction. The whole idea for the stunt had come about because a children's author had told them of the difficulty he was having finding someone to illustrate a book he was writing about the Prophet's life. (Visual depictions of Mohammed are offensive to some traditions of Islam.) Within months, the Danish newspaper's images had spread via the internet and scores of other newspapers, triggering protests in which more than 100 people died, and prompting the bombing and arson of Danish embassies, flag burning, the declaration of a fatwa by Muslim clerics and an axe attack on one of the cartoonists.

The cartoons had seemed like a good idea at the time to the newspaper's culture editor, Flemming Rose, who wanted to 'integrate Muslims into the Danish tradition of satire', as he wrote in *The Washington Post* (Rose, 2006). Rather than encouraging integration, however, the cartoons became one of the most divisive actions by a media outlet in modern history. The free expression traditions of Denmark clashed directly with an ancient Sunni Muslim prohibition on the visual illustration of Mohammed. The depiction of the Prophet with an ignited fuse in his head-dress sparked the most heated reaction from devotees.

More than a decade has passed since the cartoons were published, but the original cartoonists and editors, and those who reproduced them in other newspapers and online, still hold well-founded fears of retribution for their actions. Such fears seemed justified when in January 2015 two extremists forced their way into the offices of the satirical weekly newspaper *Charlie Hebdo* in Paris. They killed twelve people and injured eleven others. *Charlie Hebdo* had attracted controversy by republishing the Danish cartoons and subsequently publishing numerous satirical articles about Islam. A month later, an attack in Copenhagen targeted an event titled 'Art, Blasphemy and Freedom of Expression', with Swedish artist Lars Vilks—famous for his satirical drawings of the prophet Mohammed—in attendance.

The Danish cartoons episode was not the first time Muslims had taken offence at material they deemed blasphemous. The most famous fatwa was against British author Salman Rushdie in 1989, when Iranian leader Ayatollah Ruhollah Khomeini sentenced him to death for writing the book *The Satanic Verses*. The book was based loosely on the life of the Prophet. The Japanese translator was stabbed to death in 1991 and the Italian translator was also stabbed. In 1993, the Norwegian publisher of the book was shot outside his Oslo home.

All these examples illustrate the blurred divisions between free expression, hate speech and satire. Of course, no form of communication justifies violent retribution, but there is marked international variation in what level of expression is acceptable—or even legal—when it might involve racial, ethnic or religious critique.

In the eyes of the law, attacks upon others via the internet or social media go under a range of names according to their type, scale and jurisdiction. They include: cyber-bullying, cyber-stalking, online trolling, malicious online content, using carriage services to menace, harassment, hate speech, vilification, discrimination and even assault. Some are criminal offences where offenders can be fined or jailed, while others are civil wrongs where courts can award damages to victims. Some are litigated under actions we have already considered, such as defamation, privacy and breach of confidentiality.

Some are difficult to explain because the motivations are beyond the imagination of ordinary citizens. Australian 'troll' Bradley Hampson served 220 days in jail in 2011 for plastering obscene images and comments on Facebook tribute pages dedicated to the memory of two children who had died in tragic circumstances. Hampson had already been convicted of a similar offence three years earlier (*Hampson's case*, 2011).

Under First Amendment protections, even internet communications disclosing personal information about other citizens that might alarm or intimidate them or 'expose them to unwanted attention from others' is protected in the United States. The US Supreme Court hate speech judgments have found that all but communications integral to criminal conduct–fighting words, threats and solicitations–have free expression protection in America. The Court held in *The Slants case* (2017) that the US Trademarks office could not ban the registration of the name of a rock band 'The Slants'–which might seem racist and offensive to Asian Americans–because of the right to free expression under the First Amendment.

DISCRIMINATION, RACE HATE AND VILIFICATION IN AUSTRALIA

Normally, the straight reportage of racial and ethnic issues will not land a journalist or blogger in legal difficulties; however, a range of ethical dilemmas arise. Laws throughout Australian jurisdictions now specifically address discrimination at its extremities–the domain of actual vilification of people because of their racial, ethnic or religious group and the incitement to racial hatred or violence against such individuals.

The relevant Commonwealth legislation is the *Racial Discrimination Act 1975* which, in Part II, has broad prohibitions on racial discrimination in most walks of life. Of most interest to the media is Section 18C, which states in part:

> *18C (1) It is unlawful for a person to do an act, otherwise than in private, if:*
> *(a) the act is reasonably likely, in all the circumstances, to offend, insult, humiliate or intimidate another person or a group of people; and*
> *(b) the act is done because of the race, colour or national or ethnic origin of the other person or of some or all of the people in the group.*

Section 18D offers exemptions to the operation of 18C:

> *Section 18C does not render unlawful anything said or done reasonably and in good faith:*
> *(a) in the performance, exhibition or distribution of an artistic work; or*
> *(b) in the course of any statement, publication, discussion or debate made or held for any genuine academic, artistic or scientific purpose or any other genuine purpose in the public interest; or*
> *(c) in making or publishing:*
> *(i) a fair and accurate report of any event or matter of public interest; or*
> *(ii) a fair comment on any event or matter of public interest if the comment is an expression of a genuine belief held by the person making the comment.*

It was the requirement that a report be fair and accurate to earn the exemption that proved to be the main stumbling block to *Herald Sun* columnist Andrew Bolt, who famously lost an 18C case in 2011 (see Key Case 10.1). The political nature of that loss prompted several proposals to reform Section 18C, including the failed attempt in the Senate to replace the words 'insult', 'offend' and 'humiliate' with the term 'harass' in 2017 (McGhee, 2017). A similar political climate surrounded the *QUT Students' case* (2016 and 2017), which was decided in favour of the defendants (see Key Case 10.2). In the *Commonwealth Games Trade Mark case* (2017), a Gold Coast cultural heritage body opposed the registration of a trade mark to use the word 'Borobi' (meaning 'koala' in the Yugambeh language) as the koala mascot for the 2018 Commonwealth Games. One of its legal arguments was that the registration should be refused because it breached section 18C of the *Racial Discrimination Act 1975*. However, it failed to persuade the court the use of the trade mark would be likely to 'offend, insult, humiliate or intimidate another person or a group of people' (at para. 53) and that, regardless of this, the Gold Coast Commonwealth Games Corporation would qualify for the exemption under section 18D because it had acted 'reasonably and in good faith' (para. 54).

There is some debate over whether section 18C applies to Muslim people, given the ethnic and national diversity of that religion. This is because the section requires that the offensive behaviour targets 'race, colour or national or ethnic origin', but it has been held to apply to discriminatory publications about Jewish people as a race (*Holocaust cases*, 2002–09). However, alternative avenues are sometimes available for pursuing incidents of hate speech. For example, a local government councillor was reprimanded for misconduct by a judge of the Victorian Civil and Administrative Tribunal in 2017 for a tweet she posted in the midst of a debate over the building of a mosque in Bendigo. In response to a tweet from a citizen praising the idea of a mosque in the city, she posted an image of child victims of genital mutilation and suggested this would happen in Bendigo. The Tribunal upheld a Councillor Conduct Panel decision that the post constituted misconduct under the Councillor Code of Conduct (*Mosque Tweets case*, 2017).

Section 46P of the *Human Rights and Equal Opportunity Commission Act 1986* allows people to make complaints to the Human Rights and Equal Opportunity Commission (HREOC) about offensive behaviour based on racial hatred. However, while such behaviour may be an 'unlawful act', it is not necessarily a criminal offence under the legislation. Criminal charges for the most extreme forms of discrimination–urging violence against someone on the basis of their membership of a group 'distinguished by race, religion, nationality, national or ethnic origin or political opinion'–are available under the reformed 'sedition' laws of the *Criminal Code Act 1995* at section 80.2B: 'Urging violence against members of groups', with a penalty of up to five or seven years in jail.

The state and territory laws deal with the area in different ways and with varying levels of intensity, with Western Australia focusing on the publication of material intended to incite racial hatred or to harass people of a racial group. The NSW and ACT laws prohibit any public act (not just publication) inciting hatred or even severe ridicule of an individual or a group because of race. The media are protected to some extent by a provision allowing the publication of a fair report of acts of racial vilification.

Professional communicators should look to the particular legislation in their state or territory to check its breadth of operation and application to the media. The relevant Acts are as follows:

- Commonwealth: *Racial Discrimination Act 1975* and *Criminal Code Act 1995*
- Australian Capital Territory: *Discrimination Act 1991*
- New South Wales: *Anti-Discrimination Act 1977*
- Northern Territory: *Anti-Discrimination Act 1992*
- Queensland: *Anti-Discrimination Act 1991*
- South Australia: *Equal Opportunity Act 1984* and *Racial Vilification Act 1996*
- Tasmania: *Anti-Discrimination Act 1998*
- Victoria: *Equal Opportunity Act 1995* and *Racial and Religious Tolerance Act 2001*
- Western Australia: *Equal Opportunity Act 1984* and Criminal Code 1913, Chapter XI.

The laws of all jurisdictions allow for free and open coverage of the immigration and race debate. Defences of public interest, fair comment and privilege vary across jurisdictions, but usually apply in a similar way to the defamation defences. Potential difficulties arise for media outlets when reporting the views—or hosting the comments—of extremists calling for some action to be taken against a particular section of society. Letters editors, hosts of debates between ethnic groups, the editors of political and ethnic newspapers, moderators of internet forums and producers of ethnic or political programs need to obtain legal advice on how these laws relate to their particular jurisdictions so they can strike a suitable balance between free speech and sensibility.

Examples of racial vilification and racial hatred cases include the following.

ALAN JONES CASE 1 (2000)

Sydney talkback radio host Alan Jones went to air in 1995 with this rant on a discrimination case that had been decided in favour of a Dubbo woman who had been refused a rental property by an agent on the grounds of her race:

> *Now I think that's a joke. And I'll tell you why I think it is. If I owned the property on the real estate agent's list, the only property for letting and a bloke walked through the door I don't care what colour he is, looking like a skunk and smelling like a skunk, with a sardine can on one foot and sandshoe on the other and a half drunk bottle of beer under the arm, and he wanted to rent the final property available and it was mine, I'd expect the agent to say no without giving reasons. What discrimination would the agent be guilty of then?'*

He later returned to the topic with similar descriptions, and opened the lines for listeners to express their views.

The Western Aboriginal Legal Service Ltd complained to the Anti-Discrimination Board on behalf of Aboriginal people and, after five years of procedural delays and Equal Opportunity Tribunal hearings, the case came before the NSW Administrative Decisions Tribunal's Equal

Opportunities Division. The case centred on the wording of the racial vilification provisions of the NSW *Anti-Discrimination Act 1977*, mainly sections 20B, defining 'a public act' as any form of communication, and 20C, declaring racial vilification unlawful. The tribunal found that listeners would have associated the Aboriginality of the woman with Jones' derogatory remarks; that Jones and 2UE had committed a public act (the broadcast) inciting the ordinary, reasonable listener to feel serious contempt for or severe ridicule for Aboriginal people in New South Wales on the ground of their race; that despite the public interest in the issue of bad tenants, Jones had failed to establish he had acted in good faith or reasonably by linking the tenant's Aboriginality with her tenancy qualities; and that the concept of 'incitement' did not require any intent on the part of Jones—simply that the broadcast was capable of conveying to the ordinary, reasonable listener that they were being incited to hold the requisite degree of ill-feeling on the ground of race. The tribunal ordered Jones to apologise, both on air and in a letter to the complainant.

KAZAK'S CASES (2000/02)

The Australian Financial Review was found to have contravened the racial vilification provisions of the NSW *Anti-Discrimination Act 1977* by saying 'the Palestinians cannot be trusted in the peace process' and 'the Palestinians remain vicious thugs'. A public-interest defence was not available because the publication was not reasonable or published in good faith, despite an APC adjudication on the same article (Adjudication no. 1016), which found the article 'was certainly vituperative but it was published as a clearly marked opinion piece'. The decision was set aside on appeal (*Kazak's case*, 2002) on the basis that the ordinary reasonable reader would see the article as an attack on Palestinian political leadership, not on race, and that a public interest defence would apply regardless.

THE HOLOCAUST CASE (2002/03)

Founder and director of the Adelaide Institute, Dr Frederick Toben, had already been jailed in Germany in 1999 for publishing Holocaust denial material on the internet. In this Australian case, he was jailed again for contempt of court for refusing to remove similar material in defiance of a court order to do so. Toben published material on the institute's website casting doubt that the Holocaust–the murder of hundreds of thousands of Jewish people in gas chambers during World War II–actually happened, and claiming some Jewish people had exaggerated facts about it for financial gain. The president of the Executive Council of Australian Jewry, Jeremy Jones, won a finding in the Human Rights and Equal Opportunity Commission that the publication breached the *Racial Discrimination Act 1975*. He applied to the Federal Court, asking that the commission's determination be enforced. Toben was subsequently found guilty of contempt and sentenced to three months' imprisonment (see Adcock, 2009).

ALAN JONES CASE 2 (2009–13)

Opinionated Sydney talkback radio host Alan Jones devoted segments on his breakfast program on 2GB in 2005 about Lebanese males and their Muslim religion. The comments were made following a Channel Nine television current affairs show about the insulting conduct of young Lebanese men towards police at The Rocks in inner Sydney. The Administrative Decisions Tribunal found that the comments incited serious contempt of Lebanese males, including Lebanese Muslims, in breach of the NSW *Anti-Discrimination Act 1977*. It took seven years and four court cases before Jones eventually read a negotiated apology on air. He and the broadcaster also had to pay the complainant, Keysar Trad, damages of $10,000 and his court costs of more than $180,000.

ISLAM CASE (2017)

On 30 November 2015, an article under the headline 'ISLAM MUST CHANGE' appeared in the print edition of the *Herald Sun* newspaper. The article reported the comments and views of a number of federal Coalition members of parliament on the topic of the link between Islamic teaching and terrorism. Mr Aladdin Sisalem filed a complaint with the Victorian Civil and Administrative Tribunal (VCAT) alleging that publication of the article by HWT was a breach of section 8 of the *Racial and Religious Tolerance Act 2001* because the article incited, or was likely to incite, hatred against the followers of the religion of Islam. The Victoria Civil and Administrative Tribunal ruled against the complaint, on the basis that the Act does not prohibit a person from saying things about the religious beliefs of persons which are offensive to those persons, or even prohibit a person from saying things about the religious beliefs of one group of persons that would cause another group of persons to despise those beliefs. The Supreme Court of Victoria refused leave to appeal that decision.

WALL'S CASE (2018)

A woman of Māori descent complained that two cartoons published by Fairfax in the *Marlborough Express* and Christchurch newspaper *The Press* breached section 61 of the New Zealand *Human Rights Act 1993*. The cartoons were objectively insulting in that they depicted Māori and Pasifika people as negligent parents preoccupied with alcohol, cigarettes and gambling at the expense of their children's welfare. The New Zealand High Court held that the legislature's legitimate interest in enhancement of racial harmony by the suppression of so-called 'hate speech' had not specifically identified exposure to 'hatred' as the benchmark of illegality. The publications, although offensive, were not likely to excite hostility or contempt at the level of abhorrence, delegitimisation and rejection that could be considered to realistically threaten racial disharmony in New Zealand.

These cases demonstrate that professional communicators should be very careful when playing the race card in their reporting or commentary. The racial vilification and racial discrimination laws do not tolerate the linkage of race with derogatory comments about an individual unless there is some overriding public interest (e.g. where the person has made this an issue themselves), or where it is protected by the fair report or qualified privilege defences similar to those outlined for defamation in Chapter 8.

Discrimination can also centre on an individual or group's sexual orientation, with homosexual activist Garry Burns leading the charge in New South Wales with scores of anti-vilification actions spanning two decades. In 2004 and again in 2007, Burns took action in New South Wales under the anti-vilification provisions of the *Anti-Discrimination Act 1977* (NSW). In the first case (*Gay case*, 2004), involving a broadcast on radio 2UE Sydney, the complaint was sustained. Steve Price's references to 'grubby activities' and 'poofs' verged 'on the contemptuous', while John Laws' references to the homosexual partners as 'a couple of old poofs' and 'a couple of young poofs' were found capable of inciting severe ridicule among ordinary reasonable listeners. The overall effect of the conduct gave 'licence to listeners to engage in ridicule without regard to limits or boundaries, and was capable of inciting ridicule certainly to a severe degree'. In ruling that the conduct was not reasonable, the tribunal noted that both Price and Laws were experienced broadcasters who were broadcasting under the 'Commercial Radio Codes of Practice and Guidelines', which contained similar anti-vilification provisions to the *Anti-Discrimination Act 1977* (NSW). A second complaint in 2007 over remarks by Laws in 2004, which included calling the host of *Queer Eye for the Straight Guy*, a 'pompous little pansy', a 'pillow-biting pompous little prig' and a 'precious little pansy', were held to have vilified homosexuals, but to have done so within the good faith and public-interest exception in section 49ZT(2) of the NSW *Anti-Discrimination Act 1977* (*Laws case*, 2007). It has to be said that the second Laws decision is somewhat difficult to reconcile with the earlier case. By 2018, Burns had lodged an estimated 74 complaints of homosexual vilification against the owner of a website and YouTube account, John Sunol (*YouTube Gay case*, 2018, para. 5). In a five-minute video attack, Sunol called Burns a 'child molesting faggot' and made the further statement that 'homosexuals are child molesting faggots'. The Civil and Administrative Tribunal found the first statement constituted homosexual vilification, but the second statement did not, because it was not likely on the balance of probabilities to incite hatred or serious contempt for homosexuals as a group (para. 60).

INDUSTRY REGULATION OF DISCRIMINATION AND HATE SPEECH

The various professional and industry codes of practice also direct journalists and professional bloggers to avoid discriminatory and hateful communications. The MEAA Journalist Code of Ethics (see Appendix 1) makes its stance on prejudicial reportage and commentary very clear at Item 2:

> *2. Do not place unnecessary emphasis on personal characteristics, including race, ethnicity, nationality, gender, age, sexual orientation, family relationships, religious belief, or physical or intellectual disability.*

The enforcement of this self-regulatory regime is, however, problematic, and complaints about discriminatory or prejudicial material produced by journalists are more likely to be directed to the relevant industry regulator—the Australian Press Council (<www.presscouncil.org.au>) for print and online news entities, or the various broadcast industry bodies, which police their own codes of practice under the ultimate purview of the Australian Communications and Media Authority (ACMA) at <www.acma.gov.au>.

At a self-regulatory level, the APC (2001) has made a special effort to educate newspaper and online journalists and journalism students on the avoidance of discrimination and gratuitous emphasis on racial and other factors in reportage. It removed an anti-discrimination provision from its overarching Statement of Principles in a 2014 revision, but has issued special 'Advisory Guidelines' to its members on related issues including the reporting of asylum seekers, people with an intellectual disability, Nazi concentration camps, religious terms in headlines and the reporting of race. (They can be viewed at <www.presscouncil.org.au/advisory-guidelines>.)

ACMA is responsible for the regulation of the broadcast media. Under the *Broadcasting Services Act 1992*, the various broadcasting industry sectors set their own programming guidelines in the form of codes of practice. This system is explained on ACMA's website, <www.acma.gov.au>. It has registered codes of practice for all broadcasting sectors other than the ABC and SBS, which have their own codes notified to ACMA. Most of the industry codes have special requirements of news and current affairs programs, which in turn address race and ethnicity issues. Rather than explore each of the broadcasting codes, which journalists and students can do themselves by accessing the ACMA website, we focus here on the Commercial Television Code of Practice and its relevant provisions.

As ACMA explains on its website, the most recent Commercial Television Industry Code of Practice came into effect in 2015 (Free TV Australia, 2015). The code covers the matters prescribed in section 123 of the *Broadcasting Services Act 1992*, and other matters relating to program content that are of concern to the community. Section 123(3)(e) specifically states that the following is to be taken into account when such codes of practice are developed:

> *the portrayal in programs of matter that is likely to incite or perpetuate hatred against, or vilifies, any person or group on the basis of ethnicity, nationality, race, gender, sexual preference, age, religion or physical or mental disability.*

ACMA has certain requirements for the handling of complaints about such matters, with mediation between the broadcaster and the complainant being the first mechanism, working through to a determination of the matter by ACMA's own investigators. ACMA also has a range of penalties available to it under the Act, with the ultimate being the suspension of a broadcaster's licence, through to substantial fines, imposition of conditions on the licensee, down to recommendations such as the counselling and training of staff.

Similar regulations apply to radio news and current affairs. A complaint arose when the broadcaster Alan Jones yet again fuelled the fire of racial and ethnic tension in December 2005, when angry mobs in southern Sydney staged a protest then set upon youths of Middle Eastern appearance in an episode that became known as the 'Cronulla riots'. The role of the media in the lead-up to the riots, particularly that of Jones, was questioned by the ABC's *Media Watch* program (2006). In the week before the Cronulla riots, Jones described two people who were accused of assaulting some lifeguards as 'Middle Eastern grubs' and two days later continued with:

> *My suggestion is to invite one of the biker gangs to be present in numbers at Cronulla railway station when these Lebanese thugs arrive. It would be worth the price of admission to watch these cowards scurry back onto the train for the return trip to their lairs . . . Australians old and new shouldn't have to put up with this scum.*

On ensuing days, Jones agreed with listeners who called for violent retribution against youths of Lebanese origin. On 10 April 2007, ACMA formally found that Jones' comments had breached 2GB's radio licence and the Commercial Radio Codes of Practice (2004) on three separate occasions, as 'likely to incite, encourage or present for its own sake violence and brutality,' prohibited under clause 1.3 (a) of the radio code, and material 'likely to incite or perpetuate hatred against or vilify' those of Lebanese and Middle Eastern background on the basis of their 'ethnicity' prohibited under clause 1.3 (e) (now 1.1 (e)) (ACMA, 2007).

KEY CASE 10.1: *THE BOLT CASE*

Eatock v Bolt [2011] FCA 1103 (28 September 2011)
Eatock v Bolt (No. 2) [2011] FCA 1180 (19 October 2011)

FACTS

In April 2009, Melbourne's *Herald Sun* newspaper published an article by conservative columnist Andrew Bolt titled 'It's so hip to be black', and also posted it to its website with the heading 'White is the new black'. Four months later, Bolt wrote another column in the newspaper and website titled 'White fellas in the black'. The articles suggested fair-skinned Aboriginal people were not genuinely Aboriginal, but predominantly European in racial origin, yet pretended to be Aboriginal so they could access benefits and career or political advancement available to Aboriginal people. The civil action was brought by activist Pat Eatock, who was mentioned in the article along with seventeen others.

LAW

Federal Court Justice Mordecai Bromberg rejected Bolt's argument that part of the *Racial Discrimination Act* was restricted to racist behaviour based upon racial hatred. Instead, Justice Bromberg held that the articles contravened section 18C of the Act and were unlawful in that they were 'reasonably likely to offend, insult, humiliate or intimidate some Aboriginal persons of mixed descent who have a fairer, rather than darker, skin and who by a combination of descent, self-identification and communal recognition are and are recognised as Aboriginal persons'. This was because they conveyed imputations that:

(i) there are fair-skinned people in Australia with essentially European ancestry but with some Aboriginal descent, of which the individuals identified in the articles are examples, who are not genuinely Aboriginal persons but who, motivated by career opportunities available to Aboriginal people or by political activism, have chosen to falsely identify as Aboriginal; and
(ii) fair skin colour indicates a person who is not sufficiently Aboriginal to be genuinely identifying as an Aboriginal person.

Under the terms of the Act, a reason the articles were published was because 'of the race, ethnic origin or colour of those Aboriginal persons described'.

Bolt and his newspaper publisher disputed that the articles conveyed those imputations, denied they would cause offence, and claimed race, colour and ethnic origin were not motivating factors in their writing and publishing of the articles. Bolt failed in his defence that the articles were published 'reasonably and in good faith' under section 18D of the *Racial Discrimination Act 1975* (Cth):

(i) in the making or publishing of a fair comment on any event or matter of public interest; or
(ii) in the course of any statement, publication or discussion, made or held for a genuine purpose in the public interest.

Bolt failed in that defence because the articles contained 'errors of fact, distortions of the truth and inflammatory and provocative language'. Justice Bromberg ruled that beyond the 'hurt and insult', the articles were 'reasonably likely to have an intimidatory effect on some fair-skinned Aboriginal people, particularly young Aboriginal persons or others with vulnerability in relation to their identity'. The articles would embolden those with racially prejudiced views. He said he had weighed the 'silencing consequences upon freedom of expression' his ruling might have, and said:

> *At the core of multiculturalism is the idea that people may identify with and express their racial or ethnic heritage free from pressure not to do so. People should be free to fully identify with their race without fear of public disdain or loss of esteem for so identifying. Disparagement directed at the legitimacy of the racial identification of a group of people is likely to be destructive of racial tolerance, just as disparagement directed at the real or imagined practices or traits of those people is also destructive of racial tolerance.*

The judge issued a declaration of the contravention and ordered a prohibition on the articles being republished (except on their website for archival purposes) and the *Herald Sun* was ordered to publish a corrective notice next to Bolt's column, both in print and online.

LESSONS FOR PROFESSIONAL COMMUNICATORS

Justice Bromberg was at pains to stress that his ruling was more about the manner in which Bolt had presented his view rather than the nature of the view itself. It was not unlawful for writers to deal with racial identification, and 'even challenge the genuineness of the identification of a group of people'. The main lesson is to tread carefully when doing so, and to ensure your opinions are well founded upon provable facts and that such commentary is fairly presented.

By the time you read this, the legislation might have been changed. Various attempts have been made in recent years to reform racial discrimination laws, particularly sections 18B–E of the *Racial Discrimination Act* (see McGhee, 2017). It would be wise to check the current status of any reforms.

KEY CASE 10.2: *THE QUT STUDENTS' CASE*

Prior v Wood [2017] FCA 193
Prior v Queensland University of Technology & Ors [2016] FCCA 2853

FACTS

Three male students were approached by administration officer Cynthia Prior in the Oodgeroo Unit at Queensland University of Technology and asked whether they were Indigenous, and then asked to leave, with her purportedly stating: 'Ah . . . this is the Oodgeroo Unit, it's an Indigenous space for indigenous students at QUT. There are other computer labs in the university you can use. There are computers in P block or the library that you can access' (2016, para. 1). One student found a computer elsewhere and posted to a Facebook page titled 'QUT Stalker Space': 'Just got kicked out of the unsigned Indigenous computer room. QUT stopping segregation with segregation . . .?' There were other posts in reply, including:

> *I wonder where the white supremacist computer lab is.*
>
> *. . . it's white supremacist, get it right. We don't like to be affiliated with those hill-billies.*
>
> *[Name] today's your lucky day, join the white supremacist group and we'll take care of your every need!*

Ms Prior also alleged that one of respondents also posted the comment 'ITT n*****s' [an offensive racist term] to the page, but that student denied he had posted that comment and claimed someone else had posted it under his name.

LAW

Ms Prior launched action in the Federal Circuit Court against QUT and the students (including some others) seeking an apology and $250,000 damages claiming that the messages were offensive and thus breached section 18C(1) of the *Racial Discrimination Act 1975* (Cth).

Judge Michael Jarrett ruled that it was not reasonably likely that a hypothetical person in the position of Ms Prior—or a hypothetical member of the groups identified by Ms Prior who is a 'reasonable and ordinary member of either of the groups'—would feel offended, insulted, humiliated or intimidated by the comments posted by the two students who had admitted authorship (para. 49). Those two students persuaded the court that Ms Prior had no reasonable prospects of successfully prosecuting her claim because:

> *a* *the Facebook posts were not reasonably likely, in all the circumstances, to offend, insult, humiliate or intimidate another person or a group of people;*
>
> *b* *they did not make their Facebook posts because of Ms Prior's race, colour or national or ethnic origin or that of some or all of the people in the groups she identified; and*
>
> *c* *the effect of the students' conduct was not such as to engage in s 18C(1)(a) because the effect of their acts could not be seen as sufficiently profound or serious (paras 58 and 71).*

The appeal judge held that, for some of the comments, no reasonably intelligent person would have understood them 'as other than humour or irony' (2017, para. 144).

With regard to the student who allegedly posted 'ITT n*****s', both the trial judge and the appeal court held there was no evidence tendered that he was responsible for the contents of the document with his name on it, and he had denied authorship.

The court dismissed the proceedings without a full trial, holding that Ms Prior did not enjoy reasonable prospects of successfully prosecuting her case.

LESSONS FOR PROFESSIONAL COMMUNICATORS

Several important considerations emerged from this case, including:

- Both the trial judge and the appeal court judge offered a useful summary of the racial discrimination legislation and case law, which is of value to professional communicators and students.
- The courts will tolerate a certain level of humour or irony in commentary on matters of race if a hypothetical reasonable person would consider it as such.
- Clear evidence of the authorship of social media posts is needed to persuade a court that the alleged author has a case to answer.
  A postscript to this case was that a federal politician had to pay defamation damages to the student who had been alleged to have posted the 'ITT n*****s' remark because she stated on the ABC's *Q&A*

program that he was the author of the comment, despite the court having found no evidence to support that allegation (Koziol, 2016).

- The whole issue of racially discriminatory speech—and particularly the wording of the *Racial Discrimination Act*—is highly politicised. This case attracted substantial media attention and further calls for reforms of the 18C and 18D provisions.

TIPS FOR MINDFUL PRACTICE

- If you are working in the national security reporting or blogging space, you need to weigh up your ethical commitments to sources against your duty to society to protect people from terrorist attacks. Even if you do enter into confidential arrangements, the powers of surveillance, search and seizure make your communication records very easy for the authorities to monitor and seize.
- There are so many laws giving police and security agencies special powers when dealing with the media that you are strongly advised to take legal advice, as you risk heavy fines, jail terms and potential danger to your sources.
- Despite the racial vilification and discrimination legislation, the media are allowed substantial leeway in reporting the comments of others. You should draw the line at comments that are clearly aimed at creating a disturbance or inciting others to violence or hatred, or that would be reasonably likely to offend, insult, humiliate or intimidate another person or a group of people on the basis of their race, skin colour, nationality or ethnicity. The best guideline is to mention race, religion or sexual preference only if it is an actual issue in the story, as advised by the MEAA Journalist Code of Ethics, Clause 2.
- The lesson of this chapter is that you should pause and consider before you post or publish. Mindful consideration of the impact of your words upon others is the key to good journalism, blogging and professional communication on the sensitive topics of race, religion, gender, sexual orientation and a host of other points of difference between human beings.

IN A NUTSHELL

- Social and political developments over the past half-century have exposed Australian professional communicators to two expanded restrictions upon their work: national security laws and vilification laws.
- Media restrictions in the name of national security were in existence long before September 2001: sedition and treason laws date back to feudal times.
- More than 70 new anti-terror laws were passed by the Australian parliament between 2001 and 2018.
- Several cases since 2005 have highlighted the difficulties for journalists trying to report upon counter-terrorism operations and cases, particularly to do with the confidentiality of their sources being compromised and the difficulty of reporting hearings and trials because of the number of suppression orders issued.
- Each media regulatory body has codes or principles that journalists and media organisations are expected to follow, and each has a set of complaint procedures available to it.
- Laws in all jurisdictions specifically address discrimination at its extremities—the domain of actual vilification of a person because of their racial, ethnic or religious group and the incitement to racial hatred or violence against such individuals.
- The public interest exemptions to the legislation detailed under section 18D of the *Racial Discrimination Act 1975* (Cth) will normally protect journalists and bloggers going about their normal business of fair and accurate reportage and commentary.

DISCUSSION QUESTIONS

10.1 Australian media organisations have complained about the limitations anti-terrorism laws place on free expression. Is this a price worth paying in the post-9/11 era of global insecurity? How might those same laws affect bloggers and social media users? Discuss.

10.2 Do a search of anti-terrorism/national security stories over the past few months. Explain how media coverage might have been restricted because of anti-terrorism laws.

10.3 Use the <www.austlii.edu.au> database to do an advanced search for a case using the words 'terrorism', 'media' and 'suppression'. Write a case summary in the same format as the 'Jihad Jack' and Bolt cases are presented in this chapter.

10.4 Go to the ACMA website, <www.acma.gov.au>, and find some recent investigations and findings on vilification breaches. What has been the result of the complaint and decision?

10.5 Debate the topic: 'The Bolt case shows the laws of racial vilification go too far. The media should be free to air all views in society—even those that are racist.'

10.6 Find a recent example of hate speech that has resulted in legal action. Compare and contrast it with one of the cases in this chapter.

REFERENCES

Abrams, J. 2011, 'Patriot Act extension signed by Obama', *Huffington Post Politics Online*, 27 May, <www.huffingtonpost.com/2011/05/27/patriot-act-extension-signed-obama-autopen_n_867851.html>.

Adcock, B. 2009, 'Toben jailed in Germany over Holocaust website', *ABC Radio National 'PM'*, 11 November, <www.abc.net.au/pm/stories/565901.htm>.

Australian Associated Press (AAP) 2010, 'Haneef awarded $1m, India reports say', *The Australian*, 22 December, <www.theaustralian.com.au/news/nation/haneef-awarded-1m-india-reports-say/story-e6frg6nf-1225974873281>.

Australian Communications and Media Authority (ACMA) 2007, *Breakfast with Alan Jones Broadcast by 2GB on 5, 6, 7, 8 and 9 December 2005*, Investigation Report No. 1485, ACMA, Sydney.

Australian Law Reform Commission (ALRC) 2006, *Review of Sedition Laws: Discussion Paper*, Commonwealth Government, Canberra, <www.austlii.edu.au/au/other/alrc/publications/dp/71>.

Australian Press Council (APC) 2001, 'General Press Release no. 248: Reporting of "race"', *Reporting Guidelines*, <www.presscouncil.org.au/pcsite/activities/guides/gpr248.html>.

Bowcott, D. 2012, 'Twitter joke trial: Paul Chambers wins High Court appeal against conviction', *The Guardian Online*, 27 July, <www.theguardian.com/law/2012/jul/27/twitter-joke-trial-high-court>.

Clarke, M.J. 2008, *Report of the Inquiry into the Case of Dr Mohamed Haneef, Vol. 1*, Commonwealth of Australia, Canberra.

Ewart, J., Pearson, M. and Lessing, J. 2013, 'Anti-terror laws and the news media in Australia since 2001: How free expression and national security compete in a liberal democracy', *Journal of Media Law*, 5(1): 104–32, <www.ingentaconnect.com/content/hart/jml/2013/00000005/00000001/art00007>.

Four Corners 2006, 'The convert', reporter Sally Neighbour, ABC TV, 27 February, <www.abc.net.au/4corners/content/2006/s1579056.htm>.

Free TV Australia 2015, *Commercial Television Industry Code of Practice*, <www.freetv.com.au/media/Code_of_Practice/Free_TV_Commercial_Television_Industry_Code_of_Practice_2015.pdf>.

Google 2018, *Transparency Report: Requests for User Information* [Downloadable zip file], <https://storage.googleapis.com/transparencyreport/google-user-data-requests.zip>.

Hocking, J. 2004, *Terror Laws: ASIO, Counter-Terrorism and the Threat to Democracy*, UNSW Press, Sydney.

Kissane, K. 2008, 'Tip-off led to intense 16-month investigation', *The Age*, 17 September, <www.theage.com.au/national/tipoff-led-to-intense-16month-investigation-20080916-4hxp.html?page=-1>.

Kontominas, B. 2009, 'Journalists guilty of photographing army base', *Sydney Morning Herald*, 25 September, <www.smh.com.au/national/journalists-guilty-of-photographing-army-base-20090925-g5rv.html>.

Koziol, M. 2016, 'Labor frontbencher Terri Butler settles defamation suit with student over "racist smear"', *Sydney Morning Herald*, 16 December, <www.smh.com.au/politics/federal/labor-frontbencher-terri-butler-settles-defamation-suit-with-student-over-racist-smear-20161216-gtchae.html>.

Law Report 2008, 'Police raids on journalists', ABC, 30 September, <www.abc.net.au/rn/lawreport/stories/2008/2376926.htm>.

McGarrity, N. 2011, 'Fourth estate or government lapdog? The role of the Australian media in the counter-terrorism context', *Continuum*, 25(2), 273.

McGhee, A. 2017, '18C: Proposed changes to *Racial Discrimination Act* defeated in Senate', *ABC News*, 31 March, <www.abc.net.au/news/2017-03-30/18c-racial-discrimination-act-changes-defeated-in-senate/8402792>.

McNamara, L. 2009, 'Counter-terrorism laws: How they affect media freedom and news reporting', *Westminster Papers in Communication and Culture*, 6(1), 27.

Media, Entertainment and Arts Alliance (MEAA) 2005, *Turning Up the Heat: The Decline of Press Freedom in Australia 2001–2005. The Inaugural Media, Entertainment and Arts Alliance Report into the State of Press Freedom in Australia from September 11, 2001–2005*, MEAA, Sydney, <www.alliance.org.au/resources/press_freedom_reports>.

— 2006, *The Media Muzzled: Australia's 2006 Press Freedom Report. The Media, Entertainment and Arts Alliance 2006 Report into the State of Press Freedom in Australia*, MEAA, Sydney, <www.alliance.org.au/resources/press_freedom_reports>.

— 2007, *Official Spin: Censorship and Control of the Australian Press 2007. The Media, Entertainment and Arts Alliance 2007 Report into the State of Press Freedom in Australia*, MEAA, Sydney, <www.alliance.org.au/resources/press_freedom_reports>.

— 2008, *Breaking the Shackles: The Continuing Fight Against Censorship and Spin. The Media, Entertainment and Arts Alliance 2008 Report into the State of Press Freedom in Australia*, MEAA, Sydney, <www.alliance.org.au/resources/press_freedom_reports>.

— 2009, *Secrecy and Red Tape: The State of Press Freedom in Australia 2009*, MEAA, Sydney, <www.alliance.org.au/resources/press_freedom_reports>.

— 2012, *Kicking at the Cornerstone of Democracy: The State of Press Freedom in Australia*, MEAA, Sydney, <www.walkleys.com/files/media/PF2012_2.pdf>.

— 2013, *Power, Protection and Principles: The State of Press Freedom in Australia*, MEAA, Sydney, <http://pressfreedom.org.au>.

— 2017, *The Chilling Effect: MEAA's Press Freedom Report 2017*, MEAA, Sydney, <www.meaa.org/mediaroom/the-chilling-effect-meaas-press-freedom-report-2017>.

Media Watch 2006, 'Jones and Cronulla', ABC TV, 20 February, <www.abc.net.au/mediawatch/transcripts/s1574690.htm>.

Office of the High Commissioner for Human Rights (OHCHR) 1976, *International Covenant on Civil and Political Rights*, <www.ohchr.org/en/professionalinterest/pages/ccpr.aspx>.

Pacific Media Watch (PMW) 2018, *Sedition Search*, Pacific Media Centre, Auckland, <www.pmc.aut.ac.nz/search/node/sedition>.

Porter, C. 2018, 'Amendments to Espionage and Foreign Interference Bill', media release by the Attorney-General for Australia, 6 March, <www.attorneygeneral.gov.au/Media/Pages/Amendments-to-Espionage-and-Foreign-Interference-Bill.aspx>.

Pullan, R. 1994, *Guilty Secrets: Free Speech and Defamation in Australia*, Pascal Press, Sydney.

Renwick, J. 2017, *Independent National Security Legislation Monitor Annual Report 2016–2017*, Australian Government, Canberra, <www.inslm.gov.au/reviews-reports/annual-reports/independent-national-security-legislation-monitor-annual-report-2017>.

Rose, F. 2006, 'Why I published those cartoons', *Washington Post*, 19 February, <www.washingtonpost.com/wp-dyn/content/article/2006/02/17/AR2006021702499.html>.

Royes, L. 2017, 'AFP officer accessed journalist's call records in metadata breach', *ABC News Online*, <www.abc.net.au/news/2017-04-28/afp-officer-accessed-journalists-call-records-in-metadata-breach/8480804>.

Simons, M. 2011a, 'The Oz editor bargained over lives in AFP raid', *Crikey*, 2 November, <www.crikey.com.au/2011/11/02/artz-affidavit-the-oz-editor-bargained-over-lives-in-afp-raid>.

— 2011b, 'Simons: To tweet or not to tweet from court', *Crikey*, 4 November, <www.crikey.com.au/2011/11/04/simons-to-tweet-or-not-to-tweet-from-court>.

Tobias, M. 2018, 'Understanding Poland's "Holocaust law"', *Politifact*, 9 March, <www.politifact.com/truth-o-meter/article/2018/mar/09/understanding-polish-holocaust-law>.

United Nations 2011, *Universal Declaration of Human Rights*, <http://un.org/en/documents/udhr>.

CASES CITED

Alan Jones case 1: Western Aboriginal Legal Service Ltd v Jones and Radio 2UE Sydney Pty Ltd [2000] NSWADT 102 (31 July 2000), <www.austlii.edu.au/au/cases/nsw/NSWADT/2000/102.html>.

Alan Jones case 2: Trad v Jones & Anor (No. 3) [2009] NSWADT 318 (21 December 2009), <www.austlii.edu.au/cgi-bin/viewdoc/au/cases/nsw/NSWADT/2009/318.html>; *Trad v Jones (No. 4)* [2012] NSWADT 265 (12 December 2012), <www.austlii.edu.au/cgi-bin/sinodisp/au/cases/nsw/NSWADT/2012/265.html>; *Trad v Jones (No. 5)* [2013] NSWADT 127 (5 June 2013), <www.austlii.edu.au/cgi-bin/sinodisp/au/cases/nsw/NSWADT/2013/127.html>.

Artz's case: Director of Public Prosecutions v Artz [2013] VCC 56, <www.countycourt.vic.gov.au/files/DPP%20v%20Artz%20%5B2013%5D%20VCC%2056.pdf>.

Baladjam's case: see Operation Pendennis cases

Benbrika's case: see Operation Pendennis cases

Bolt case: Eatock v Bolt [2011] FCA 1103, <www.judgments.fedcourt.gov.au/judgments/Judgments/fca/single/2011/2011fca1103>; *Eatock v Bolt* (No 2) [2011] FCA1180 <www.austlii.edu.au/cgi-bin/viewdoc/au/cases/cth/FCA/2011/1180.html>.

Commonwealth Games Trade Mark case: Jabree Ltd v Gold Coast Commonwealth Games Corporation [2017] ATMO 156 (14 December 2017), <www.austlii.edu.au/cgi-bin/viewdoc/au/cases/cth/ATMO/2017/156.html>.

Gay case: Burns v Radio 2UE Sydney [2004] NSWADT 267, <www.austlii.edu.au/cgi-bin/sinodisp/au/cases/nsw/NSWADT/2004/267.html>.

Hampson's case: R v Hampson (2011) QCA 132 (21 June 2011).

Haneef case: Haneef v Minister for Immigration and Citizenship [2007] FCA 1273, <www.austlii.edu.au/au/cases/cth/FCA/2007/1273.html>; *Minister for Immigration & Citizenship v Haneef* [2007] FCAFC 203, <www.austlii.edu.au/au/cases/cth/FCAFC/2007/203.html>.

Holocaust cases: Jones v Toben [2002] FCA 1150, <www.austlii.edu.au/au/cases/cth/federal_ct/2002/1150.html>; *Toben v Jones* [2003] FCAFC 137 (27 June 2003), <www.austlii.edu.au/cgi-bin/sinodisp/au/cases/cth/FCAFC/2003/137.html>; *Toben v Jones* [2009] FCAFC 104 (13 August 2009), <www.austlii.edu.au/cgi-bin/sinodisp/au/cases/cth/FCAFC/2009/104.html>.

Holsworthy Barracks cases: R v Fattal & Ors [2011] VSC 681 (16 December 2011), <www.austlii.edu.au/cgi-bin/sinodisp/au/cases/vic/VSC/2011/681.html>; *Fattal & Ors v The Queen* [2013] VSCA 276 (2 October 2013), <www.austlii.edu.au/cgi-bin/sinodisp/au/cases/vic/VSCA/2013/276.html>.

Islam case: Sisalem v The Herald & Weekly Times Pty Ltd [2017] VSC 254 (18 May 2017), <www.austlii.edu.au/cgi-bin/viewdoc/au/cases/vic/VSC/2017/254.html>.

'Jihad' Jack cases: R v Thomas (No. 3) [2006] VSCA 300 (20 December 2006), <www.austlii.edu.au/cgi-bin/sinodisp/au/cases/vic/VSCA/2006/300.html>; *Thomas v Mowbray* [2007] HCA (2 August 2007), <www.austlii.edu.au/au/cases/cth/HCA/2007/33.html>; *R v Thomas (No. 4)* [2008] VSCA 107 (16 June 2008), <www.austlii.edu.au/cgi-bin/sinodisp/au/cases/vic/VSCA/2008/107.html>; *R v Thomas* [2008] VSC 620 (29 October 2008), <www.austlii.edu.au/cgi-bin/sinodisp/au/cases/vic/VSC/2008/620.html>.

Kazak's cases: Kazak v John Fairfax Publications Ltd [2000] NSWADT 77, <www.austlii.edu.au/au/cases/nsw/NSWADT/2000/77.html>; *John Fairfax Publications Pty Ltd v Kazak (EOD)* [2002] NSWADTAP 35 (25 October 2002), <www.austlii.edu.au/cgi-bin/sinodisp/au/cases/nsw/NSWADTAP/2002/35.html>.

Laws case: Administrative Decisions Tribunal Equal Opportunity Division (No. 2) [2007] NSWADT 47.

Mosque Tweets case: Chapman v Greater Bendigo CC (Review and Regulation) [2017] VCAT 417 (23 March 2017), <www.austlii.edu.au/cgi-bin/viewdoc/au/cases/vic/VCAT/2017/417.html>.

Operation Pendennis cases: R v Benbrika & Ors (Ruling No. 33) [2008] VSC 487 (15 September 2008), <www.austlii.edu.au/cgi-bin/sinodisp/au/cases/vic/VSC/2008/487.html> (*Benbrika's case*); *Regina (Cth) v Baladjam & Ors* [2008] NSWSC 714, <www.austlii.edu.au/cgi-bin/sinodisp/au/cases/nsw/NSWSC/2008/714.html> (Baladjam's case).

QUT Students' case: Prior v Wood [2017] FCA 193, <www.austlii.edu.au/cgi-bin/viewdoc/au/cases/cth/FCA/2017/193.html>; *Prior v Queensland University of Technology & Ors* [2016] FCCA 2853, <www.austlii.edu.au/cgi-bin/viewdoc/au/cases/cth/FCCA/2016/2853.html>.

Slants case: Matal v Tam 137 S. Ct 1744 (2017), <www.supremecourt.gov/opinions/16pdf/15-1293_1o13.pdf>.

Wall's case: Wall v Fairfax New Zealand Limited [2018] NZHC 104 (12 February 2018), <www.austlii.edu.au/cgi-bin/viewdoc/nz/cases/NZHC/2018/104.html>.

YouTube Gay case: Burns v Sunol [2018] NSWCATAD 10 (10 January 2018), <www.austlii.edu.au/cgi-bin/viewdoc/au/cases/nsw/NSWCATAD/2018/10.html>.

PART 5

KEY ISSUES FOR THE DIGITAL ERA

CHAPTER 11

Intellectual property: Protecting your work and using the work of others

KEY CONCEPTS

Intellectual property (IP)
Legally protected creations of the mind, including literary and artistic works, music, inventions, designs, symbols, names and images.

Copyright
Legal protection of the form of expression of a work such as an article or an image.

Trade mark
A sign used to distinguish goods or services dealt with or provided in the course of trade by a person from goods or services of the same kind provided by others.

Fair dealing and fair use
Exceptions and defences to copyright infringement (the former narrower and the latter broader) available to those using a copyright work in a fair and attributed way.

We live in an age of 'cut and paste', where boundaries between 'borrowing' and 'stealing' are blurred. Increasingly in developed nations, less wealth stems from the labour of blistered hands than from the creativity and originality of the mind. Works of literature, drama, music, art, multimedia and software have spawned major industries. Their commercial and legal value has appreciated radically. Over the past decade, it has become incredibly easy to incorporate someone else's work—an extract of text, a photograph or a sound grab—into our own. At the same time, new multimedia and multi-platform roles expose professional communicators to a new level of legal complexity.

This chapter begins by looking briefly at some ethical objections to plagiarism before moving on to the main areas of intellectual property (IP) law of concern to journalists. We take a short tour of trade marks, patents, the action of 'passing off' and a related action under section 18 of the Australian Consumer Law (ACL) before considering in more detail the law of copyright.

As a professional communicator—whether a journalist, public relations consultant, blogger or citizen journalist—you can find yourself on either side of the intellectual property fence. If you place a high value on the merit of your words or images, you are probably not impressed when you discover someone else has cut and pasted them and pretended they are their own creations. On the other hand, you will often want to draw upon someone else's work and might even want to reproduce it in full. In a legal sense, sometimes you might be a plaintiff wanting to stake your own claim to intellectual property rights, while on other occasions you might be a defendant needing to justify your use of someone else's material.

INTERNATIONAL CONTEXT AND BACKGROUND

Professional communicators deal with sound, text and images—all of them subject to various forms of IP protection. Other types of intellectual property you might encounter include performances and broadcasts, inventions and discoveries, industrial designs, trade marks and commercial names—all listed in the Convention Establishing the World Intellectual Property Organization (WIPO) in 1967 (WIPO,

1979a). Put simply, IP comprises 'creations of the mind': inventions, literary and artistic works, and symbols, names, images and designs used in commerce, which have found actual material expression. Intellectual property laws are meant to protect our exclusive right to exploit the array of creative outputs we might produce as human beings.

Intellectual property is a strange legal beast. It has a strong international foundation in treaties and conventions, with some common elements that apply no matter where you are based or where your material is read. Most of the world's nations are members of the Geneva-based WIPO and are signatories to the major treaties. International cooperation on IP laws dates back to the creation of the first international conventions covering industrial property in Paris in 1883, and literary and artistic works in Berne in 1886.

But elements of the law and its level of enforcement vary markedly between nations. IP can be one of the most complex areas of law, with specialists earning their living from advising clients on the intricacies of IP in particular jurisdictions, particularly as new technologies spawn an array of new creations and the internet highlights technical differences that result in bewildering new interpretations from the courts. It all means that you really do need to seek expert legal advice if you are considering pushing the boundaries of IP law in your writing or if you have already been threatened with legal action. You can find information about the IP laws of various countries by browsing the *Directory of Intellectual Property Offices* (WIPO, 2011). The US Copyright Office, for example, has a useful introduction to that area of IP law and details US requirements at <www.copyright.gov>.

As a professional communicator, the IP area you have likely heard about is copyright, which covers creative works like writing, music and images, and in many countries also includes works of technology like computer programs and databases. As a creator, you are granted rights over your outputs, as embodied in their form of expression—although if you are producing them as an employee, these might belong to your employer.

The starting point for understanding copyright is that it does not protect an *idea* alone. (You need to look to industrial property laws for protection of inventions or ideas via patent law.) Copyright will only protect the *form of expression* used to convey your idea. So you might tweet about a brilliant concept you have for a new television drama series and then feel betrayed when someone beats you to the network to pitch that same proposal. The courts will just say 'bad luck' unless you can show that your rival has copied a substantial part of your original treatment. The lesson here is that you shouldn't use blogs or social media to float ideas you want to protect.

The WIPO (2016) booklet *Understanding Copyright and Related Rights* is an excellent entry-point for learning about the basic copyright principles applying globally. It explains that 'copyright' translates into 'author's rights' in many other languages because it is the creator of the work—the 'author' of written works—who holds the right to reproduce their outputs. The word 'copyright' in English refers to that act itself—the 'right' to 'copy' something you have created. As the holder of that right, you have the legal power to license others to do so as well. An excellent international example of the principle that copyright rests with the creator of a work was the *Monkey case* (2018). In 2011, an Indonesian monkey named Naruto—a crested black macaque—took a 'selfie' with camera equipment set up by wildlife photographer David Slater. Monkey see, monkey do. Slater complained to Wikimedia Commons after the images were posted there, but they refused his demand that he take them down, arguing he did not hold copyright in the images because he did not actually take them—the monkey did (Wikimedia Foundation, 2014). The basic principle stood: copyright rests with the human creator of a work (*Monkey case*, 2018). However, the monkey did not get to claim damages for the photographer's use of the work. The US Ninth Circuit Court of Appeals denied an application by an animal rights group to have the monkey's copyright in the images formally acknowledged, stating that animals did not have standing. The photographer and the monkey (represented by animal rights group PETA) negotiated a settlement (Toliver, 2017).

Most countries confer upon you a right to the exclusive use of your literary or artistic work the instant you create it—without the need for any kind of registration of the work as your own. You can use it in any way you like—as long as you do not break other laws in the process—and also have the exclusive right to authorise others to use it and to charge them for that use. You can prohibit or authorise the reproduction of your work in a range of formats, the distribution of copies of your work, its public performance, its broadcast or communication to the public in other ways, its translation into another language or its adaptation from one format to another.

First up, let's dispel a myth. A work does *not* have to display the copyright symbol '©' to be protected by copyright. Of course, it doesn't hurt to include it alongside your name and the year of creation, because there are still a few countries that are not signatories to the Berne Convention (WIPO, 1886, 1979b), which did away with the need to display it. Inserting '©' at least signals your claim of authorship to anyone who might think that because you posted material on the internet or in social media you are giving up your rights to its use. But a word of caution here: the terms and conditions of various social media sites—Facebook being one example—typically provide (depending on your privacy settings) that you give a royalty-free, worldwide licence to use any IP content that you post. That means, for example, that the default position is that Facebook can license any of your copyright material to others—including for money—which then goes to Facebook, and not to you.

An important difference between countries' copyright laws is duration. Under international conventions, your communication outputs will remain in copyright until at least 50 years after your death, although that is exactly half a century more than should worry you. But some countries—including the United States and Australia, as well as all nations in the European Union—have extended this term to 70 years after the death of the creator. Of course, this rule is more relevant if you want to reproduce the work of a famous writer, artist or musician in your own blog. You will need to check whether enough time has passed since the author has died for the work to have entered the public domain or whether the creator has voluntarily waived their rights by assigning a general licence to a copyright-free organisation.

The not-for-profit Creative Commons is a good example. Founded in 2001, it promotes the 'creative re-use of intellectual and artistic works', whether owned or in the public domain. It offers free copyright licences enabling creators to grant a voluntary 'some rights reserved' approach as an alternative to the traditional 'all rights reserved' default system of copyright law. Its public domain tools allow works that are free of known copyright to be easily searched online and provides a mechanism for rights holders to dedicate their works to the public domain. Wikimedia Commons is similar.

Some countries, such as the United States, offer you several advantages if you have paid to register your copyright work with a federal government agency. For example, you can't file suit for infringement of your copyright in the United States unless you have paid the registration fee.

The law in most places allows for certain situations where you can copy parts of other creators' material without their authorisation/permission but with appropriate attribution. WIPO gives three key examples of such 'free use', which cover the purposes of many bloggers:

- quoting from a protected work, provided that the source of the quotation and the name of the author are mentioned, and that the extent of the quotation is compatible with fair practice
- use of works by way of illustration for teaching purposes
- use of works for the purpose of news reporting.

Some countries extend this to 'fair use' or 'fair dealing' exceptions. Of course, the courts and legislators in different countries vary in the way they interpret your 'fair' practice in borrowing such material, especially in relation to the proportion of the material you are copying, and its significance in the context of the work as a whole. They also take into account how you have used the material, your purpose in doing so, the type of work you are copying, whether you are doing it for commercial gain and the impact of your use upon the future commercial worth of the material. Fair dealing exceptions can apply to reporting of news and current affairs, criticism and review, parody and satire, and education—depending on the jurisdiction and its laws.

There are differences between 'fair use' (broader and more flexible) and 'fair dealing' (narrower and specified). The Australian Law Reform Commission (ALRC, 2014) weighed the pros and cons of the two types of exceptions and recommended a change that built the 'fair use' exception into Australian law, but this had not yet been actioned at the time this edition went to press. There was strong lobbying by publishers' and creators' representatives against any such change.

We return to the particularities of Australian copyright law later in the chapter.

ETHICAL AND SELF-REGULATORY CONSIDERATIONS

Intellectual property rights present a moral issue. Can we borrow someone else's creative work without owing a moral debt–at the very least, crediting them? Australian copyright law includes moral rights, which we detail later in this chapter, in acknowledgement of the fundamental moral questions surrounding the theft or misuse of someone else's creative work.

Most professional communicators now have a tertiary education, and universities are vigilant about plagiarism. Under their academic integrity policies, they hand out penalties ranging from failing an assignment to expulsion. Yet, even in the academic environment, plagiarism is sometimes hard to pin down. When we move to the professional ethical level, item 10 of the MEAA Journalist Code of Ethics (see Appendix 1) states simply, 'Do not plagiarise'. In discussing the code, the MEAA's Ethics Review Committee (1996) explained the risk of plagiarism occurring in a journalist's work:

> *Plagiarism offends the values of honesty, fairness, independence and respect for the rights of others. It can occur in many ways, including (but not limited to): when secondary sources are relied on too heavily; when material from wire services is fused with the work of staff reporters; because of the ease with which words can be 'cut' and 'pasted' by computer; and when the words of a public relations copywriter are reproduced from a press release verbatim without attribution to the source.*

As we observed above, the moral dimension of intellectual property rights is embodied in the *Copyright Act*: 'moral rights' are legally enforceable rights—for example, the right of attribution, recently discussed briefly in the *Corby case* (2013).

More worrying for most journalists and professional bloggers might be the prospect of being 'outed' as a plagiarist. Just how deeply affronted journalists feel by such an accusation was illustrated when *60 Minutes* reporter Richard Carleton (now deceased) sued the ABC's *Media Watch* for saying that he and his team had plagiarised a BBC documentary (see *Carleton's case*, 2002, profiled in Chapter 8). Justice Higgins described the allegation of plagiarism as being 'regarded by journalists and, indeed, many others as an accusation of disgraceful and reprehensible conduct' (at para. 105). While he found the allegations against Carleton and *60 Minutes* untrue, he decided that *Media Watch* had established a defence of fair comment.

Why is it, then, that some reporters and columnists seem ready to steal the words of others? Why do editors and news directors turn a blind eye? Why do those same people take umbrage at others lifting their work?

Journalists often have a fairly 'loose' attribution style, sometimes resorting to expressions as vague as 'sources said' or 'media outlets reported'. Some fall back on 'everybody else steals *our* copy', excusing their plagiarising today of *The New York Times* or Wikipedia because yesterday the local radio station had 'ripped and read' the story they had written. Yet it is a huge leap from poor attribution to no attribution at all—parading the intellectual property of others as your own work.

INTELLECTUAL PROPERTY LAW

While the ethical consequences of plagiarism can be embarrassing, the legal consequences can be expensive. The *Butterworths Encyclopaedic Australian Legal Dictionary* (Butt and Nygh, 2004) defines intellectual property as:

> *A group of legislative and common law rights affording protection to creative and intellectual effort and includes laws on copyright,*

> *design, patent, circuit layouts, plant varieties, confidential information, trade mark and business reputation (passing off and trade practices).*

Professional writers and editors will be concerned mostly with the law of copyright, which forms the bulk of discussion in this section, but it is worthwhile looking briefly at some aspects of the laws of trade marks, 'passing off' and consumer law.

TRADE MARKS

A trade mark, according to section 17 of the *Trade Marks Act 1995* (Cth) is:

> *a sign used, or intended to be used, to distinguish goods or services dealt with or provided in the course of trade by a person from goods or services so dealt with or provided by any other person.*

Corporations are very protective of their trade marks. The masthead of a newspaper or the various permutations of a media organisation's name might be registered as a trade mark under the *Trade Marks Act*. News Corporation has had the trade mark 'Newspoll' registered since 1984 to protect a subsidiary business of that name, which conducts and reports public opinion polls. In our globalised commercial world, the wrongful use of a company's name is of special concern to multinational corporations. Many company names have become so commonly used that they have morphed in the language to mean the generic type of product or process rather than the specific brand. The US *Columbia Journalism Review* sometimes runs ads from major companies and the International Trademark Association (INTA) to warn against the misuse of brand names. Examples—which often have an air of practical unreality about them—are complaints about the word 'Velcro' being used instead of 'separable fasteners', 'Ray-Ban' in place of 'sunglasses' and 'iTunes' instead of 'audio data computer software'. In the end, it is really quite simple: if you want to err on the safe side, select your words carefully and only use a brand name if you have done your research and are referring to that specific brand intentionally.

If not, it is usually better look to a more descriptive expression for that class of product, service or phenomenon. This might also avoid other legal actions that could result from your disparagement of a particular brand or process (by the misuse of the trademarked name) when you really intended to target the broader class of product or service.

If you do receive a threatening letter, however, it is important to take a deep breath and recall that trade mark registration does not confer copyright protection. Use in editorial copy of a word that has trade mark registration does not amount to trade mark infringement, nor does it breach anyone's copyright. Even if copyright were to exist in a single word, its use in Australia in an editorial context would almost inevitably be protected under the 'fair dealing' exceptions in the *Copyright Act*, with which we deal below.

The cases in which use of a trademarked expression can amount to infringement will not typically involve professional communicators, as opposed to business competitors. In the *Malishus case* (2018), a person registered a trade mark in Australia. Two other Australian residents then incorporated a company in New Zealand using a name that was identical to a word ('Malishus') included in the trade mark, and registered it in New Zealand, the United States of America and the United Kingdom. The question for the Australian courts became whether the (mere) *uploading* of the claimed infringing trade mark (the word 'Malishus') on Facebook arguably constituted a use of the trade mark, directed to Australia, and for that reason was capable of infringing the trade mark previously registered in Australia. The Federal Court held that uploading the word 'Malishus' on social media was directed to jurisdictions that *included* Australia, and for that reason it was capable of constituting a use of the word 'Malishus' as a trade mark in Australia, where that word already had trade mark protection. The *Malishus* decision is interesting, insofar as it focuses on *uploading* with an *intent* to target Australian audiences as the test, in contrast to the law as we saw it apply in the case of defamation, in which it is the fact and location of proven *downloading* that is relevant, and where *intent* as to the place of publication plays no part in establishing the action. (Although it may be relevant, if downloading in Australia is actually proven, to the question of malice and aggravated damages.) The lesson here is that, at least where paid branded content ('advertorial') is involved, it would be wise to tread carefully.

'PASSING OFF' AND CONSUMER LAW

Two other important avenues for protection of intellectual property may be available to those who feel their work has been unfairly exploited: the action for 'passing off' and protection under section 18 of the Australian Consumer Law set out in Schedule 2 of the *Competition and Consumer Act 2010* and its state equivalents, known as trade practices and/or fair-trading legislation.

In common law countries such as Australia and the United Kingdom, there is an action called 'passing off', which can be launched against you if you have used someone's name or likeness to imply that they have entered into some commercial arrangement to endorse your product or service in some way. In its basic form, it offers simple protection to businesses against those who pretend to have some connection with them or endorsement from them. It has been extended in the creative arts to protect newspaper columnists from deceptive parodies of their work being published under their names in competing publications and also to protect the 'pen-names' of authors being used by their former employers after they have moved on to another title.

The ingredients of passing off were stated in the *Cricketer case* (1974, at 478):

> *First, that the plaintiff has a business; secondly, that it has a reputation in a name or use of a name in the sense that the particular name is distinctive of the plaintiff; and thirdly, that there is a real probability that the plaintiff's clients or prospective clients will be deceived by believing that the defendant's goods are the plaintiff's, causing him damage.*

The action can cover the claim of a false connection, as with a celebrity endorsement (Van Caenegem, 2001: 226), and can protect goodwill and reputation (Walker, 2000: 945). The action was used in Australia to protect the pen-name 'Pierpont' in the *Penname case* (1977), after the business journalist who used that *nom de plume*—Trevor Sykes—moved from *The Australian Financial Review* to *The Bulletin* magazine. His column continued for another 40 years, first at *The Bulletin* and then back at *The Australian Financial Review*.

Many parts of the world put limitations on how you can use the name and image of another—particularly if you are making a profit from it. These are often called 'personality rights'. In European and other civil law jurisdictions, there are tough limits on how you can use the likenesses of others—all bundled up in the laws of privacy. You can't just cut and paste someone's photo from the internet and use it in your blog—especially if it appears to be endorsing your enterprise in some way. The United States offers a property right known as the 'right to publicity', and several states have passed laws to extend its basic common law protections. It gives people the right to protect their name, image and other identifying features against commercial exploitation by others. However, like so many areas of US law, it is limited by the free speech protections given by the First Amendment, so it usually only encompasses blatant cases of exploitation that lack a free expression rationale.

Section 18 of the Australian Consumer Law (and its state equivalents) prohibits conduct, in trade or commerce, that is 'misleading or deceptive or is likely to mislead or deceive'. Journalists are most likely to encounter it in the domain of misleading advertising or advertorials—and it also applies to social media communications. Actions for misleading and deceptive conduct and passing off can also arise in the field of public relations. In the *Essential Media case* (2002), examined in Chapter 13, Essential Media Communications won an injunction restraining another public relations firm from using the acronym 'EMC2' in connection with its business.

Professional communicators who work in PR or advertising, or who use their journalistic talents as researchers or script consultants on docudramas or 'faction' (*Constable Wendy case*, 2010), also need to be aware that while 'character rights' do not exist in Australia, to prevent anyone profiting by the publicity attracted by the mere use of or reference to an established fictional character, passing off principles can extend to such use. In the *Crocodile Dundee case*, an advertisement for Grosby shoes which partially re-created the knife scene from *Crocodile Dundee*, using an actor dressed in a costume similar to the one Paul Hogan wore in the 1986 film, was held to have amounted to passing off, on the basis that viewers would have inferred a connection with or approval from Hogan, which did not exist.

While Australian IP laws do not protect character rights, they do protect rights in formats–an area of particular concern to media professionals working in 'reality' shows on TV, or creating their own online 'shows'. In the *MKR case* (2015), Channel Seven broadcast a reality television cooking program called *My Kitchen Rules (MKR)* over six consecutive seasons, and announced that it would introduce another reality television cooking program into its broadcast schedule, to be called *Restaurant Revolution*, which had a format different from *MKR*. Meanwhile, Nine began broadcasting a reality television cooking program called *The Hotplate*. Seven alleged that by producing and broadcasting episodes of *The Hotplate*, Nine was infringing Seven's copyright in *MKR*. The court held that the formats of *MKR* and *The Hotplate* were very similar, and was also satisfied that Seven had an arguable case that this close similarity was (at least to some extent) the result of copying. Nine said that the *MKR* format was largely unoriginal, and that *MKR* was a 'successful but nonetheless unimaginative collection of unoriginal ideas and situations found in earlier reality television programs'. Looking at the balance, the court refused to grant an injunction to Seven preventing Nine continuing to broadcast the program. The lesson here, of particular importance for media professionals working in the broadcast or online spaces, is that the format within which material is presented can itself be protected by intellectual property law.

FOCUS CASE 11.1: *CLARK'S CASE*

Clark v Associated Newspapers Ltd [1998] EWHC Patents 345 (21 January 1998)

FACTS

Alan Clark was a politician and author of diaries that ventured into very revealing aspects of his private life and fantasies. He wrote a regular column for London's *News of the World*. A rival newspaper, the *Evening Standard*, attempted to parody Clark's column by running a mug shot of the politician with the logo 'Alan Clark's Secret Election Diary' (and later 'Alan Clark's Secret Political Diary'). The standfirst (lead-in) to the column always attributed the material to the journalist Peter Bradshaw 'imagining' what such a diary might contain.

LAW

Clark sought an injunction to stop the newspaper parading the column as his own and an award of damages, on two grounds:

- the law of passing off
- a section of the *Copyright Designs and Patents Act 1988* (UK) that conferred a right not to have a work falsely attributed to him as author (moral rights).

In finding for Clark, Justice Lightman ruled that while the newspaper had the right to parody the work of the plaintiff, it had to package or present it in such a way that it did not deceive readers into thinking the articles were in fact written by him: 'A parody which occasions only a momentary and inconsequential deception is both successful and permissible; but a parody which occasions an enduring deception is neither' (at para. 19).

LESSONS FOR PROFESSIONAL COMMUNICATORS

This is an instructive case for journalists: many an editor has been tempted to satirise an author's work by presenting material as though they had written it. It requires finesse, because making the imitation too realistic can run foul of both the law of passing off and the moral rights of authors, which were introduced to Australia in December 2000. Under section 195AC of the *Copyright Act 1968*, authors now have the right not to have authorship falsely attributed, just as Clark had in the United Kingdom.

When considered alongside *Hanson's case* in Queensland in 1998 (see Chapter 8), in which an injunction was upheld stopping the playing of a satirical recording of a politician's voice, the *Copyright Act* protections have stood as a warning to journalists to take care with satire and parody; more recently, changes to the *Copyright Act* to introduce a new 'fair dealing' exception for parody and satire have gone some way towards redressing the balance, as we learn below in the *Pokémon case* (2017), although we will have to wait to see the full impact of the amendments (s 41) in case law.

THE LAW OF COPYRIGHT

Australian copyright law is embodied in the *Copyright Act 1968* (Cth). It is less fragmented than the law of defamation—which has both statutory and common law elements—or freedom of information—which has different legislative instruments in each state and territory. We will examine important sections of the Act that affect you as a professional communicator, study the wording of the legislation, consider some important court cases that cast light on the topic and weigh up the implications for you in your reporting.

Of the twelve Parts to the *Copyright Act*, four are of most significance to journalists and other professional communicators. These are:

- Part III—dealing with copyright in original literary, dramatic, musical and artistic works
- Part IV—dealing with copyright in subject matter other than works, such as broadcasts
- Part V—outlining the remedies and offences applying, and
- Part IX—stating the enforceable moral rights of authors.

Various other provisions are also relevant, and will be mentioned where appropriate.

COPYRIGHT IN ORIGINAL LITERARY, DRAMATIC, MUSICAL AND ARTISTIC WORKS

Even though some news stories are far from 'literary', print and online journalists' work fits within this category. In section 31, the *Copyright Act* defines copyright as the exclusive right to reproduce literary, dramatic, musical and artistic works as well as compilations such as films, sound recordings, published editions and broadcasts. Because 'literary work' includes compilations, a newspaper or magazine falls under this category, as does a script for radio or television. Copyright in a broadcast rests with the creator of the program as a whole.

In the case of literary works, section 31(1)(a) defines copyright as the exclusive right:

- to reproduce the work in a material form;
- to publish the work;
- to perform the work in public;
- to communicate the work to the public;
- to make an adaptation of the work.

The central concept is that copyright does not protect an idea. It protects the material expression of an idea–for example, in words. An idea itself cannot be protected by copyright law, only the work to which it has given rise. It follows that there is nothing in copyright law to prevent professional communicators from gleaning ideas or information from other sources when creating their own work. But when such 'gleaning' becomes copying another person's work–in part or in whole–the law of copyright comes into play. In other words, copyright operates to protect the 'work' of its creator, not the ideas or facts on which that work is based. It protects the form of expression of the idea rather than the idea itself.

Under Australian law, copyright protection is automatic from the instant a work is created. All that is required under section 32 is that the work be published first in Australia or that the creator of the work is 'an Australian citizen, an Australian protected person or a person resident in Australia' and that the work is 'original'–that is, the result of the author's own efforts and skill. The work is then protected in most countries under a series of international treaties.

Under section 33(2), copyright in a literary work continues until the expiration of 70 years after the author dies. Subject to some exceptions, copyright in photographs lasts for 70 years after the photographer's death. Once copyright has expired, the work is in the 'public domain', meaning that permission is no longer required to use it.

Despite the use in the legislation of terms like 'original', 'artistic' and 'literary', copyright law does not operate merely to protect works of great creativity or imagination. Originality means only that the work must result from its creator's own efforts and must not have been copied from another source.

COPYRIGHT IN JOURNALISTS' WORK

If you are a blogger or journalist working for a media corporation or selling your work on a freelance basis, you might not qualify for copyright payments. This is because some countries—including Australia—have passed laws to assign the employer automatic copyright in work done in the scope of your employment.

In Australia, the basic rule of copyright under section 35 is that ownership is held by the creator from the time the work is created (ACC, 2014a: 2). However, where print media employees (including journalists, photographers or artists) produce the work as part of their work contracts for inclusion in a newspaper, magazine or periodical, the employee owns the right to reproduce the work for inclusion in a book and to reproduce the work for photocopying purposes, and the media employer retains all other rights, such as the right to reproduce the work in electronic databases or on the internet (ACC, 2014a: 2–3). Freelance reporters and photographers hold copyright for all uses unless their contracts state otherwise. Contracts with major news organisations almost invariably confer those rights on the publisher, so it pays to check before signing.

Like other property, copyright can be transferred to others. Importantly, however, section 196(3) of the Act provides that an assignment of copyright (whether total or partial) does not have effect unless it is in writing signed by or on behalf of the assignor.

This final aspect is particularly important for journalists and photographers, because they often make or receive requests to use copyright material. A newspaper journalist or photographer may get a call from a colleague asking for permission to use a photograph. Unless they are working for the same umbrella organisation, permission has to be given in writing by a representative authorised to assign copyright on behalf of the company. The issue of assignment of copyright arose in the *Kokoda Trail case* (2005), in which Channel Seven won an injunction to stop Channel Nine screening footage of a Kokoda Trail walk by a group of disadvantaged boys. Channel Seven had funded a freelance camera crew to accompany the youths, and had paid for some of the equipment. Later, the group's organiser authorised a production company to make a television documentary, to be screened on Nine. The Full Court upheld Seven's appeal on the grounds that Seven had not assigned its share of the joint copyright to the organisation's leader, Mr Brett Murray, and had not granted Mr Murray a licence to authorise Nine's broadcast of the film.

REPRODUCING THE WORK OF OTHERS: KEY CONSIDERATIONS

Professional communicators often need to draw on the work of others when reporting, commenting on or creating publications, broadcasts or material for websites. There is even more pressure to do so now that sites like Buzzfeed.com have built their business model around the curation of online material and its repackaging into their own lists and collections of images and footage; there are also online mastheads that profit from doing little more than repackage unattributed content, including both text and images, from other print and online publications.

The following basic questions offer an introductory guide:

- Has the copyright period expired? (Has the creator been dead for more than 70 years?)

- Has the copyright holder 'assigned' copyright to you? (This is a full transfer of ownership of the material and proof of assignment.)
- Has the copyright holder 'licensed' you to use the material? (This might be a restricted permission to use the material, such as for a certain time or for a particular purpose.)
- If none of the above, do you plan to use a 'substantial' or significant or important portion of the work?
- If so, does one of the 'fair dealing' exceptions apply, such as the exception for the purpose of criticism or review, reporting news, or 'parody or satire'?

If the work has not been made available through either assignment or licence, and if you plan to use a substantial part of the work, you have to be willing to pay for the use, or be able to work within one of the fair dealing exceptions.

One difficulty is that, when the legislation uses the expression 'substantial part', it does not define what is meant by that term. As we will see, the courts have interpreted it to mean any significant or important part of the work, no matter how large or small a portion it might represent. This was an important aspect of the *Panel case* (2005—see Key Case 11.1). The courts are concerned more with the inherent 'quality' of the portion used rather than the amount of it that is used (Ross, 2002).

This remains a vexed area, in particular regarding coverage of public spectacles such as sporting events. In the *Sky Television case* (2007), the New Zealand High Court refused to grant an interim injunction stopping Sky's broadcast of the Rugby World Cup using TV3 footage, even though the court held that the extent of the use might well have exceeded fair dealing. The court suggested that it would be in the interests of the industry as a whole if an agreed convention could be developed as to what is fair dealing with material to which another media organisation holds exclusive rights, in the context of sports reporting (at para. 121). The court suggested that it was likely to continue to be one of the 'most vexed areas' in the application of fair dealing exceptions.

FAIR DEALING EXCEPTIONS

Once it is established that a 'substantial' part of the copyright work—an element of the work that goes to its heart or is significant or important to it (*Panel cases*, 2005)—has been used, professional communicators have to look for an exception or a defence if they choose to proceed without assignment or licence. The three exceptions most commonly relied on by news organisations are fair dealing for the purposes of criticism or review (s 41), fair dealing for the purpose of reporting news (s 42) and fair dealing for the purpose of parody or satire (s 41A).

The first two exceptions require that 'sufficient acknowledgement' be made. That term is defined in section 10(1) as:

> *an acknowledgement identifying the work by its title or other description and, unless the work is anonymous or pseudonymous or the author has previously agreed or directed that an acknowledgement of his or her name is not to be made, also identifying the author.*

This might present a hurdle for some media organisations, who are reluctant to acknowledge the source for commercial reasons (even when they have used a substantial portion of someone else's work) or whose house style minimises the attribution given. An acknowledgement stating 'a news site reported yesterday' would not be enough, whereas 'Bridie Jabour reported in *The Guardian Australia* yesterday' would acknowledge both the author and the outlet.

Fair dealing for criticism or review

The *Copyright Act 1968* uses a single paragraph to outline the exception. It states at section 41:

> *A fair dealing with a literary, dramatic, musical or artistic work, or with an adaptation of a literary, dramatic or musical work, does not constitute an infringement of the copyright in the work if it is for the*

> *purpose of criticism or review, whether of that work or of another work, and a sufficient acknowledgement of the work is made.*

The key criteria here are that the dealing be 'fair', that a 'sufficient acknowledgement' be made and that the use serves the purpose of criticism or review. A columnist may review a book or a film and reproduce passages or photographic stills, as long as they sufficiently indicate the source and do not use too much of the work in the review. How much is fair? The courts will determine this on a case-by-case basis, but will obviously be reluctant to allow large excerpts or whole works to be replicated to attract readers, viewers or listeners.

A landmark case was the *Clippings case* (1990), in which two newspaper journalists claimed successfully that a press clipping service had photocopied and sold their articles in breach of copyright. The clipping service, Neville Jeffress Pidler, failed to convince the court that it had copied the articles under the fair dealing provisions. The judge drew upon the *Macquarie Dictionary* definitions of 'criticism' and 'review' (paras 39–43):

> *The Macquarie definition of 'criticism' includes the following:*
>
> *'1. The act or art of analysing and judging the quality of a literary or artistic work, etc.: literary criticism. 2. The act of passing judgment as to the merits of something . . . 4. A critical comment, article or essay; a critique.'*
>
> *In my opinion, 'criticism' in the context of s 41 is used in these senses. It has been held that criticism of any kind, and not only literary criticism, is within the provision . . .*
>
> *The Macquarie definition of 'review' includes the following:*
>
> *'1. A critical article or report, as in a periodical, on some literary work, commonly some work of recent appearance; a critique . . . '*
>
> *In my opinion, 'review' is used in s 41 in this sense. It would seem that the word 'review' in the sense in which it is to be understood in s 41 is cognate with the word 'criticism'. It may be said that one is the process and the other is the result of the critical application of mental faculties.*

Under these definitions, a broad range of journalistic tasks might fall within the realm of criticism or review, including dining reviews, book reviews and letters to the editor. Most that might earn the 'honest opinion' or 'fair comment' defence in defamation would qualify, so long as the use was 'fair'. However, as the Federal Court decided in the *Panel cases* (2002), and as we will see later in relation to parody, the primary *purpose* of the use of the copyright material must indeed be the kind of use relied upon. In the *Panel cases*, the court held that the defence was lost because the material had really been used 'for its own sake, either as something worth seeing again, or for the benefit of those who had missed it when it was originally broadcast by Nine' (at para. 112)—not 'criticism or review' as claimed.

Fair dealing for the purpose of reporting news

The second exception available to journalists is fair dealing for the purpose of reporting news, set out in section 42:

> *(1) A fair dealing with a literary, dramatic, musical or artistic work, or with an adaptation of a literary, dramatic or musical work, does not constitute an infringement of the copyright in the work if:*
> *(a) it is for the purpose of, or is associated with, the reporting of news in a newspaper, magazine or similar periodical and a sufficient acknowledgement of the work is made; or*
> *(b) it is for the purpose of, or is associated with, the reporting of news by means of a communication or in a cinematograph film.*
>
> *(2) The playing of a musical work in the course of reporting news by means of a communication or in a cinematograph film is not a fair dealing with the work for the purposes of this section if the playing of the work does not form part of the news being reported.*

The key elements are again the operation of the words 'fair' and 'sufficient acknowledgement'. Section 42(2) allows for the incidental recording of music being played as part of a live news event, in a film or online, but not for the dubbing of copyright music over a news item.

Clearly, the fairness of the use and the sufficiency of any acknowledgement are going to be key issues of concern to media workers. Coverage accepted as fair dealing for the reporting of news has included the use of a 30-second extract of a broadcast of an interview with a woman pregnant with eight embryos in a news item criticising the practice of 'chequebook journalism' (*Embryo case*, 1999).

Fair dealing for the purpose of parody or satire

In the wake of the High Court's judgment in the *Panel cases* (2004—see Key Case 11.1), in 2006 the federal government enacted an additional fair dealing exception for the purpose of 'parody or satire', to redress the problems raised in that case. It said copyright would not be infringed if the use for parody or satire amounted to a special case, did not conflict with the normal exploitation of the work and did not unreasonably prejudice the legitimate interests of the owner of the work. The exception is stated simply in section 41A:

> *A fair dealing with a literary, dramatic, musical or artistic work, or with an adaptation of a literary, dramatic or musical work, does not constitute an infringement of the copyright in the work if it is for the purpose of parody or satire.*

See also the related provision, section 103AA:

> *A fair dealing with an audio-visual item does not constitute an infringement of the copyright in the item or in any work or other audio-visual item included in the item if it is for the purpose of parody or satire.*

As the Australian Copyright Council (2014b: 3) points out, drawing upon dictionary definitions, a parody may be thought to be an imitation of a work that may need to draw upon parts of the original to be effective. The concept of satire is more difficult to define:

> *The purpose of satire, on the other hand, is to draw attention to characteristics or actions—such as vice or folly—by using certain*

forms of expression—such as irony, sarcasm and ridicule. It seems that both elements are required: the object to which attention is drawn (vice or folly, etc.) and the manner in which it is done (irony, ridicule, etc.). It is not clear, for example, that a cartoon which uses irony or ridicule about characteristics or actions other than something like vice or folly would be satirical.

Ensuing cases will determine whether the use of copyright work for parodic or satirical purposes has been 'fair' under the copyright provisions or 'reasonable' under the moral rights provisions of the Act. In the *Pokémon case* (2017), the Federal Court looked at the parody defence when it was raised by a business called Redbubble, which had created an internet marketplace for 'print-on-demand' personalisation services for customers who wanted a product with an image or word that had been created by an artist or designer. Some of the designs made available by Redbubble through its 'internet market place' included designs featuring Pokémon characters. The court had to decide whether Redbubble had authorised infringement of copyright in those characters and, if so, whether it could claim that infringement was excused under the fair dealing parody exception. The court held (consistently with the approach in the *Panel cases* to criticism or review) that what must be shown is that the use made of the work was both fair and for the *purpose* of parody and satire, and not just that what was produced might in the eyes of some *be* parody or satire. The company that owned the Pokémon rights won the case, but only received nominal damages of $1.

BROADCAST JOURNALISTS, ONLINE EDITORS AND THE USE OF AUDIO-VISUAL ITEMS

Radio, television and online journalists and PR personnel creating audio-visual material need to note the provisions in Part IV of the *Copyright Act 1968* dealing with 'copyright in subject matter other than works', which covers the use of 'audio-visual' items. Section 100A defines an audio-visual item as 'a sound recording, a cinematograph film, a sound broadcast or a television broadcast'.

The wording of the fair dealing exceptions for the use of audio-visual items is similar to that examined above applying to 'works'. The Act states:

> 103A Fair dealing for purpose of criticism or review. *A fair dealing with an audio-visual item does not constitute an infringement of the copyright in the item or in any work or other audio-visual item included in the item if it is for the purpose of criticism or review, whether of the first-mentioned audio-visual item, another audio-visual item or a work, and a sufficient acknowledgement of the first-mentioned audio-visual item is made.*
>
> 103AA Fair dealing for purpose of parody or satire. *A fair dealing with an audio-visual item does not constitute an infringement of the copyright in the item or in any work or other audio-visual item included in the item if it is for the purpose of parody or satire.*
>
> 103B Fair dealing for purpose of reporting news
> *(1) A fair dealing with an audio-visual item does not constitute an infringement of the copyright in the item or in any work or other audio-visual item included in the item if:*
> *(a) it is for the purpose of, or is associated with, the reporting of news in a newspaper, magazine or similar periodical and a sufficient acknowledgement of the first-mentioned audio-visual item is made or;*
> *(b) it is for the purpose of, or is associated with, the reporting of news by means of a communication or in a cinematograph film.*

Section 87 confers on the copyright holder in a television or sound broadcast the exclusive right to copy images and sound contained in it, and to rebroadcast it or otherwise communicate it to the public. Section 91 limits copyright for television and sound broadcasts to those holding a licence under the *Broadcasting Services Act 1992* or to the ABC or SBS.

Division 4 of the Act sets out the different periods for copyright to continue in audio-visual items (reflecting changes made in 2004 as part of the Australia–United States Free Trade Agreement):

- 70 years after the calendar year in which sound recordings or films were first published (ss 93 and 94)
- 50 years after the expiration of the calendar year in which a sound or television broadcast was made (s 95).

The Free Trade Agreement also impacted upon the rights held by performers in sound recordings of live performances. Under the complex wording of sections 100AA–AH, the performers share the copyright to the audio in such broadcasts, meaning broadcast or online journalists wishing to use such material in their stories will have to deal with both the performer and the person who owns the recording medium (the master).

A new free trade agreement, the Comprehensive and Progressive Agreement for Trans-Pacific Partnership (TPP-11), was signed in Santiago, Chile, on 8 March 2018 between Australia, Brunei Darussalam, Canada, Chile, Japan, Malaysia, Mexico, Peru, New Zealand, Singapore and Vietnam. This agreement is a separate treaty that incorporates, by reference, the provisions of the Trans-Pacific Partnership (TPP) Agreement (signed but not yet in force), with the exception of a limited set of provisions.

Under TPP-11, all of the parties including Australia agree to ratify a number of intellectual property treaties, including the Berne Convention for the Protection of Literary and Artistic Works (WIPO, 1979b) and the World Intellectual Property Organization (WIPO) Copyright Treaty (1996) and Performances and Phonograms Treaty (1996).

Under the Intellectual Property Chapter of TPP-11, Australian copyright owners receive the same treatment as nationals of other TPP countries, subject to Australia retaining its existing copyright exceptions. TPP-11 protects copyright and related rights of authors, performers and producers with respect to reproduction, communication, distribution and broadcasting of their works, performances and phonograms, in general for a term of the author's life plus 70 years, but at the same time requires its signatories to achieve an appropriate balance in their copyright systems, including through limitations and exceptions, covering legitimate purposes such as criticism, comment and news reporting.

KEY CASE 11.1: *THE PANEL CASES* (2002, 2004 AND 2005)

TCN Channel Nine Pty Ltd v Network Ten Pty Ltd [2002] FCAFC 146 (22 May 2002)

Network Ten Pty Ltd v TCN Channel Nine Pty Ltd (2004) 78 ALJR 585; [2004] HCA 14 (11 March 2004)

TCN Channel Nine Pty Ltd v Network Ten Pty Ltd (No. 2) [2005] FCAFC 53 (26 May 2005)

FACTS

Network Ten featured a weekly program, *The Panel*, which involved a panel of comedians and guests commenting on recent events and people in a humorous way. It was a precursor to the successful evening format of *The Project* on the same network. The program typically contained excerpts of footage from news events and other television stations' programs, which formed the basis of critique, satire or simply conversation points. The competing network, Channel Nine, claimed Channel Ten had breached its copyright by using excerpts from several of its programs on *The Panel*.

LAW

On appeal from the trial judge, the Full Court of the Federal Court substantially agreed with Channel Nine's argument that Ten had breached its copyright, holding that:

(a) The nature of copyright in a television broadcast differs from other kinds of material such as films, in that the rebroadcasting of each component image and sound can be a breach of copyright in its own right, without having to consider the program as a whole.

(b) The defence of fair dealing for the purposes of criticism or review or for the purposes of reporting of news under sections 103A and 103B of the *Copyright Act* needs to be considered on a case-by-case basis for each segment broadcast, rather than for the program as a whole.

(c) The fair dealing defence failed for several of the items, because they were broadcast for their sheer entertainment value rather than genuinely for the reporting of news or for criticism or review.

The Full Court upheld Network Ten's fair dealing defence for nine of the twenty excerpts used in the program.

Ten won its appeal to the High Court. A majority held that copyright law should not be applied by reference to every single, separate image in a broadcast, but in terms of the overall program. The copyright was protecting the cost and skill involved in preparing and transmitting the overall program. The High Court referred back to the Federal Court the question of whether the excerpts represented 'substantial' parts of the program.

A majority of the Full Court held that Ten had used a 'substantial part' in only six of the remaining eleven broadcasts, for which the fair dealing defence had originally failed. Importantly, it found that the test of substantiality was not merely a quantitative one. It was very much a matter of quality—whether the excerpt, no matter how small—was a significant or important ingredient of the program.

LESSONS FOR PROFESSIONAL COMMUNICATORS

The question of 'substantiality' applies across media, and professional communicators can take from this case that their use of any significant portions of someone else's work can be a breach of copyright—even though the proportion taken compared to the total work might be small. After the *Panel cases*, a fair dealing defence covering parody or satire was introduced as section 103AA of the *Copyright Act.* This has yet to be fully developed in case law, but it perhaps explains why satirical teams have continued to be able to build clips from other networks into their news/comedy programs.

Broadcast journalists and online editors need to pay heed to finer aspects of the *Panel* decision on substantiality. They should look carefully at the Full Federal Court's 2002 and 2005 decisions for examples of excerpts complying with, and breaching, the requirements.

The principles from the *Panel cases* were applied in the *Thoroughvision case* (2005), in which the Federal Court refused an injunction against Sky Television to stop it using parts of broadcasts originally transmitted by Channel Seven. The judge decided there was a serious chance Sky might win the case by arguing it had not taken a 'substantial' part, or by using one of the fair dealing exceptions.

DIGITAL DIMENSIONS

Almost everything you might include in a blog or on a website is likely to be covered by copyright law—either yours or someone else's. That could include the words you compose, illustrations or cartoons you draw, photographs or moving footage you upload, plans you draft, annotated lists you compile and music you share. Most laws and treaties do not mention multimedia products, but experts agree that their unique arrangement of sound, text and images as they are presented on websites also qualifies for copyright protection as creative works.

A range of new considerations have arisen with the advent of the internet, Web 2.0 and the unique forms of communication it has facilitated on social media platforms. Professional communicators should resist the temptation to cut and paste the words, images and sounds created by others into their work, because they will most likely be infringing the rights of a copyright owner.

There is debate over this, with some claiming the posting of material to the internet gives an 'implied licence' to others to use it. On using material from the internet, the Australian Copyright Council (2015: 2–3) offers this advice:

> *You will have an 'express' permission if, for example, there is a statement on the site which states that you may do certain things (for example, download a document for personal or non-commercial uses). Some material made freely available on the internet is distributed by its creators under Creative Commons licences. There are several versions of the licences containing express permissions to use the material in certain ways, usually indicated by the Creative Commons' logo, and a link to the relevant terms or conditions . . .*
>
> *You will also have an 'express' permission if, for example, you email for permission and get a reply which expressly allows you to use the material. Your right to use the material, however, will be limited by the terms of the permission granted, and/or by any conditions which the copyright owner imposes.*
>
> *An 'implied' permission, on the other hand, is a permission which is not spelled out, but which is implied from all the circumstances. Generally, implied permissions are very limited in scope.*

The site has to imply clearly a permission (for example, it could have a button that says 'printer friendly version' or 'email to a friend'). In the case of these two examples, it is unlikely that you could imply a permission to use the material on the site for a commercial purpose: if you want to use material for a commercial purpose, look for an express permission on the site, or email the website for permission.

Moral rights amendments to the *Copyright Act 1968* were partly a response to the propensity of internet users to cut, paste and appropriate the work of others. The *Copyright Amendment (Digital Agenda) Act 2000* (Cth) introduced changes to copyright law to address those problems. A series of High Court and Federal Court copyright cases have dealt with some of the more complex intellectual property issues in the digital era. The case law in this area is developing rapidly, and there have also been legislative interventions. These developments include the following:

- *The Kazaa cases (2005, 2006).* Kazaa was a peer-to-peer file-sharing system, operated by Sharman Networks. The operators infringed copyright by authorising users to copy sound recordings. Despite warnings against copyright breaches on the website, the court held that Sharman Networks knew its users were sharing copyright files and did not take steps to prevent it. The record companies reached an out-of-court settlement in 2006 involving A$151 million and agreements to convert the operation to include filtering systems.
- *Cooper cases (2005, 2006).* Cooper operated a website that linked to infringing copies of popular sound recordings. The court found he was not liable for breaching exclusive rights to communicate material to the public (because the sound files did not download directly from his site), but was liable for authorising the infringement by allowing others to insert links on his site to infringing material. The ISP was also held liable for authorising the infringements because it received a financial benefit in the form of free advertising and because, despite being aware of the infringements, it had failed to stop the website operator. This was

an interesting finding, because amendments to the *Copyright Act* to comply with the Australia–United States Free Trade Agreement had introduced a 'safe harbour' scheme protecting ISPs from litigation through their mere hosting of an infringing service if certain conditions were satisfied. This decision appeared to mean that the ISP was not protected if it benefited from an infringement, or knew about it and did not stop it (and had the power to stop—see section 101A); however, see the *iiNet case*, below.

- *Mobile League case (2007).* Telstra failed to obtain an injunction, despite submitting that continuous on-demand content highlights from Premier Media—half-owned by News Limited, which in turn half owned the National Rugby League (NRL), which Telstra had paid for the rights—were unfair.
- *Twin of Brothers case (2009).* The principles in the *Cooper* case were followed in 2009: TVBO had copyright in 42 episodes of *Twin of Brothers*, about two men who are the most wanted people in the martial arts world. Sky Net infringed copyright by transmitting a pirated version, which had been obtained via interception in Taiwan, to pay television subscribers in Australia.
- *iiNet case (2012).* Users of iiNet (an ISP) infringed copyright in films by making them available using the BitTorrent peer-to-peer system. Thirty-four Australian and US companies claimed iiNet infringed copyright in thousands of commercially released films and television programs by authorising its users' infringing acts. Although iiNet had purportedly taken no action in response to notices alleging copyright infringement, the High Court held that it did not authorise the infringements. It did not have any direct power to prevent the infringements from occurring, and to say it did would place obligations on ISPs that the *Copyright Act* does not impose.
- *BitTorrent case (2014).* The owner of copyright in the film *Dallas Buyers Club*, which won a Golden Globe award, sued 31 BitTorrent users, identified by their IP addresses, for breach of copyright in

the US District Court. This is just one of many what have become known as 'copyright troll' cases in the United States.

- *ISP cases (2016)*. Proceedings were brought by Village Roadshow and other copyright owners against a large number of Australian ISPs, on the basis that they should be ordered to take reasonable steps to disable access to various online locations, including The Pirate Bay, TorrentHound and isoHunt, which infringed or facilitated the infringement of copyright. In granting injunctions and making those orders, the Federal Court held that it was satisfied that if the ISP provided access to an online location outside Australia, whose primary purpose was to facilitate the infringement of copyright, it was not necessary for the applicant to establish knowledge or intention on the part of the ISP itself.

In 2013, the ALRC recommended the repeal of the existing fair dealing provisions and the introduction of a more flexible fair use exception as a defence to copyright infringement, extending to a new fair use exception for 'quotation'. In February 2014, it delivered its final report in its copyright inquiry (ALRC, 2014), confirming that recommendation. It stated (at paras 6.18–6.19):

> *This Report recommends the introduction of a fair use exception, which has a number of advantages over a confined fair dealing exception. Despite the many benefits common to both fair use and fair dealing, a confined fair dealing exception will be less flexible and less suited to the digital age than an open-ended fair use exception. Importantly, with a confined fair dealing exception, many uses that may well be fair will continue to infringe copyright, because the use does not fall into one of the listed categories of use. For such uses, the question of fairness is never asked.*

There are many situations in the 24/7 newsroom where there is a temptation to just 'grab' material—particularly from social media platforms like Facebook. But such usage needs to fall within the copyright guidelines stated above if you are to escape liability. For example, a crime victim's Facebook page or Twitter profile might feature their photograph—but if it is not a 'selfie' (self-taken), then the copyright in the image rests with another person—the photographer who took the image. While the practice is common, and in some circumstances there will be a fair dealing exception available, your safest course is always to get the permission of the creator to reuse their material or to pay them for it. Often that means some detective work on your part because images in particular are copied so quickly on the internet that it can be difficult to find out who is the original creator or copyright holder.

The very nature of platforms such as Twitter, Facebook and Instagram as social media—where you expect and hope your banter will be re-posted—raises questions over the extent of attribution necessary and even possible. Nevertheless, full attribution of the creator is always essential to a fair use argument. The BBC was criticised in the *British Journal of Photography* for crediting only Twitpic and not the actual creators of the photographs it had broadcast during the London riots in 2011. While many editors and news directors choose to take the risk of breaching other people's copyright on commercial grounds, as this edition went to press media organisations were reporting an alarming growth in payments to the creators of material—particular photographs—stolen from the internet and social media by cavalier editors. Journalists take the high ground on some ethical issues like confidentiality of sources so it is surprising they are so willing to plagiarise the work of others, which is not only unlawful but in breach of their ethical codes.

Haitian photographer Daniel Morel, who took spectacular photographs of the earthquake in Haiti in 2010 and posted them to social media via Twitpic, won a copyright case in New York in 2013. The images were re-posted by another Twitter user and then sold by Agence France Presse and Getty Images to mainstream media outlets globally (Balasubramani, 2013). Digital 'theft' of creative work is rampant on the internet and in social media, as most of us know from the music, gaming and software piracy programs that have emerged over recent years. Some operators have been pursued in court in either criminal prosecutions or civil actions. Both options are open. Authorities will normally only prosecute under the criminal law, and fine or jail the perpetrators, if the infringement has happened on a large commercial scale. But private individuals and companies have the option to sue for damages for breach of copyright in their courts if they can identify and serve a defendant (and can afford the legal costs). And that is often the problem—finding the John or Jane Doe who has reproduced the material without your permission and then, even if you do win a judgment, actually extracting compensation from them where they might reside may not recognise the validity of Australian court judgments, or allow you to enforce them in other jurisdictions.

The enforcement of intellectual property laws varies markedly throughout the world, as you may have witnessed in the form of pirated labelled clothing and bootleg DVDs openly on sale in the streets of some developing countries. For some creators, there is little that can be done to preserve the creative value of their work once it has been reproduced brazenly online. As a professional communicator, it is often as much a moral obligation you have to your fellow creators to only draw upon their work under the allowable fair dealing provisions and with full and thorough acknowledgement of their original authorship.

Courts throughout the world have turned their attention to whether you are breaching copyright by linking to copyright material or linking to other sites that in turn infringe on someone else's copyright. There has been a wide range of outcomes, however, and taking into account all the linking that happens on an hourly basis via social media like Facebook and Twitter, there seems to be very little risk in the practice for any single amateur blogger. Most of the cases have centred on large-scale deep-linking to commercially valuable material within competitors' websites, particularly when it involves the 'mining' of other people's information for new business purposes. 'Deep links' are links to specific pages or audio-visual material within a larger website, bypassing the 'home page' URL, which was long considered the usual entrée to a site.

Actually reproducing the complete works of others is another matter, and several bloggers have been pursued in recent years for running copies of whole articles and photographs on their sites. Such lawsuits have become a mini-industry and even a business model for one company—the former US-based Righthaven—which sued about 275 bloggers and websites that had reproduced material from the newspaper groups it represented.

The issue of passing off frequently arises in the internet environment, in particular in domain name (www) registration, with some opportunists tempted to exploit the system by registering famous people's and companies' names as website URLs and social media handles. Trade marks, business names and domain names all involve different registration processes through separate bodies. According to IP Australia (2016), the agency responsible for administering patents, trade marks and designs, 'Domain names are issued by private internet companies and registered by the .au Domain Administration. The purpose of a domain name is to secure the web URL only.' The .au Domain Administration Ltd (auDA) was formed in 1999. It develops domain name policy, licenses registry operators, accredits and licenses registrars and facilitates a dispute-resolution process. Despite its efforts, numerous disputes have ended up in the courts. A '.com' domain name can be registered almost at will, as Tasmanian mine disaster survivors Brant Webb and Todd Russell found in 2006 when their .com domains were snapped up by internet entrepreneurs (Miller, 2006). We deal with this issue—known as 'cyber-squatting'—in greater detail in Chapter 13, when we look at the legal implications of this practice for public relations practitioners, freelancers and new media entrepreneurs.

REMEDIES: COMPENSATION FOR COPYRIGHT BREACHES

Part V of the Act deals with remedies and offences for copyright breaches, which can have civil or criminal consequences. Under section 115, remedies available include an injunction and either damages or an 'account of profits', the payment by the infringer of any profits made from the copying. Additional damages can be awarded depending upon the flagrancy of the infringement among other things.

If there is a commercial element to the infringement, breach of copyright can also be a criminal offence, with section 132(1) of the Act making the sale or hire, exhibition or import of an article in breach of copyright an offence 'if the person knows, or ought reasonably to know, the article to be an infringing copy of the work'. Under section 133, the court can order the destruction or surrender of any infringing articles to the copyright owner (known as 'delivery up'). This can also apply to any devices used for copying. Under section 132AC, criminal offences apply to 'substantial infringement on a commercial scale'. In the wash-up of the *Kazaa case* (2005), the record companies unsuccessfully sought a determination that what they alleged was continuing infringing conduct amounted to contempt of the Federal Court (*Kazaa case*, 2006).

MORAL RIGHTS OF AUTHORS

International conventions and Australian law grant you 'moral rights' over your work in addition to economic rights. They give you the right to claim authorship of your work through attribution, and also the right to object to any changes others might make to your work that might damage your integrity as the creator.

Even if you transfer the copyright in your work to someone else–as you might do as a freelancer or if you are writing as an employee in a government or media organisation–you still retain your moral rights as an author. This means you can take action against those who might put their own names to your work or those who have put your name to the work but have changed it to your disadvantage. It operates in part to protect you from unfair attacks and parodies where your work has been mutilated, distorted beyond recognition or reproduced in a thoroughly inappropriate context that damages your honour.

It won't protect 'reasonable' criticism of your work or any critique to which you have agreed. It also does not prevent employers or clients leaving your name off work if you have contracted to allow them to do so. But it sends a warning to others that they shouldn't mess with your work or republish it without giving you due credit. As a blogger, it also means you should be careful when writing parodies pretending to be someone else or denigrating their content and style by chopping and changing it to your satirical ends.

The Australian government introduced moral rights for creators in 2000 which now make up Part IX of the Act. Under section 189, 'moral right' means:

> *(a) a right of attribution of authorship; or*
> *(b) a right not to have authorship falsely attributed; or*
> *(c) a right of integrity of authorship.*

Division 4 deals with the right of integrity of authorship, which under section 195AI states:

> *(1) The author of a work has a right of integrity of authorship in respect of the work.*
> *(2) The author's right is the right not to have the work subjected to derogatory treatment.*

Effectively, this attempts to prevent unfair attacks on the work. The ACC (2001: 2) points out that derogatory treatment 'might involve a mutilation or a material distortion of a work, or using a work in a context which prejudices the author's honour or reputation'.

Moral rights apply to literary works, as well as musical, dramatic, artistic works and films. They remain with the creator, or the creator's heirs, for the same period as copyright.

While 'reasonable' criticism of an author or an author's work is acceptable, as is criticism consented to by the author, the Act also considers industry practice and work. A case in which breach of moral rights occurred is the *Corby case* (2013). Publishers Allen & Unwin published photographs taken by family members of convicted Bali drug smuggler Schapelle Corby in a book *Sins of the Father*, without asking permission. The publisher relied upon the fact that the copyright owners had previously given permission, including in one case to the book's author, allowing publication of the photographs. The court found that the permission was for another purpose, unconnected with production of the book. Allen & Unwin was liable for breach of copyright, and for infringing the moral rights of the members of Corby's family who took the photographs, which were not attributed to them. The $54,250 in damages awarded included $45,000 for 'flagrant disregard' of the Corby family's copyright.

In the *PI case* (2015), *The Sun-Herald* newspaper published a report on a private investigator that referred to him as a 'liar, cheat and unlicensed private investigator' who was 'again using aliases to scam unsuspecting clients'. The article featured what appeared to be a professionally created photograph of the PI's partner posed on a bed and semi-naked from the waist up. The PI did not sue for defamation, but asked the court to follow *Corby* and award damages for breach of copyright in the photograph, and also to award damages for a breach of moral rights–in this case, a breach of attribution of authorship. The court ruled a person could not be said to have suffered loss for non-attribution where they would not have wished their 'name to be published in connection with a photograph of which they were the author, thereby suggesting they were somehow implicated in, or receiving credit for, reproduction of the photograph in connection' with the publication, As the PI had said the publication made him angry and upset, and consistently with that evidence it should follow that he would not want to have been connected with the publication of the photograph within it, so the court found no breach of his moral rights. He was not 'injured in any professional calling as a photographer' (at para. 31), so no moral rights injury had occurred. He was, however, awarded $10,001 in damages for breach of his copyright in the image.

In the *Happy Herb case* (2017), a photographer sued for the use of an image of camomile flowers that had been uploaded onto a commercial website. He was a professional photographer and a citizen of the United States, whose works had been published in books, magazines and calendars as well as on greeting cards, postcards and posters. A portfolio of some of his works was on display at his website, where a copyright notice was displayed on each page of the website and watermarked on each work published on that website. He was not aware of the infringement for some time, and the photograph was immediately taken down when he claimed breach of copyright. Because the photographer admitted that his photographs, including this particular photograph, had been distributed widely on the internet without attribution or his authority and could be downloaded freely, the court declined to award anything for breach of his moral rights.

In the course of its judgment, the court noted that an offer of $10 made for the unauthorised use of the photograph was 'derisory' and made the following useful observation, which should be heeded by any professional communicator faced with a claim of this kind:

> *It is a pity that it has taken a contested hearing in order to provide Mr Briner with appropriate compensation for the use of the Work. Persons downloading photographs from the internet should recognise that there may be a risk of copyright infringement and, once notified of an infringement, they should act promptly and reasonably in order to arrive at an appropriate fee as compensation for the use of the Work. (para. 37)*

TIPS FOR MINDFUL PRACTICE

- Careful and sensible operation within the available defences and exceptions should ensure that the professional communicator minimises the likelihood of having to defend an intellectual property action.
- As creative professionals, we should respect the intellectual property of others. This is reinforced by the presence in the legislation of protection for the moral rights of authors.
- 'Freely viewed' does not equal 'freely used'. Check who owns material you find online and via social media. If it is worth lifting, it might command a price you should be paying. If you cannot afford to pay, it is wiser to link through to the copyright holder's site than to just plunder it for your own use.
- Take your own photos, or use Creative Commons sources such as Wikimedia.

- Full attribution will not guarantee you immunity from copyright action, but it is good ethical practice and a great start. If you have drawn upon a primary source for your material—for example, a government media release or a speech—then cite it and offer your audience a link to the original.
- Avoid using trade mark terms generically. Only use them if you are referring to that very product.
- Misrepresenting someone's work can breach their moral rights, and setting up fake accounts, impersonating them or 'passing off' your relationship for commercial gain might land you in court.
- The key message is that you will probably stay out of trouble if you give due credit and respect to the creative work of others.
- If you think your own work has been lifted by others, by all means seek advice on your options, but remember that legal action can be complex and expensive.

IN A NUTSHELL

- Intellectual property comprises 'creations of the mind': inventions, literary and artistic works, and symbols, names, images and designs used in commerce. IP laws are meant to protect our right to the exclusive use of the array of creative outputs we might produce as human beings.
- You can encounter IP laws when you reproduce the work of others or if they steal your creative output.
- The journalist or professional communicator, as both a creator of original material and a user of others' work, could be destined for either the plaintiff's or the defendant's role in a court case.
- Your form of expression can be protected by copyright, but not your ideas.
- The not-for-profit Creative Commons promotes the 'creative re-use of intellectual and artistic works', whether owned or in the public domain.

It offers free copyright licences, enabling creators the option of a voluntary 'some rights reserved' approach.

- The three exceptions to breach of copyright most commonly cited by news organisations are fair dealing for the purposes of criticism or review (s 41); fair dealing for the purpose of reporting news (s 42); and fair dealing for the purpose of parody or satire (s 41A).
- There are differences internationally between 'fair use' (broader and more flexible) and 'fair dealing' (narrower and specified) as defences to breach of copyright.
- International conventions and Australian law grant you 'moral rights' over your work in addition to your actionable economic rights.
- Corporations are protective of their trade marks—symbols used to distinguish their products, services or corporate regalia from others.
- Litigants might also turn to the law of 'passing off' or the consumer law 'misleading and deceptive conduct' provisions to pursue an action over the wrongful use of commercial names and materials.

DISCUSSION QUESTIONS

11.1 Debate the topic: 'The internet and social media have rendered copyright pointless.'

11.2 List three situations where professional communicators might want to use someone else's intellectual property in their work and three situations where professional communicators might want to defend their own intellectual property against misuse. Explain each.

11.3 The MEAA Journalist Code of Ethics states, 'Do not plagiarise'. But how 'loosely' are journalists allowed to attribute information, compared with academics? What risks do they face by offering little or no attribution?

11.4 Give three examples of sentences where a company's trade mark might mistakenly be used instead of a product or a process. Explain the basis of the confused meaning.

11.5 What are the consequences of plagiarism at your university or in your newsroom or workplace? Find out what the policy is and summarise it.

11.6 Think of five ways a journalist or blogger working for an online outlet might encounter copyright issues and explain the best way for them to handle each situation.

11.7 You are a blogger or influencer who wants to create your own YouTube presence or following, and you set out to create a series of posts, videos or blogs loosely based on an overseas reality show format about the day-to-day lives of celebrity husbands married to successful career women. Is there anything to be concerned about?

11.8 You are a police reporter, invited along by border security on one of a series of high-profile raids on factories employing illegal workers, when in the rush to flee, one of the workers runs out on to the street where you are standing and accidentally drops a family photograph, which you pick up. Your news editor wants to use the photograph to illustrate a front-page story about the raids. What, if anything, do you tell the editor?

REFERENCES

Australian Copyright Council (ACC) 2001, *B59v3—Journalists and Copyright Supplement*, Australian Copyright Council, Sydney.

—— 2014a, *Information Sheet: Journalists and Copyright*, Australian Copyright Council, Sydney, <www.copyright.org.au/>. Search for 'journalists & copyright'.

—— 2014b, *Parodies, Satire and Jokes*, Australian Copyright Council, Sydney, <www.copyright.org.au/>. Search for 'parodies, satire and jokes'.

—— 2015, *Internet: Copyright & Downloading*, Australian Copyright Council, Sydney, <www.copyright.org.au>. Search for 'Internet copying & downloading'.

Australian Law Reform Commission (ALRC) 2014, *Copyright and the Digital Economy: ALRC Report 122*, Commonwealth Government, Canberra, <www.alrc.gov.au/publications/copyright-report-122>.

Balasubramani, V. 2013, '*AFP v Morel*—lawsuit over Haiti photos taken from Twitter/Twitpic goes to trial', *Technology Marketing and Law Blog*, 13 November, <http://blog.ericgoldman.org/archives/2013/11/afp-v-morel-lawsuit-over-haiti-photos-taken-from-twittertwitpic-goes-to-trial.htm>.

Butt, P. and Nygh, P. 2004, *Butterworths Encyclopaedic Australian Legal Dictionary*, LexisNexis, Sydney.

IP Australia 2016, IP Australia Media Centre, 'Trade mark basics', <www.ipaustralia.gov.au/trade-marks/understanding-trade-marks>.

MEAA Ethics Review Committee 1996, *Ethics Review Committee Final Report*, MEAA, Sydney.

Miller, N. 2006, 'Celebrities may be able to reclaim domain from cybersquatters', *Age Online*, 19 September, <www.theage.com.au/news/technology/celebrities-may-be-able-to-reclaim-domain-from-cybersquatters/2006/09/18/1158431644946.html>.

Ross, J. 2002, 'The *Panel case* and the desirability of harm as a requirement of copyright liability', *Deakin Law Review*, 9, <www.austlii.edu.au//cgi-bin/disp.pl/au/journals/DeakinLRev/2002/9.html>.

Toliver, Z. 2017, 'Settlement reached: "Monkey selfie" case broke new ground for animal rights', PETA, <www.peta.org/blog/settlement-reached-monkey-selfie-case-broke-new-ground-animal-rights>.

Van Caenegem, W. 2001, *Intellectual Property*, Butterworths, Sydney.

Walker, S. 2000, *Media Law: Commentary and Materials*, Law Book Company, Sydney.

Wikimedia Foundation 2014, 'Monkey selfie', *Wikimedia Foundation Transparency Report*, <https://transparency.wikimedia.org/stories.html>.

World Intellectual Property Organization (WIPO) 1886, *Berne Convention for the Protection of Literary and Artistic Works*, <www.wipo.int/treaties/en/ip/berne>.

—— 1979a, *Convention Establishing the World Intellectual Property Organization*, <www.wipo.int/treaties/en/text.jsp?file_id=283854#P50_1504>.

—— 1979b, *Berne Convention for the Protection of Literary and Artistic Works*, <www.wipo.int/treaties/en/text.jsp?file_id=283698>.

—— 2011, *Directory of Intellectual Property Offices*, <www.wipo.int/directory/en/urls.jsp>.

—— 2016, *Understanding Copyright and Related Rights*, 2nd edn, <www.wipo.int/edocs/pubdocs/en/wipo_pub_909_2016.pdf>.

CASES CITED

BitTorrent case: Dallas Buyers Club LLC v Does 1–31, US District Court, Southern District of Texas, case no. 14-cv-00248, <https://law.justia.com/cases/federal/district-courts/washington/wawdce/2:2014cv01819/207565/59>.

Carleton's case: Carleton v ABC [2002] ACTSC 127 (18 December 2002), <www.austlii.edu.au/au/cases/act/ACTSC/2002/127.html>; *Carleton v ABC* [2003] ACTSC 28 (2 May 2003), <www.austlii.edu.au/au/cases/act/ACTSC/2003/28.html>.

Clark's case: Clark v Associated Newspapers Ltd [1998] EWHC Patents 345 (21 January 1998), <www.bailii.org/cgi-bin/markup.cgi?doc=/ew/cases/EWHC/Patents/1998/345.html>.

Clippings case: Re De Garis and Moore and Neville Jeffress Pidler Pty Ltd, No. G1319 of 1988 FED No. 352 Copyright 18 IPR 292 (1991) 20 IPR 605 (1990) 37 FCR 99, <www.austlii.edu.au/cgi-bin/viewdoc/au/cases/cth/FCA/1990/218.html>.

Constable Wendy case: Hatfield v TCN Channel Nine Pty Ltd [2010] NSWCA 69 (8 April 2010) at [111], <www.austlii.edu.au/cgi-bin/viewdoc/au/cases/nsw/NSWCA/2010/69.html>.

Cooper cases: Universal Music Australia Pty Ltd v Cooper [2005] FCA 972 (14 July 2005), <www.austlii.edu.au/au/cases/cth/federal_ct/2005/972.html>; *Cooper v Universal Music Australia Pty Ltd* [2006] FCAFC 187 156 FCR 380, <www.austlii.edu.au/au/cases/cth/FCAFC/2006/187.html>.

Corby case: Corby v Allen & Unwin Pty Limited [2013] FCA 370 (24 April 2013), <www.austlii.edu.au/cgi-bin/viewdoc/au/cases/cth/FCA/2013/370.html>.

Cricketer case: The Cricketer Ltd v Newspress Pty Ltd and David Syme & Co Ltd [1974] VR 477.

Crocodile Dundee case: Pacific Dunlop Ltd v Hogan (1989) 23 FCR 553; 87 ALR 14; 14 IPR 398; [1989] AIPC 90-578; [1989] ATPR 40-948 (FC), <www.austlii.edu.au/cgi-bin/viewdoc/au/cases/cth/FCA/1989/185.html>.

Embryo case: Pro Sieben Media AG v Carlton UK Television Ltd and Twenty-Twenty Vision Ltd [1999] EMLR 109, <www8.austlii.edu.au/cgi-bin/LawCite?cit=%5b1999%5d%201%20WLR%20605>.

Essential Media case: Essential Media Communications Pty Ltd v EMC2 & Partners [2002] VSC 554 (10 December 2002), <www.austlii.edu.au/cgi-bin/disp.pl/au/cases/vic/VSC/2002/554.html>.

Hanson's case: ABC v Hanson [1998] QCA 306, Appeal no. 8716 of 1997 (28 September 1998), <https://archive.sclqld.org.au/qjudgment/1998/QCA98-306.pdf>.

Happy Herb case: Briner v The Happy Herb Company & Ors [2017] FCCA 1854 (11 September 2017), <www.austlii.edu.au/cgi-bin/viewdoc/au/cases/cth/FCCA/2017/1854.html>.

iiNet case: Roadshow Films Pty Ltd v iiNet Ltd [2012] HCA 16 (20 April 2012), <www.austlii.edu.au/au/cases/cth/HCA/2012/16.html>.

ISP cases: Roadshow Films Pty Ltd v Telstra Corporation Ltd [2016] FCA 1503 (15 December 2016).

Kazaa cases: Universal Music Australia Pty Ltd v Sharman License Holdings Ltd [2005] FCA 1242 (5 September 2005), <www.austlii.edu.au/au/cases/cth/federal_ct/2005/1242.html>; *Universal Music Australia Pty Ltd v Sharman Networks Ltd* [2006] FCA 29, <www.austlii.edu.au/au/cases/cth/FCA/2006/29.html>.

Kokoda Trail case: Seven Network (Operations) Ltd v TCN Channel Nine Pty Ltd [2005] FCAFC 144 (8 August 2005), <www.austlii.edu.au/au/cases/cth/FCAFC/2005/144.html>.

Malishus case: Lamont v Malishus & Ors [2018] FCCA 423 (14 March 2018), <www8.austlii.edu.au/cgi-bin/viewdoc/au/cases/cth/FCCA/2018/423.html>.

MKR case: Seven Network (Operations) Limited v Endemol Australia Pty Limited [2015] FCA 800 (6 August 2015), <www.austlii.edu.au/cgi-bin/viewdoc/au/cases/cth/FCA/2015/800.html>.

Mobile League case: Telstra Corporation Pty Ltd v Premier Media Group Pty Ltd [2007] FCA 568, Federal Court of Australia (18 April 2007), Allsop J, <www.austlii.edu.au/cgi-bin/sinodisp/au/cases/cth/FCA/2007/568.html>.

Monkey case: Naruto Monkey PETA v Slater CA9 No. 16-15469 D.C. No. 3:15-cv-04324-WHO Opinion 04 23 18, <www.documentcloud.org/documents/4444209-Naruto-Monkey-PETA-v-Slater-CA9-Opinion-04-23-18.html>.

Panel cases: TCN Channel Nine Pty Ltd v Network Ten Pty Ltd [2002] FCAFC 146 (22 May 2002), Federal Court of Australia, <www.austlii.edu.au/au/cases/cth/FCAFC/2002/146.html>; *Network Ten Pty Ltd v TCN Channel Nine Pty Ltd* (2004) 78 ALJR 585; [2004] HCA 14 (11 March 2004), High Court of Australia, <www.austlii.edu.au/au/cases/cth/high_ct/2004/14.html>; *TCN Channel Nine Pty Ltd v Network Ten Pty Ltd (No. 2)* [2005] FCAFC 53 (26 May 2005), Federal Court of Australia, <www.austlii.edu.au/au/cases/cth/FCAFC/2005/53.html>.

Penname case: Sykes v John Fairfax & Sons Ltd [1977] 1 NSWLR 415.

PI case: Monte v Fairfax Media Publications Pty Ltd [2015] FCCA 1633 (7 August 2015), <www.austlii.edu.au/cgi-bin/viewdoc/au/cases/cth/FCCA/2015/1633.html>.

Pokémon case: Pokémon Company International, Inc. v Redbubble Ltd [2017] FCA 1541 (19 December 2017).

Sky Television case: Media Works NZ Ltd & TV Works Ltd v Sky Television Ltd, HC AK CIV 2007-404-5674 [2007] NZHC 924 (18 September 2007) at [121], <www.austlii.edu.au/cgi-bin/viewdoc/nz/cases/NZHC/2007/924.html>.

Thoroughvision case: Thoroughvision Pty Ltd v Sky Channel Pty Ltd [2005] FCA 1527 (28 October 2005), <www.austlii.edu.au/au/cases/cth/federal_ct/2005/1527.html>.

Twin of Brothers case: TVBO Production Ltd v Australia Sky Net Pty Ltd [2009] FCA 1132, <www.austlii.edu.au/au/cases/cth/FCA/2009/1132.html>.

CHAPTER 12
Privacy

KEY CONCEPTS

Breach of privacy
'[D]isclosure or observation of information or conduct [which] would be highly offensive to a reasonable person of ordinary sensibilities' (Gleeson, CJ, *Lenah Game Meats case*, 2001)

Trespass
Entering land or premises without actual or implied permission, staying there after being asked to leave, or placing a recording device on someone's property.

Data protection
Information privacy laws controlling the collection and storage of personally identifiable information.

Surveillance
The monitoring of people's lives or data using human observation, or analogue or digital technologies and applications.

Constraints upon the media in the name of individual privacy have been growing for more than a century, and the pressure has mounted in the digital era. Journalists and marketers are being called to account for decisions that intrude into the private lives of citizens, even though they might believe such intrusions are in the 'public interest'. Politicians, judges, regulatory bodies and reform inquiries like the Leveson Inquiry (2012) in the United Kingdom and the Finkelstein (2012) and Convergence (2012) reviews in Australia demanded news organisations explain their internal processes for decisions that had legal and ethical consequences.

The privacy debate has advanced markedly over recent years, particularly with the advent of new surveillance technologies. This chapter traces the background and international context of the debate, explores the social media and digital dimensions of the issue, and explains the key laws and regulations that affect journalists and professional communicators.

PRIVACY: BACKGROUND AND INTERNATIONAL CONTEXT

Just over a century ago, there was no notion of a formal 'right to privacy'. The practice of gentlemen duelling to the death over matters of pride was masterfully recorded by the writer Alexandre Dumas in his novel *The Three Musketeers*. In real life, Dumas lived the extravagant lifestyle of the famous author in an era when the stars of print were the equivalent of screen idols today. He was besotted with 32-year-old actress Adah Isaacs Menken—the Paris Hilton of her time—regarded by some as the first female cult celebrity. The lovebirds posed for some saucy photographs (she in her underwear and he without the compulsory gentleman's jacket) but the photographer then tried to trade on their celebrity by registering copyright in the images. Dumas felt aggrieved but, as James Q. Whitman explained in the *Yale Law Journal*, the court held that his property rights had not been infringed. However, the judge decided Dumas did have a right to privacy that trumped any copyright the photographer might have held. With that French decision in 1867, privacy was born as a right in the legal world.

While the French courts were developing privacy law in the 1860s, there was no notion of a formal 'right to privacy' in the English-speaking world. Laws in the United States, Britain and its former colonies had evolved over centuries to protect the individual's space and reputation in several ways, including defamation, copyright, trespass, nuisance and confidentiality. In 1888, Michigan Supreme Court Justice Thomas Cooley wrote of a 'right to be let alone'. Then, in a landmark *Harvard Law Review* article in December 1890, the great US jurist Samuel D. Warren and future Supreme Court Justice Louis D. Brandeis announced a new 'right to privacy' in an article by that name. Warren had been angered when a daily newspaper published the guest list of a high society dinner party his family had hosted at his Boston mansion, which he saw as a gross invasion of his privacy. The right to privacy owes its existence to a wealthy lawyer who resented the media prying into his personal life.

Warren and Brandeis wrote, 'The press is overstepping in every direction the obvious bounds of propriety and of decency. Gossip is no longer the resource of the idle and of the vicious, but has become a trade, which is pursued with industry as well as effrontery.' Their words mirror those of the critics of celebrity gossip mags and websites today, particularly in the wake of the UK phone hacking scandal (Leveson, 2012).

The Americans proceeded to develop their new right to privacy over the next century, but the First Amendment to the US Constitution limited its impact on the media in that country, rendering the citizen's right to privacy merely a shield against overly intrusive government interference.

INTERNATIONAL PRIVACY PROTECTIONS

The legal right to privacy is recognised in nearly every national constitution and in most international human rights treaties. Privacy wins protection at the highest international levels. It is included in the Universal Declaration of Human Rights (Article 12), the International Covenant on Civil and Political Rights (Article 17), the European Convention on Human Rights (Article 8), the American Declaration of the Rights and Duties of Man (Article V) and the American Convention on Human Rights (Article 11). A right to privacy has been upheld in the European Court of Human Rights and by the United Nations (UN) Human Rights Committee.

The International Covenant on Civil and Political Rights states at Article 17:

> 1 *No-one shall be subjected to arbitrary and unlawful interference with his privacy, family, home or correspondence, nor to unlawful attacks on his honour and reputation.*
> 2 *Everyone has the right to protection of the law against such interference or attacks.*

Privacy gained traction in the Organization for Economic Cooperation and Development (OECD)'s Privacy Principles, which have provided the platform for basic data protection regimes internationally. While most nations and regional governance bodies agree, at least publicly, that personal data should not be misused by governments, in June 2013 *The Guardian* and *The New York Times* published articles based on information supplied by former US National Security Agency contractor Edward Snowden, exposing widespread warrantless collection and storage of electronic communications by US government agencies.

Continental Europe features systems of civil law with strong privacy protections under their law of 'delict' (similar to the common law of 'torts'), where citizens can seek compensation for infringements of their personality rights. German law divides privacy into the 'intimate', the 'individual' and the 'private'. In France, specific rights of personality are identified, including the 'right to confidentiality of correspondence', the 'right to privacy of domestic life' and the 'right to a person's name'. Many countries have reinforced the law of delict with privacy clauses in their constitutions and offences in their criminal law.

CELEBRITY ACTIONS

For several decades, the right to sue over breaches of privacy failed to take hold in the United Kingdom or other common law jurisdictions such as Australia and New Zealand; the public interest in free expression held sway. A major turning point came in Britain and Europe with the death of Princess Diana in Paris in 1997 after a car chase involving paparazzi.

In 1998, the United Kingdom passed its *Human Rights Act*, which incorporated the European Convention on Human Rights into British law, including a right to privacy (Article 8) and a right to free expression (Article 10). From that moment, the approach of the UK courts started to take on the flavour of their continental European neighbours.

Many of the UK judges avoided the words 'right to privacy', preferring to bend and stretch the ancient action of 'breach of confidence' to suit. Most of the litigants in the United Kingdom and Europe have come from the ranks of entertainment, sports and royalty. Actors Michael Douglas and Catherine Zeta-Jones convinced the High Court that *Hello!* magazine had breached their confidence by publishing unauthorised photographs of their wedding taken by a paparazzo who posed as a guest (*Douglas Wedding case* 2001). In 2004, the House of Lords found against the *Mirror* for publishing a photo of supermodel Naomi Campbell leaving a drug addiction clinic because, despite being taken in a public place, it revealed confidential information about her medical condition (*Supermodel case* 2004). The European Court of Human Rights went a step further by finding that Princess Caroline of Monaco had a right to privacy when she was photographed using a long lens while holidaying on a public beach (*Princess case* 2004). While such photographs did not contribute to public debate on the role of the princess, the court subsequently ruled in 2013 that a different photograph published in an article about the rich renting out their holiday houses did: the princess and her husband were public figures who could not claim protection of their private lives in the same way as private individuals (*Princess case*, 2013).

Some argued that the developing privacy laws were justified when, in January 2007, the royal editor of the tabloid *News of the World* was jailed for four months under phone-tapping laws for intercepting the mobile phone messages of Prince William (Leveson, 2012). In 2008, Britain's High Court of Justice awarded Formula One boss Max Mosley (son of 1930s British fascist Sir Oswald Mosley) £60,000 for invasion of privacy over a *News of the World* story headed 'F1 boss in Sick Nazi Orgy with Hookers' and 'Son of Hitler-loving Fascist in Sex Shame', based on clandestine filming and subsequent publication of a sado-masochism session (*Mosley case*, 2008). In the same year, Hugh Grant, Elizabeth Hurley and her husband Arun Nayar received a settlement of £58,000 over publication of photos taken while they were on holiday.

It really is a list of the who's who of the rich and famous, and while the decisions concerned the traditional media, the principles apply equally to bloggers and social media users: unlike in the United States, courts in the United Kingdom and Europe will not tolerate salacious intrusion into the lives of very public figures. The decisions were reinforced throughout 2010 and 2011 when the UK courts issued at least eighteen non-publication injunctions ordering that the identities of several high-profile people be kept secret when exposés of their private lives were about to be revealed in the media. Some even fell into the category of 'super injunctions'—where it was prohibited to even reveal that an injunction had been issued. One celebrity injunction—the *Three-way case*—broke new ground in 2016 when the Supreme Court of the United Kingdom allowed the injunction to stay in force even though the material had spread throughout the internet. The celebrity, 'PJS', married to another entertainment personality, YMA, won the order to stop the details of a sexual encounter between him and two others—described by the court as a 'three-way'. The court decided it was reasonable to maintain an order despite the fact that people might still go searching for the material online and find it, because at least it was not plastered all over the front pages of tabloid newspapers and their digital equivalents. The court ruled that what little public interest there was in the free expression of material about people's private sexual encounters was outweighed by the participants' right to privacy (para. 24). Media lawyer David Engel told the BBC that the decision represented a distinction between the laws of confidentiality and privacy in that the material was no longer technically confidential but the courts acted to restrict its dissemination because it was private (Stillito, 2016).

The New Zealand Court of Appeal turned its attention to the right to privacy in 2004 in the *Hosking Twins case*. It decided by a three-to-two majority to move ahead with a privacy tort, although the minority were extremely vocal in their criticism of the development and launched a strong defence of press freedom. The New Zealand test, as outlined by Gault P (at para. 117), is that the two fundamental requirements for a successful claim for interference with privacy are:

> 1 *the existence of facts in respect of which there is a reasonable expectation of privacy; and*
> 2 *publicity given to those private facts that would be considered highly offensive to an objective reasonable person.*

The Hoskings were media personalities who had adopted twins and later separated. They asked for their privacy, but a magazine photographer snapped the mother walking the twins in their stroller in a public place. The court ultimately decided this fact scenario did not meet its new test of privacy invasion, but in the course of saying so developed the elements of the new tort. A new right to privacy had been established in New Zealand.

Celebrity cases have also emerged in Australia, although most have been in the realm of defamation law, involving sports personalities and entertainers like Bec Hewitt, Rebel Wilson, Geoffrey Rush and Chris Gale, covered in Chapters 7 and 8. Yet celebrities have also started defending their privacy and confidentiality. In 2013, the NSW Supreme Court refused an injunction from the actress Holly Candy over a magazine that showed her heavily pregnant because it would be futile to try to stop the publication since thousands of magazine copies were already in the late stages of distribution (*Holly Candy case*, 2013). However, the court said she might still win substantial damages for breach of confidence.

DIGITAL DIMENSIONS

Blogs, social media and online media outlets seem just as obsessed with celebrities and gossip as the mainstream media, and privacy protection is as much about the settings on social media platforms as it is about international law.

In 2011, a court in London acted to protect the privacy of an extra-marital love affair between two modern-day celebrities, but their identities went viral on social media, rendering the court order embarrassingly ineffective. Former reality TV contestant Imogen Thomas told *The Sun* newspaper about her sexual liaison with an unnamed footballer in a 'kiss-and-tell' account. She demanded tens of thousands of pounds from Manchester United superstar Ryan Giggs to keep the affair secret, and set up meetings in hotel rooms so they could be photographed by paparazzi (*Thomas's case*, 2011). Mr Giggs rushed to court and won an interim injunction banning publication of his identity or details of his relationship with Ms Thomas, but more than 70,000 Twitter users defied the order, as well as the *New Sunday Herald* in Scotland from beyond the reach of the English court's jurisdiction. Despite this level of coverage, High Court Justice Eady extended the injunction on the grounds that Giggs' identity was not yet sufficiently in the 'public domain'. He said that while possible blackmail was at play, his main concern was in protecting the privacy of the footballer for the sake of his wife and children, in line with earlier European privacy decisions. Within days, a British journalist was being threatened with a contempt of court action for using Twitter to reveal the name of a different footballer and his lover who had won a similar injunction to protect their identities after a different affair (Gunter, 2011). Not all the injunctions concerned the rich and famous, and they were even extended by a judge to include social media users in mid-2011. Court of Protection Justice Baker banned Facebook and Twitter users from identifying a brain-damaged woman in a case where her mother was applying to withdraw her life support (Reuters, 2011).

DATA-PROTECTION LAWS

A large area of privacy law is built around the storage and handling of personal data by governments and corporations. There are data-protection laws in most countries, typically restricting the use of your private details to a narrow set of circumstances related to that department or organisation's business. They need your permission to use the private facts, and then need to comply with regulations on their secure storage.

You will often hear stories about breaches of data protection laws, either in a physical or digital form. Blogger Elisa D. Cooper became the first individual targeted by the California Department of Managed Health Care in 2005 after she posted a link to the private medical records of about 140 clients of the health plan where she had worked. Her former employer, Kaiser Permanente Health Group, had inadvertently uploaded the material to its website (Pwenneke, 2005). She was the group's former website designer, who was so angry about their practices that she set up the blog and called herself the 'Diva of the Disgruntled'. The company was fined $200,000 and then launched an action against Cooper to take down her blog.

The US Supreme Court decided in 2011 that the term 'personal privacy' applied only to 'natural persons', and not to corporations trying to avoid the release of sensitive internal data in answer to freedom of information requests.

The volumes of private information held on every UK citizen by governments and corporations was highlighted in the documentary *Erasing David*, where the lead character went into hiding and hired some of Britain's top investigators to try to find him by discovering everything they could about him via public and private files. He found it was impossible to lead a private and anonymous existence in the early twenty-first century.

Our digital trail extends wherever and whenever we conduct business on the internet. The typical web browser allows countless 'cookies' that track many of our online activities. Search engines, app stores, airlines, travel booking agencies and numerous other online entities hold all sorts of digital information about us that may or may not be secure or subject to legal discovery in the case of a court action. The onus is on individual users to become acquainted with the terms of use of the platform they are using and to ensure their privacy settings are fixed at a suitable level.

Social media platforms added exponentially to the scale of private data held and traded globally by companies, political organisations and governments. An international backlash against Facebook resulted from the Cambridge Analytica scandal in 2018, when it was revealed that the data analytics firm had harvested personal information from the Facebook profiles of more than 50 million people to influence elections internationally (including the 2016 US presidential election and the UK Brexit referendum) and to target fake news at the accounts of swinging voters (Greenfield, 2018).

As the US-based Pew Research Center reported in 2011, more than half of all people online had uploaded photos to be shared with others. As facial recognition ('tagging') is combined with geo-location capabilities, it means we are leaving a digital footprint via our images and other metadata.

Fairfax Media reporter Ben Grubb won an appeal to the Privacy Commissioner in 2015 against a Telstra refusal to release his 'personal information' in the form of 'metadata' that the telecommunications giant held about him—a decision overturned in 2017 by the Federal Court. His original request came in the midst of public debate over federal government's data-retention laws introduced as amendments to the *Telecommunications (Interception and Access) Act 1979*, requiring telecommunications companies to retain metadata for at least two years (see Chapter 10). The Privacy Commissioner ruled that Telstra had to freely provide Grubb with:

- Internet Protocol (IP) address information
- Uniform Resource Locator (URL) information
- cell tower location information beyond the cell tower location information that Telstra retains for billing purposes;
- but not the phone numbers of incoming callers. (*Grubb case no. 1*, at para. 172).

However, in 2017 the full court of the Federal Court dismissed the Privacy Commissioner's argument on the basis that the technical information could not be demanded under the privacy principle because it was not personal information 'about an individual' (*Grubb case no. 2*, para. 80).

TROLLING, CYBERSTALKING AND BULLYING

Another type of privacy breach takes the form of harassment. Things can get pretty heated in cyberspace and the Twittersphere, but most people know when to walk away from an online disagreement. Stalking laws in many countries extend to digital intimidation.

Sometimes there is a fine line between satire or parody and cyber-bullying, particularly when they stem from relationships that have turned sour. Fake Facebook pages or Twitter accounts sometimes include false private details of the target's sex life or private affairs, triggering legal action. A UK court awarded damages for breach of privacy and libel in 2008 over a bogus Facebook page that falsely claimed a television executive was gay. The case was interesting because it showed that even publication of false private information could be considered a breach.

The digital era has involved a marked increase in the phenomenon of 'revenge pornography'—the 'non-consensual distribution of nude or sexual images online or via mobile phones' (Henry, Powell and Flynn, 2017: 3). A 2017 study found one in five Australians—equally divided between men and women—had experienced distressing image-based abuse and that 80 per cent of Australians agreed it should be a crime to share sexual or nude images without permission (Henry, Powell and Flynn, 2017: 2).

Cyber-bullying and related crimes are dealt with at Commonwealth level under the Criminal Code 1995, with the main offences carrying two- to ten-year jail terms under:

- section 478.1(1)—unauthorised access to, or modification of, restricted data
- section 477.3(1)—unauthorised impairment of electronic communication
- section 474.17—using a carriage service to menace, harass or cause offence.

A recent development has been the establishment of an Office of the eSafety Commissioner in 2015 under the *Enhancing Online Safety Act 2015*, with a mandate to coordinate and lead online safety efforts across government, industry and the not-for-profit community. It was amended in 2017 to expand the Commissioner's remit to promote and enhance online safety beyond children to include Australians of all ages. The scheme features mechanisms for complaints handling and removal of material from participating social media services. The Commissioner also administers an image-based abuse portal with reporting options, support and resources for victims of image-based abuse, and their families and friends.

PRIVACY LAW IN AUSTRALIA

There was still no common law right to privacy in Australia in 2018, although a number of laws went part-way to protecting the privacy of citizens. The interplay between the Australian media and privacy laws has long been a struggle between free expression and the citizen's desire for seclusion and confidentiality.

Complaints about media intrusion date back to the early nineteenth century. According to *Historical Records of Australia* (Series 1, vol. 13), as early as 1827 NSW Chief Justice Francis Forbes rejected Governor Ralph Darling's proposal for legislation licensing the press, stating that, 'the press of this Colony is licentious may be readily admitted; but that does not prove the necessity of altering the laws'.

Three years later, *The Sydney Gazette and New South Wales Advertiser* (1830) published an extract from London's *New Monthly Magazine* on the prying nature of the British press compared with its European counterparts, stating that, 'The foreign journals never break in upon the privacy of domestic life.' But the London newspapers would hound a 'lady of fashion' relentlessly:

> *They trace her from the breakfast table to the Park, from the Park to the dinner-table, from thence to the Opera or the ball, and from her boudoir to her bed. They trace her everywhere. She may make as many doubles as a hare, but they are all in vain; it is impossible to escape pursuit.*

In 1847, New South Wales became the first Australian state to add 'public benefit' to its defence of truth for libel—essentially a privacy element in defamation law (ALRC, 1979: 117). In 1882, the first identified use of the phrase 'right to privacy' appeared in an Australian newspaper. Commenting on a major libel case, the *South Australian Weekly Chronicle* (1882: 5) stated that, 'A contractor having dealings with the Government or with any public body has no right to privacy as far as those dealings go.' Following publication of the landmark 'A Right to Privacy' *Harvard Law Review* article in 1890 (Warren and Brandeis, 1890), the usage of the phrase escalated in the colonial press.

In the 1937 *Victoria Park Racing case,* the High Court decided by a three-to-two majority that a radio station that broadcast horse race calls from a platform on a property overlooking the track did not unlawfully interfere with the racing club's use of its property. The station had not breached any 'right to privacy'. But the comments of dissenting Justice George Rich were prescient: 'Indeed, the prospects of television make our present decision a very important one, and I venture to think that the advance of that art may force the courts to recognise that protection against the complete exposure of the doings of the individual may be a right indispensable to the enjoyment of life.' Over the ensuing 75 years, support for an actionable right to privacy increased as the concept gained currency internationally.

In 2001, the High Court revisited its 1937 *Victoria Park Racing* privacy decision in the *Lenah Game Meats case* (see Key Case 12.1). It rejected the claim of a Tasmanian abattoir that it had a right to privacy that animal liberationists breached when trespassing to film the slaughter of possums, which the ABC planned to broadcast. However, the court refused to rule out the potential for a right to privacy under a different fact scenario. Intermediate court decisions in Queensland in 2003 and Victoria in 2007 awarded plaintiffs damages for invasion of privacy. In Queensland, a District Court judge ruled that the privacy of former Sunshine Coast mayor Alison Grosse had been invaded by an ex-lover who harassed her after their affair had ended. She was awarded $108,000 in damages (*Sunshine Coast Mayor case*, 2003).

Four years later, Victorian County Court Judge Felicity Hampel held that a rape victim's privacy was invaded when ABC Radio broadcast her identity, despite state laws banning the identification of sexual assault complainants. She was awarded $110,000 damages (*Jane Doe case*, 2007).

These decisions were not appealed, which left the issue undecided by a superior court until in 2008 the Victoria Court of Appeal held that, while a jilted lover's distribution of secretly made sex tapes was a breach of confidence, it was not a breach of privacy because there was no invasion of privacy tort in Australia (*Sex Tapes case*, 2008). Despite that, in 2013 a Queensland District Court judge refused to deny a girl with a disability an opportunity to sue Yahoo! for breach of privacy after her image was used to post offensive messages under the name 'Spastic Legs' (*Disability case*, 2013).

The line of thinking in Australia has been similar to the British approach in the historic celebrity cases mentioned earlier, in adapting the equitable remedy of breach of confidence to invasions of privacy. It was followed in Western Australia in 2015 when the Supreme Court awarded $48,404 in damages to a woman whose former lover–a co-worker at a mine site–had posted intimate images and videos of her to Facebook in an act of revenge after she ended their relationship. The court also issued an injunction ordering him not to post any further intimate images of her (*Revenge Porn case*, 2015). The case offers a concise summary of the application of the equitable remedy of breach of confidence (explained in Chapter 9) to a privacy matter. Justice Robert Mitchell explained how the act of posting the indecent material constituted a breach of the man's equitable obligation, owed to his ex-partner, to maintain the confidentiality of the images (para. 55). The images had the 'necessary quality of confidence about them', the circumstances in which they were obtained conveyed an obligation of confidentiality, and they had been posted on Facebook to the detriment of the plaintiff (paras 56–9). Justice Mitchell drew on historical cases where the breach of confidence action had been used to restrain a defendant from publishing private material, including the 1849 case over etchings created by Queen Victoria and Prince Albert for their own use, which had been secretly copied from the original plates and were about to be published by a London printer (*Royal Etchings case*, para. 48).

In 2018, the Australian Information Commissioner used the 'right to privacy' as one of the grounds to reject the ABC's freedom of information application for reports, correspondence and other communication from the Department of Home Affairs about an individual who may have faced disciplinary action over their role at Australia's immigration detention centre in Nauru. He decided that the individual's right to privacy, the management function of the agency and the interests of an individual or groups of individuals outweighed the factor in favour of disclosure of the information (*Nauru Detention case*, 2018, para. 24).

A similar reason was given in the appeal against the Queensland Information Commissioner's ruling allowing the release to *The Australian* newspaper of Department of Justice and the Attorney-General correspondence with Supreme Court justices about a secret and embarrassing recording of a conversation between two of the judges and the former Chief Justice, Tim Carmody. Justifying his decision overruling the release of the correspondence, Justice Cliff Hoeben ruled that he should give 'significant weight to the public interest in protecting the privacy interests of the applicant in respect of the personal information contained in the Information in Issue' (*Judges Tapes case no. 2*, at para. 71). He noted that the right to privacy was one of the factors listed in Part 3 of the *Right to Information Act 2009* (Qld), favouring non-disclosure of information in the public interest, and he defined the right to privacy as 'the right of an individual to preserve their personal sphere free from interference from others' (at para. 32).

However, while privacy remained an element, a related request by *The Courier-Mail* newspaper for the actual tape of the judges' conversation was rejected predominantly on other public interest grounds. Justice Hoeben stated:

> *Of those factors, the most important is the public interest harm likely to arise from the loss of confidence in the judiciary and interference with the proper administration of justice in Queensland*

> *should the documents in dispute be made available. Without being specific, it is difficult to accept that anything other than harm would be caused by allowing into the public domain what could only be described as rancorous exchanges between the then Chief Justice and other judges of the Supreme Court. No educative function would be achieved. Such disclosure would do nothing other than satisfy a prurient interest in what was an unfortunate period in the Supreme Court's history. (at para. 167)*

The best that can be said as this book went to press is that further development of privacy law is likely—either at common law or via the introduction of State or Commonwealth-based statutory torts for the serious invasion of privacy.

KEY CASE 12.1: *LENAH GAME MEATS CASE*

ABC v Lenah Game Meats Pty Ltd (2001) 208 CLR 199 (15 November 2001)

FACTS

In early 1998, there was a break-in at the Lenah Game Meats abattoir in Tasmania. Someone trespassed into the meatworks and planted secret cameras that recorded the killing of brush-tailed possums for export. There was nothing illegal about the company's operations, and it followed best practice standards in its processes. The vision was delivered to the ABC, which proposed to broadcast it on its current affairs program *The 7.30 Report*.

LAW

The company sought injunctions stopping the ABC from broadcasting the video, requiring the ABC to deliver up all copies of the film in its possession, and also sought damages and costs. The Supreme Court of Tasmania refused an interim injunction to stop the broadcast, but the Full Court of the Supreme Court later agreed to grant one. (Meanwhile, the ABC had broadcast excerpts of the film.) The ABC appealed to the High Court to have the injunction lifted. It succeeded in its appeal by a five-to-one majority, although the justices varied markedly in their reasons.

Especially controversial was Justice Ian Callinan's minority argument that the modern media had changed so significantly that they might not be worthy of many of the protections previously afforded, that the implied constitutional freedom was wrongly derived, that there were arguments for a tort of privacy even extending to corporations and that the doctrine against prior restraint in defamation trials placed too much emphasis on free expression. The main elements of the judgments relevant to privacy were as follows:

- A separate wrong of invasion of privacy was a possibility. The majority decided it was best left open for a more suitable test case involving a natural person rather than a company.
- It was unlikely that any such action for invasion of privacy would extend to corporations.
- Showing a film of the processes used by the abattoir was not a breach of confidence, because the processes themselves were not sufficiently confidential, despite the film being made on private premises.
- Despite the fact that the footage was obtained illegally via trespass by unknown parties, its publication by a third-party broadcaster was not 'unconscionable'.

The majority of the High Court discharged the injunction on the grounds that the lower court did not have authority in equity to grant it, but in the process raised the prospect of developing a form of privacy action. Gleeson CJ and Callinan J favoured the English approach of extending the breach of confidence action to apply to the filming of private activities, an approach reflected in more recent decisions.

LESSONS FOR JOURNALISTS

The case is important reading for journalists and students because it canvasses a range of issues relevant to media law topics covered in this chapter, and earlier in this book. These include:

- the principle of prior restraint and interlocutory injunctions in defamation cases
- whether Australian law recognises a tort of invasion of privacy
- whether corporations have a right to privacy
- relevance to privacy of the implied constitutional freedom of political communication
- trespass to land and whether the owner of premises has a right to restrain publication of film gained while a trespass is being committed.

A key lesson of relevance to this chapter is that the High Court approved the use of material by the media that might have been gained illegally by an unknown third party. If the ABC had been involved in the trespass in any way, the court might have restrained the publication—particularly if the broadcast contained confidential information, such as a secret technique of processing or equipment.

PRIVACY ACT 1988

In 1979, the Australian Law Reform Commission (ALRC) released a major report on privacy, *Unfair Publication: Defamation and Privacy*, recommending that a person be allowed to sue for damages or an injunction over publication of 'sensitive private facts' relating to health, private behaviour, home life, and personal or family relationships, which were likely to cause distress, annoyance or embarrassment. Defences were proposed if the publication was relevant to a topic of public interest (ALRC, 1979: 124–5).

A second law reform report in 1983, *Privacy*, recommended a *Privacy Act* to establish information privacy principles, and the appointment of a Privacy Commissioner. This was implemented in the *Privacy Act 1988*, which at first applied only to personal information held by Australian government departments and agencies, but was extended to larger private sector organisations in 2000. Media organisations were exempted from the provisions for their news operations as long as they ascribed to privacy standards published by their representative bodies.

The amendments established a separate set of privacy principles, known as the National Privacy Principles (NPP), which applied to the private sector. Designed mainly to protect consumers from having their personal details released to direct marketers, the changes gave ordinary citizens new data protections and imposed obligations upon the private sector for the protection of their clients and customers that previously were required only of government agencies. In 2014 the Australian Privacy Principles replaced the National Privacy Principles and the Information Privacy Principles. The new principles apply to both Australian government agencies and private-sector organisations covered by the *Privacy Act 1988*. The main updates included changes to data retention regulations, and the collection and storage of personal and other sensitive information (OAIC, 2014). The *Privacy Amendment (Notifiable Data Breaches) Act 2017* established the Notifiable Data Breaches (NDB) scheme, applying to all agencies and organisations with existing personal information security obligations under the *Privacy Act 1988*. It introduced an obligation to notify individuals whose personal information was involved in a data breach that was likely to result in serious harm. The Australian Information Commissioner must also be notified. The regime applied to Australian government agencies, businesses and not-for-profit organisations with an annual turnover of $3 million or more, credit reporting bodies and health service providers, among others.

'Personal information' was redefined after the reforms to mean:

> *information or an opinion about an identified individual, or an individual who is reasonably identifiable:*
> *(a) whether the information or opinion is true or not; and*
> *(b) whether the information or opinion is recorded in a material form or not.*

The changes gave citizens new powers to access information about themselves, to find out how it was being used and disclosed, to ensure that such information was accurate, to complain about its improper use and to get damages for hurt feelings if it had been used improperly. The Act applied to information collected during business transactions as well as information about people's private affairs. Full details of the requirements can be found at the Office of the Australian Information Commissioner's website, <www.oaic.gov.au/privacy/about-privacy>.

The site also lists determinations by the Privacy Commissioner. *LA's case* (2017) offers an example of someone winning compensation over a data breach. A retired Royal Australian Air Force employee won $12,000 in non-economic damages from the Department of Defence for interference to his privacy plus $3420 after his entire service medical records—including specialist appointments and assessments—were released to his son without his permission. The Privacy

Commissioner found Defence had failed to comply with Australian Privacy Principle 6 (APP 6), which provides that 'if an APP entity holds personal information about an individual that was collected for a particular purpose, the entity must not use or disclose the information for another purpose unless the individual has consented to the use or disclosure of the information' (*LA's case*, 2017, at 3).

THE JOURNALISM EXEMPTION AND THE PUSH FOR REFORM

When the *Privacy Act 1988* was first introduced, citizens obtained a right to approach an organisation and obtain any personal information held on them. The obligations had a substantial impact on media organisations, as advertising, marketing and circulation departments of media outlets have always made extensive use of direct marketing techniques and kept all sorts of information about their clients, advertisers, readers, viewers and listeners. However, their greater concern was the obligation to follow all of the new privacy protocols in the collection, storage and retrieval of information about people mentioned in their news stories. This would have put a prohibitive obligation on news outlets. After substantial lobbying by media companies and organisations such as the Australian Press Council (APC), a media exemption was developed. The new section 7B(4) of the *Privacy Act 1988* was titled 'Journalism', and read:

> *An act done, or practice engaged in, by a media organisation is exempt . . . if the act is done, or the practice is engaged in:*
> *(a) by the organisation in the course of journalism; and*
> *(b) at a time when the organisation is publicly committed to observe standards that:*
> *(i) deal with privacy in the context of the activities of a media organisation (whether or not the standards also deal with other matters); and*
> *(ii) have been published in writing by the organisation or a person or body representing a class of media organisations.*

Those representative bodies were the APC and the various broadcasting industry groups whose policies were registered with ACMA.

Importantly, the *Privacy Act* also respected the confidentiality that journalists owed to their sources. Under section 66(1A) of the Act, a journalist has a reasonable excuse for not giving information or answering a question, 'if giving the information, answering the question or producing the document or record would tend to reveal the identity of a person who gave information or a document or record to the journalist in confidence'. This was a welcome recognition of the importance of the journalist-source confidentiality relationship in a major piece of Commonwealth legislation.

In 2008, the ALRC recommended legislation creating a statutory cause of action for breach of privacy—a tort—where an individual had a 'reasonable expectation of privacy', with a cap for non-economic loss of $150,000 (ALRC, 2008). The Commission expressed concerns about the journalism exemption in the *Privacy Act 1988*, particularly with its broad scope, loose criteria and a lack of independent assessment of industry bodies' privacy standards. The Commission also questioned whether new media, such as internet publications and social media, would be covered by the exemptions (ALRC, 2008, para. 42.35); however, the journalism exemption survived intact.

In 2011, the federal government released an Issues Paper outlining a possible Commonwealth cause of action for a serious invasion of privacy (Commonwealth of Australia, 2011). Law reform bodies recommended similar state-based legislation in South Australia and Victoria in 2013 (ALRC, 2014, paras 1.46–1.47). The Convergence Review in 2012 flagged the withdrawal of the *Privacy Act* exemptions from media outlets that refused to join its proposed news standards regulatory system (Convergence Review, 2012). Those recommendations were not implemented.

An ALRC report in 2014 recommended that any new tort for the serious invasion of privacy should cover two types of behaviour—'intrusion upon seclusion' and 'misuse of private information' (ALRC, 2014, Recommendation 5-1). It would only be actionable where the plaintiff had a 'reasonable expectation of privacy in all the circumstances (Recommendation 6-1) and might be balanced by a court against freedom of expression and media freedom among other public interest factors (Recommendation 9-2).

The ALRC conducted an inquiry in 2015 into the encroachment by Commonwealth laws into traditional rights and freedoms. With regard to the relationship between privacy and free speech, it concluded: 'In the ALRC's view, there is no reason to suggest that privacy regulation unjustifiably interferes with freedom of speech' (ALRC, 2015: 122).

The NSW Standing Committee on Law and Justice published a report in March 2016 recommending legislation to protect individuals from serious invasions of privacy such as revenge porn. A Private Member's Bill entitled 'Civil Remedies for Serious Invasions of Privacy' was introduced to the NSW Parliament but lapsed later that year.

TRESPASS

A journalist has no special right of entry to someone else's property beyond that of an ordinary citizen. Under the tort of trespass, every person who is in possession of premises has the right to refuse others entry. You are liable for trespass if you:

- enter land or premises without the consent of the occupier
- remain there when permission to be there has been withdrawn, or
- place an object like a listening device or a camera on someone else's land or in their premises (Walker, 2000: 878).

The basic rule is that once the occupier has asked a journalist to leave the premises, the journalist should leave immediately or will be committing a trespass from that moment. Once an owner has asked someone to leave the premises and that person refuses, the owner can use reasonable force to remove them. The owner can also place certain conditions on granting access to the property. For example, an exclusive occupier of premises may impose a condition, enforceable by injunction, that an entrant not take photographs while the entrant remains on the premises (*Our Dogs case*, 1916).

A landmark case in the field was the *A Current Affair case* (2002), in which a reporter and film crew from Channel Nine's *A Current Affair* joined NSW Environment Protection Authority (EPA) staff in a raid on a property to determine whether environmental offences had occurred. The crew had cameras rolling as they entered the property and confronted the owner. He sued for damages to compensate him for his distress and mental trauma, and the trial judge awarded him $100,000, including aggravated and exemplary damages. The Court of Appeal agreed there had been a trespass without licence, but reduced the damages to $25,000, denying the landowner exemplary damages. The court held the following:

- The fact that the owner had not locked the gate to the property did not constitute an implied licence to enter and film.
- The film crew should reasonably have known that the owner would not consent to a film being taken during such a raid on his property.
- There was an implied licence for journalists to enter the land to request permission to film, but not to film without permission.
- Although the owner did make the statement, 'Right, I think that you'd better hang on until I've got a statement to make' and then 'I want no people here unless *A Current Affair* are prepared to do a deal with me' after the crew were already filming, he withdrew that within a few seconds—this brief exchange did not constitute an express licence to trespass.

The court warned public authorities not to invite journalists on such raids, known as 'ride-alongs'.

In short, there is an implied licence to enter a property to ask permission to conduct an interview or film, as long as there are no clear warning signs to the contrary. However, journalists should not interpret an official agency's invitation to accompany them on a raid as conferring any immunity from action for trespass, and media organisations can expect to pay substantial damages for the distress and humiliation they cause to someone as a result.

It is useful to look at this law in a positive rather than a negative light. Essentially, the law of trespass allows journalists to enter a person's property to seek an interview unless the interviewee has specifically restricted the purpose for which access to the property has been granted or has previously refused to be interviewed. It also allows journalists to interview, photograph and film people or their property from outside their land. If a neighbour grants you permission to use their property to do so, or if you capture the image while on public property, you are committing no trespass. (But be careful here, as other laws might apply—for example, Chief Justice Gleeson ruled in the *Lenah Game Meats case* in 2001 (at para. 34) that a photograph 'illegally or improperly or surreptitiously obtained, where what is depicted is private, may constitute confidential information'.)

Courts can award damages—even aggravated and exemplary damages—against trespassers, and in extremely rare circumstances can issue injunctions to prevent broadcast or publication of film taken by trespassers, and even information gained in interviews conducted while trespassing. The damages would be limited to those needed to compensate the plaintiff as a result of the trespass. Courts will normally issue such injunctions only if they believe publication would be 'unconscionable' and that irreparable harm would result.

For example, the NSW Supreme Court awarded $15,000 in general damages (plus special damages) against activists who trespassed into a piggery to film the state of the animals on behalf of the head of Animal Liberation NSW so he could make a cruelty report to the RSPCA. The trespassers convinced the court that their prime purpose was to expose allegedly cruel behaviour to the authorities and that they were unaware that Animal Liberation would issue media releases on the matter potentially damaging the commercial reputation of the pig farm operator. However, the piggery failed in its attempts to win an injunction to get possession of the video and photographs taken because the trespass did not meet the criteria for breach of confidence or unconscionability. The piggery also failed to have the copyright in the video and images assigned from the creators to them because of the trespass (*Piggery case*, 2011).

The law of trespass applies just as much to the hidden camera as it does to the obvious 'walk-in'. A sign prohibiting filming in premises is enough to render any film obtained in contravention of the sign the fruits of a trespass and potentially subject to an injunction restraining broadcast if the conduct was 'unconscionable' or involved a breach of confidence, and perhaps also the award of damages (Leder, 1994). Journalists also need to be aware of the impact of state legislation, such as the NSW *Surveillance Devices Act 2007*, on surreptitious filming.

NUISANCE

Nuisance protects an occupier's use or enjoyment of their land from unreasonable interference. Again, an injunction is the usual remedy sought, although damages can also be awarded. It will succeed only where the defendant has interfered with an interest of an occupier recognised by the courts. As with trespass, an injunction will be granted to prevent the publication of material obtained through nuisance, but only if publication would be 'unconscionable'. Generally, publication will go ahead on the basis that damages will be an adequate remedy, with the publisher facing the consequences later.

Essentially, the nuisance has to be persistent and annoying for it to be actionable. The rights of an occupier do not include a freedom from the view of neighbouring properties. However, constant, systematic surveillance, as might occur in a 'stake-out' by a group of noisy journalists just outside someone's home, with photographers continually filming into that person's premises, could be deemed nuisance. Continuous telephone calls that persist despite requests for them to cease could be considered a nuisance, while a series of phone calls merely seeking an interview for a story would not normally be considered as such (Walker, 2000: 881). Sometimes an apprehended violence order (AVO) is used as an alternative. In 2005, actress Nicole Kidman won a temporary restraining order against two magazine photographers who camped outside her Sydney property and followed her in a vehicle (Pearson, 2005). She planned to follow this up with an apprehended violence order, but her lawyers reached a confidential agreement with the photographers, under which they agreed not to take photographs near her home.

A classic Australian case in nuisance, as it is in privacy, is the *Victoria Park Racing case* (1937). The defendant Taylor's land overlooked a racecourse. He built a platform from which he allowed a radio station to broadcast its call of the races. This affected the racing club's attendances. The club sued, claiming nuisance in that the platform comprised an unlawful interference with its use of the racetrack. The court held that the mere overlooking of the land did not constitute an unlawful interference with the racing club's use of its property. It certainly affected its profitability, but this was a different issue. There was no detraction from the natural rights of enjoyment of the occupier. The crucial finding was that observation of someone from outside the bounds of their property would not normally be considered nuisance unless the behaviour was such that it was interfering with their enjoyment of that property.

West Australian Supreme Court Justice Kenneth Martin offered an excellent summary of nuisance law in the *Car Park case* (2016), where a company operating a public car park brought an action in private nuisance against the public transport authority to stop it removing a right-turn entry into its facility from an adjoining road. In refusing the application, Justice Martin traced the history of the case law in the area, including nuisance by picketing unionists—the closest equivalent to a pack of journalists occupying the footpath outside a residence.

Nuisance was also mentioned in the *Brown Protest case* in 2017, where the High Court ruled the anti-protest provisions of the Tasmanian *Workplaces (Protection from Protesters) Act 2014* (Tas) were invalid because they burdened the implied constitutional freedom to communicate on matters of politics and government. In his dissenting judgment, Justice Stephen Gageler pointed out that a forestry company could succeed in an action for nuisance against protesters whose conduct on business premises prevents, hinders or obstructs—interferes with—its business activity: 'There must be a material interference, beyond what is reasonable in the circumstances, with the plaintiff's use or enjoyment of the land or of the plaintiff's interest in the land.' He said picketing was not necessarily a nuisance and unlawful unless it became obstruction and besetting (*Brown Protest case*, paras 385–6). A similar line of argument might be applied to a media pack gathered outside someone's home or business, obstructing traffic and disturbing their access to their premises–although such behaviour would seemingly need to be continuously undertaken by the identifiable party being sued.

Professional communicators working internationally also need to be aware of a host of laws that might apply to their reporting methods or publishing procedures in other countries–which sometimes go well beyond the laws of trespass or nuisance. The journalist and three crew of the Nine Network current affairs program *60 Minutes* were arrested in Lebanon and spent two weeks in jail on kidnapping charges over their 2016 abduction in a Beirut street of children who were at the centre of a custody dispute between their Australian mother and Lebanese-Australian father, who was holding them in his care there. Only after extended diplomatic and legal representations did the team manage to return to Australia to face an internal review over the tactics they had used, with the producer losing his job over his role in the story (Ward, 2016).

SURVEILLANCE AND LISTENING DEVICES

Federal and state laws affect the use of surveillance and listening devices, and place a range of restrictions on the publication of reports gained by their use. Under Commonwealth law, it is an offence to intercept (listen to or record) a communication passing over a 'telecommunications system' without the knowledge of the person making the communication. This is detailed in section 7(1) of the *Telecommunications (Interception and Access) Act 1979*, which states:

> *A person shall not: (a) intercept; (b) authorize, suffer or permit another person to intercept; or (c) do any act or thing that will enable him or her or another person to intercept; a communication passing over a telecommunications system.*

A high-profile example of this was the interception of an uncomplimentary mobile phone conversation between former Victorian premier

Jeff Kennett and then federal shadow minister Andrew Peacock about future prime minister John Howard in 1987. Scanner enthusiasts recorded the very frank late-night chat, which caused a political uproar when it subsequently appeared on newspaper front pages.

Each of the states and territories also has legislation restricting the recording of a private conversation without the consent of all parties to the conversation by someone who is not a party. In Victoria, the law allows recording by a party to a conversation, as do the Northern Territory, New South Wales, South Australia, Tasmania and the ACT, subject to a twofold test: reasonable necessity, and no intention to re-publish. Northern Territory laws allow a party to record in the case of urgent public interest.

The legislation is called, in the respective states and territories:

- *Surveillance Devices Act* (Vic., WA, NT, NSW, SA)
- *Listening Devices Act* (Tasmania and ACT)
- *Invasion of Privacy Act* (Qld).

The NSW *Surveillance Devices Act* was updated in 2007 to reflect modern surveillance devices. It states in section 11 that:

> *A person must not publish, or communicate to any person, a private conversation or a record of the carrying on of an activity, or a report of a private conversation or carrying on of an activity, that has come to the person's knowledge as a direct or indirect result of the use of a listening device, an optical surveillance device or a tracking device in contravention of a provision of this Part.*

The general prohibition on listening devices applies to hidden tape recorders and cameras as well as emergency services radio scanners, illegal private eye-type bugging devices, and recording applications on smartphones and tablets: it applies to any equipment used to record or listen to a private conversation.

When surveillance devices are accompanied by other deception, criminal laws can come into play, as they did with a story by Channel

Nine's *A Current Affair* in 2002. The ABC's *Media Watch* reported that the program had hired undercover operatives to go into doctors' surgeries in Brisbane, Adelaide and Perth to try to expose the ease with which GPs issued medical certificates to 'sick' employees wanting some time off work. After a complaint from one of the doctors stung by the set-up, one of the undercover operatives was arrested and convicted of '[imposing] upon any person . . . by any false or fraudulent representation either orally or in writing . . . with a view to obtain money or other benefit or advantage' and fined $100 (*Media Watch*, 2002).

In 2005, paparazzo photographer Jamie Fawcett, was accused of planting a listening device outside actor Nicole Kidman's Sydney property. Police dropped the charges against him because they believed there was not enough evidence to satisfy a jury beyond reasonable doubt that Fawcett had planted the bug. When Fawcett later sued Fairfax, publisher of *The Sun-Herald* newspaper, for defamation, a Supreme Court justice found on the lower civil 'balance of probabilities' test that it was true that Fawcett had planted the bug. He lost the case (*Snapper case*, 2008).

In June 2007, Channel Seven Perth was prevented from broadcasting a private conversation between an employer and employee, which it had obtained using a hidden camera. The Court of Appeal held that even though the hidden camera recording confirmed that the employee had been terminated after informing a manager that she was pregnant, which the court found was a matter of proper and legitimate public interest, the issue could have been covered adequately without the broadcast of the secret recording (*Pregnant case*, 2007). That decision was followed in 2018 by another decision, when the Western Australian Supreme Court of Appeal dismissed the ABC's appeal against a trial judge's refusal to allow the broadcaster to show video footage of cattle being dehorned, secretly recorded by a cattle station employee in contravention of that state's *Surveillance Devices Act*. The court held that even though the footage had been played in open court during the trial of the animal cruelty case, it was open to the trial judge to conclude that publication of the illegally recorded footage would not materially enhance public debate on the issue (*Dehorning case*, 2018, para. 93).

Quinn (2011) points to other examples of Australian media use of surveillance techniques, including the following:

- *A Current Affair* reporter Ben Fordham and producer Andrew Byrne were charged in 2009 over the secret filming of a man as he ordered a $12,000 contract killing. They were found guilty in July 2010 of breaching the NSW *Listening Devices Act 1984*, but the charge was later dismissed.
- Private investigators hired by the rival tabloid television program *Today Tonight* posed as potential buyers of a helicopter owned by Larry Pickering, former cartoonist for *The Australian*. They secretly filmed and recorded Pickering piloting the helicopter.
- Investigative journalist Paul Barry used a hidden camera when interviewing serial killer Charles Sobraj in an Indian prison.

A surreptitious 'prank call' recording by DJs Mel Greig and Michael 'MC' Christian on Sydney's 2DAY-FM in 2012 made international news when they managed to get connected through to a nurse in a London hospital who was caring for the Duchess of Cambridge, then suffering morning sickness during her pregnancy with Prince George. The DJs put on voices purporting to be those of the Queen and Prince Charles. The global prank turned sour when the duty nurse who had connected the call through to the ward committed suicide and left a note blaming the humiliation of the episode for her despair. ACMA launched an investigation into whether the radio station had breached a condition of its licence prohibiting it from using its broadcasting service in the commission of an offence. The offence in question was a breach of the *Surveillance Devices Act 2007* (NSW). The station owner took ACMA to the Federal Court in 2013 to try to prevent it investigating the alleged breach, but Justice Edmonds ruled that the investigation could proceed. The High Court unanimously upheld his decision on appeal, ruling that ACMA did indeed have power to make an administrative determination that a licensee had committed a criminal offence as part of its processes, despite the fact that no court had found the offence proven (*Today FM case*, 2013 and 2015).

Whatever recording is done, it is likely to come under close scrutiny and legal advice should be sought before setting up or carrying out any form of phone recording, video surveillance or data-tracking. You should also avoid accessing people's internet and social media accounts without their permission. Hacking into someone's account to bypass their privacy settings can be a simple but illegal process, as detailed above.

OBSCENITY AND INDECENCY

The laws of obscenity and indecency are as much an issue of public taste as they are of privacy, and are of more concern to new media entrepreneurs, publishers and producers than to working journalists. Most news media reportage is done within the bounds of normal community standards, the yardstick the courts use to determine whether material is obscene or indecent. A range of provisions applies to control the circulation and broadcast of indecent material. The common law offence of publishing obscene material is only one.

State and territory criminal laws also typically prohibit obscene or indecent behaviour. For example, section 17(1) of the *Summary Offences Act 1966* (Vic) provides:

> *(1) Any person who in or near a public place or within the view or hearing of any person being or passing therein or thereon—*
> *(a) sings an obscene song or ballad;*
> *(b) writes or draws exhibits or displays an indecent or obscene word figure or representation;*
> *(c) uses profane indecent or obscene language or threatening abusive or insulting words; or*
> *(d) behaves in a riotous indecent offensive or insulting manner—*
> *shall be guilty of an offence.*

In 2014, an anti-abortion protester was convicted of displaying an obscene figure in a public place—the East Melbourne Fertility Clinic—

contrary to section 17(1)(b). She had been carrying placards featuring graphic images of the body parts of aborted foetuses. She appealed to the Victorian Supreme Court, arguing that the section should be ruled invalid because it unreasonably burdened her implied freedom of political communication. After reviewing the constitutional implied freedom case law, Justice Karin Emerton dismissed the appeal, concluding:

> *In my view, the prohibition of the display of obscene images in public places achieves an appropriate balance between freedom of political communication and the need to protect the public from unwitting and unwelcome exposure to images that are at the highest end of what is disgusting, repulsive, repugnant and offensive, having regard to contemporary standards.* (Foetus case, *2017, at para. 107)*

The decision should sound a warning to bloggers and alternative media producers at the protest/dissident end of the spectrum and to journalists reporting upon their activities, particularly if they wish to use offensive images or footage in their coverage.

Other restrictions on indecent or obscene material apply via the regulations under which material is allowed to be broadcast or printed. For example, the *Broadcasting Services Act 1992* attaches conditions to broadcasting licences (see <www.acma.gov.au>). The Commonwealth agency Australian Classification works with state and territory governments to patrol the classification of films, computer games and publications (see <www.classification.gov.au>).

PRIVACY AND THE ETHICAL REGULATORS

The question of intrusion into the lives of celebrities and public figures is as much an ethical question as it is a legal one. Much of the debate about privacy is in the realm of ethics rather than law, and the enforcement of such ethical standards is in the province of self-regulatory bodies like the APC rather than in the laws of the land. As we saw earlier, section 7B(4) of the *Privacy Act* offers a journalism exemption from onerous record-keeping obligations to large media companies, as long as they subscribe to the privacy standards of their representative bodies. In broadcast journalism, such transgressions fall within codes of conduct of industry groups regulated by ACMA.

Privacy also features in the MEAA Journalist Code of Ethics. In 1984, the Australian Journalists' Association (AJA) revised its 1944 Code of Ethics to include a new clause (9) requiring journalists to 'respect private grief and personal privacy' and providing that they 'shall have the right to resist compulsion to intrude on them' (MEAA, 1996). It preserved these elements at Clause 11 of a 1999 revision of the Code, which was the version in existence in 2018.

Most newspaper publishers are members of the Australian Press Council (APC), whose Statement of General Principles was revised in 2014 (see Appendix 2). The privacy general principles read as follows:

> Privacy and avoidance of harm
>
> 5 *Avoid intruding on a person's reasonable expectations of privacy, unless doing so is sufficiently in the public interest.*
>
> 6 *Avoid causing or contributing materially to substantial offence, distress or prejudice, or a substantial risk to health or safety, unless doing so is sufficiently in the public interest.* (APC, 2014)

Its extended 'Statement of Privacy Principles' is published at <www.presscouncil.org.au/statements-of-principles>.

ACMA is responsible for the regulation of the broadcast media. Under the *Broadcasting Services Act 1992*, the various broadcasting industry sectors set their own programming guidelines in the form of codes of practice, outlined on ACMA's website at <www.acma.gov.au>. ACMA has registered codes of practice for all broadcasting sectors other than the ABC and SBS, which have their own codes notified to ACMA. Most of the industry codes have special requirements relating to news and current affairs programs, which in turn address privacy as an issue.

ACMA has certain requirements for the handling of complaints about such matters, with mediation between the broadcaster and the complainant being the first mechanism, working through to a determination of the matter by ACMA's own investigators. ACMA has a range of penalties available to it under the Act, with the ultimate being the suspension of a broadcaster's licence, through to substantial fines, imposition of conditions on the licensee, and down to counselling and training of personnel.

The main broadcasting industry codes covering privacy are Free TV Australia's Code of Practice, Commercial Radio Australia's Code of Practice, the ABC's Editorial Policy and its Charter of Editorial Practice, and the SBS Codes of Practice.

ACMA published an updated set of *Privacy Guidelines for Broadcasters* in 2016, providing an overview of how ACMA assesses complaints by listeners or viewers that allege breaches of the privacy provisions in the codes. The 2016 updates incorporated amendments to codes of practice since the last major revision in 2011, included new case studies of key ACMA privacy investigation decisions; updated references to personal information; and clarified ACMA's approach to consent, material in the public domain and children's privacy (ACMA, 2016). Importantly, the guidelines stated that someone could withdraw their consent before broadcast if it was reasonable to do so (2016: 4). Further, special care needs to be taken when using material about a child or a 'vulnerable' person—who might, for example, have a mental illness or perhaps be traumatised by a distressing news event (2016: 5).

TIPS FOR MINDFUL PRACTICE

- Do not enter someone's property for an interview without their permission—leave when asked to do so.
- Research and comply with data-protection laws if you plan to collect or trade in personal information. Public relations and marketing personnel will not usually qualify for the journalism exemptions to *Privacy Act* requirements.
- Never breach a court order banning someone's identification.
- Blog, tweet and report on matters that are clearly in the public domain, not about people's private lives.

- Always identify yourself as a journalist (if you are one) when about to conduct an interview; do not commence recording until the interviewee has given their permission, and ask them to repeat their assent once recording has started.
- Carefully study the privacy clauses in the codes of ethical practice applying to your medium.

IN A NUTSHELL

- There is no common law right to privacy in Australia, although a number of laws go part of the way to protecting the privacy of citizens, and there are moves towards establishing such a right, especially in the wake of the 2001 *Lenah Game Meats case*.
- The *Privacy Act 1988* features some exemptions for journalism, but is generally a block to the free flow of information. Recent law reform reports have recommended narrowing the media exemption or making compliance part of a new media regulatory system.
- The internet and social media raise privacy concerns at an international level.
- A journalist has no special right of entry to someone else's property above that of an ordinary citizen. Under the law of trespass, every person who is in possession of premises has the right to refuse others entry to those premises.
- The basic rule of trespass is that, once the occupier has asked someone to leave their premises, the person should do so or they will be committing a trespass.
- Nuisance is an area of the law that protects an occupier's use or enjoyment of their land from unreasonable interference. It might only be applied to the media in extreme circumstances of disruption or blockage to access.
- Under federal law, it is an offence to intercept (listen to or record) a communication passing over a 'telecommunications system' without the knowledge of the person making the communication.

- Each of the states and territories also has a *Surveillance Devices Act* or equivalent that prohibits the recording of a private conversation without the consent of all parties to the conversation, in particular by someone who is not a party to the conversation. This is subject to some narrow exceptions.
- Several provisions apply to control the circulation and broadcast of indecent material. The common law offence of publishing obscene material is only one. Others operate via the regulations under which material is allowed to be broadcast or printed.
- Each of the main industry bodies has codes or principles that journalists and media organisations are expected to follow, and each has a set of privacy requirements and complaint procedures.

DISCUSSION QUESTIONS

12.1 You work for the leading celebrity news blog eXposed! The 21-year-old daughter of your city mayor is rumoured to have been involved romantically with a married international football star. Your sister happens to be her Facebook 'friend', and she shows you several images from her social media page of the pair taking cocaine and in intimate embraces at a Pacific island resort. Your eXposed! editor demands you use the photos and screen captures of the social media evidence in an exclusive scoop on the celebrity affair. What is your legal position?

12.2 Identify a new portable communication technology or application that has just come on the market. List the ways journalists might be able to use this in their reportage, and also list the dangers they might present under the listening devices and surveillance legislation in your jurisdiction.

12.3 Buy or borrow a celebrity gossip magazine. Find three examples of privacy intrusion and explain how they could breach the law or the various codes of ethics or practice. Think of public-interest arguments that an editor might use to justify their publication.

12.4 Search online to find a recent example of an intrusion into privacy that has prompted legal action. Compare and contrast it with one of the cases in this chapter.

REFERENCES

Australian Communications and Media Authority (ACMA) 2016, *Privacy Guidelines for Broadcasters*, ACMA, Melbourne, <https://acma.gov.au/theACMA/Library/Industry-library/Broadcasting/privacy-broadcasting>.

Australian Law Reform Commission (ALRC) 1979, *Unfair Publication: Defamation and Privacy*, ALRC, Canberra, <www.alrc.gov.au/report-11>.

—— 1983, *Privacy*, ALRC, Canberra, <www.alrc.gov.au/report-22>.

—— 2008, *For Your Information: Australian Privacy Law and Practice*, ALRC, Canberra, <www.alrc.gov.au/publications/report-108>.

—— 2014, *Serious Invasions of Privacy in the Digital Era*, ALRC, Canberra, <www.alrc.gov.au/publications/serious-invasions-privacy-digital-era-alrc-report-123>

—— 2015, *Traditional Rights and Freedoms: Encroachments by Commonwealth Laws—Final Report*, December 2015, ALRC, Sydney, <www.alrc.gov.au/sites/default/files/pdfs/publications/alrc_129_final_report_.pdf>.

Australian Press Council (APC) 2014, *Statements of Principles*, APC, Sydney, <www.presscouncil.org.au/statements-of-principles>.

Commonwealth of Australia, Department of Prime Minister and Cabinet 2011, *Issues Paper: A Statutory Cause of Action for Serious Invasion of Privacy*, Commonwealth Government, Canberra, <www.ag.gov.au/Consultations/Documents/Righttosueforseriousinvasionofpersonalprivacy-issuespaper/Issues%20Paper%20-%20Statutory%20Cause%20of%20Action%20-%20Serious%20Invasion%20of%20Privacy%20-%20PDF.pdf>.

Convergence Review 2012, *Convergence Review: Final Report*, Department of Broadband, Communications and the Digital Economy, Canberra, <www.dbcde.gov.au/__data/assets/pdf_file/0007/147733/Convergence_Review_Final_Report.pdf>.

Finkelstein, R. 2012, *Report of the Independent Inquiry into the Media and Media Regulation*, Department of Broadband, Communications and the Digital Economy, Canberra, <www.archive.dbcde.gov.au/2013/august/independent_media_inquiry>.

Greenfield, P. 2018, 'The Cambridge Analytica files: the story so far,' *The Guardian*, 26 March, <www.theguardian.com/news/2018/mar/26/the-cambridge-analytica-files-the-story-so-far>.

Gunter, J. 2011, 'Journalist could face jail over alleged injunction breach on Twitter', <www.journalism.co.uk/news/journalist-could-face-jail-over-alleged-injunction-breach-on-twitter/s2/a544262/>.

Henry, N., Powell, A. and Flynn, A. 2017, *Not Just 'Revenge Pornography': Australians' Experiences of Image-based Abuse—A Summary Report*, RMIT University, Melbourne, <www.rmit.edu.au/content/dam/rmit/documents/college-of-design-and-social-context/schools/global-urban-and-social-studies/revenge_porn_report_2017.pdf>.

Leder, R. 1994, 'The law of the hidden camera', *Medialine*, 1: 7.

Leveson, B. 2012, *Report of An Inquiry into the Culture, Practice and Ethics of the Press*, The Stationery Office, London, <www.official-documents.gov.uk/document/hc1213/hc07/0780/0780.asp>.

Media, Entertainment and Arts Alliance (MEAA) 1996, 'AJA Code of Ethics 1944', in *Ethics Review Committee Final Report*, <www.gwb.com.au/99a/ethics.html>.

Media Watch 2002, 'Sickie sneaky', 12 August, <www.abc.net.au/mediawatch/transcripts/120802_s2.htm>.

NSW Standing Committee on Law and Justice 2016, *Remedies for the Serious Invasion of Privacy in New South Wales*, NSW Government, Sydney, <www.parliament.nsw.gov.au/committees/DBAssets/InquiryReport/ReportAcrobat/6043/Report%20no%2057%20Remedies%20for%20the%20serious%20invasion%20of%20.pdf>.

Office of the Australian Information Commissioner (OAIC) 2014, 'Privacy fact sheet 17: Australian privacy principles', <www.oaic.gov.au/privacy/privacy-resources/privacy-fact-sheets/other/privacy-fact-sheet-17-australian-privacy-principles>.

Office of the High Commissioner for Human Rights 1976, *International Covenant on Civil and Political Rights*, <www.ohchr.org/en/professional interest/pages/ccpr.aspx>.

Pearson, M. 2005, 'Press freedom suffers for celebrity security', *The Australian*, 3 February.

Pwenneke, S. 2005, 'Kaiser Permanente sues blogger over patient information', <www.blogherald.com/2005/03/18/kaiser-permanente-sues-blogger-over-patient-information>.

Quinn, K. 2011, 'Private eyes and media lies', *The Age*, 23 July, <www.theage.com.au/national/private-eyes-and-media-lies-20110722-1hsvb.html#ixzz1T4Tg57oy>.

Reuters 2011, 'UK Twitter users banned from identifying brain damaged woman', *Sydney Morning Herald*, 16 May, <www.smh.com.au/technology/technology-news/uk-twitter-users-banned-from-identifying-braindamaged-woman-20110516-1eow5.html>.

South Australian Weekly Chronicle 1882, 'The Late Libel case', 22 April, <http://trove.nla.gov.au/ndp/del/article/91293216>.

Stillito, D. 2016, 'Celebrity injunction: PJS cannot be named, says Supreme Court', *BBC News*, 19 May, <www.bbc.com/news/uk-36329818>.

Sydney Gazette and New South Wales Advertiser 1830, 'Varieties', <http://trove.nla.gov.au/ndp/del/article/2194344>.

United Nations 2011, *Universal Declaration of Human Rights*, <www.un.org/en/documents/udhr>.

Walker, S. 2000, *Media Law: Commentary and Materials*, Law Book Company, Sydney.

Ward, M. 2016, '*60 Minutes* producer exits as internal review finds major faults with Lebanon story', *Mumbrella*, 27 May, <https://mumbrella.com.au/60-minutes-producer-exits-internal-review-finds-major-faults-story-369843>.

Warren, S. and Brandeis, L. 1890, 'The right to privacy', *Harvard Law Review*, 4(5): 193–220.

CASES CITED

Brown Protest case: Brown v Tasmania [2017] HCA 43, <www.austlii.edu.au/cgi-bin/viewdoc/au/cases/cth/HCA/2017/43.html>.

Car Park case: Shogunn Investments Pty Ltd v Public Transport Authority of Western Australia [2016] WASC 42, <www.austlii.edu.au/cgi-bin/viewdoc/au/cases/wa/WASC/2016/42.html>.

A Current Affair case: TCN Channel Nine Pty v Anning [2002] NSWCA 82 (25 March 2002), <www.austlii.edu.au/au/cases/nsw/NSWCA/2002/82.html>.

Dehorning case: Australian Broadcasting Corporation v Sawa Pty Ltd [2018] WASCA 29, <www.austlii.edu.au/cgi-bin/viewdoc/au/cases/wa/WASCA/2018/29.html>.

Disability case: Doe v Yahoo!7 Pty Ltd & Anor; Wright v Pagett and Ors [2013] QDC 181, <www.austlii.edu.au/au/cases/qld/QDC/2013/181.html>.

Douglas Wedding case: Douglas v Hello! Ltd [2001] 2 WLR 992; [2001] 2 All ER 289.

Foetus case: Fraser v County Court of Victoria & Anor [2017] VSC 83, <www.austlii.edu.au/cgibin/viewdoc/au/cases/vic/VSC/2017/83.html>.

Grubb case: no. 1—Ben Grubb and Telstra Corporation Limited [2015] AICmr 35, <www7.austlii.edu.au/cgi-bin/viewdoc/au/cases/cth/AICmr/2015/35.html#fnB3>; *no. 2—Privacy Commissioner v Telstra Corporation Limited* [2017] FCAFC 4, <www.judgments.fedcourt.gov.au/judgments/Judgments/fca/full/2017/2017fcafc0004>.

Holly Candy case: Candy v Bauer Media Limited [2013] NSWSC 979 (20 July 2013).

Hosking Twins case: Hosking & Hosking v Simon Runting & Anor [2004] NZCA 34 (25 March 2004), <www.austlii.edu.au/nz/ cases/NZCA/2004/34.html>.

Jane Doe case: Jane Doe v Australian Broadcasting Corporation [2007] VCC 281, <www.glj.com.au/files/doevabcjudg.pdf>.

Judges' Tapes cases: no. 1—Carmody v Information Commissioner & Ors [2018] QCATA15, <https://archive.sclqld.org.au/qjudgment/2018/QCATA18-015.pdf>; *no. 2—Carmody v Information Commissioner & Ors* [2018] QCATA 19, <www.austlii.edu.au/cgi-bin/viewdoc/au/cases/qld/QCATA/2018/19.html>.

LA's case: 'LA' and Department of Defence [2017] AICmr 25, <www.oaic.gov.au/resources/privacy-law/determinations/2017-aicmr-25.pdf>.

Lenah Game Meats case: ABC v Lenah Game Meats Pty Ltd (2001) 208 CLR 199, <www.austlii.edu.au/au/cases/cth/high_ct/2001/63.html>.

Mosley case: Mosley v News Group Newspapers Ltd [2008] EWHC 1777 (QB) High Court of Justice, Eady J (24 July 2008), <www.bailii.org/ew/cases/EWHC/QB/2008/1777.html>.

Nauru Detention case: Australian Broadcasting Corporation and Department of Home Affairs (Freedom of information) [2018] AICmr 24 (20 February 2018), <www.austlii.edu.au/cgi-bin/viewdoc/au/cases/cth/AICmr/2018/24.html>.

Our Dogs case: Sports and General Press Agency Ltd v 'Our Dogs' Publishing Co. Ltd [1916] 2 KB 880.

Piggery case: Windridge Farm Pty Ltd v Grassi and Ors [2011] NSWSC 196, <www.austlii.edu.au/cgi-bin/viewdoc/au/cases/nsw/NSWSC/2011/196.html>.

Pregnant case: Channel 7 Perth Pty Ltd v 'S' (A Company) [2007] WASCA 122 (12 June 2007), <www.austlii.edu.au/au/cases/wa/WASCA/2007/122.html>.

Princess cases: von Hannover v Germany (Application No. 59320/00) 2004 ECHR 294 (24 June 2004), <www.worldlii.org/eu/cases/ECHR/2004/294.html>; *von Hannover v Germany (No. 3)* [2013] ECHR 835, <www.bailii.org/eu/cases/ECHR/2013/835.html>.

Revenge Porn case: Wilson v Ferguson [2015] WASC 15, <www.austlii.edu.au/cgi-bin/sinodisp/au/cases/wa/WASC/2015/15.html>.

Royal Etchings case: Prince Albert v Strange [1849] EngR 255; (1849) 1 Mac & G 25; 41 ER 1171, <www.worldlii.org/int/cases/EngR/1849/255.pdf>.

Sex Tapes case: Giller v Procopets [2008] VSCA 236 (10 December 2008), <www.austlii.edu.au/cgi-bin/sinodisp/au/cases/vic/VSCA/2008/236.html>.

Snapper case: Fawcett v John Fairfax Publications Pty Ltd [2008] NSWSC 139 (27 February 2008), <www.austlii.edu.au/cgi-bin/sinodisp/au/cases/nsw/NSWSC/2008/139.html>.

Sunshine Coast Mayor case: Grosse v Purvis [2003] QDC 151 (16 June 2003), <www.austlii.edu.au/au/cases/qld/QDC/2003/151.html>.

Supermodel case: Campbell v MGN Ltd [2004] UKHL 22, <www.bailii.org/uk/cases/UKHL/2004/22.html>.

Thomas's case: NewsGroup Newspapers Limited v Imogen Thomas (2011) EWHC 1232 (QB) 2011 HQ11XO1432.

Three-way case: PJS v News Group Newspapers Ltd [2016] UKSC 26, <www.supremecourt.uk/cases/docs/uksc-2016-0080-judgment.pdf>.

Today FM case: Today FM (Sydney) Pty Ltd v Australian Communications and Media Authority [2013] FCA 1157, <www.judgments.fedcourt.gov.au/judgments/Judgments/fca/single/2013/2013fca1157>; *Australian Communications and Media Authority v Today FM (Sydney) Pty Ltd* [2015] HCA 7, <www.austlii.edu.au/cgi-bin/viewdoc/au/cases/cth/HCA/2015/7.html>

Victoria Park Racing case: Victoria Park Racing and Recreation Grounds Co. Ltd v Taylor (1937) 58 CLR 479, <www.austlii.edu.au/au/cases/cth/HCA/1937/45.html>.

CHAPTER 13

The law of public relations, freelancing and new media entrepreneurship

KEY CONCEPTS

Negligence
A legal action available to someone who has suffered damage as a result of the defendant's breach of duty to take reasonable care where the defendant should have been be able to foresee that the plaintiff might risk injury.

Contract
A legally enforceable promise that is central to the operations of business, requiring an intention to contract, an agreement between the parties (an offer and a matching acceptance) and 'consideration'—something of value exchanged to demonstrate commitment to the contract.

Unfair dismissal
An employee has been unfairly dismissed if the Fair Work Commission finds that their dismissal was harsh, unjust or unreasonable, and that it was not a case of genuine redundancy. Some cases following an employee's misuse of social media have been upheld as justifiable dismissals.

Professional indemnity insurance
Insurance policies covering the insured professional up to an agreed limit for legal costs, damages awards or settlement payouts, typically covering negligence, incompetence, intellectual property infringements including breach of copyright, missed deadlines, breaches of consumer law, defamation, breach of privacy and breach of confidence.

While this book is titled *The Journalist's Guide to Media Law*, its subtitle—'A handbook for communicators in a digital world'—reflects the broad range of professionals who now need a basic understanding of media law and related legal risks they may encounter. Some of you are journalists who have applied your skills to new fields after careers in traditional news media. Others are journalism students who have seized an opportunity in an allied field of public relations, media relations or government communications after graduation. And of course there are those of you whose training or career has been in another field but who now work full or part time as specialist bloggers or freelance writers in your areas of expertise, or who are engaged as entrepreneurs in news-related digital media ventures. This chapter introduces legal topics important to each of these occupations—and also provides students with an important revision of key media law principles as they apply to these professional communication contexts.

BACKGROUND AND INTERNATIONAL CONTEXT

For most of the past century, there has been considerable cross-pollination between careers in journalism, public relations, and government and business affairs. Journalists have switched to become media advisers to politicians, or to start their own public relations consultancies. Many have been hired as communications officers with government departments and agencies. Reporters have carved out successful freelance careers as photojournalists or stringers for international wire agencies, or as specialist writers or commentators in their niche fields in sports, science, finance or politics. A select few have started with a single media operation or an idea for a media business and have built that into a successful financial enterprise. International media mogul Rupert Murdoch inherited ownership of Adelaide newspaper *The News* in 1953 and over six decades built that into the multinational media conglomerates News Corp and 21st Century Fox, as we know them today. We are starting to see digital equivalents, such as Greek-born Arianna Huffington who transcended traditional media by surfing the rise of the internet with the establishment of the *Huffington Post* (now *Huffpost*), which alongside *BuzzFeed* is regarded as one of the most successful digital news start-ups; in 2018 these two publications had a combined value of more than $1 billion.

The worlds of the internet and social media cover a gamut of news-related platforms, applications and operations, many created by journalists who have seen a chance in the new media environment and grabbed it. The team behind the Dublin-based social media news agency Storyful is an excellent example. Foreign correspondent and news anchor Mark Little watched the Arab Spring unfold on YouTube and brought together other journalists and technology experts to create a successful business model combining the best aspects of twentieth-century news agency systems with the exciting new field of citizen journalism and crowd-sourcing of news and information. They sold to News Corp in 2013 for $25 million.

Audience adoption of digital technologies heralds the new era of interactive media, where innovative models of news-gathering and delivery have their own legal challenges. The changing landscape was summed up by the Senate Select Committee on the Future of Public Interest Journalism:

> *Perhaps the most common theme in evidence received from the media sector was the struggle to adapt to new business models, including the implications of the move away from a reliance on revenue from advertising and newspaper sales, toward monetising the publication of material on masthead sites, and through the aggregators. (Senate Select Committee, 2018: 25)*

This dynamic environment positions audiences in the box seat to choose the content they want—and rewards adaptable communicators and entrepreneurs who can navigate the law in a range of new media and business situations.

All three careers—public relations, freelancing and media entrepreneurship—entail some distinct but overlapping legal considerations. Some involve unique applications of the media laws we have covered in this book, including defamation, confidentiality, privacy and intellectual property. New legal dilemmas arise from the digital environment in which we now work; others involve commercial law issues associated with establishing and operating any small business—consumer law, contract, negligence and employment law. Government regulatory, co-regulatory and self-regulatory regimes also come into play. The scope of these sometimes disparate areas of law means that a comprehensive account of all of them is well beyond the capacity of this chapter—but we hope to offer a starting point for students still weighing up career choices, and for qualified journalists who might be considering a career change.

Public relations professionals, freelancers and new media entrepreneurs cannot be legal experts unless they have completed a law degree and spent many years practising or teaching law, but they should have a basic understanding of the areas of law that affect their work, so they can hear the alarm bells and seek expert legal advice when a situation is escalating into a genuine legal problem. This is a crucial part of risk identification and crisis management—key elements of business administration and public relations courses.

MEDIA LAW PERSPECTIVES FOR PUBLIC RELATIONS PRACTITIONERS, FREELANCERS AND NEW MEDIA ENTREPRENEURS

In this section, we pick up on some of the topics from previous chapters and consider special issues that arise for those working in public relations, freelancing or starting their own new media businesses. The media laws we have been examining throughout this book can certainly affect public relations consultants when they are performing journalism-type tasks—perhaps when writing and sending media releases as media relations officers or when creating internal and external publications, videos and social media postings as government communications personnel. Of course, freelance journalists encounter the same areas of media law as their colleagues, who are full-time employees of media corporations—although, as we will see, they may not always have the same protections. And new media entrepreneurs need to be across media and publishing laws internationally: their business model depends upon it.

DEFAMATION AND INJURIOUS FALSEHOOD

Public relations involves the management of many reputations—those of key personnel, corporations and brands—and as we learned in Chapters 7 and 8, defamation is all about reputations. When a personal or corporate reputation is damaged by some kind of publication—or when a business loses money because of fake news—we enter the legal domains of defamation and injurious falsehood. As a public relations practitioner, you may encounter these from either side: you or your client might end up bringing an action, or may be the target of one.

Media relations can be a particular area of concern: words spoken at media conferences in Adelaide and Perth were at the centre of defamation actions in 2012 and 2017. In the *Nightclub case*, a Hindley Street nightclub owner called a press conference to announce an initiative to increase public safety and reduce violence in the central Adelaide precinct. Almost two years later, he sued a neighbouring travel agency operator over a statement he alleged she had uttered in the midst of that media conference. He claimed the travel agency owner had announced loudly to the media gathered at the conference that he—the nightclub owner—was responsible for all the violence in Hindley Street. After hearing from several witnesses (including the nightclub's public relations consultant), the District Court judge found for the defendant. He said it was more likely the interjector had not made such a blatant defamatory allegation against the nightclub owner and, even if she had, he would only have awarded $7500 in damages. There was no evidence of a recording having been made of the words she had spoken.

However, words spoken by a detective in a media conference resulted in Western Australia's highest award of defamation damages in 2017. Detective Senior Sergeant Jack Lee had described Perth barrister Lloyd Rayney as the 'prime' and 'only' suspect in widely broadcast press conferences about the investigation into his wife Corryn's 2007 murder (*Barrister's Wife case*, 2017). Rayney was acquitted of her murder in 2012 in one of the state's highest profile cases. He then proceeded to sue the state over the detective's comments in those media conferences back in 2007 and won $2.623 million in damages. The Western Australian

Supreme Court held that the state was not entitled to the qualified privilege defence because Detective Lee had gone

> *far beyond what was appropriate in the circumstances with which he was confronted, and, especially having regards to the seriousness of the offence being investigated and the obvious professional damage that loose language would inflict on Mr Rayney. (para. 165)*

Errors and misstatements meant the detective had not exercised reasonable care in his responses to questions, losing the statutory qualified privilege defence, and went beyond a police officer's duty to keep the public informed, thus forfeiting the common law qualified privilege defence (para. 173). (The quantum of damages was subject to appeal when this edition went to press.)

This followed the line of reasoning by the South Australian Supreme Court's Full Court when it rejected the SA Police use of the qualified privilege defence in a defamation case brought by a former newspaper photographer who was a suspect in a murder (*Murder Suspect case*, 2015). The court held that a media release and a press conference hosted by police 'fell wholly outside the interest or duty of the police to provide information necessary to obtain such assistance from the public as may potentially be available and outside the interest of members of the public to receive such information'. There was no public interest to be served by police going into the details of the crime or the state of their investigation or the fact of their suspicions at that time in relation to the suspect (at paras 437–8).

The NSW Supreme Court held in the *Councillor's case* (2017) that giving an interview to a journalist or hosting a press conference renders whoever is speaking responsible for any defamatory material conveyed in that interview or press conference because they 'both intended its republication and understood it would be republished, either in whole or in part' (at para. 64). The court ruled that, 'In the circumstances of a press conference, or interview by the press, express authority or a request to publish is not necessary' (at para. 65).

In the *Born Brands case* (2013), two media releases had vastly different consequences for the manufacturers of a device to help better position infants during sleep. The first was particularly successful, generating a news segment on *Brisbane Extra* about its Babywedge product and an appearance on national morning television (at para. 8). But the second media release–emanating from the US Consumer Product Safety Commission (CPSC)–caused unexpected damage because it warned consumers against using infant sleep positioners. Babywedge then featured on a Channel 9 news segment among other such products in a story about the potential dangers of infant sleep positioners (at para. 14). As part of the fallout from the crisis, Born Brands sued the Nine Network for both defamation and injurious falsehood, claiming the news item damaged its reputation as a small corporation (fewer than 10 employees) and that it contained false statements, published with malice, which had caused it actual financial loss (injurious falsehood). However, the company found no relief because the television network managed to defend both actions successfully, with the court finding the statements were not false and no malice was proven (paras 184–9).

We learned in Chapter 7 that 'defamatory matter' can include all kinds of published material, including emails or social media communications–broadly, anything you or your client might produce for distribution. In the *DVD case* in Western Australia in 2006, the consultancy Professional Public Relations (PPR) was ordered to provide all records it had about a DVD recording that criticised a proposed brickworks: the director of a building materials company claimed the DVD conveyed defamatory statements about him and his company. He suspected a rival building materials company–a client of PPR–was behind the production, and wanted this confirmed so that he could commence legal action.

We explained in Chapter 7 that a plaintiff can sue anyone responsible for a publication–and that might include the freelancer who has written the piece as well as the media outlet that publishes it. Freelance journalists need to be extra cautious about potential defamation actions because they may not have the backing of a major media organisation when trying to defend a lawsuit. This is particularly the case if they are reporting for a foreign media outlet or a small online start-up that might not have the resources to defend an action brought against it, in which case the journalist can expect to be sued personally. Freelancers can also be caught out if they have not yet sold their story to a media outlet and they are sued over their other communications about their work—especially tweets that might not give the full context of a story, or contain sufficient context to qualify for a defence (as we saw in the *Treasurer case* in Chapter 7). Some freelancers post 'teasers' about their work on their private blog posts or use crowd-funding software to showcase their stories to potential buyers. These can leave the individual as a target for a defamation suit. All of this is even more reason to ensure that you are covered by professional liability insurance, either through an organisation like the MEAA's Freelance Pro (MEAA, 2018) or privately through an insurance broker.

NEW MEDIA PLATFORM RESPONSIBILITY AND THE COMMENTS OF THIRD PARTIES

New media entrepreneurs need to be mindful of the decisions in the *Search Engine cases* (2012–18). Melbourne man Michael Trkulja won $200,000 in damages from Google and $225,000 from Yahoo! after his image and name appeared in search results for underworld criminal figures and the multinational outlets refused to remove them when asked. After a separate action over further instances of search results for Melbourne underworld figures showing images of him, and autocomplete predictions on a search for his name prompting an association with criminal identities, in 2018 Mr Trkulja won a High Court appeal against a Victorian Court of Appeal ruling that he had no real prospect of success proving any of the imputations were capable of being conveyed by the search engine results.

The ruling is particularly relevant to new media start-ups developing software, applications or even games that might associate identifiable people with damaging key words, or with others who may have dubious reputations. While the *Broadcasting Services Act 1992* provides a degree of protection to internet service providers and content hosts from state and territory laws, including the law of defamation, it is crucial to observe that any protection stops at least from the moment you become aware of the nature of the offending content: if in doubt, block it or take it down while you investigate. In some cases—depending upon your level of involvement with the publication—you might be held responsible at an earlier juncture.

The main decision on this was the *Allergy Pathway case* (2011—see Key Case 1.1), which centred on a breach of consumer law. Justice Ray Finkelstein ruled that a company was responsible for statements made by others on its website and social media pages. We turn to this case as the major precedent examining the responsibility of social media hosts and website publishers for the comments of third parties on their platforms. Regulatory bodies such as the Advertising Standards Bureau have since followed this decision in subsequent cases. The extent to which you might be immediately liable for an offending comment or whether you would be protected by taking it down within a 'reasonable' time have yet to be determined. Certainly, Justice Finkelstein's decision suggests you would need to take reasonable steps to remove any such comments the instant they are brought to your attention; in the contempt space, a *sub judice* contempt charge will focus upon how long the comments remained available, and how likely it was that a potential juror or witness would have seen them.

A series of cases since *Allergy Pathway* have further refined publisher responsibility for third-party comments. Some have harked back to a 1937 English case, the *Golf Club case*, where the secretary of a golf club and its owner were found liable for a poem defaming a member of the club that had been pinned to the club's noticeboard. The court deemed them 'secondary publishers' of the notice because they failed to remove it after they had been notified of its content.

This approach has been echoed in recent cases involving internet search companies, with the courts holding them liable, considering them 'secondary publishers' if they do not take down the material within a reasonable time after it has been brought to their attention.

However, the roles of publishers across media and social media platforms can vary markedly, so Australian courts have opted to consider the facts of the particular internet publishing scenario and the publisher's role in the process, a course of action advised by the New Zealand Court of Appeal in *Murray's case*:

> *[W]e think it is important to focus on the particular factual situation before the Court. Our analysis of the authorities shows how sensitive the outcome can be to the particular circumstances of the publication. The fact that many of the authorities relate to publication in one form or another on the internet does not provide any form of common theme, because of the different roles taken by the alleged publisher in each case. (at para. 125)*

The special nature of responsibility for publishing a Facebook page came under the microscope in 2015 in the *Facebook Page case*. There, Justice John Dixon applied these five key principles when considering publisher liability on Facebook (at para. 37):

- *a* *A defendant who has not authored or been first publisher of defamatory material might still be a primary publisher if they were complicit in authorising the communication or failed to take reasonable care to prevent its publication. The defendant needed to know of the content, though not necessarily that it was defamatory.*
- *b* *A defendant can still be a primary publisher if they were not complicit in its creation but had the ability to control whether publication occurred if they exercised control over publication independently of the author at the time of publication.*
- *c* *A defendant would be a subordinate (secondary) publisher if they acquired knowledge of the defamatory material (such as a defamatory comment posted to Facebook).*
- *d* *A defendant would be a subordinate publisher if they failed to remove or terminate a defamatory communication if they are responsible for, or ratify, the continued publication.*
- *e* *Such ratification will depend on the manner in which the internet platform is structured, how it is operated or controlled by its sponsor and the role of the defendant in this, including how the material got onto the site, how the defendant became aware of it, the requirements for removing it and how it remained there after the defendant learned of it.*

The High Court's decision in the *Search Engine case* (2018) sent a clear warning to such platforms that they could be held responsible for defamatory material on their sites in a range of situations and that an innocent dissemination defence would not necessarily apply.

CONTEMPT OF COURT

As we learned in Chapter 5, you are liable for *sub judice* contempt if you publish material that could, as a matter of practical reality, prejudice a trial. The most famous *sub judice* contempt in a public relations context remains *Wran's case*, from 1987. Then NSW Premier Neville Wran called a media conference at which he stated that he believed his friend, High Court Justice Lionel Murphy, was innocent of serious charges he was then facing. Sydney's *Daily Telegraph* published the comments under the heading 'Murphy innocent—Wran. Court Orders Retrial'. Both Wran and *The Daily Telegraph* were convicted of contempt, with Wran fined $25,000 and the newspaper $200,000.

Many Australian courts, at least at the Supreme Court level, have communications officers who have been appointed to help manage publicity and deal with media inquiries. They are usually known as 'public information officers' (PIOs). You would be wise to work closely with the PIO in your jurisdiction if you plan to issue any statement related to a current or forthcoming trial: a contempt conviction can involve a stiff fine and even a jail sentence. Freelance journalists and bloggers should also work through PIOs if they are covering a particular court case and do not routinely work from that court. Some privileges may be offered to the media to assist them with their court coverage—such as special seating, note-taking, permission to record proceedings for non-broadcast purposes and permission to tweet from court in some jurisdictions. Freelancers and bloggers may face a stern warning or even a contempt charge if they do any of these things without the permission of the presiding officer. Such a warning was issued to media academic and *Crikey* correspondent Margaret Simons in 2011 when she tweeted her reportage of preliminary magistrates court proceedings in the *Artz case* (2013), discussed below.

As flagged above, public relations practitioners responsible for social media moderation, bloggers and new media start-ups also need to take particular care with the comments of third parties and other user-generated content about criminal trials.

CONFIDENTIALITY

Public relations practitioners and freelance journalists have an obligation to respect confidences. We have already considered the journalist's obligation under Clause 3 of the MEAA Journalist Code of Ethics (see Appendix 1). For PR practitioners, this duty sits at Clause 4 of the Public Relations Institute of Australia (PRIA) Code of Ethics, requiring practitioners to 'safeguard the confidences of both present and former employers and clients, including confidential information about employers' or clients' business affairs, technical methods or processes, except upon the order of a court of competent jurisdiction' (see Appendix 3). It is the latter part of that clause that differs from the journalist's obligation, which prevents them from disclosing their sources even when ordered to do so by a court. Journalists have been prepared to go to jail to protect their sources, who might at times themselves be public relations practitioners or communications officers in a government department. As we learned in Chapter 9, most jurisdictions now have shield laws offering a degree of protection to journalists loath to reveal a confidential source in court. We also learned that it will generally be unlawful to disclose confidential information without an overriding public interest—which the courts have defined narrowly. Disclosure of information may also result in criminal charges if it is in breach of state or federal laws. All jurisdictions make it a serious crime for a public servant to release confidential information—section 70 of the Commonwealth *Crimes Act 1914* makes it an offence for present and former public servants to disclose any fact or document that they have acquired through being a public servant, and that they had a duty not to disclose; section 79 goes much further and criminalises the receipt or retention of such documents if they carry even a relatively low-level 'secret' classification. You can also be sued for breach of confidence if you reveal private or corporate secrets. As noted above, public servants are bound by strict confidentiality laws, and those who disseminate government secrets can face dismissal, fines and even jail. That happened to Victorian detective Simon Artz in 2013 when he lost his job and was given a suspended jail sentence for disclosing information about a planned raid on a terrorist cell—all because he had developed a friendship with then associate editor of *The Australian*, Cameron Stewart (*Artz case*, 2013).

PRIVACY

All government departments and corporations with a turnover of more than $3 million per annum are required to abide closely by regulations controlling the capture, storage and dissemination of private information about individuals under the *Privacy Act 1988.* As detailed in Chapter 12, there are some exceptions to its operation (including journalism), and many smaller media start-ups, freelance journalists and bloggers will be exempt from its requirements because their turnover will not reach the threshold. Nevertheless, the law effectively requires most larger PR consultancies and practitioners working within government and larger businesses to be very careful in managing the information they collect about people. Special restrictions apply to 'sensitive' information such as medical data—and there are strict protocols about how people's private data can be used for marketing purposes and in direct marketing campaigns. It is worth looking closely at the Act and at the numerous fact sheets prepared by the Office of the Australian Information Commissioner (2018).

INTELLECTUAL PROPERTY AND COPYRIGHT

We have explained the basic principles of intellectual property and copyright law in Chapter 11, but it is worth reinforcing them here in the context of public relations, freelancing and new media entrepreneurship. Each involves unique work contexts where such issues may arise. A public relations consultant may be tempted to copy the work of others and use it without attribution simply to save time and energy in preparing a media release, a brochure or an in-house publication. Copyright law applies in all of these situations. Freelancers can be lured into extensive borrowing of the words of others, as pay rates per word drop in a competitive media environment.

Those working in the realm of gossip or 'celebrity' journalism need to take special care when dealing with the endorsements and images, particularly of international celebrities. Many parts of the world, including Australia, have limitations on how you can use the name and image of others—particularly if you are making a profit out of it. These are often called 'personality rights', but may also involve breaches of the Australian Consumer Law, relating to misleading and deceptive conduct. They may even involve a defamation claim: in the *Golfer case* (1931), an amateur golfer sued over the use of his image in an illustration advertising Fry's chocolates, on the basis that it suggested that he had breached his amateur status by taking paid endorsements. Satirists need to beware of the action in 'passing off', which can be brought against someone who has falsely represented their work or business as that of another—as in the case of a 'spoof' website. In common law countries like Australia and the United Kingdom, such an action can be commenced against you if you have used someone's name or likeness to imply they have entered into a commercial arrangement to endorse your product or service in some way. In its basic form, the passing-off action offers simple protection to businesses against those who try to trade off their reputation by pretending to have some connection with them, or endorsement from them. Similar protections exist under the Australian Consumer Law and, while there is an exemption for information providers, the exemption does not extend to promotions of your own business or advertising.

Another area of intellectual property of particular relevance to public relations practitioners and new media entrepreneurs is trade mark law. In our globalised commercial world, the unauthorised use of a product name is of special concern to multinational corporations. Many company names have become so commonly used that there is often a question of whether they have become a 'generic' description of a type of product or process. The International Trademark

Association (INTA, 2018) warns against the misuse of brand names. As noted in Chapter 11, it gives recommendations–some verging on the ludicrous–including that the phrase 'separable fasteners' should be used in place of the trade mark 'Velcro' and that 'audio data computer software' should be used instead of the generic use of 'iTunes'. Bear in mind that a trade mark does not amount to worldwide literary copyright: it is designed to protect against others applying the same trade mark to other goods competing in the same market. Despite routine flurries of correspondence from firms of US attorneys, your descriptive use of a trademarked name in a piece of content is unlikely to lead to action: companies keep these letters on file as evidence that they have been vigilant in policing the generic use of product names. You need to step carefully with the use of trademarked logos, however, and entrepreneurs should avoid using an existing trade mark for their own start-up internet business: if in doubt, consult a trade mark lawyer.

DIGITAL DIMENSIONS IN PR, FREELANCING AND NEW MEDIA ENTREPRENEURSHIP

In Chapter 1, we reviewed a range of legal issues arising in the digital and social media environment, some of which have special relevance to the broader realm of professional communication beyond journalism. Some of these digital issues are particular to the roles of public relations consultant, freelancer or new media entrepreneur.

Jurisdiction–the place where a law applies–is an issue of special relevance in the Web 2.0 environment, where a simple press of a 'send' button means your post is available to be read in far-flung places throughout the world. As we learned in other chapters, internet and social media communications bring their own array of interstate and international legal pitfalls because most jurisdictions–including Australia–make you legally liable for whatever you have published or posted under the law that applies at the location where it is downloaded–not just where you are based (*Gutnick's case*, 2002). Public relations consultancies, freelance bloggers and new media start-ups operating internationally need to take legal advice on the ramifications of their actions in other jurisdictions in which they do business, or in which it is likely that their product will be consumed. Acceptable practices in Australia can be illegal in other parts of the world that have different cultural traditions or harsher forms of government censorship.

It is also worth reinforcing the issue of your responsibility for the comments of others on your website, web page or social networking sites. It is important for a public relations consultancy or a new media start-up to commit staff to routine and effective moderation of comments, which can get quite heated and polarised when topics like politics, religion, human rights, the environment and even sport are being debated. Comments posted by others can leave such organisations exposed to a range of legal actions, including defamation, contempt and racial vilification, for statements made by angry people they interview or who leave comments on social media sites: the fact of a publisher having actively encouraged comment is now often included in defamation claims as having caused additional hurt to feelings, and warranting an award of aggravated damages. Not-for-profit and boutique operations are rarely as well resourced as government and major corporations, and may not have the financial and legal muscle to defend and appeal a case stemming from a staffer's ignorance or poor judgement.

So-called 'cyber-squatting' can also be an issue. Since the advent of the internet, profiteers have tried to exploit the registration of domain names of unwitting celebrities, businesses and organisations. Law-makers are still trying to work out how to deal with this problem: quite often there is nothing the courts can do because the offender lives in a different jurisdiction. Disputes often end up in the hands of international and national domain name-registration agencies, which engage in arbitration between the parties to try to resolve the argument over who is really entitled to the name. The Internet Corporation for Assigned Names and Numbers (ICANN) will work with national bodies to withdraw a domain name from a cyber-squatter. It is in your best interests as a blogger, PR consultancy or media entrepreneur to keep a close eye on your domain name registration and to register in advance any close wording variants, especially if you are using your blog to achieve a commercial end. You never actually 'own' your URL—you are only licensed to use it for a certain period by the registration body. Cyber-squatters keep a close eye on the registration process and pounce once a popular name becomes available. They then may use it to sell advertising or try to sell it back to you at an inflated price. You can't register every possible variation on the spelling of your name so some spyware and phishing operators register common misspellings of the URLs of famous people and corporations—a practice known as 'typo-squatting'. Even trade mark law is inconsistent in its application to the area of domain names, and the courts will often not grant relief unless someone clearly demonstrates intent in 'bad faith' to profit from the deception within the same jurisdiction as the victim. The international dispute-resolution processes for domain names might be less expensive than litigation, but they can still be beyond the means of the ordinary blogger or small business. WIPO's Arbitration and Mediation Center charges between US$1500 and US$5000 for its services, depending upon how many domain names are contested and the number of independent panelists needed for the adjudication. It claims it can process such matters within two months of filing. The domain name cases it has handled—listed at <www.wipo.int/amc/en/domains/casesx/all.html>—make for interesting reading and feature many of the world's leading brands winning their legitimate URL registration back from shysters and spammers from remote corners of the planet (WIPO, 2018).

AUSTRALIAN BUSINESS LAW FOR PUBLIC RELATIONS PRACTITIONERS, FREELANCERS AND NEW MEDIA ENTREPRENEURS

An array of business laws confronts public relations practitioners, freelancers and new media entrepreneurs when they are establishing and operating their own commercial enterprises. We do not have sufficient space to go into them in detail here—in fact, the business law texts cited here would make excellent reference works if you decided to go into business (Gibson and Fraser, 2011; Griggs, Clark and Iredale, 2009). It is vital, however, that you adopt sensible and safe commercial practices to minimise legal risk. These include deciding upon the most suitable legal entity for your commercial operations (individual, partnership, company or trust); complying with the reporting obligations under taxation law; dealing with immigration laws as they apply to foreign employees; ensuring any company directors operate within their corporations law powers and fulfil the legal duties expected of them; and being across international legal e-commerce requirements. A shortage of start-up capital can tempt small business operators to cut corners, which can later have serious legal implications. For example, a partnership structure might be a cheaper option at the outset, but risks leaving the personal finances of partners exposed as a result of the acts or omissions of other partners.

Business law is a vast field, and there is typically at least one catch-all subject in a typical MBA degree. Four key business law topics are crucial for all three of the occupations targeted in this chapter—public relations consultant, freelancer and new media entrepreneur. They are the legal specialty fields of contract law, negligence, consumer law and employment law. We deal briefly with each of these in turn.

CONTRACT LAW

A breach of an important contract can be devastating to the financial viability of a public relations consultancy or freelance writer, and it can ruin the prospects of a start-up media venture getting off the ground. While the law of contract can get very complex, the basic concept of a contract is fairly simple: *a contract is a legally enforceable promise.* It is something crucial to the effective operation of a business because our financial system operates on the principle of promises being kept rather than broken, so that there is an element of trust and predictability in our dealings. Contracts play a role in a variety of situations in the public relations and news business. They can cover the terms of employment for a freelance journalist or other staff, the terms of an advertising agreement with a client, the agreed price and timelines for professional services being offered, and the division of royalties that might flow to investors from a creative news product you are bringing to market. Gibson and Fraser (2011: 305–6) list the essential elements of a contract:

- an intention to contract
- an agreement between the parties (including an offer and acceptance)
- 'consideration'—what Gibson and Fraser (2011: 305–6) describe as 'something of value passing from one party to another in return for a promise to do something'.

Contract law can be a specialised area, and constitutes a subject in law degrees—partly because there is a body of case law related to the circumstances in which a contract might be deemed valid by a court. In determining a contract's validity, a court will consider the legal capacity of the parties who have entered into the contract, evidence of their consent, the legality of the purpose of the contract and the form the contract takes (Gibson and Fraser, 2011: 307). The action for 'breach of contract' arises when one or more terms of the contract have not been met—which might include work not being completed within an agreed timeline. This is usually where lawyers enter the fray, and a contract dispute can involve long and expensive court action, although alternative forms of dispute resolution are becoming more common. Griggs, Clark and Iredale (2009: 85) recommend that managers follow these steps when they are drawing up a business contract:

- reducing the agreement to writing and ensuring it contains all the agreed terms
- drafting it in plain English that does not require interpretation
- ensuring it contemplates obvious problems and presents a process for a solution
- ensuring compliance with any relevant legislation
- limiting exposure to liability
- identifying the law that should apply, particularly in international contracts.

A complex sub-branch of the law of contract is the law of agency—the term used to describe the authority you might assign to someone to enter into contracts on behalf of your business.

An example of a contract dispute over public relations services was a West Australian District Court case involving a consultant to a South African mining company considering buyouts or mergers with other mining companies (*Mining PR case*, 2004). The dispute surrounded a 'partly written, partly oral and partly implied' agreement to provide 'public relations, lobbying, consulting, networking, facilitating and co-ordinating' services. The problem was that very little was detailed in the agreement, forcing the judge to look at previous work done by the consultant and to come to an estimate of the number of hours he had worked and their value on this occasion. The consultant was awarded $830 per day for eight weeks, totalling $33,200 plus expenses.

NEGLIGENCE

The tort of negligence is a legal action available to someone who has suffered damage as a result of a breach of duty to take reasonable care, owed to them by the defendant, who should have been able to foresee that the plaintiff might risk injury (Gibson and Fraser, 2011: 163). The crucial point that the court needs to decide often turns on whether or not a reasonable person might have foreseen that there was a risk of injury in the particular circumstances of the case. It also requires that the risk was not an insignificant one, and that a reasonable person in the defendant's position would have taken precautions (Gibson and Fraser, 2011: 165).

Many of the earlier cases concerned actual physical injury caused to people through the negligence of others, but later the courts began to award damages for economic loss, not just for physical damage to a person or their property. Since the 1960s, the courts have upheld liability for negligent misstatements that result in economic loss (Griggs, Clark and Iredale, 2009: 127). This means that public relations consultants and new media start-up companies can be liable for bad advice if someone acts upon it to their detriment. Special standards and duties of care apply to professionals, by reference to their professional body's standards (Griggs, Clark and Iredale, 2009: 127). In the case of public relations consultants, the key document is PRIA's Code of Ethics (see Appendix 3). A public relations consultant's exposure to professional negligence claims can be closely linked to the terms of their contract for services and the adequacy of their professional indemnity insurance. It is sensible to take legal advice on the wording of such a contract so that your role and services are precisely defined and the boundaries of your responsibilities and liabilities are specified. Other professionals—in particular lawyers—may have their liability limited in accordance with a scheme approved under their own professional standards legislation.

CONSUMER LAW

In Chapter 3, we looked briefly at the role of the Australian Competition and Consumer Commission (ACCC), which polices section 18 of the Australian Consumer Law, set out in Schedule 2 to the *Competition and Consumer Act 2010*, targeting misleading and deceptive conduct in trade or commerce. Here we consider aspects of the ACCC's purview that impact upon public relations consultants, freelancers and new media entrepreneurs.

Section 18 of the Australian Consumer Law prohibits corporations from engaging in conduct that is 'misleading or deceptive or is likely to mislead or deceive'. Public relations practitioners and new media entrepreneurs need to be on the alert against making claims about their own products or services—or those of their clients—that might mislead or deceive consumers. Such claims might arise in corporate promotional material, on websites and in social media, in advertisements and in 'advertorials' or 'advertising features' in the mainstream media. Media releases making unverified claims about products or services are a special risk in this category.

In the *Essential Media case* (2002), the public relations consultancy Essential Media Communications used the state-based Victorian equivalent version of the Commonwealth consumer protection laws to win a Supreme Court injunction to stop another PR firm—EMC2—from using that abbreviation of their name. Essential Media claimed the use by its competitor of the abbreviation could 'mislead and deceive' clients, some of whom already knew them by that acronym. The court accepted, in addition, that EMC2 might have been 'passing off' its business as that of Essential Media Communications. The Federal Court issued an injunction in similar circumstances in the earlier *Weston case* (1985) to stop a public relations company using the name 'Weston' when an existing consultancy was already operating under that name.

News organisations have a 'safe harbour' exemption to some of these provisions under the 'prescribed information provider' exception (s 19), which had been introduced into the current legislation's predecessor, the *Trade Practices Act*. The exemption acknowledges the fact that news organisations cannot possibly vouch for every claim made by those quoted in their news columns or stories (Applegarth, 2008). Freelancers, bloggers and new media start-ups need to consider their business structures and work practices in relation to the media safe harbour exemption, which requires them to establish that they are a 'prescribed information provider' to engage the protection. In the *Carlovers case* (2000), a freelance journalist was categorised as a 'prescribed information provider' because he was in the process of preparing articles for such providers, namely established media. One prominent litigant failed in his attempt to use the consumer law against a freelance journalist. Entrepreneur the late Alan Bond and mining company Lesotho Diamond Corporation, to which he consulted, tried to use the misleading and deceptive conduct provisions to sue then freelance journalist and Bond biographer Paul Barry over an article making serious allegations against them, which they claimed were false. They were the sorts of allegations that might normally have formed the basis of a defamation action. Federal Court Justice French struck out the consumer law action as having no prospects for success because Barry, as a freelance journalist, would qualify for the media safe harbour immunity (*Bond Diamond case*, 2007, at para. 43). On appeal, the Full Court agreed that freelancers would qualify for immunity, and went further to say that media organisations should not be held responsible for freelancers' misleading and deceptive conduct unless they knew of that behaviour when publishing the material (at para. 66).

In the *Sponsored Links case* (2013), Google Inc. won an appeal against the Australian Competition and Consumer Commission (ACCC), which had claimed the search engine should be legally accountable under the misleading and deceptive conduct provisions of consumer law for representations in sponsored links from advertisers highlighted at the top of search results. The High Court held that Google did not create the sponsored links that it displayed. The court decided that ordinary and reasonable users of the Google search engine would have understood that the representations in the sponsored links were those of the advertisers, not necessarily endorsed by Google. Thus the High Court held unanimously that Google did not engage in conduct that was misleading or deceptive. This may be instructive for new media entrepreneurs, depending upon their own level of knowledge of the contents of advertisements and other material they might be posting.

Of particular interest to public relations consultants is the question of whether celebrities' use of social media and blogs without disclosing secret sponsorships or payments can be in breach of laws against misleading and deceptive conduct. In 2012, the ACCC issued a warning to celebrities that their tweets endorsing certain products and services might be prosecuted under the consumer law. The South Australian Tourist Commission had paid celebrities, including singers Kate Ceberano and Shannon Noll, to tweet to their followers that they had visited Kangaroo Island and had a great time. The ACCC said celebrities did not have to disclose they had been paid for such endorsements, but should not mislead followers into thinking that they had been somewhere if they had not (von Muenster, 2012).

There are also self-regulatory constraints on celebrities and so-called 'influencers' endorsing brands on social media without disclosing any vested interest, such as the Australian Association of National Advertisers (AANA) revised rules requiring them to do so within four weeks. Clause 2.7 of its Code of Ethics requires that 'advertising or marketing communication must be clearly distinguishable as such to the relevant audience' (AANA, 2018; Canning, 2017).

The US Federal Trade Commission has extended the principle to bloggers who parade as independent reviewers while really being paid for their endorsements with cash or rewards, as happens with some restaurant, travel and fashion reviews; and generally brands who do not disclose sponsored posts. So too has the UK Advertising Standards Authority (Canning, 2017).

EMPLOYMENT LAW

Employment law—covering workplace relations, human resources and their associated contracts and policies—is an important area of commercial law affecting public relations consultants, freelancers and new media entrepreneurs.

Effective social media policies are now an essential element of employment law in Australia. PR firms and new media entrepreneurs need to get their social media policies right, check that they are updated, and ensure that their employees are trained in their terms if they expect to be able to rely upon them to discipline or dismiss staff for misuse of their social networking accounts. If you are a public relations consultant or a freelancer, you need to read your employers' social media policies thoroughly and comply with their terms. The wording of a social media policy can be used against you if you are fired for inappropriate use of social media and you have neglected to become familiar with the workplace policy on its use. Comedian and freelance columnist for *The Age*, Catherine Deveny, was dismissed in 2010 for a series of offensive tweets about child celebrity Bindi Irwin from the Logies Awards ceremony (Farmer, 2010). This was followed by other episodes involving journalists and their social media posts, including *Sydney Morning Herald* columnist Mike Carlton, who resigned in 2014 following an uproar after he exchanged insults with readers over his position on the always controversial topic of Israel and Palestine (*ABC News*, 2014). The following year, SBS dismissed sports reporter Scott McIntyre over a series of critical tweets he made about Anzac Day, resulting in his settling an unfair dismissal action against his employer (Visentin, 2016). In a different example, the ABC did not take action against social commentator Yassmin

Abdel-Magied over her Facebook post criticising the Australian government's policy on immigration detention centres on Anzac Day 2017 on the rationale that she was a part-time employee expressing her private views, which were not representative of the national broadcaster (Carmody, 2017).

The lesson here is that you should endeavour to draw a clear distinction between your private and work social media accounts, carefully adjust your privacy settings to a suitable level for the content you are sharing and only post on the assumption that your colleagues, clients and competitors might well see everything you post, regardless of those precautions. While it sometimes takes an admirable level of self-control, you should refrain from getting personal with your comments and responses on your social media account, even if something someone has said really offends or annoys you. These kinds of strategies help to minimise the legal risks in your social media use.

Decisions by Fair Work Australia (now the Fair Work Commission) have been very clear about the fact that a clear and reasonable social media policy is essential if a company wishes to dismiss an employee for online misbehaviour. Key Case 13.1, the *Facebook Abuse case*, reinforces the need for clarity in a social media policy and training on its terms, and underscores the importance of employees not using their private Facebook accounts to criticise fellow employees or clients—even after work hours.

Public servants can face consequences for their use of social media, particularly if the lines are blurred between private and public accounts. If you are given a social media editing or monitoring role in a government department, it is essential that you familiarise yourself with any social media policy in operation and ensure the tasks you are being asked to perform do not run counter to it. For example, tweeting your personal opinion about a political issue on your own account or the department's account would usually breach the entity's social media policy, and likely the relevant public service code of conduct. This would leave you subject to disciplinary action, and perhaps personally liable for any damage you have caused some other person or company.

In the *Immigration Tweeter case*, a public affairs officer with the Commonwealth Department of Immigration and Citizenship, Michaela Banerji, failed in her bid in the Federal Circuit Court in 2013 to prevent her employer from dismissing her over anonymous tweets she had sent criticising various political figures, employees of the department, the government's immigration policies and an immigration detention centre security company. She failed to convince the court that her implied right to communicate on matters of politics and government should prevent her dismissal. However, when she appealed over her compensation to the Administrative Appeals Tribunal in 2018, that body found that the 'act of termination unacceptably trespassed on the implied freedom of political communication, (and) it follows that the act of termination was unlawful' (at para. 128). That decision was subject to a High Court appeal in 2018 after a reference from the Commonwealth Attorney-General.

In the *Centrelink case* (2016), the Fair Work Commission found that reasonable criticisms of management of the Department of Human Services by an employee were acceptable because of the common law right to freedom of expression and the implied freedom to communicate on matters of politics and government (para. 72). However, the employee's social media descriptions of Centrelink clients as 'spastics and junkies', 'whinging junkies' and 'junkies'; allegations that many clients' claims of depression were not genuine; and criticism of the department's processing times as 'utterly disgraceful' were valid reasons for dismissal because they breached the Australian Public Service (APS) Code of Conduct under section 13 of the *Public Service Act 1999* and the public service social media policy (at para. 78).

KEY CASE 13.1: *FACEBOOK ABUSE CASE*

Cameron Little v Credit Corp Group Ltd [2013] FWC 9642 (U2013/11522), 10 December 2013

FACTS

Mr Little had worked as a customer relationship manager for Credit Corp Group for three years when, in June 2013, he used his personal Facebook account to criticise an organisation (Christians Against Poverty, or CAP) with which he dealt on behalf of his employer and to make sexually suggestive comments about a new colleague. Little had listed his employment on his Facebook account as a 'Dinosaur Wrangler' at 'Jurassic Park', but other details on his page made it possible to identify him as an employee of the Credit Corp Group. He dealt with CAP when the not-for-profit group was negotiating new debt arrangements with Credit Corp on behalf of its clients. He posted to their page:

> *For reals bro, you should put a little more of funding into educating consumers on how the world works rather than just weaseling them out of debt, blah blah blah, give a man a fish/teach a man to fish.*

and

> *No thanks, just take my advice and try to educate people about things like 'interest' and 'liability' rather than just weasel them out of contracts. #simple*

Little posted the following comment about his new work colleague:

> *On behalf of all the staff at The Credit Corp Group I would like to welcome our newest victim of butt rape, [colleague's name]. I'm looking Forward to sexually harassing you behind the stationary cupboard big boy.*

The day after the posts came to the attention of his employer, he was called to a meeting where his employment was terminated. Two weeks later, he filed a claim for unfair dismissal.

LAW

Fair Work Commission Deputy President Peter Sams ruled that the dismissal had been fair, pointing to the following relevant factors:

- Little had been issued with the Employee Handbook and the Employee Code of Conduct and made aware of their contents.
- He had attended an induction at the commencement of his employment in 2010 and a 'Working Together' module in August 2012.
- His employment contract stated that the company's policies and procedures were directions from the employer to the employee.
- He had the ability to access and change the privacy settings for his account.
- It was irrelevant that Little had created the social media posts out of work hours.
- It was implausible that Little believed his Facebook page was 'private' and he did not understand how Facebook worked.
- He had been formally warned about an earlier incident where he had posted an inappropriate comment to a website.

LESSONS FOR PROFESSIONAL COMMUNICATORS

The decision affirmed earlier Fair Work Commission decisions in the *Good Guys case* (2011) and the *Linfox case* (2012). Those in the position of employer need to ensure all staff are fully aware of—and trained in—the organisation's social media policy, and that it is fair and up to date. Employees need to keep abreast of their organisation's social media policy, ensure their social media accounts are set to private and avoid posting material related in any way to their work—certainly not anything that is discriminatory or critical of colleagues, management or clients. This applies both during work hours and when off duty.

ESCALATION PROCEDURES FOR LEGAL THREATS

An important law-related policy area for public relations consultancies and new media start-ups is to ensure that they have a detailed outline of 'escalation procedures' in the instance of a threat of legal action. Every company should have written policies detailing the steps to be taken once a legal threat has been received—who needs to be advised within the organisation, who has the authority to engage and deal with lawyers, and the protocols for gathering and storing evidence related to the matter. It is vital, for example, that notes and recordings are not tampered with, deleted or edited in any way. Those involved with the incident are likely to be interviewed by management and lawyers, and may be required to write down as much as they can about the incident and associated conversations while these are still fresh in their memory. Records of phone calls and emails may be required. It is much better that such considerations are spelt out in detail, and that staff are trained in the policies well before the legal crisis arises—because it may be damaging to a case (or expose people to the risk of action for contempt of court) if you have lost or destroyed crucial evidence. In the defamation context, this occurred in the *Cougar case* (2012), in which the plaintiff claimed that she had been defamed as a 'pub slut' and a person who 'engages in disgraceful and sexually promiscuous conduct by accepting semen in all her orifices'. The plaintiff lost her appeal against a judge's decision to strike out her claim when she claimed to have lost two mobile phones, allegedly containing pornographic texts and photos involving various NRL players.

INSURANCE NEEDS

By now, you should appreciate the importance of being insured adequately if you are operating as a freelancer, PR consultant or as the principal of a new media start-up. Any of the traps outlined in this chapter can spark legal action, which can be expensive in terms of both court costs and damages awards—and it is only sensible you have a professional indemnity insurance policy to cover you so that you do not lose your business and personal wealth over a legal mishap. Product and public liability, workers' compensation and professional indemnity insurance policies are essential for any small communication business engaged in publishing. Between them, they cover physical accidents and injuries to third parties and employees, along with the legal liability for things that can go wrong with your professional behaviour: incompetent or negligent strategies and advice, intellectual property infringements, missed deadlines causing financial loss, breaches of consumer law, defamation actions, and breach of privacy or confidentiality by either the principals or their employees.

It is best to consult with experts from a professional body like PRIA or the MEAA about the most suitable policies for freelancers and small consultancies. Sometimes they may be able to negotiate discounts for members with insurance brokers; the MEAA (2018) advertises such services in its Freelance Pro scheme. The public relations practitioner working in a government department has many of the benefits of being a public servant, including security in the knowledge that government-funded legal resources will likely be available to defend them if their work-related behaviour attracts litigation.

REGULATION AND SELF-REGULATION OF PUBLIC RELATIONS, FREELANCING, BLOGGING AND NEW MEDIA

There are many self-regulatory codes and co-regulatory bodies that may apply to the work of public relations consultants, freelance journalists and bloggers, and new media entrepreneurs—again depending upon their specialty area of operation.

At the self-regulatory level, PRIA determines the ethical standards of consultants through its Code of Ethics (PRIA, 2015a) (see Appendix 3) and the Consultancy Code of Practice (PRIA, 2015b). As explained in Chapter 3, breaches can result in members being censured, fined, suspended or expelled from the association, as detailed in the complaints procedure at <www.pria.com.au/aboutus/ethics-complaints-and-enquiries>.

Freelancers and professional bloggers who are members of the MEAA ascribe to the MEAA Journalist Code of Ethics (see Appendix 1), and the disciplinary processes applying to it are also explained in Chapter 3. The journalists' union has recently made a concerted effort to bring serious bloggers into its fold through its Freelance Pro initiative (MEAA, 2018). Freelance Pro is a new category of MEAA membership offering professional indemnity and public liability insurance, contract advice, a media access card, the 'Freelance Pro trustmark' and accredited training in the MEAA Code of Ethics and media law. Membership requires bloggers to commit to a 'respect for truth and the public's right to information' and the core principles of honesty, fairness, independence and respect for the rights of others.

Specifically, they must subscribe to the twelve key journalists' ethical principles of fair and accurate reporting, anti-discrimination, source protection, refusal of payola, disclosure of conflicts of interest, rejection of commercial influences, disclosure of chequebook journalism, using honest news-gathering methods and protecting the vulnerable, disclosing digital manipulation, not plagiarising, respecting grief and privacy, and correcting errors (MEAA, 2001; see Appendix 1). These can be overridden only for 'substantial advancement of the public interest' or where there is 'risk of substantial harm to people'. However, we learned in Chapter 3 of the low level of enforcement of this code by the MEAA, which may have a bearing on public and judicial perceptions of journalists' accountability.

Ad Standards <www.adstandards.com.au> (the Advertising Standards Bureau) administers a national system of advertising self-regulation with a range of ethical codes including the Australian Association of National Advertisers Code of Ethics (AANA, 2018). Ad Standards handles consumer complaints about advertisements across a range of media. It operates both an Ad Standards Community Panel and an Ad Standards Industry Jury to adjudicate consumer and competitive complaints against the advertising self-regulatory Codes. For example, a complaint about the Facebook page for the beer Victoria Bitter in 2012 was upheld on the grounds that people had posted comments to the social networking site that were in breach of advertising standards. They included coarse language, sexual references and comments demeaning of women and homosexual people. Comments on the page were managed by an agency under the supervision of the Carlton and United Breweries marketing team, which agreed to improve its frequency and effectiveness of comment moderation after the decision (ASB, 2012).

Several co-regulatory bodies hold powers that can impinge on the work of public relations consultants, freelancers and new media entrepreneurs. They include the following:

- *The Australian Communications and Media Authority (ACMA),* *<www.acma.gov.au>*. This broadcasting regulator's powers can impact upon public relations consultants, freelancers and new media entrepreneurs in a range of ways. Public relations consultants need to ensure that their audio packages and video news releases (VNRs) comply with the code of conduct and classification requirements of the particular broadcast media they are targeting (community, commercial radio, pay television, etc.). ACMA also administers the national Do Not Call Register, where citizens withdraw their phone numbers from telemarketing dial-ups, and polices the *Spam Act 2003*—the legislation ensuring customers can unsubscribe from junk mail posts to their email, mobile phone and messaging services. It is important that public relations consultants and new media startups work within the bounds of this legislation, at the risk of facing heavy fines. For example, in 2017 TPG Internet paid a $360,000 infringement notice from ACMA for continuing to send SMS commercial electronic messages to consumers who had withdrawn their consent by unsubscribing (ACMA, 2017).

- *The Classification Board, <www.classification.gov.au/About/Pages/Classification-Board.aspx>*. This is a unified system of classification of films, video games and some publications, established under the *Classification Act 1995*. Public relations consultants and new media entrepreneurs need to be aware of its requirements because almost all films and computer games have to be classified before they can legally be made available. The board (ACB, 2018) decides which of the classifications should apply, based on issues such as violence, sex, language, themes, drug use and nudity. The board also classifies material submitted by the police, customs and ACMA, including internet sites, imported publications, films and computer games.
- *Therapeutic Goods Administration (TGA), <www.tga.gov.au>*. The TGA is a Commonwealth government agency with the power to regulate therapeutic goods (medicines, medical devices and blood products). Some advertisements directed at consumers require approval before they can be broadcast or published, while advertising prescription-only and some pharmacist-only medicines

to the general public is prohibited. The term 'advertisement' is defined broadly in the *Therapeutic Goods Act 1989* to include 'any statement, pictorial representation or design, however made, that is intended, whether directly or indirectly, to promote the use or supply of the goods'. This can cover public relations material and advertorials, and freelance health writers and public relations consultants to pharmaceutical companies need to be well versed in its requirements and restrictions.

- *Australian Securities and Investments Commission (ASIC), <http://asic.gov.au>*. ASIC (2017) is an independent Commonwealth entity operating as Australia's corporate, markets and financial services regulator. Its role is to ensure Australia's financial markets are fair and transparent, supported by confident and informed investors and consumers. It is set up under the *Australian Securities and Investments Commission Act 2001* (ASIC Act), and enforces large sections of the *Corporations Act*. Public relations consultants, freelance financial reporters and new media entrepreneurs need to be especially cautious about restrictions on 'rumour-trage'—the spreading of false or misleading rumours about a company's float or performance that are associated with market manipulation—and ASIC's policing of the powers and duties of company directors.

  It also has tough requirements that advertisements for financial products do not mislead. For example, in 2017 Financial Choice Pty Ltd, an Australian financial services provider, paid two ASIC infringement notice penalties totalling $21,600 for making misleading representations in marketing emails sent to consumers and on its website. As a result of the investigation Financial Choice:

  - agreed to stop sending communications that stated or implied that Financial Choice was seeking consumers' opinions because superannuation funds had asked it to do so, and
  - removed the misleading statements from the Find My Super website (ASIC, 2017).

ASIC also imposes strict conditions on claims being made in documents associated with company floats in their prospectuses and initial public offering (IPO) announcements. These are known to tread a fine line between marketing, sales and compliance, and ASIC has powers to pursue marketers, public relations consultants and journalists who do not ensure statements about future outcomes are reasonably based and that major risks are disclosed in print, broadcast, online and in social media statements. Special concerns in the corporate sector relate to securities law and directors' powers and duties. For example, before a press release is sent out quoting the managing director of a listed company, advisers need to ensure it is not exposing the managing director to legal action over a statement that should have been notified to the stock exchange, or that suggests the managing director should have declared some conflict of interest in relation to the company's dealings. The media release can itself prompt a PR and legal crisis for the firm. A case in which a draft news release and a draft announcement to the Australian Stock Exchange generated significant litigation was the *Asbestos case* (2010), which related to approval of an announcement of a 'fully funded' trust to meet future asbestos related liabilities.

TIPS FOR MINDFUL PRACTICE

- Legal pitfalls of public relations, freelancing and new media entrepreneurship can be complex, but you will be more likely to stay out of trouble if you give due credit and respect to the creative work of others, are transparent in your dealings with sponsors and create a firewall between your private and professional social media usage.
- Remember to renew your domain name registration, or it might be poached by cyber-squatters.
- Distinguish your work and home personas, and use your blogs and social media accordingly.

- Always disclose any rewards or incentives you might have received from a sponsor, and do not pretend you are offering an independent endorsement if you have received anything in return.
- An early apology, settlement or a negotiated solution to the point of dispute can leave all parties reasonably satisfied and much better off financially than they would have been if the legal dispute had been allowed to escalate.
- Appreciate the importance of being insured adequately as a consultant, freelancer or entrepreneur.
- Ensure you and your staff are aware of the powers of the various self-regulatory and co-regulatory bodies and the specific government agencies that might impact on your work.
- Reflect upon the ethical standards and professional values of your occupation and consider whether your words and actions honour them.

IN A NUTSHELL

- A range of laws apply to public relations consultants, freelancers and new media entrepreneurs, including defamation, confidentiality, privacy and intellectual property, consumer law, contract, securities law and negligence.
- Several co-regulatory and self-regulatory bodies can have disciplinary powers over public relations consultants, freelancers and new media entrepreneurs, including the PRIA, MEAA, ACMA, ASIC, Ad Standards, the Classification Board and the ACCC.
- Be mindful of the impact of your publications upon others. Draw upon the moral framework of your culture and/or religion, and become familiar with the ethical code of your occupation as a public relations consultant, a freelance journalist or a new media business operator. While there are some exceptional situations, sound moral and ethical practice usually helps to limit your legal exposure.
- A contract is a legally enforceable promise—crucial to the effective operation of a business, because our financial system relies on the principle of promises being kept rather than broken.

- The tort of negligence is a legal action available to someone who has suffered damage as a result of the defendant's breach of duty to take reasonable care where they should have been able to foresee that the plaintiff might risk injury.
- Section 18 of the *Competition and Consumer Act 2010* prohibits conduct that is 'misleading or deceptive or is likely to mislead or deceive'.
- Employment law covers workplace relations, human resources and their associated contracts and policies.
- Product and public liability, workers' compensation and professional indemnity insurance policies are essential for any small communication business.
- Every business has, or should have, written escalation or 'upward referral' policies outlining the steps to be taken once a legal threat has been received.

DISCUSSION QUESTIONS

13.1 You are about to be hired into a position in an occupation related to the media—as a public relations practitioner, a freelance blogger or a team member of a new media start-up firm. Make a table summarising the top three legal topics that might be relevant to each, and justify your selections.

13.2 How might the law of contract impact on the legal relationships and work practices of the public relations professional, the blogger or the new media entrepreneur?

13.3 You have been asked to write the social media policy for a new not-for-profit political blogging agency. What are the top five elements you should include in that social media policy?

13.4 You own a boutique social media news agency. An employee has just written a Facebook post under her personal account calling her editor a bitch and questioning her sexual behaviours. She has her privacy settings on maximum, but has two colleagues as Facebook 'friends' and one of them has sent you a screen capture of the post. What options are available to you?

13.5 Go to <www.austlii.edu.au> and search for a recent case involving a public relations consultant. Compare and contrast it with one of the cases in this chapter.

REFERENCES

ABC News 2014, '*Sydney Morning Herald* columnist Mike Carlton resigns following furore over Gaza column', 7 August, <www.abc.net.au/news/2014-08-06/smh-columnist-mike-carlton-resigns-following-gaza-column-furore/5651470>.

Advertising Standards Bureau (ASB) 2012, *Case Report—Case 0271/12: Foster's Australia, Asia and Pacific*, 11 July, <http://ms.adstandards.com.au/cases/0271-12.pdf>.

Applegarth, P. 2008, 'How deep is the media safe harbour?', *Gazette of Law and Journalism* 23, <http://archive.sclqld.org.au/judgepub/2008/How%20deep%20is%20the%20safe%20media%20harbour.pdf>.

Australian Association of National Advertisers (AANA) 2018, *Code of Ethics*, <http://aana.com.au/content/uploads/2017/09/AANA-Code-of-Ethics-as-at-01.03.2018.pdf>.

Australian Classification Board (ACB) 2018, 'About', <www.classification.gov.au/about/pages/classification-board.aspx>.

Australian Communications and Media Authority (ACMA) 2017, 'TPG pays $360,000 price for spam breaches', media release 36/2017—3 November, <www.acma.gov.au/Industry/Marketers/Anti-Spam/Ensuring-you-dont-spam/tpg-pays-360000-price-for-spam-breaches>.

Australian Securities and Investments Commission (ASIC) 2017, '17-248MR Financial Choice pays $21,600 in penalties for false and misleading representations', media release, 25 July, <http://asic.gov.au/about-asic/media-centre/find-a-media-release/2017-releases/17-248mr-financial-choice-pays-21-600-in-penalties-for-false-and-misleading-representations>.

Canning, S. 2017, 'Influencers must reveal sponsors, but TV shows can keep quiet about product placement, say new advertising rules', *Mumbrella*, 31 January, <https://mumbrella.com.au/asb-aana-influencers-rules-distinguishable-ads-product-placement-423251>.

Carmody, B. 2017, 'ABC stands by Yassmin Abdel-Magied after Facebook post sparks Anzac Day outrage', *smh.com.au*, 26 April, <www.smh.com.au/entertainment/tv-and-radio/abc-stands-by-yassmin-abdelmagied-after-facebook-post-sparks-anzac-day-outrage-20170426-gvsehn.html>.

Farmer, G. 2010, 'Wrong, Deveny, Twitter is not just passing notes', *Sydney Morning Herald*, 5 May, <www.smh.com.au/federal-politics/society-and-culture/wrong-deveny-twitter-is-not-just-passing-notes-20100505-u7nb.html>.

Gibson, A. and Fraser, I. 2011, *Business Law*, 6th edn, Pearson Education, Sydney.

Griggs, L., Clark, E. and Iredale, I. 2009, *Managers and the Law: A Guide for Business Decision Makers*, 3rd edn, Thomson Reuters, Sydney.

International Trademark Association 2018, 'Overview', <www.inta.org/about/pages/overview.aspx>.

Media, Entertainment and Arts Alliance (MEAA) 2001, *MEAA Journalist Code of Ethics*, <www.alliance.org.au/hot/ethics code.htm>.

—— 2018, 'Freelance Pro', <www.meaa.org/meaa-media/freelance-pro>.

Office of the Australian Information Commissioner 2018, 'Privacy fact sheets', Commonwealth Government, Canberra, <www.oaic.gov.au/individuals/privacy-fact-sheets>.

Public Relations Institute of Australia (PRIA) 2015a, *Code of Ethics*, <www.pria.com.au/documents/item/6317>.

—— 2015b, *Registered Consultancy Code of Practice*, Melbourne, <www.pria.com.au/aboutus/consultancy-code-of-practice>.

Senate Select Committee on the Future of Public Interest Journalism 2018, *Report*, Commonwealth of Australia, Canberra, <www.aph.gov.au/Parliamentary_Business/Committees/Senate/Future_of_Public_Interest_Journalism/PublicInterestJournalism/Report>.

Visentin, L. 2016, 'Sacked reporter Scott McIntyre and SBS resolve dispute over Anzac Day tweets', *Sydney Morning Herald*, 11 April, <www.smh.com.au/business/companies/sacked-reporter-scott-mcintyre-and-sbs-resolve-dispute-over--anzac-day-tweets-20160411-go37vt.html>.

Von Muenster Solicitors & Attorneys 2012, 'Cash for tweets: What is the price you might pay?', <www.vmsolicitors.com.au/tag/twitter-kangaroo-island-misleading-and-deceptive-conduct-advertising>.

World Intellectual Property Organization (WIPO) 2018, 'Domain name dispute resolution', <www.wipo.int/amc/en/domains>.

CASES CITED

Allergy Pathway case: Australian Competition and Consumer Commission v Allergy Pathway Pty Ltd (No. 2) [2011] FCA 74, <www.austlii.edu.au/cgi-bin/sinodisp/au/cases/cth/FCA/2011/74.html>.

Artz case: Director of Public Prosecutions v Artz [2013] VCC 56, <www.countycourt.vic.gov.au/files/DPP%20v%20Artz%20%5B2013%5D%20VCC%2056.pdf>.

Asbestos case: Morley & Ors v Australian Securities and Investments Commission [2010] NSWCA 331 (17 December 2010), <www.austlii.edu.au/cgi-bin/sinodisp/au/cases/nsw/NSWCA/2010/331.html>.

Barrister's Wife case: Rayney v The State of Western Australia [No. 9] [2017] WASC 367, <www.austlii.edu.au/cgi-bin/viewdoc/au/cases/wa/WASC/2017/367.html>.

Bond Diamond case: Bond v Barry [2007] FCA 1484, <www.austlii.edu.au/au/cases/cth/FCA/2007/1484.html> [16 February 2010]; *Bond v Barry* [2008] FCAFC 115, <www.austlii.edu.au/cgi-bin/sinodisp/au/cases/cth/FCAFC/2008/115.html>.

Born Brands case: Born Brands Pty Ltd v Nine Network Australia Pty Ltd (No. 6) [2013] NSWSC 1651, <http://classic.austlii.edu.au/cgi-bin/sinodisp/au/cases/nsw/NSWSC/2013/1651.html>.

Carlovers case: Carlovers Carwash Ltd v Sahathevan [2000] NSWSC 947 (13 October 2000), <www.austlii.edu.au/au/cases/nsw/supreme_ct/2000/947.html>.

Centrelink case: Daniel Starr v Department of Human Services [2016] FWC 1460, <www.fwc.gov.au/documents/decisionssigned/html/2016fwc1460.htm>.

Cougar case: Palavi v Queensland Newspapers Pty Ltd & Anor [2012] NSWCA 182, <www.austlii.edu.au/cgi-bin/sinodisp/au/cases/nsw/NSWCA/2012/182.html>.

Councillor's case: Milne v Ell [2017] NSWSC 555, <www.austlii.edu.au/cgi-bin/viewdoc/au/cases/nsw/NSWSC/2017/555.html>.

DVD case: BGC (Australia) Pty Ltd v Professional Public Relations Pty Ltd & Anor [2006] WASC 175, <www.austlii.edu.au/cgi-bin/sinodisp/au/cases/wa/WASC/2006/175.html>.

Essential Media case: Essential Media Communications Pty Ltd v EMC2 & Partners [2002] VSC 554, <www.austlii.edu.au/cgi-bin/sinodisp/au/cases/vic/VSC/2002/554.html>.

Facebook Abuse case: Cameron Little v Credit Corp Group Ltd [2013] FWC 9642 (U2013/11522), 10 December 2013, <http://decisions.fwc.gov.au>.

Facebook Page case: Von Marburg v Aldred & Anor [2015] VSC 467, <http://classic.austlii.edu.au/cgi-bin/sinodisp/au/cases/vic/VSC/2015/467.html>.

Golf Club case: Byrne v Deane [1937] 2 All ER 204; [1937] 1 KB 818.

Golfer case: Tolley v J.S. Fry & Sons Ltd [1931] AC 333.

Good Guys case: O'Keefe v Williams Muir's Pty Limited T/A Troy Williams The Good Guys [2011] FWA 5311–11 August 2011, <www.fwc.gov.au/decisionssigned/html/2011fwa5311.htm>.

Gutnick's case: Dow Jones & Company Inc. v Gutnick [2002] 210 CLR 575 (10 December 2002), <www.austlii.edu.au//cgi-bin/disp.pl/au/cases/cth/HCA/2002/56.html>.

Immigration Tweeter case: Banerji v Bowles [2013] FCCA 1052; *Banerji and Comcare (Compensation)* [2018] AATA 892.

Linfox case: Linfox Australia Pty Ltd v Glen Stutsel [2012] FWAFB 7097 (C2011/6952), <www.fwc.gov.au/fullbench/2012fwafb7097.htm>.

Mining PR case: Newshore Nominees Pty Ltd as Trustee for the Commercial and Equities Trust v Durvan Roodepoort Deep, Limited [2004] WADC 57, <www.austlii.edu.au/cgi-bin/sinodisp/au/cases/wa/WADC/2004/57.html>.

Murder Suspect case: Sands v State of South Australia [2015] SASCFC 36.

Murray's case: Murray v Wishart [2014] NZCA 461; [2014] 3 NZLR 722.

Nightclub case: Tropeano v Karidis [2012] SADC 29, <www.austlii.edu.au/cgi-bin/sinodisp/au/cases/sa/SADC/2012/29.html>.

Search Engine cases: Trkulja v Yahoo! Inc. & Anor [2012] VSC 88, <www.austlii.edu.au/au/cases/vic/VSC/2012/88.html>; *Trkulja v Google Inc. LLC & Anor (No. 5)* [2012] VSC 533 (12 November 2012), <www.austlii.edu.au/cgi-bin/sinodisp/au/cases/vic/VSC/2012/533.html>; *Trkulja v Google LLC* [2018] HCA 25 (13 June 2018), <http://eresources.hcourt.gov.au/showCase/2018/HCA/25>.

Sponsored Links case: Google Inc. v Australian Competition and Consumer Commission [2013] HCA 1 (6 February 2013), <www.austlii.edu.au/cgi-bin/viewdoc/au/cases/cth/HCA/2013/1.html>.

Treasurer case: Hockey v Fairfax Media Publications Pty Limited [2015] FCA 652, <www.austlii.edu.au/cgi-bin/sinodisp/au/cases/cth/FCA/2015/652.html>.

Weston case: Re Weston Communications Pty Ltd v Fortune Communications Holdings Limited and the Weston Company Limited [1985] FCA 426, <www.austlii.edu.au/cgi-bin/sinodisp/au/cases/cth/FCA/1985/426.html>.

Wran's case: Director of Public Prosecutions (Cth) v Wran (1987) 7 NSWLR 616.

APPENDIX 1

MEAA Journalist Code of Ethics

Respect for truth and the public's right to information are fundamental principles of journalism. Journalists search, disclose, record, question, entertain, comment and remember. They inform citizens and animate democracy. They scrutinise power, but also exercise it, and should be responsible and accountable. MEAA members engaged in journalism commit themselves to:

- honesty
- fairness
- independence
- respect for the rights of others

Journalists will educate themselves about ethics and apply the following standards:

1. Report and interpret honestly, striving for accuracy, fairness and disclosure of all essential facts. Do not suppress relevant available facts, or give distorting emphasis. Do your utmost to give a fair opportunity for reply.
2. Do not place unnecessary emphasis on personal characteristics, including race, ethnicity, nationality, gender, age, sexual orientation, family relationships, religious belief, or physical or intellectual disability.
3. Aim to attribute information to its source. Where a source seeks anonymity, do not agree without first considering the

source's motives and any alternative attributable source. Where confidences are accepted, respect them in all circumstances.

4. Do not allow personal interest, or any belief, commitment, payment, gift or benefit, to undermine your accuracy, fairness or independence.
5. Disclose conflicts of interest that affect, or could be seen to affect, the accuracy, fairness or independence of your journalism. Do not improperly use a journalistic position for personal gain.
6. Do not allow advertising or other commercial considerations to undermine accuracy, fairness or independence.
7. Do your utmost to ensure disclosure of any direct or indirect payment made for interviews, pictures, information or stories.
8. Use fair, responsible and honest means to obtain material. Identify yourself and your employer before obtaining any interview for publication or broadcast. Never exploit a person's vulnerability or ignorance of media practice.
9. Present pictures and sound which are true and accurate. Any manipulation likely to mislead should be disclosed.
10. Do not plagiarise.
11. Respect private grief and personal privacy. Journalists have the right to resist compulsion to intrude.
12. Do your utmost to achieve fair correction of errors.

GUIDANCE CLAUSE

Basic values often need interpretation and sometimes come into conflict. Ethical journalism requires conscientious decision-making in context. Only substantial advancement of the public interest or risk of substantial harm to people allows any standard to be overridden.

APPENDIX 2

Australian Press Council Statement of General Principles

Publications are free to publish as they wish by reporting facts and expressing opinions, provided they take reasonable steps to comply with the following Principles and the Council's other Standards of Practice:

ACCURACY AND CLARITY

1. Ensure that factual material in news reports and elsewhere is accurate and not misleading, and is distinguishable from other material such as opinion.
2. Provide a correction or other adequate remedial action if published material is significantly inaccurate or misleading.

FAIRNESS AND BALANCE

3. Ensure that factual material is presented with reasonable fairness and balance, and that writers' expressions of opinion are not based on significantly inaccurate factual material or omission of key facts.
4. Ensure that where material refers adversely to a person, a fair opportunity is given for subsequent publication of a reply if that is reasonably necessary to address a possible breach of General Principle 3.

PRIVACY AND AVOIDANCE OF HARM

5. Avoid intruding on a person's reasonable expectations of privacy, unless doing so is sufficiently in the public interest.
6. Avoid causing or contributing materially to substantial offence, distress or prejudice, or a substantial risk to health or safety, unless doing so is sufficiently in the public interest.

INTEGRITY AND TRANSPARENCY

7. Avoid publishing material which has been gathered by deceptive or unfair means, unless doing so is sufficiently in the public interest.
8. Ensure that conflicts of interests are avoided or adequately disclosed, and that they do not influence published material.

[Effective 1 August 2014]

APPENDIX 3

Public Relations Institute of Australia (PRIA) Code of Ethics

PRIA is a professional body serving the interests of its members. PRIA is mindful of the responsibility which public relations professionals owe to the community as well as to their clients and employers.

PRIA requires members to adhere to the highest standards of ethical practice and professional competence. All members are duty-bound to act responsibly and to be accountable for their actions.

The following code of ethics binds all members of PRIA:

1. Members shall deal fairly and honestly with their employers, clients and prospective clients, with their fellow workers including superiors and subordinates, with public officials, the communication media, the general public and with fellow members of PRIA.
2. Members shall avoid conduct or practices likely to bring discredit upon themselves, the Institute, their employers or clients.
3. Members shall not knowingly disseminate false or misleading information and shall take care to avoid doing so inadvertently.
4. With the exception of the requirements of Clause 9 members shall safeguard the confidences of both present and former employers and clients, including confidential information about employers' or clients' business affairs, technical methods or processes, except upon the order of a court of competent jurisdiction.
5. No member shall represent conflicting interests nor, without the consent of the parties concerned, represent competing interests.

6. Members shall refrain from proposing or agreeing that their consultancy fees or other remuneration be contingent entirely on the achievement of specified results.
7. Members shall inform their employers or clients if circumstances arise in which their judgment or the disinterested character of their services may be questioned by reason of personal relationships or business or financial interests.
8. Members practising as consultants shall seek payment only for services specifically commissioned.
9. Members shall be prepared to identify the source of funding of any public communication they initiate or for which they act as a conduit.
10. Members shall, in advertising and marketing their skills and services and in soliciting professional assignments, avoid false, misleading or exaggerated claims and shall refrain from comment or action that may injure the professional reputation, practice or services of a fellow member.
11. Members shall inform the Board of the Institute and/or the relevant State/Territory Council(s) of the Institute of evidence purporting to show that a member has been guilty of, or could be charged with, conduct constituting a breach of this Code.
12. No member shall intentionally injure the professional reputation or practice of another member.
13. Members shall help to improve the general body of knowledge of the profession by exchanging information and experience with fellow members.
14. Members shall act in accord with the aims of the Institute, its regulations and policies.
15. Members shall not misrepresent their status through misuse of title, grading, or the designation FPRIA, MPRIA or APRIA.

INDEX